for Michael Schmidt

Contents

1160499

PILLING, J.

FIFTY MODERN EUROPEAN POETS
28/02/83
JM

809·1034
PILLING, J.
Reader's guide to
50 modern European
poets £9.50
1160499

Please renew/return this item by the last date shown.

So that your telephone call is charged at local rate,
please call the numbers as set out below:

	From Area codes 01923 or 020:	From the rest of Herts:
Renewals:	01923 471373	01438 737373
Enquiries:	01923 471333	01438 737333
Minicom:	01923 471599	01438 737599

L32   www.hertsdirect.org

A Reader's Guide to
Fifty Modern European Poets

Reader's Guide Series
General Editor: Andrew Mylett

A Reader's Guide to
Fifty Modern European Poets

by John Pilling

Heinemann – London
Barnes & Noble – Totowa, New Jersey

Heinemann Educational Books Ltd
LONDON EDINBURGH MELBOURNE AUCKLAND HONG KONG
SINGAPORE KUALA LUMPUR NEW DELHI IBADAN NAIROBI
JOHANNESBURG KINGSTON PORT OF SPAIN

First published 1982 by Pan Books as
An Introduction to Fifty Modern European Poets
in the Pan Literature Guides Series
First published in this casebound edition 1982

British Library CIP Data
Pilling, John
  A reader's guide to fifty modern European poets.
  1. Poetry, Modern—20th century—History and
  criticism
  I. Title
  809.1'034   PN1261

  ISBN 0-453-18724-4

Library of Congress CIP Data
Pilling, John.
  A readers guide to fifty modern European poets.
  (Reader's guide series)
  Bibliography: p.
  Includes index.
  1. European poetry—19th century—Translations into English.
2. European poetry—20th century—Translations into English.
3. English poetry—Translations from foreign languages.
I. Title.
PN6101.P454 1982   808.81'034   82-11363

  ISBN 0-389-20241-X

Published in Great Britain by
Heinemann Educational Books Ltd
22 Bedford Square, London WC1B 3HH
Published in the U.S.A. 1982 by
Barnes & Noble Books

Printed and bound in Great Britain by
Biddles Ltd, Guildford and King's Lynn

Preface

In the years since the Second World War the poetry reader in this country and in America has taken an unprecedented interest in the work of poets writing in languages with which he is either partially or totally unfamiliar, the so-called 'modern languages' of a Europe which, though occupying only a small portion of it, has culturally dominated the world. It is a peculiar phenomenon, not least insofar as poetry is generally, and surely rightly, considered as language at its most expressive, and therefore strictly untranslatable into any other tongue. Anyone with a smattering of a given language can see, usually at a glance, how much has been lost in bringing over – the root meaning of the word 'translation' – a poem from that language into English; one famous definition of poetry is 'that which gets lost in translation'. Yet the poetry reader derives a satisfaction from translated poetry that differs in degree rather than in kind from that which he is accustomed to feel when reading poetry in his own language; it is possible to argue that there is a substratum present in every poetic utterance which enables it to withstand and survive translation. The evidence for the latter position is surely quite as strong, indeed in some ways stronger, than it is for the former; the vast majority of poetry readers, after all, possess nothing like the amount of linguistic expertise which would enable them to read all the significant European poetry of the last hundred and fifty years or so in the five major and countless minor languages in which it was originally written. In practice even exceptional linguists are occasionally dependent on translated materials. It is not surprising that in recent years there should have been several attempts to show that each act of reading is essentially, whether or not we are conscious of it, an act of translation. The difference between a second-order activity (in which we read the poetry of our native language) and a third-order one (in which we read the modern poetry of Europe in more or less serviceable translations) cannot, of course, be conjured away, and even bilingual editions, desirable though they are, leave some readers with an unbridgeable gap. But literature, and poetry in particular, seems to possess some unnamable and indescribable agent which ensures that the pleasure principle, though not without a struggle, is finally triumphant over the reality principle, as I expect most of my readers will be ready to agree.

There exist many critical introductions to modern European poetry, of which the most significant are listed in my bibliography. In none of them, however, whatever their respective merits, has an attempt been made to give an idea of an individual author's whole *oeuvre* considered independently of any thematic strain which he may be taken as representative of. This I have tried to provide in what follows, by taking fifty poets whose stature, either in national or international terms, cannot seriously be questioned. The choice of such figures obviously becomes more contentious with living poets (roughly one-fifth of those I deal with) or with those born in the last eighty years (roughly one-third). But well over thirty of the poets considered here, perhaps even as many as forty, effectively demand inclusion in an enterprise of this kind, and will raise few eyebrows. I have tried to approach each poet in a manner which, without unduly fragmenting the book, seemed proper to a preliminary investigation, an introduction on which readers, with or without the help of the books listed in the bibliography, might build in the light of their own responses. It is the common reader with whom I am concerned; those with an expert scholarly knowledge of the material treated here should not expect to find any judgements or analyses that they have not previously worked out for themselves or encountered elsewhere.

It hardly seems necessary to defend the decision to begin

with Baudelaire; the whole of a distinctively 'modern' litera-
ture – whether or not we elect to call it 'Modernist' – can be
traced back to him in one way or another. It is an accident of
history, but one which we may be forgiven for thinking
meaningful, that none of the poets with anything like a prior
claim to be considered 'modern' – Goethe, Hölderlin, Leo-
pardi, Pushkin, Heine – lived to see the first publication in
volume form in 1857 of Baudelaire's *Les Fleurs du Mal.* Less
defensible, perhaps, is the decision to include four poets who
derive from Spanish America and a poet born in Germany
who writes in Hebrew, none of whom may strictly be termed
'European'. However, most anthologies of European poetry
permit themselves a similar degree of latitude, at least as far
as poetry in Spanish is concerned, and once again I have
allowed the pleasure principle, conditioned by the intrinsic
interest of the poets in question, full rein. Least defensible of
all is the decision to dispense with quotations from the original
languages. But I cannot expect the common reader to be pro-
ficient in more than one (and I cannot know which one) of the
major languages of Europe (French, German, Italian,
Spanish and Russian), and to have quoted in Portuguese,
Polish, Modern Greek, Hungarian, Serbo-Croat and Modern
Hebrew would have been even more pointless, even assuming
I could have deceived my readers into thinking that I had any
acquaintance with them. It would have unnecessarily im-
poverished this book to have omitted the eight poets writing
in the minor languages simply because I could not read them
in the original, and I have been more than content to use the
available translations which almost all my readers will also
avail themselves of. However, I have felt it necessary to make
my own versions of the lines I wished to quote from poetry
written in the major European languages, convinced that I
could otherwise never have come close to feeling, rightly or
wrongly, that I had begun to understand the poems. I have
used all the books listed in the bibiliography as aids in what
inevitably made an already difficult task into an extremely
demanding one, but in the cases of Borges and Brodsky, who
have supervised the translation of their poems into English,

I have accepted what they themselves would have been well able to alter if they had so wished. Since I am not primarily concerned with generalized themes and individual native traditions, I have preferred to follow chronology even when it permits certain figures to intrude in what might otherwise have been, notably in the case of the Russian poets born between 1889 and 1893, significant clusters. Within an inevitably heterogeneous structure a certain homogeneity seems nevertheless to emerge.

The reader will decide upon the strengths and weaknesses of the book as a whole. The essays, brief as they are, are meant to encourage him to read or re-read the poetry to which they refer. If anything I write should discourage him from doing so, I hope he will turn to the poems themselves, in whatever form he finds them most accessible, and share my conviction that the last century and a quarter has been one of the most fertile periods for poetry in the long history of European literature.

Reading, 1981

Charles Baudelaire (1821–67)

Born in Paris, the son of a retired senator and a soon-to-be-widowed mother. Sent to boarding-school in Lyons after his mother's remarriage to a colonel in the army with whom he later quarrelled. An avid reader of the Romantic poets during his adolescence; a brilliant but unruly pupil at the celebrated Lycée Louis-le-Grand. Enrolled as a law student in 1839 but preferred the Bohemian life of the Latin Quarter. Sailed to Mauritius and Réunion in 1841 under duress from his stepfather, and later claimed to have reached as far as India. Financially independent at his majority, he became a fashionable figure in the Quarter on his return to Paris, where he cultivated the 'dandy' image afterwards inseparably associated with him. In the early 1840s began to compose the poems later collected in *Les Fleurs du Mal* and to live with the 'black Venus' Jeanne Duval, a liaison which was to last intermittently almost until his death. In 1844 his financial affairs were taken out of his hands by his mother and stepfather. Made a profound impact with his art criticism in the later 1840s and supported the radical cause in the Revolution of 1848. Began to experiment with hashish and to think of himself as the literary descendant of Edgar Allan Poe, whom he translated. Deeply influenced by the mystical writings of Swedenborg, which prompted him to develop an aesthetic based on 'correspondences' in the years 1852–4, the period of his friendship with Madame Sabatier. Published his one collection of poems, *Les Fleurs du Mal*, in 1857 and was immediately accused of blasphemy and obscenity; fined three hundred francs on being found guilty of the latter. In poor health from 1860 onwards, with complaints of syphilitic origin. Reissued an expanded version of *Les Fleurs du Mal* in 1861, which is generally considered superior in structure to the 1857 edition. Disappointed in his campaign to gain entry to the French Academy, he embarked on a disastrous lecture tour of Belgium, where his condition deteriorated rapidly. Died in a Parisian nursing-home. Recognized on the centenary of his birth as the greatest French poet of the century, though his influence on Verlaine, Mallarmé and Rimbaud began as early as the 1860s.

In an essay on Baudelaire added to the third edition of *The Symbolist Movement in Literature* (1919) Arthur Symons writes:

He spent his whole life in writing one book of verse (out of which all French poetry has come since his time), one book of prose in which prose becomes a fine art, some criticism which is the sanest, subtlest and surest which his generation produced, and a translation which is better than a marvellous original.

Symons's remarks have the virtue of reminding us that the poet of *Les Fleurs du Mal* was also the prose poet of *Spleen de Paris*, the critic of *L'Art Romantique* and the translator of Edgar Allan Poe. Any one of these diverse but intimately related activities would have ensured Baudelaire a permanent place in the literature of his country and his continent; taken together, they make him the single most important literary figure of the nineteenth century. For Anglo-American readers the most perishable part of his output is inevitably his translations of Poe, though their decisive influence on the subsequent developments of Mallarmé and Valéry, and Poe's presence as one of the two authors who (as Baudelaire admitted) 'taught me how to reason', ensure that they will never be entirely neglected. His essays on Delacroix, Daumier, Manet, Flaubert and Wagner – all written at a time when there was very little criticism of any value on the artists concerned – have long been recognized as among the most intelligent and profound responses to the great figures of nineteenth-century culture. His fifty or so prose poems – 'without rhythm and rhyme, supple enough and rugged enough to adapt ... to the lyrical impulses of the soul, the undulations of reverie, the jibes of conscience' – constitute the first significant, and in some respects unsurpassed, ventures into what is now one of the most distinctive genres of modern literature. And his 'one book of verse' (first published in 1857, and again four years later in an expanded and revised edition) has been one of the most influential volumes of poetry of all time. The very archetype of the modern poet – isolated, rebellious, anguished, self-destructive – derives largely from Baudelaire. It is natural, therefore, that commentators should regard the history of modern poetry as essentially the history of footnotes to a figure notorious in his lifetime and now of almost legendary stature.

Baudelaire inherited the essentially Romantic fascination for the exceptional figure who, alone upon earth, is in quest of the means whereby he may transcend terrestrial reality and find a more or less unorthodox salvation. But he lacked the consistency of purpose which had enabled his forbears to find transcendence in joyous moments of expanded consciousness and to conjure figures of intercession to ratify them; he possessed the more troubled temperament of the confirmed sceptic. Out of his scepticism certain positives emerged, though they were often in competition with one another. He told Flaubert, for example, that his ambition was to become 'a pure will constantly in motion', but one of his favourite quotations was Emerson's dictum 'the hero is he who is immovably centred'. His scepticism was evidently of the thoroughgoing kind which makes the achievement of absolutes at once imperative and impossible. Convinced of the reality of sin on an earth which he saw as essentially purgatorial, he was equally convinced of the impossibility of grace. He was left 'posting between earth and heaven' like a modern Hamlet, without any prospect of inhabiting either for any length of time.

In an attempt to bring his helpless oscillations under control Baudelaire began to contrive a method which might permit a definitive transcendence to take place. This method is perhaps best seen as a kind of secular equivalent to the spiritual exercises of an ascetic, with a belief in beauty and the poetic imagination replacing the saint's belief in God. It is the origin of later attempts to promote ideas of 'art for art's sake'. However, for Baudelaire such a method contained a moral element which later exponents of it were prepared to dispense with. In Baudelaire's view, as his essay on Théophile Gautier indicates, '[the artist is] the slave of his duty, because he does not cease to obey the obligations of his calling, because the love of beauty is for him a matter of destiny, because he sees his duty as irresistible compulsion'. A similarly homiletic tone is detectable at the end of the essay 'Of The Essence Of Laughter', where one of the obligations of the artist's calling is identified: 'the artist is an artist only on condition that he is dual and that he is ignorant of none of the phenomena of his dual nature'. Baudelaire's own dualistic temperament clearly dictated that this would have to be his primary article of faith. But it was a belief rather than a method, and therefore in need of supplementation. Precisely because Baudelaire saw himself as 'a slave to his duty' he needed to evolve some system whereby he could also be master of it.

Baudelaire's first attempt at mastery was to propose, in the words of a famous letter to the naturalist Toussenel, that 'Imagination is the most *scientific* of the faculties, because it alone understands *universal analogy*, or what a mystic religion calls *correspondence*.' Of the many authors from whom he might have derived this idea it is clear that the mystical writings of Swedenborg and the speculative stories and essays of Edgar Allan Poe were of paramount importance to him. However, his sceptical temperament prevented him from believing in the unaided powers of the imagination; when the imagination failed, its 'scientific' properties required artificial resuscitation. Through the agency of narcotics and stimulants he was offered access to what he knew to be 'artificial paradises', but the inherent ephemerality of such paradises left him overwhelmed by enslavement to the very stimulants which had provoked them. His incessant and ironical self-scrutiny obliged him to adopt a tone at once cold and passionate even in his intimate journals. But one of the entries in 'My Heart Laid Bare' shows him unmistakably aware of how his cultural fetishes (the origin of his celebrated advocacy of 'the dandy' as a modern hero) had only cloaked, and not supplanted, the nature underneath:

I have cultivated my hysteria with delight and terror. Now I suffer continually from vertigo, and today, the 23rd of January 1862, I have received a singular warning: I have felt the wind of the wings of madness pass over me.

He came finally to acquiesce in what he saw as 'a destiny eternally solitary'. But it could not disguise the absolute absence of any curative strategies, as a passage in one of his prose 'Squibs' indicates:

For myself, who feel within me sometimes the absurdity of a prophet, I know that I shall never achieve the charity of a physician. Lost in this vile world, elbowed by the crowd, I am like a worn-out man, whose eyes see, in the depths of the years behind him, only disillusionment and bitterness, ahead only a tumult in which there is nothing new, whether of enlightenment or of suffering.

It is in the poems of *Les Fleurs du Mal*, which the poet told his mother were 'created with passion and deliberation', that the drama of Baudelaire's life takes on its most concentrated and crystalline form. He had praised the painter Delacroix for his 'disdain for the superfluous' and to achieve something comparable in poetry he chose forms for his abrasively contemporary subject matter which were mainly conventional and classical. Like Mallarmé after him, he had a marked preference for what he called the 'Pythagorean beauty' of the sonnet. One of the fragments of 'My Heart Laid Bare' reads: 'the grand style (nothing more beautiful than the commonplace)', and *Les Fleurs du Mal* represent an unprecedently sustained attempt to perceive the beautiful in the commonplace and to clothe it with the noble eloquence of 'the grand style'. This is made plain in the poem 'The Sun', usually taken to be one of the earliest poems in the collection, which describes how the setting sun 'ennobles the destiny of the meanest things' and explicitly relates this to the activity of the poet. Another early poem ('Alas! who has not groaned ...') suggests that to perform such a transformation the poet must 'raise his eyes to the cloudless vaults', hoping to find there a consolation which will make the suffering of 'the meanest things' meaningful. In an age of bourgeois materialism such an act must, in Baudelaire's scheme of things, make the poet as despised a creature as the people he would celebrate. And if in one sense this is an imprisonment (in one poem he feels himself 'caged in a noisome hovel' like the Italian poet Tasso in Delacroix's painting), in another respect it liberates him; he can even imagine that he dominates the Underworld like the 'man of stone' Don Juan. Implicit in this latter stance (dramatized in the poem 'Don Juan In The Underworld') is the idea that the poet must undertake a spiritual journey, like his Romantic forebears (Shelley in 'Alastor', for example), and the poem 'Evaluation' is evidently one of Baudelaire's first attempts at such a journey. But in all these early poems his attachment to the physical and material world, a fallen world of sin and fleshy delights, keeps him earthbound; he is doomed, like the lesbians of 'Damned Women', to be 'a seeker after the infinite' along paths that are tragically finite. Perhaps the most memorable of Baudelaire's expressions of this theme is in the emblematic poem 'The Albatross': the giant wings which made the bird 'a prince of the clouds' inhibit its ability to perform the ordinary act of walking. In moments of ecstasy Baudelaire could put words into the mouth of an infinite and statuesque goddess who was a constant reminder of what he himself would never attain:

To hypnotize my docile lovers I
Possess pure mirrors beautifying all things:
My eyes, large eyes of timeless radiance.

                                        ('Beauty')

But his own eyes could see nothing but 'madness and horror'; *he* was afflicted with 'nocturnal visions' that no such beatitude could lighten ('The Diseased Muse').

    Baudelaire suggested in his bitterly ironic 'Consoling

Maxims On Love' (1846) that it was man's ability to exercise his freedom of choice which offered him the possibility of salvation: 'it is necessary, therefore, to choose one's loves'. In his own case he chose precisely one of the commonplace and despised creatures around whom his ideas of beauty and nobility revolved: the poor and profligate 'black Venus', Jeanne Duval. The poems in which he celebrated all her physical charms not unnaturally provoked an extreme reaction from a public in whom *pudeur* was uppermost. But, as in the case of her infinite counterpart Beauty, it was not so much her flesh as her eyes (dark and sunken and lacking all radiance) which most transfixed him. Thus hypnotized he was led to identify the lesser good with the greater and to find himself confused as to which was which, commencing an ultimately wearying quest within the confines of a vicious circle. Yet something of the Petrarchan tradition, in which the inaccessible beloved occasionally shows a kindness commensurate with her cruelty, survives in some of these poems. The major difference is that the docile, passive, masochistic and oddly chaste poet finds suffering superior to satisfaction. The very sterility of Baudelaire's passion, nowhere more dramatically rendered than in 'A Carrion', became its *raison d'être*. But it widened the gulf – an obsessive word with Baudelaire – between the bliss of paradise and the unrelieved horrors of the underworld. The voyage of the soul beyond the transient pleasures of the sensibility continued to conjure up the prospect of a landfall like that hypothesized in 'The Lock of Hair', 'a reverberating port in which my soul may drink/ Huge waves of perfume, sound and colour'. But the Ideal of Beauty came more and more under pressure from a sterile reality, and in the gulf between them Baudelaire began to choose death as the only certain prospect that could please.

It was in the poems first published in April 1851 under the title 'Limbos' that the horizon of death decisively supplanted Beauty as the ideal to which Baudelaire aspired. But, as 'The Death of Artists' shows, the survival of an ideal, however sterile an ideal it may seem, requires the idealist to hope

it may be realisable. 'The Death Of The Poor' ends with an
ecstatic welcoming of death as:

The glory of the gods, the mystic granary,
The poor man's purse and ancient origin,
The gate that opens onto unknown skies.

As with other ecstasies, it obliged him to experience equally
powerful moments of agony. 'A Voyage To Cytherea' (the
island of Venus in Greek mythology) paints a much darker
portrait, confronting the poet with an ideal become reality:

The sky was pleasant, and the sea was calm;
But all, alas!, was dark and stained with blood
For me, and, as in a thick winding-sheet
My heart was buried in that allegory.

O Venus! On your island I found only
A symbolic gibbet where my image hung ...
Give me, O heavenly father, strength to look
Without disgust upon my heart, my flesh.

It is unclear whether Baudelaire himself would have con-
sidered that his prayer had been answered. But in the poems
inspired by his chaste love for the actress Madame Sabatier
the disgust recorded in the Jeanne Duval poems has effec-
tively disappeared. It would seem from the poem 'To One
Who Is Too Gay' that at first Madame Sabatier's cheerful-
ness inspired in him feelings akin to those aroused by the
saturnine Jeanne Duval. However, in one of the poems that
he sent her ('What will you say tonight ...') she plainly as-
sumes a trinity of roles – Muse, Madonna and Guardian
Angel – that had been beyond the capacity of the 'black
Venus'. The Sabatier eyes 'shine with the mystic clarity/Of
candles in daylight'; to Baudelaire they apparently seemed
an earthly counterpart of the eyes of ideal Beauty. Under this
new dispensation he was able to think more of the rising sun
than of twilights, and even to find harmony in evenings
through which 'the memory of you gleams like a monstrance'.
But the dawn proved a false one, primarily – or so it is sup-
posed – because Madame Sabatier wanted more tangible

proofs of affection than veneration. The most positive aspect of the Sabatier interlude was that it enabled Baudelaire to face the ensuing void with something approaching equanimity.

Confronted by what the poem 'The Irremediable' calls 'a heart become its own mirror' – subsequently an obsessive theme in Mallarmé and Valéry – Baudelaire's mood was less turbulent, more stoically resigned. He was still determined to prove the architect of his own salvation by making the void a substitute for the absence of the 'correspondences' with which he had begun his enterprise. But a poem of 1859 ('The Labouring Skeleton') records his recognition that he had deluded himself: 'all things, even death, lie to us'. If he remained, as the famous last line of 'The Voyage' suggests, in permanent quest of the New, it was in a quite different spirit from that later adopted by Apollinaire; it helped him to defer the conviction that there could be no remedy, that no change was possible. Such a conviction gave rise to one of his finest poems, 'The Swan', which resembles his earlier poem on the albatross, but is much more complex. The second section of the poem dramatizes how, despite the fact that 'everything becomes an allegory for me', the reality remains unaltered by such transformations:

Paris changes. But in my melancholy
Nothing moves.

It was out of this trough of self-absorption that Baudelaire, in his poems about the widowed, the old and the sightless, came close to achieving what he thought he never would possess: the 'charity of the physician'. His response to them was, like their passage through the streets, 'stoical and uncomplaining'. And it was a mood which the greater flexibility of the prose poem, so much closer to ordinary discourse, was especially well adapted to sustain. The 'Draft Of An Epilogue' for the second edition of *Les Fleurs du Mal* suggests that Baudelaire was even hoping to achieve the tranquillity of mind associated with the sage. A great late sonnet depicts this most memorably:

Be wise, my Sorrow, and more still.
You cried for night; it falls; and it is here.

It is possible – though this is still a matter of dispute – that, having found what he called his 'calmative', the poet whose name had become synonymous with Satanism was able to return to the Catholicism he had abandoned. A shrewd associate of Baudelaire's suggested that the author of *Les Fleurs du Mal* had only two choices left: to become a Christian or to blow his brains out. He did not blow out his brains, though his life, like that of Edgar Allan Poe, bears some of the marks of a long, slow, suicide. As for becoming a Christian, the best evidence would seem to be in the poem 'The Unforeseen', though Baudelaire's own note on it exposes it to his usual inflexion of irony:

Here the author of *Les Fleurs du Mal* is turning towards the eternal life. It had to end like that. Let us note that, like all new converts, he is very strict and very fanatical.

It seems appropriate that a poet who had indeed been both strict and fanatical, in accordance with his belief that the artist should be 'ignorant of none of the phenomena of his dual nature', should have left the matter open to the partisans to settle.

One cannot hope to do justice to Baudelaire in the space of a few paragraphs; he demands the same concentration that he employed as a method. 'It must be very obvious', he told his mother in 1865, 'that the little I have done is the result of a very painful effort'. André Gide wrote of Baudelaire in his journal for 1920: 'incomparable distress of that soul, every one of whose efforts is a desperate one'. Baudelaire's centrality for successive generations of readers, however, has consisted in the way his poems and prose poems objectify that distress and make coherent art out of the fragments of a life. One of the poet's most memorable utterances on the fate of Edgar Allan Poe suggests he would have understood and condoned this 'redemptive' attitude to his own work: 'a part of what is today the source of our enjoyment is what killed him'.

Stéphane Mallarmé (1842–98)

Born in Paris, the son of a government official. Lived with his grandparents for a year after the death of his mother in 1847. Sent to boarding-school and afterwards to *lycées* where his academic performance was unexceptional. Composed a considerable amount of juvenilia in the years 1854–60, much of it under the influence of Victor Hugo. Profoundly distressed by the death of his sister in 1857. Decisively influenced by Baudelaire, whom he read for the first time in 1861. Married a woman of German extraction in London in 1863, where he had gone to learn English, primarily (as he told Verlaine) in order to read Poe in the original. Began the composition of the works by which he is remembered whilst teaching English at *lycées* in Tournon, Besançon and Avignon from 1863 to 1870, when he was in an almost unrelieved condition of spiritual torment. Returned to Paris in 1871 to teach English at the Lycée Condorcet and Collège Rollin until five years before his death. In 1874 moved to an apartment in the rue de Rome, which after 1880 became famous for the Tuesday night gatherings held there, the meeting-place for all those interested in Symbolism. His poems were privately printed in 1887; he became notorious for his obscurity on the publication in 1892 of a selection of his verse and prose. Invited in 1894 on the strength of his Parisian fame to lecture in Oxford and Cambridge, where the audience found him largely incomprehensible. Little is known of his personal life, and his liaison with Méry Laurent, whom he first met at Manet's studio in 1881, does not appear to have left its mark on his poetry, except in the case of one of his famous 'Fan' poems. Died in his summer retreat at Valvins of a long-

standing respiratory complaint. Regarded with suspicion in
French academic circles for many years after his death, but
a great influence on modern French writing, especially in the
years since the Second World War.

No modern poetry is more forbidding at first glance, even for
those with an excellent command of French, than Mal-
larmé's. The very qualities for which the French language is
famed, its clarity and its logic, seem to have been flagrantly
and wilfully flouted and enveloped in a cloak of impenetrable
mystery. It was Mallarmé's intention, expressed in a line
familiar to readers of Eliot's *Four Quartets*, to 'give a purer
sense to the words of the tribe' (to purify their 'dialect' as Eliot
has it). But his quest for purity was so extreme and unremit-
ting that, apart from those who gathered round him in his
last twenty years, the tribe may scarcely be said to have
benefited from his experiment. He was much more concerned
with words – he even wrote an eccentric study of English
words – than with people, and especially with words that
would approximate his ideal of 'pure' poetry. Such an atti-
tude led him to adopt an unprecedented aesthetic position
– perhaps the ultimate position that an 'aesthete' might oc-
cupy – whereby 'all earthly existence must ultimately be con-
tained in a book'. This amounted to nothing less than a
deification of language itself: 'If the poem is to be pure, the
poet's voice must be stilled and the initiative taken by the
words themselves, which will be set in motion as they meet
unequally in collision'. It is a prescription which sounds
faintly like an obsessive linguist's account of the creation of
the world. A similar note is struck in a lecture Mallarmé
gave to a bewildered audience at the University of Oxford
in 1894: 'I am asking for a total restoration ... whereby the
mind may seek its own native land again'. Mallarmé's native
land was, like the paradise of the theologians, a place of the
utmost perfection. But it was both unimaginable and indes-
cribable. In this respect his deification of language was in-
sufficient, despite his belief in its omnipotence, to provide him

with access to it. The supreme language, he was forced to admit, was missing: 'the diversity of languages on earth means that no one can utter words which would bear the miraculous stamp of Truth Herself Incarnate'. Insofar as there was an unbridgeable gulf between words and truth, all utterance became provisional. And in the face of the object – whether in the normal sense of something perceived in the external world or in the philosophical sense of something presented to the mind – all speech became periphrasis. This is the origin of Mallarmé's celebrated dictum that the artist must 'describe not the object itself, but the effect it produces'. Had he been concerned with the external world, he might have become something like a poetic equivalent of his favourite Impressionist painter, Claude Monet. But his 'object', in both senses of the word, was the inner world of his imagination, within the imprisoned orbit of which his words were born and died. He told his Oxford audience that their ambition should be to 'prove to the satisfaction of our soul that a natural phenomenon corresponds to our imaginative understanding of it', almost as if to console them with the familiar claim that literature's task was to hold 'a mirror up to nature'. But he added a tell-tale admission which indicates where his true interest lay: 'And our hope, of course, is that we may ourselves be reflected in it.'

To hold the mirror up to the inner world of the self and the mind might not have been so pressing a concern of Mallarmé's if he had not suffered, while teaching English at a *lycée* in Tournon, a partly religious, partly ontological crisis known as the 'nights of Tournon'. Its results are easier to describe than its causes or symptoms. It involved an 'assumption' in which personal identity was lost and the poet became 'one of the ways which the Spiritual Universe has found to see Itself'; an elevation to a transcendent and eternal world of Beauty; a dream-like synthesis in which all self-division was overcome; and an intimation of rebirth from a point of origin. Its primary cause would appear to have been intense scrutiny of his own thought-processes in monastic seclusion, and its primary symptom a sensation of absence, of void, of nothing-

ness: 'in order to perpetuate the indelible idea of pure Noth-
ingness, I had to fill my brain with the sensation of absolute
Emptiness'. The literary analogue for such a shipwreck was
almost certainly the peculiar encounter with a substantial
void which concludes Poe's *Narrative of Arthur Gordon Pym*; the
philosophical analogue was presumably Hegel's *Phenomenology
of the Spirit*, in which Hegel proposes that, by means of ne-
gation, an object becomes a concept. But the experience was
clearly one which Mallarmé would have suffered without ever
reading Poe or Hegel, and he certainly made it the basis for
the whole of his subsequent poetic activity. For the experience
of Nothingness filled him with horror, and thereafter lan-
guage – which possessed the properties of a substantial Noth-
ing – had to be brought in to occupy the vacuum, to temper
the void and to clothe its nakedness. In this way, in the
manner of what mathematicians call an inverse proof (as he
himself told a correspondent), he conjured a landfall out of
a shipwreck; 'the dream that destroyed me will restore me'.
Judged by the number of poems he was able to write after
the crisis – some forty in thirty years, together with a few
prose poems – not to mention the fact that 'The Book' (as
he came to call it) remained unfinished, the restoration was
less total than he might have wished for; no doubt this is why
it figured in his Oxford lecture. In the event the restoration
that had grown out of destruction retained destruction as its
primary feature, so that each poem thereafter became a kind
of repeated shipwreck, a stain on the silence that was the only
pure index of 'Truth Herself Incarnate'. 'My work was
created only by *elimination*,' he told a friend; 'destruction was
my Beatrice'. The primary casualty of such an approach
was what we ordinarily understand by 'physical reality'; as
late as 1891 he was still admonishing a fellow-poet to 'gnaw
and reduce' the real world and to pursue the secret and
hidden identities of a mysterious inner world. Mallarmé's hero
was explicitly the man who 'keeps looking up at the sky as he
dies of hunger'. But to defer death by inanition he contented
himself and sustained himself by looking in at the imaginary
universe which offered the nearest human approximation to

the infinite horizons suggested by, and at the same time ob-
scured by, the sky.

'Things already exist; we don't have to create them', Mal-
larmé told an interviewer in 1891; 'we simply have to see their
relationships'. Far from wishing to create things he wished
to negate them, or rather believed that language could not
do otherwise:

> Why should we perform the miracle by which a natural object is
> almost made to disappear beneath the magic waving wand of the
> written word, if not to divorce that object from the direct and the
> palpable, and so conjure up its *essence* in all purity?
>   When I say: 'flower', then from that forgetfulness to which my
> voice consigns all floral form, something different from the usual
> calyces arises, something all music, essence and softness: the flower
> which is absent from all bouquets.

As this passage shows, Mallarmé was not really intent
(though he used the analogy) on being a modern alchemist,
turning base metal into gold as Baudelaire had found beauty
in ugliness. He thought of himself as a kind of verbal magi-
cian, who could make real things disappear and reappear as
either more real or less real, or both at once. 'Our eternal
and only problem', he said in his Oxford lecture, 'is to seize
relationships and intervals, however few or multiple. Thus,
faithful to some special vision deep within, we may extend
or simplify the world at will.' It was natural for Mallarmé,
with beliefs of this kind, to take an interest in art-forms which,
by comparison with 'The Book' he could not write, were in-
herently ephemeral: the performing arts of the theatre, the
concert-hall, the ballet, even the fashion-show. It was his
abiding belief that 'to create is to conceive an object in its
fleeting moment, in its absence':

> To do this, we simply compare its facets and dwell lightly,
> negligently, upon their multiplicity. We conjure up a scene of
> lovely, evanescent, intersecting forms.

As a poet, however, the 'intersecting forms' which most
intrigued him were those of syntax itself, especially when
placed under the constraints of the sonnet, and made more

difficult still by *recherché* rhymes and a virtual absence of punctuation. At the opposite pole from the silence which would be the 'supreme language' Mallarmé situated the game carried out for the sheer pleasure of participating in it. And to those who wanted to know what the rules of the game were he would reply 'Syntax', knowing full well that his syntax was so fluid it would permit unrelated or mutually exclusive readings to be made. For Mallarmé this 'game' aspect enhanced the poem and made it at once more fragile and more self-sustaining, like a spider's web or a piece of music. A 'series of decodings' was more important to him than a single para-phrasable meaning, and since there was no cipher other than that which the syntax at once pointed towards and away from, the series of decodings was potentially infinite. It was his hope that the decodings were fragments of what, *sub specie aeternitatis*, would be revealed as a synthesis:

During the last twenty-five years poetry has been visited by some nameless and absolute flash of lightning . . . revealing that, in general, all books contain the amalgamation of a certain number of age-old truths; that actually there is only one book on earth; that it is the law of the earth, the earth's true Bible. The difference between individual works is simply the difference between individual interpretations of one true and established text.

This, as other remarks of Mallarmé confirm, is an aesthetic position analogous to that of the Orphic cults of early Greek religion: it makes language and universe, word and world, co-extensive and retroactive upon each other. Anyone wishing to defend Mallarmé against the obvious charge of obscurity that he does nothing to discourage is effectively forced to adopt a similar stance, like Paul Valéry, his most devoted and most gifted disciple:

[These crystalline constructions] have not the transparency of glass, no doubt; but in that they somehow break habits of mind on their facets and on their concentrated structure, what is called their obscurity is only, in reality, their *refraction*.

However, the difficulty with Mallarmé is not the recognition that refraction is taking place, but rather to recognize

the norm (or 'true, established text') against which the devi-
ation is to be measured. One cannot help feeling that more
accessible amalgamations of age-old truths would not have
had to wait so long for recognition and could have been more
effortlessly achieved. The shortcomings of 'pure poetry' have
become clearer with the passage of time and the continuing
impurity of things other than poetry; it yields to no other type
of poetry in beauty, but it seems to lack a fundamentally
human dimension.

The absence of a human dimension is less marked in Mal-
larmé's pre-crisis poems, which represent about one third of
his poetic *oeuvre*. Many of them, like 'Anguish', 'Renewal',
'The Ringer' and 'The Azure', are effectively confessional, a
lament at the apparently unbridgeable gulf between a miser-
able terrestrial world and the evidences of a purely transcen-
dent one. But in two of the finest ('Sea Breeze' and 'The
Windows') Mallarmé envisages the kind of journey that
might enable him to traverse the intervening space, together
with its consequences. The last stanza of 'The Windows' is
representative:

Is there a way, O Self who knew bitterness,
To smash the crystal by the monster soiled

And flee on my threadbare wings
– At the risk of falling for eternity?

There *was* a way, as the great crisis poems 'Herodias' and
'A Faun's Afternoon' demonstrated. But it involved the cre-
ation of what Valéry was to call 'crystalline constructions'
quite as much as it involved smashing crystals. In the case
of 'Herodias' Mallarmé was unable to complete such a con-
struction to his satisfaction, despite obsessive work on the
poem; had it been completed, it seems probable that it would
have dramatized a self's confrontation with, and conquest of,
its 'otherness'. As it stands it is, like the Hamlet-like pro-
tagonist of Mallarmé's prose fragment 'Igitur', 'rendered un-
stable by the malady of the ideal'. 'A Faun's Afternoon', the
mood of which is captured and rendered more accessible by
Debussy's music, represents something of a convalescence;

despite the faun's presentiment of 'certain doom', his languid insouciance as to whether he has created or reflected the nymphs he has been addressing seems to betoken a more relaxed state of mind, a diminution of bitterness. Unlike the pre-crisis poems, however, 'Herodias' and 'A Faun's Afternoon' do all they can to discourage a reading of them in terms of a specifically human drama; in each case the central figure is emblematic of an essence, an almost perfect representative of an ideal. The same is true of the non-fictional beings, all artists and all dead, whom Mallarmé takes as the pretext, in sonnets of great formal grandeur, for his ideas on poetry: Poe, Baudelaire, Wagner and Verlaine. They have reached a perfection in death that Herodias and the faun cannot achieve; they are, as the famous first line of 'The Tomb of Edgar Poe' obliquely suggests, 'Such as at last Eternity changes into Itself'. Those left alive are, by comparison (as the 'Funeral Toast' for Gautier reminds us), 'the sad solidity of our future ghosts'.

It is into such a ghostly world that the late poems of Mallarmé take us, a world of smoke-rings, lace-curtains, sprays of foam, and flutterings of fans. All of these dramatic props in Mallarmé's imaginary universe seem to offer intimations of the covenant between the nothing that man is and the great Nothing that he must become; they are what Mallarmé called 'the trembling of the veil of the temple – meaningful folds and a little tearing'. The desire for a transcendent world is overwhelming and never more powerfully expressed than in the famous 'Swan' sonnet, where the constellation Cygnus seems to mock the whole enterprise. But the language employed begins to approach Mallarmé's ideal of autonomous utterance, so that most readers remain trapped in its 'folds' and ill-equipped to perpetrate 'a little tearing'. This is even more true of Mallarmé's last composition, *A Dice Throw*, still – after nearly a century – the *ne plus ultra* of strangeness, or estrangement, in modern poetry. Here it is less the 'folds' than the 'tearing' which we are required to take account of, for the creative act is exposed as an unavoidable shipwreck; the reader is left – like the writer – with only a handful of enigmatic spars to cling to. To think (or to imagine, or to create) is acknowledged to be a hopeless gesture, an act which 'will never abolish chance' (or death, or the absolute). Yet insofar as 'Typography becomes a ritual' (as Mallarmé intended it should in this poem), the blank spaces which surround it may be presumed to play a part comparable to the pause in a drama or in a piece of music. Paul Valéry reacted to this extreme experiment in an unambiguously positive manner: 'He has raised, I thought, a page to the power of the starry sky'. But few readers have been able wholeheartedly to endorse this famous judgement, and there seems to be no way in which these constellations of words could be made to yield up their secrets to everyone's satisfaction.

'I may someday deserve to be considered as an amateur, but no more than that', Mallarmé wrote to a friend in 1864. He has come, on the contrary, to be thought of as literature's most Olympian professional, and was considered as such by the group of disciples and acolytes who gathered round him at the end of his life. There have always been dissenting voices, however: the Jules Renard who considered him 'untranslatable, even into French'; the Tolstoy who, faced with a particularly formidable sonnet, said 'this poem is not exceptional in its incomprehensibility; I have read several other poems by Mallarmé and they also had no meaning whatsoever'. It is in the nature of the case that he should continue to be both deified and derided; there has yet to be an account of him that does not gravitate towards one pole or the other, perhaps because – as befits so thought-tormented a man – he was his own best reader.

Paul Verlaine (1844–96)

Born in Metz, the only child of an army captain and a bourgeois mother who doted on him. Inspired to become a poet by reading Baudelaire's *Les Fleurs du Mal* in the year of its publication. Published his first collection, *Poèmes saturniens*, in 1866, by which time his dependence on alcohol, later to reach gargantuan proportions, was established, as were his bisexual tastes. Soon after the publication of his second collection (*Fêtes galantes*, 1869) he met the woman he was to marry, after a protracted courtship, in 1870. Worked halfheartedly in the administration of the Paris Commune. First met Rimbaud in 1871, after which he effectively abandoned his wife and child. Lived more or less turbulently with Rimbaud until 1873, when he fired a pistol at him, injuring Rimbaud's hand. Imprisoned in Belgium on a charge of attempted murder; reconfirmed his Catholicism whilst in prison at Mons. On release returned to England, which he had visited with Rimbaud, to teach French at Stickney Grammar School in Lincolnshire, where he struggled to remain sober and pious. At the time of the appearance of the volume *Sagesse* (1876) – variously regarded as the culmination of his achievement and the beginning of his decline – he was teaching at a private Catholic school in Bournemouth. Taught in the Ardennes, where he began a passionate friendship with a young male pupil who accompanied him to England. Having failed to find settled employment, he returned to provincial France and worked on the book which was ultimately to make Corbière, among others, famous: *Les Poètes maudits* (1884). After the death of his mother in 1886 he sought comfort from a series of motherly whores and became physically, morally and, with very few exceptions, poetically degenerate, though continuing to be admired for the verbal beauty of his earlier verse. Died bedridden in Paris at the height of his notoriety and fame, since when the interest aroused by his work has fluctuated.

Of the great French poets who decisively redirected the course of poetry in the latter half of the nineteenth century, only Verlaine has fallen from the position of eminence which, at the end of his life, led to him being granted the unofficial title of 'Prince of Poets'. The final *coup de grâce* came at a time when the leading spokesman for the new Surrealist movement was intent on the elevation of the most important figure in Verlaine's life, the poet Rimbaud: 'the overestimation of Verlaine', said André Breton, 'was the great error of the Symbolist epoch'. Verlaine was, for a time, much the most influential of the French Symbolists, inspiring any number of poets to emulate his achievement in their native languages. Yet the qualities of his best work were strictly inimitable, as he himself – in a long and painful decline – had occasion to discover. And if with hindsight he does indeed seem slightly less compelling than Baudelaire, Mallarmé or Rimbaud, it is only because he did not sustain his early promise and achievement. Verlaine's temperament and intellect look febrile and rather conservative when placed beside those of his great contemporaries. But the shortcomings of his intellect are best regarded as strengths rather than weaknesses in the career of a poet for whom cerebral activity was always far less important than surrender to those impulses of sensation which defined the essential and timeless structures of the sensibility. Verlaine's greatness as 'the first poet in the world, in some things' (as Ben Jonson said of Donne) has, in fact, never been seriously questioned. Indeed his position as the most musical of French poets, the most subtle exponent of 'nuance' (as he called it in his famous 'Art Poétique' of 1874), seems to grow more rather than less secure, however little of the contemporary limelight he may occupy. His virtuoso experiments with versification have tended to matter more to experts and to literary historians than to the common reader, and his musicality effectively resists translation into a non-Romance language. But insofar as the identification of (and response to) nuance remains an inseparable part of any reader's experience of poetry Verlaine is obviously a much less negligible figure than André Breton would have had him be, with a much more widespread and permanent appeal than Breton himself could ever enjoy.

In an essay which was one of the first serious assessments of Baudelaire's greatness, Verlaine spoke of the 'deceptive and difficult' elements inherent in what Baudelaire had contrived to make 'so simple in appearance'. Verlaine's own simplicity is not without its 'deceptive and difficult' facets. These are visible in some, if not all, of the poems in his first volume, the *Saturnine Poems* of 1866. The 'Prologue' rather misleadingly tries to place this collection under the sign of the chiselled and marmoreal Parnassians, but the adjective in the title, and the character of the best poems, identify these early manifestations of Verlaine's spirit – very early, if we can believe Verlaine's claim to have written them at the age of sixteen – as primarily indebted to Baudelaire. Even here, however, there are poems like the famous 'Chanson d'automne' which are of uniquely Verlainean inspiration. Like many of the 'Sad Landscapes' among which it is placed, this poem effectively erases the distinction between self and world in order to articulate, as precisely and at the same time as indefinitely as possible, the intangible and yet fundamental faculty with which Verlaine was always primarily concerned: the poet's soul. The first stanza presents a typically Verlainean languor inspired by 'the long sobs/Of violins' which are quite as much metaphorical as they are real. The second records the poet's tears as prompted by the chime of a clock (once again only dubiously real) which has enabled him to elude the passive suffocation of the present but at the cost of reminding him of the past. The third and final stanza transforms the poet into a dead leaf swept away by a gust of wind and left without even his initial languor, however monotonous it may have been. The poet's physical presence in this poem is as tenuous as that of the objects on which he fixes his attention. Verlaine himself is even less present in the poem 'Mystic Twilight'; here the sudden rekindling of an impersonal Hope at sunset is immediately rendered diaphanous, as the soul, reason, and sensibility of the poet experience a kind of immense swoon which envelops all rational discriminations. The beautiful 'Sunsets' poem effectively glosses this by suggesting that the setting sun is an emblem of the heart that ceases to be aware of itself, a heart which is surrendering to a reverie more consoling than even the 'sweet songs' of melancholy offer access to. In some of these poems ('The Hour Of The Shepherd' for example,) there is actually no human heart materially present, or the heart becomes indistinguishable (as in 'The Nightingale') from 'the tree that trembles and the bird that weeps'. The primary cause of Verlaine's desire to disappear from reality altogether is made plain in the aptly-titled 'Melancholia' section of the *Saturnine Poems*. In the autumnal 'Nevermore' he is haunted by a dream-image which comes to him unbidden; in 'Three Years Afterwards' he is haunted by the faint aroma of mignonette. In both, the absence of a beloved object is suddenly brought home to him. Only in dream images, as the poignant 'My Familiar Dream' indicates, could the poet find 'a woman I love, who loves me' and whose voice ('calm, remote and grave') possessed the 'inflexion of dear dead voices'. In the absence of this insubstantial figure (as in 'Anguish'), reality was so barren that only the preparation of his soul for 'frightful shipwrecks' – quite how frightful Verlaine could never have guessed – made it meaningful for the poet.

It is usual to ascribe Verlaine's early melancholy primarily to his literary sources, and to compare the darker tones of his subsequent *Fêtes galantes* (1869) with those of the painter Watteau, whose enigmatic eighteenth-century world the *Fêtes* reproduce so delightfully. However, the 'Walpurgis Night' poem in his first volume asks questions of a similar world in a manner that shows both are distinctively Verlainean and peculiar to him.

These agitated ghosts, are they then projections
Of the drunken poet, or his regret, or his remorse,
These agitated ghosts in measured throng,
  Or simply the dead?

The famous 'Clair de lune' poem which opens the *Fêtes*
confirms unequivocally that the 'chosen landscape' on which
these 'enclosing masques and bergomasques' are being played
out is the poet's soul; the imaginary figures cannot quite
believe their happiness and in the moonlight their songs fade.
The 'Sentimental Colloquy' which ends the collection is even
gloomier, with the two speakers explicitly dead, and the dark-
ness their only audience. 'Clair de lune' and 'Sentimental
Colloquy' effectively frame the whole collection. But between
these two poems the mood is somewhat lighter, for Verlaine
is also taking an impish delight in his ability to conjure an
imaginary and ancient world. The impishness cannot conceal
the numerous intimations of disquiet: the Columbine figure
in the delicate 'Pantomime' is awakened from her dream by
the sudden and disturbing presence of voices in the breeze;
the speaker in 'The Shells' is troubled by the unspoken impli-
cations of what he finds 'in the grotto where once we loved';
the nightingale of 'Muted' cannot quite banish the despair
which the lovers feel as night falls; and in 'The Faun' the
lovers are reminded of the passage of time by the clatter
of a tambourine. Only in 'To Clymene', where the poet sur-
renders to the 'tones and aromas' which bemuse his reason,
are there intimations of permanent remedy, and even here
Verlaine contrives, by his favourite device of making the
poem one long sentence, to place all the weight on the final
line – 'So be it!' – with its faintly fatalistic tinge.

In 1870 Verlaine published a collection inspired by the
woman he had married and was soon, under the pressure of
his passion for Rimbaud, to leave. Most of these pious poems,
prophetic of some of his very weak later poetry, are negligible,
with Verlaine no longer occupying that shadowy and insub-
stantial world which was uniquely his, but preferring to bask
in the sun of a reciprocated love. Having found the soul for
which, as the opening poem of the volume acknowledges, his

own soul had longed, Verlaine's ability to portray the inner drama of his sensibility seems temporàrily to have deserted him. The best that can be said of *La Bonne Chanson* is that it inspired Fauré to write one of his loveliest song-cycles. In the *Songs Without Words* of 1874, Verlaine coarsened his poetry still further (in the section called 'Birds In The Night') when he tried to accuse his wife and to justify his own behaviour in the interim. Yet *Songs Without Words* contains some of Verlaine's most wonderful and accomplished poems, especially in the 'Forgotten Ariettes' with which it opens. These poems have given rise to considerable critical debate as to whether they were inspired by Rimbaud or by the poet's wife, although this is plainly immaterial to the quality of Verlaine's achievement. Indeed what makes these poems so powerful is the way Verlaine has refined certain motifs and situations which, quickened though they may have been by the traumas of his triangular relationship, were present in his poetry long before he had met either Rimbaud or his wife. The 'drowned hopes' of poem IX (another powerful 'soul-landscape') originate in 'Mystic Twilight'; the birds in the trees – an habitual image with Verlaine – recall 'The Nightingale'. In poem VII, the soul's inability to answer the question posed it by the heart has many antecedents in Verlaine's earlier poetry, though none are quite so trenchant in their expression of 'exile'. The languor of poem III is reminiscent of the famous 'Chanson d'automne', although once again the emotions seem to have taken on a more crystalline focus than in the earlier poem. The famous poem VIII, which transfers the poet's *ennui* to a flat landscape on which the snow gleams like sand, brilliantly embodies the poet's sense of imprisonment by repeating its initial two stanzas in reverse order later in the poem. The most surprising but least characteristic images in these ariettes are those presumed to have been inspired by Rimbaud, the 'double eye' of poem II, for example.

The ariettes are the closest that *Songs Without Words* comes to justifying its title (borrowed from Mendelssohn), and nothing else in the volume quite measures up to their simultaneously fragile and high-tensile power. He was only occasionally thereafter to achieve the flawless and infinitely suggestive simplicity of poems that make words sing without any of the strain that usually accompanies such an activity. His dereliction at being imprisoned for firing shots at Rimbaud was total, and enforced separation from him seems to have permanently damaged his spirit. It was whilst in prison that he reaffirmed the Catholicism of his childhood, and two years after his release he published his last important volume (*Sagesse*, 1876). *Sagesse* has been extravagantly admired by some French critics, and it is no disparagement of the collection to say, with Rémy de Gourmont, that Verlaine 'always sings the same love song, whether his love is love of a woman or of the angels, and it is almost the same sensuality'. The sacred poems of *Sagesse* are sensual and yet innocent; the reference in poem V to a 'childlike heart' sets the volume's keynote. But it is possible to regret the absence of the 'deceptive and difficult' elements of his earlier poems. The special naïveté which Verlaine valued so highly – his first letter to Mallarmé in 1866 makes mention of how important he considered 'naïveté' to be – comes over best in the sequence 'My God Said To Me'. Here Verlaine's previously melancholy addresses to an auditor only shadowily present are given an unexpectedly, but not unreservedly, positive colouring. And there is a residual intimation of dialogue in the very beautiful sonnet beginning 'Hope gleams like a blade of straw in the stable', the syntax of which has all the tense and tranquil properties of Verlaine's most memorable poems. There are examples in part three of *Sagesse* (where most of the best poems in the volume are to be found) of what one can only call 'songs without words', a genre to which, even in his decline, Verlaine could occasionally contribute. But the volumes after *Sagesse* are throttled by a distressing inability to write much more than mere words, deprived of the music and nuance with which his name is synonymous.

When his sensuality was engaged, as in the clandestine and pornographic poems which are still not included in the definitive edition of Verlaine's *Complete Works*, Verlaine could still write with something like his old verve. And though he abused his frame with a ferocious and almost vocational attraction for dissipation, there were still moments in his later years when he could speak trenchantly. His reaction to someone who was intent on labelling him a Symbolist is particularly shrewd, and deserves to be better known: 'When I suffer or rejoice or weep, I know quite well that that isn't a symbol'. Verlaine remains, despite his shortcomings, the supreme exponent of a poetry of feelings which was bound to prove vulnerable to the aggressive and fundamentally intellectual theoretical stances of those who came after him, but which is obviously addressed to the permanent features of anyone's sensibility, which do not alter very much.

Tristan Corbière (1845–75)

Born Édouard-Joachim Corbière near Morlaix in Brittany, the son of a sea-captain who published poems and novels. Suffered from rheumatism as a child and from tuberculosis from the age of fifteen. A celebrated eccentric and practical joker in the Roscoff of his young manhood, where he fell in love with the Italian actress mistress of a French Count, who removed her to Paris in 1871. Himself moved to Paris in early 1872, where he spent much of his time with the Count and his mistress. Returned to Brittany, where his father paid for the printing of his solitary collection of poems *Les Amours Jaunes* (1873), which was completely ignored by the public. Became gravely ill in Paris, and was taken home by his mother to Morlaix, where he died a few months before his father. Discovered by Verlaine in 1883, who included him in *Les poètes maudits* (1884), and later by the young T. S. Eliot. Much admired by the Surrealists, but still an equivocal figure for the majority of the French literary establishment. A recurrent minor presence in Anglo-American literature where he tends, however, to be overshadowed, by the equally short-lived and equally unconventional Jules Laforgue.

Corbière's life and work conform so exactly to the received idea of the *poète maudit* or 'cursed' poet that it seems natural to regard him as a kind of archetype defining an otherwise superfluous, or at best inexact, descriptive term. It was not until nine years after his death, in 1884, that Corbière was rescued from oblivion and assured of something resembling a posterity by Paul Verlaine, who included an essay on him and a selection from his work in the book which gave the term currency: *Les poètes maudits*. In 1873 Corbière had published his solitary volume of poems, *Les Amours Jaunes*, with funds provided by his father, and been completely ignored. And even in the past hundred years there have been attempts to dislodge him from the marginal and vulnerable position in literary history which he inevitably occupies. Corbière seems, in fact, to have mattered more to Anglo-American readers than to most of the pillars of the French literary establishment. In England and America he is known, where he is known at all, as one of two shadowy and short-lived French nineteenth century poets – the other being Jules Laforgue – who influenced the early poetry of T. S. Eliot; but since Laforgue was the greater influence, it is Corbière's name rather than his poetry that is most often cited. Laforgue himself compared Corbière to 'a pirate on the prowl' and it is no doubt proper that he should have remained a kind of pariah in the history of modern poetry. To have been granted such a posterity at all, would presumably in any case have been greeted by Corbière with one of the jaundiced laughs (*rires jaunes* in French idiom) which are the hallmarks of his poetry and which, with the added implication that it is 'yellowback' pornographic literature, provided him with a title for it. Yet this 'amateur succeeding by strokes of genius' (as Edgell Rickword has called him) can command an affection that his more famous and more substantial contemporaries do not always inspire. There is something very human in the way Corbière adopted as his Christian name an archetypal emblem of sadness, whether in Arthurian romance or in Wagnerian opera, and yet completely scorned the sublimities associated with it. What little we know of his one major love affair suggests that it possessed none of the tragic grandeur of Tristan's. And his own reckless journeys by boat in all weathers, his only companion a wretched spaniel (Tristan II) for whom he obviously reserved his greatest affection, seem to have been motivated, quite unlike his namesake's, primarily by disgust with himself. His rejection of his bourgeois origins was pretty well total, though he evidently admired his father; he not only went sailing in his boat but, together with his dog, used to sleep in it on the beach near his Breton birthplace. Corbière was supremely gifted in puncturing not only the pretension he abhorred in others but also his own pretension to be writing poetry at all. Yet he is far from being a merely satiric poet; the novelist Huysmans aptly compared the cries of pain which issue from his dry and abrasive manner to the breaking of a violin string.

Corbière is the poet of one volume and a few stray 'comb-and-paper' pieces (or *mirlitons*) which might have gone towards the making of another. No principle of development is discernible in *Les Amours Jaunes*, and no date or place of composition is to be trusted. And yet the seven sub-divisions of the book possess a certain logic, to which even the poems which he himself did not include (but which since have been added by editors) can be relatively easily assimilated. The first section of *Les Amours Jaunes* ('That?') establishes the mood which will undergo only a very slight degree of alteration in the subsequent pages. The title poem of this section, with its absurd epigraph from Shakespeare – 'What?' – is a kind of *ars poetica* in which Corbière disclaims that he is either an artist or a poet. Self-confessedly 'jerky' and 'haphazard', the poem is actually organized around a sequence of internal oppositions, which culminate in a final line which epitomizes the whole poem: 'Art doesn't know me. I don't know art'. This artless art which openly acknowledges its own irony as a pose is also found in the poem 'Epitaph', which pursues a similar mélange of paradoxes. The first of Corbière's many attempts at a species of self-portraiture, it enables the poet to view himself, as he often did, as already dead. 'That?' and 'Epitaph' are both poems which, by the multiplication of vicious circles, at once conceal and reveal the personality that is caught in them. Their objectivity is plainly bogus, and yet the mask is never quite discredited. They arouse the attention as poems that are utterly unlike what we normally agree to call poetry; but they do not quite rivet it, and they are only a foretaste of what is to come.

Most of the poems in the second section (which gives its

title 'Yellow Loves' to the book as a whole) are sonnets in varying stages of disrepair. Here the stance of irony gives way to an exasperated bitterness which takes womankind for its primary target. In poems like 'To A Comrade' and 'Good Luck And Fortune', the poet plays a dual role; he is at once abject and outraged, a beggar and a scourge in equal measure. And in 'Feminine Singular' and 'To The Eternal Madam' Corbière makes general an indictment which obviously originated in a personal and specific deprivation. In the poem 'Woman' he even dons a female mask in order that the whole sex should stand forth self-condemned; a similar 'wild beast' is the speaker in 'Poor Chap'. But no amount of ventriloquism can conceal the fact that these female speakers – comparable with those in 'Decline' and 'Good Evening' – are merely stalking-horses from behind which, and through whose agency, Corbière can contemplate his profound disgust with himself. This self-disgust reaches a kind of climax, albeit a muted one, in the octosyllabic sonnet 'The Toad'. Here, as in 'Insomnia' and 'The Poet's Pipe', only the prospect of sleep seems to offer much hope of relief. (Four of the five 'Rondels For After' also view the sleep of death as the only permanent refuge from the squalor and hardships of life.) Deprived of sleep, Corbière characteristically does one of three things: he either harangues an absurdly *chic* Bohemia, or anatomizes bad poets, or sets himself up – like the hermit on the Armorican seacoast of 'The Contumacious Poet' – as an unheroic hero, perverse and stubborn, yet justified in his contempt of others. The third of these strategies is of particular interest, and there is a certainty of purpose about 'The Contumacious Poet', reflected in Corbière's mastery of narrative momentum, which makes comparison with Villon inevitable and justified. This is certainly one of the greatest of Corbière's testaments, less ambitious than 'The Travelling Minstrel', but like that poem superbly focussed, nowhere more so than in the final stanza, where the poet destroys the edifice he has been labouring to construct:

His lamp was dying. He opened the window.
The sun was rising. He looked up at his letter,

Laughed and ripped it up . . . The small white bits
In the fog seemed a flight of gulls.

None of the 'Serenades' which follow are so powerful, al-
though (like the 'Rondels for After') they do possess a kind
of plaintive and refractory music; they are poems that remind
us of Corbière's fondness for the fiddle and the hurdy-gurdy.
The same is true of the fourth section of *Les Amours Jaunes*
('Flukes') though these poems are less like songs and revert
to the genre of disguised self-portrait. The exclamatory
'Litany Of Sleep', indeed, is agonizingly personal; it was a
poem much admired by the Surrealists. At the same time,
however, 'Litany' is too rhapsodic to be truly successful; it
is much more rhapsodic, in fact, than the chilling 'Rhapsody
Of A Deaf Man'. There are poems in this section so precisely
designated by their titles – 'Despondent'. 'Truncated Idyll'
and 'Pariah', for example – that the poems themselves can
add little to them. Yet Corbière is never, even here, as
straightforward as he seems. 'Poor Man's Funeral Procession'
has, for example, often been taken at face value as an index
of Corbière's sympathy and affection for the oppressed and
the dispirited, though it is perfectly possible, and perhaps pre-
ferable, to read it as a companion piece with those other
poems of his in which he allegorically expresses the plight of
the kind of artist he was. Corbière does not often go outside
himself for his subjects, though when he does do so – as in
'Twin Brother And Sister' – he can write a 'fluke' of such
tremendous precision and restraint that many calculated
works, placed beside it, look threadbare.

It is ironic, therefore, that the two sections of *Les Amours
Jaunes* in which Corbière most often goes outside himself
('Armorica' and 'Seamen') should have been the ones which
have found most favour with generations of readers. 'Armo-
rica' is dominated by the long poem 'The Travelling Minstrel
And The Pardon Of Saint Anne', where Corbière's fascin-
ation with the latter proves ultimately less tenacious than his
obsession with the misery of the former. Two short poems in
this section – 'Evil Landscape' and 'Still Life' – are also of
the highest quality, both very statemental, but with each unit

of utterance in them of perfect weight and gravity, and in each case the 'amateur' Corbière accomplishes a sophisticated correlation between the objects of his perception and the sonorous words with which he describes them.

'Seamen' is also dominated by a long poem, indeed Corbière's longest, 'The Hunchback Bitor'. Unlike 'The Travelling Minstrel', this is essentially a narrative poem, with the same qualities as 'The Contumacious Poet' but raised to a new level – it is arguably Corbière's most brilliant and inexhaustible poem – by the poet's wholehearted involvement in the life and death of someone other than himself. The harbour background is painted with an eye for detail and an economy that few Realist painters could match, yet it is not primarily a pictorial poem. The strength of this great poem resides in its macabre mixture of tragic and comic elements, and in Corbière's brilliant mastery of demotic speech. The 'sheepish happy' Bitor, little more than 'a paring's end', is seen by Corbière as an absurd and pitiful creature who, like himself in the 'Yellow Loves' section, is cruelly made fun of by the whores he lusts after. And yet the tragic dénouement ennobles Bitor even as it diminishes him by its acknowledgement that, in his death as in his life, he has never been more than a piece of human flotsam. 'This wretched body had known love' Corbière concludes, with a quiet sympathy which is not only uncompromised by his habitual irony but manages to coexist in perfect harmony with it.

There are two short poems in 'Seamen' that are not dwarfed by this extraordinary poem. 'The End' is a critique of Victor Hugo's famous but sentimental poem 'Oceano Nox', which restores an ordinary humanity to the drowned sailors whom Hugo had treated in his customarily sublime manner. 'To Old Roscoff' is reminiscent of the poems earlier in the volume in which Corbière has seen sleep as the only refuge from the miseries of living. But this poem has a warmth, a fellow-feeling, a gentleness almost, that the earlier poems do not possess. The Breton seacoast of this poem remains a point of reference in the best of the Paris poems 'Paris By Night', none of which were included in the edition of *Les Amours Jaunes* published in Corbière's lifetime; it was obviously the only place where Corbière could feel something akin to happiness. Paris was clearly nothing more than a place of utter anguish. The 'Paris By Night' poems look slight and insubstantial when placed beside the poems of Baudelaire, though there are many signs that the suffering they record is much more than a merely literary appropriation of Baudelaire's. As in the poems of 'Armorica' and 'Seamen', Corbière seems uncharacteristically detached from himself, as if seeking a defence that might prove a bulwark against the horrors of city life.

Of these maverick poems, if one can so distinguish them (for almost all of Corbière could be so described), it is 'On A Portrait of Corbière' which gives us, appropriately enough, our most abiding impression of the poet: self-regarding but not self-deluded:

I'd like to be a whore's dog,
Licking a little love that wasn't paid for;
Or a goddess with flowing mane on the coast of Africa,
Or mad, but properly; mad, not half-crazy.

There is a famous maxim of Chamfort's which states that 'if Diogenes had lived in our time, his lantern would have to have been a dark lantern'. A line in Corbière's 'Rhapsody Of A Deaf Man' suggests the poet may have known this maxim. But whether he did or not, and however much he himself might have wanted to deny it, his poems certainly offer his readers a light which, without dispersing the gloom, pierces it unforgettably, with all the febrile persistence that this profoundly paradoxical man could muster.

Arthur Rimbaud (1854–91)

Born in Charleville, the second son of an army lieutenant and a severe and bigoted mother. Prodigally gifted as a school-boy, he soon grew irritated by conventional bourgeois pro-vincial life, and ran away to Paris without a penny in his pocket. Returned home to run away again repeatedly, until finally installing himself in Paris and in the affections of Ver-laine in 1871. Continued in the company of Verlaine the pat-tern of vagrancy which was to mark his life after he had abandoned poetry; wrote almost all the poems now associated with him (except 'Le Bateau ivre') during his troubled period with Verlaine. Within a short time of separating from him abandoned poetry unequivocally, and showed no interest when a decade later literary Paris was impressed by what it took to be the posthumous publication of *Les Illuminations* (1886). Printed *Une Saison en Enfer* at his own expense in 1875, though is generally presumed to have written at least some of the *Illuminations* after completing this work in the summer of 1873. Redirected his energies to the study of music and the acquisition of languages before enlisting in the Dutch Colonial Army, becoming a building foreman in Cyprus and finally a trader and explorer in the Middle East and East Africa, where he is believed to have married. Finally laid low by a cancer in the leg which necessitated amputation on his return to Marseilles, where he died. With the much in-ferior Lautréamont a profound influence on the Surrealists, since which time his poetry and his legendary life have come to seem representative of a visionary strain in modern liter-ature.

The life and poetry of Rimbaud are without precedent or parallel in the history of modern literature, and have been extensively mythologized. One does not have to succumb to the myths to be sure that as a 'child Shakespeare' – Victor Hugo's description, in a letter which Rimbaud characteristically ignored – he has no rivals. The whole of his contribution to literature was composed between the ages of fifteen and twenty, after which he repudiated it utterly, in favour of hectic travel, dubious enterprises in Africa (including gun-running and slave-trading) and money-making schemes which all failed lamentably. His brief commitment to literature and his prolonged and total abandonment of it were each pursued with the passion for extremity which we associate more readily with the man of action than with the man of letters, and must obviously be considered two sides of the same coin. Only at the end of his life, dying in great pain, did he show any regret at not having married, sired a family and been an unimpeachable bourgeois. All the rest of his time on earth had been an insatiable quest either for the highest ideals or for the lowest common denominators, of which it is the former, despite and because of his rejection of them, which have ensured his permanent survival as one of the representative figures of the modern imagination. Brought up in a claustrophobic and provincially pious milieu, from which his father had absconded, Rimbaud dedicated himself from an early age, in an archetypally rebellious spirit, to the vision of a transformed reality which would possess the same undifferentiated and magical qualities as the events experienced by a child. He was not, as it sometimes seems, an artist by accident, but by design; and he abandoned art when the design for which he had adopted it had, in his opinion, been proven vain by his own efforts. One only has to read his letters in the last seventeen years of his life to see that the designs to which he dedicated himself in his adulthood were of a quite untranscendental nature, and of consequence to posterity only because of his incomparable adolescence.

The earliest poem of Rimbaud's to have survived is an astonishingly proficient Latin composition on a pastoral theme. It won him a school prize and abundantly justifies his later description of himself (in the poem 'Seven-year-old Poets') as 'very intelligent'. It serves to remind us that beneath the volatile and dynamic surface of the later poetry there is an astonishingly precocious intellect at work. But the poem is primarily of interest as an index of the fourteen-year-old's sensibility, his desire to escape into a sensual and beneficent natural world and to become thereby an inspired and pro- phetic poet, a modern Orpheus. In the event the fact that he ends the poem feeling free from care is less prophetic than the fatigue after long wanderings to which he also admits. But the mood of the French poems he wrote prior to leaving home for the first time, if not completely carefree, is basically optimis- tic. They confirm the idea he was trying to counter in the poem 'Romance': 'You're not serious when you're seventeen'. The desire to strip off (both literally and figuratively) the protective coverings of unaccommodated man (in 'Tartuffe's Punish- ment') and unaccommodating woman (in 'First Evening') seems to stem primarily from curiosity; even the attack on the bourgeoisie in 'By The Bandstand' has the lightweight quality of raillery about it. Rimbaud's most ambitious attempt to be 'serious' at this time was the long poem 'Sun And Flesh' (first called 'Credo In Unam'), which embodies his own substitute for the Apostolic Creed: a pagan world of pleasure in which mankind participates on an equal footing with his gods. He found such a world, for perhaps the only time in his life, by running away from home for the first time, and recorded what he found in the poems he wrote: 'The Tease', 'At The Green Cabaret', 'Wandering' and most memorably in 'What Nina Answered' in which (as in 'First Evening') the female of his affections proves unexpectedly recalcitrant. On his next sally – at the time of the Paris Commune – Rimbaud found only pain and death. Yet it is noticeable that the dead soldier of 'The Sleeper In The Valley' has the same repose as the drowned Ophelia of an earlier poem, and there is still a hope that the forces of nature will prove beneficent in 'The Crows'. On his third excursion, in the depraved May of 1871, he seems to have suffered a shock from which he may never have fully recovered, and wrote poems of a scatological character, concerned almost exclusively with the sexual and excretory functions of the body: 'The Sitters', 'Squatting', 'My Little Lovelies' and the grotesque 'Venus Anadyomene'. This latter poem is a record of his revulsion from the naked female form he had celebrated (in wish-fulfilment perhaps) in 'First Evening'. His excoriation of womankind continued in 'The Sisters Of Charity', 'The Ladies Who Look For Lice' and 'First Communions'. A few months later he began a homosexual relationship with Paul Verlaine from which he emerged, apart from a bullet in the wrist, relatively unscathed; though it is customary to date Verlaine's poetic decline from their separation, and Rimbaud's abandonment of literature – in so far as it can be accurately dated – followed hard upon it.

In a poem written in the spring of 1871 ('The Cheated Heart') Rimbaud is to be found asking himself the sinner's question: 'What must I do to be saved?' An orthodox religious answer was plainly out of the question: he was only to accept the Catholic church on his death-bed. His salvation (and, as it transpired, his damnation) was to be of his own making; he would become a *voyant*, a visionary. He outlined his plan in the famous letter of 15 May 1871 to his friend Paul Démeny:

the first task of the man who wants to be a poet is to study his own awareness of himself, in its entirety; he seeks out his soul, he inspects it, he tests it, he learns it. As soon as he knows it, he must cultivate it.

Thus far, as he effectively admitted later in the letter, the programme is not dissimilar to Baudelaire's, though more excitedly expressed. Even the celebrated contention that '*I* is an other' can be derived from Baudelaire. And the 'long, boundless, and systematized *disorganization* of *all the senses*' had also been indulged in by his predecessor, an expert in the construction of 'artificial paradises'. In two respects only – though both were to be crucial in his development of a 'visionary' attitude – did Rimbaud transcend Baudelaire: by rejecting all conventional forms ('The inventions of the unknown demand new forms') and by thinking of art as a species of action

('Poetry will no longer give rhythm to activity; it will be *in the vanguard*'). In the case of the first the 'visionary' has to remain true only to his vision: 'if what he brings back from *beyond* has form, he gives it form; if it has none, he gives it none'. (This later proved immensely attractive to the Surrealists, who regarded Rimbaud as their patron saint.) In the case of the second the 'visionary', having transformed his vision into action, becomes 'responsible for humanity, for *animals* even', like Orpheus: he will 'make precise the quality of the unknown arising in his time in the universal soul' and at the same time be '*a multiplier of progress*'. Much of Rimbaud's subsequent activity as a poet was devoted to the combined aim of multiplying and making precise, and even with his prodigious ability this was a process of trial and error.

The most famous product of his 'visionary' programme was 'The Drunken Boat', a poem which would resemble other Romantic quest-voyages were it not for the fact that the 'I' which narrates it is literally an 'other': the boat itself. Almost all the items encountered by the boat occur in plural forms, as if in accordance with Rimbaud's desire to be a 'multiplier of progress'. But the poem is more often rhetorical than precise, as even some of its more fervent admirers have admitted. Its most touching moment is its most singular, when – as is often the case with Rimbaud's best poetry – he is reaching back to his childhood:

I've cried too much, true enough; the dawns are heartrending.
Each moon is bitter and each sun is sour:
An acrid love has swollen me with torpors.
Let my keel split! Let me shipwreck!

If I desire a European shore,
It is the black cold pool where, in the odour
Of evening, a child squats full of sorrow
Launching a boat as frail as a May butterfly.

There is a greater concentration of precision in the famous 'Vowels' sonnet, an instance of what Rimbaud later called 'verbal alchemy'. But many have doubted, however, whether the poem is meant to be taken as seriously as it sometimes has been. Much more obviously serious is the prose poem 'The Deserts Of Love' which, like 'The Drunken Boat', ends with the 'visionary' having to come to terms with the inescapable disintegration of his ecstasy and the chill return of reality. The same is true of 'Michel and Christine' and also of 'Memory', one of the finest fantasies ever to have arisen out of Rimbaud's contemplation (or imaginative projection) of the healing balm of water. Rimbaud achieves great precision in this poem, without forfeiting any of his suggestive powers; it is much less enigmatic than the song-like sequences 'The Comedy Of 'Thirst', 'The Triumph Of Patience' and 'The Triumph Of Hunger'. Even in these latter cases, however, there is little that is actually obscure when Rimbaud's fundamental difficulty – how to sustain the vision against its moment of disappearance – is at issue.

The heartrending dawns which reduce the Promethean hyperbole of 'The Drunken Boat' to a tragic acknowledgement of frailty are an index of the hard-headed realism that underpins Rimbaud's most fantastic imaginings. He is always effectively saying – as at the end of the untitled poem beginning 'What do we care, my heart . . .' – '*It is nothing: I am here: I am still here*'. Whether this recognition was the predisposing force behind his repudiation of literature is obscured by the impossibility of determining a chronology whereby he did so. Of his two most challenging and brilliant works, *A Season In Hell* (written April–August 1873) was the only one he cared enough about to see through the press; the collection of *Illuminations* was not published until 1886, by which time he had lost all interest in them and was presumed in Parisian intellectual circles to be dead. Some critics place the latter before *A Season In Hell*, some after; still others place a number of them before and a number of them after, but there is no agreement as to how they should be distributed. What is clear is that Rimbaud, preparatory to abandoning literature altogether, abandoned verse in favour of the prose poem; there are arguably no finer examples of the genre in French literature than the 'stories' (as Rimbaud called them) of *A Season In Hell* and the 'coloured plates' (as Verlaine called them) of *Illuminations*. The prose poem evidently gave

Rimbaud a special purchase on the 'something new' that his
letter to Paul Démeny was so insistent about. And *A Season In
Hell* is certainly a critique of even that part of his past pro-
duction which, a year or so before, must have seemed to him to
represent 'something new'. The voices of the past are in fact
locked in battle with the disabused voice of the present. The
conflict is so terrible and turbulent that the work comes as close
to being an act as literature perhaps ever can. And it is
essentially an act of confession performed in the hope of pur-
ification. For although in the prologue Rimbaud addresses
himself to Satan, he is writing in the hope of discovering a
divine love and a banquet of beauty. To be worthy of it, he must
revisit the darknesses and deliriums of a soul which has willed
its own damnation. Two deliriums in particular haunted him:
the liaison with Verlaine (the 'foolish Virgin' in whose com-
pany he himself had been 'the infernal Bridegroom') and the
vain dream of a verbal alchemy in which he very plainly no
longer believed: 'I flattered myself that I had invented a poetic
language accessible, some day or other, to all the senses ... I
adopted the most absurd and exaggerated mode of expression
conceivable ... That's all past. I now know how to salute
beauty.' In the section 'Morning' the salute seems to be one of
greeting; this dawn, unlike those of 'The Drunken Boat', is
marked by intimations of harmony. But the final section is
unequivocally a 'Farewell', and the only promise of beauty to
be found in it is his new dream, supplanting that in which '*I* is
an other': 'now it will be permitted me to *possess truth in one soul
and one body*'. There are certainly apprehensions of a tragic
loneliness at the end of *A Season In Hell*, but also of a tragic
grandeur, as Rimbaud struggles to believe his vigil may be,
even has been, rewarded: 'for I can say that victory is mine'.
The Surrealists took Rimbaud's claim in the prologue to have
'torn these few hideous pages out of my notebook' as a rationale
for their own practice of automatic writing; but the 'victory', if
such it is, could not have been automatically achieved without
losing its penitential character. If these were the last literary
words that Rimbaud wrote before his African experiment, we
cannot but feel that the victory was followed by a defeat; but if

the *Illuminations* post-date *A Season In Hell* his belief that he had achieved a victory was abundantly confirmed.

There is an 'illumination' called 'Vigils' which may or may not be contemporaneous with Rimbaud's season in hell, but which also ends with a kind of victory, a glimpse of dawn to offset the cold dream with which it has begun. The difficulty in 'late' Rimbaud is to decide whether the dominance of the real over the ideal is to be considered a victory or a defeat. Yet many writers after Rimbaud – notably Claudel – found in him an inspiration enabling them to return to Catholicism. What saves the *Illuminations* from the desolation of Rimbaud's inferno is their translucency, their comparative tranquillity, their enigmatic simplicity. The titles of the poems – usually one word, and often in the plural form that Rimbaud was so attracted by – are aptly pictorial, and the poems themselves summon up images in nearly every line. Rimbaud describes himself in one of them ('Vagabonds') as 'impatient to find the place and the formula', but no formula has emerged from this collection, and the places (as in 'Dawn', 'Mystique' and 'Bridges', or indeed in almost every individual poem at some point or other) are always prone to prove a phantasm.

Not all the *Illuminations* are of the highest quality, but there is general agreement that the last three – in the sequence of the first edition – are particularly fine. 'Genie' is certainly a key utterance in respect of Rimbaud's feelings on the subject of love, a subject which, in one form or another, dominates his whole *oeuvre*. 'Love must be reinvented', the infernal Bridegroom had told the foolish Virgin in *A Season In Hell*. 'I shall never be able to throw love out of the window', he had told himself in the illumination 'Sentences'. In 'Lives' he prides himself on an achievement that is quite free of his tendency to adolescent boasting:

[I am] a musician ... who has discovered something like the key-signature of love.

The last paragraph of 'Genie' suggests that this is indeed the case:

He has known us all and loved us all. May we know, this winter
night, from promontory to promontory, from the tumultuous pole
to the chateau, from the crowd to the beach, from glances to
glances, strengths and tired feelings, to hail him and see him and
send him once again on his way and, under the tides and atop the
deserts of snow, to follow his visions, his breathings, his body,
his light.

'Youth' also speaks of a labour that has been brought to
fruition, and in lines 'neither fixed nor forced' which give the
impression that they are truly a labour of love. The last words of
'Youth', however, describe yet another departure. There is a
certain logic, therefore, whether or not Rimbaud himself ever
intended it, in ending the *Illuminations* with the poem
'Clearance Sale', a selling-off of stock preparatory to giving up
the business.

The end of Rimbaud's poetic career is a lot less clear than its
beginnings, which is one reason why the mystique which has
grown up around his name is in no danger of diminishing. It is
not known, and presumably now never will be, whether
Rimbaud abandoned literature in despite of having 'reinven-
ted' love or in despair of doing so. Even in default of any
definitive solution to the problems that his meteoric career
throws up, it seems certain that Rimbaud will continue to be
the cardinal modern example of the two polarities available to
poets of a kindred disposition: to transform the world and to
keep silent.

Constantine Cavafy
(1863–1933)

Born in Alexandria into a Greek merchant family with offices in England. After the death of his father in 1870 the family moved to Europe, residing in Liverpool from 1873 to 1877. Thereafter he lived in Alexandria except for three years (1882–5) in Constantinople, where he wrote many poems, some in English, and began definitively to identify himself as a homosexual. Worked for a time as a journalist and as a broker and finally took up a post as a civil servant in the Ministry of Public Works which he kept until retirement. Passed his leisure hours in reading, gambling and satisfying his sybaritic appetites. Considered his mature poetry to have been written after 1910 and resisted attempts to have his juvenilia reprinted. Printed all his poems privately in limited editions and took little interest in the fame he was beginning to acquire. Generally considered the greatest Greek poet of modern times. Not a writer who encourages or rewards attempts to scrutinize his personal life, of which little is known.

Few modern poets have equalled Cavafy's capacity, in E. M. Forster's famous phrase, for 'standing absolutely motionless at a slight angle to the universe'. Yet even this characterization seems too grandiose to describe the greatest Greek poet of modern times. 'I only speak,' Cavafy wrote in a personal note of 1902, 'but I don't think my words useless. Someone else will act. And my words – coward that I am – will assist his energy. They clear the ground.' Cavafy's words do indeed clear the ground, repeatedly dismantling the fragile and precarious edifices which the human heart builds as protection against the unpleasant realities of its conditions. In a language so laconic that, in translation at least, it scarcely seems to warrant the title of poetry, Cavafy lays bare the timeless structures of the sensibility, its longings, its disappointments, its strategies for survival and its propensity to self-delusion. In this respect he resembles a classical or neo-classical moralist; yet he signally lacked a great moralist's consistency of purpose, knowing his own life and his exclusively homosexual affiliations to be so pleasure-orientated that a properly ethical stance was out of the question. As a substitute Cavafy developed an aesthetic position beyond good and evil: 'The true artist', he wrote, 'does not have, like the hero of a myth, to choose between vice and virtue, but both will serve him and he will love both equally.' As an apologist for 'an infinite compassion which ignores the small distinctions of just and unjust', Cavafy valued above all the human tolerance which 'forgives, justifies and includes everything, because it understands'. In other poets such a stance might be part of an attitude of 'art for art's sake', and in what little we know of Cavafy's personal life it would seem as if he moved in the kind of hothouse circles in which aestheticism and his own sexual predilections might be least embarrassing. But when not in pursuit of male beauty he was, as Seferis was to observe, 'condemned to the truth', and he lived for most of his life in a poor quarter of Alexandria which daily reminded him of the unbeautiful. 'Where could I live better?' he is reported to have said; 'below, the brothel caters for the flesh. And there is the church which forgives sin. And there is the hospital where we die.' His conversation was evidently as free from embellishment as his poetry; he seems to have been incapable of the large and extravagant gesture. He does not even appear to have cared much whether his poetry was read and admired outside his own small circle; most of it was published privately or in limited editions. Attempting to alter the sexual prejudices of the public at large, as modern homosexuals have been keen to do, was plainly foreign to him. His poems suggest that a critique of other prejudices was more important to him: of the need to think well of oneself, of the need to believe that someone or

something in a hypothetical future would give meaning to the
inexorable passage of time, and of the need to console oneself
for irreparable losses with pleasures that might temporarily
offset regretful backward glances. In his quiet way he addressed
himself to timeless and fundamental issues, 'substantives' as he
called them, without possessing, or passing on to others, any
body of doctrine which would finally make sense of them, his
primary relief consisting in having cast light upon them in his
own peculiarly angular manner.

Cavafy himself vigorously and justifiably repudiated the
poetry he wrote before the age of thirty as 'trash'; sentiment-
ality, triteness and self-indulgence – the hallmarks of this early
poetry – also appear from time to time in the one hundred and
seventy-four poems which make up the accepted canon of his
verse. But it is clear from some of the poems casually dated
'Before 1911' in the *Collected Poems* that in young middle age he
was intent on turning from a confessional mode of utterance to
a more impersonal manner. Only three of the 'Before 1911'
poems present an 'I' figure who is unmistakably the poet
himself – 'Walls', 'Candles' and 'The Windows'. All three show
him to have been inconsolably miserable, timidly immured in
himself, helplessly inert and oppressed by the meaningless
passage of time. The poem 'Monotony' presents feelings that
are plainly too deep-seated to be easily remedied:

One monotonous day follows another
identically monotonous. The same things
will happen to us again and again,
the same moments come and go.

A month passes by, brings another month.
Easy to guess what lies ahead:
all of yesterday's boredom.
And tomorrow ends up no longer like tomorrow.

Even in a powerful poem like this, Cavafy seems too content to
make merely descriptive statements; 'Voices' and 'Longings'
are other poems of which the same might be said. His style
quickens only when he thinks of the horizon of death that brings
all tomorrows to an end, especially when (as in 'The Horses Of

Achilles' and 'The Souls Of Old Men') it is with the deaths of
other people that he is concerned. Cavafy is reminiscent here of
T. S. Eliot in his 'agèd eagle' persona; but he has none of Eliot's
resources of self-possession. Like Eliot, however, he makes use
of *personae* to distance himself from his own malaise; and it is this
device which makes any number of his miniature dramas into
universal statements. One of the most attractive of the early
poems is 'That's The Man', in which a poet worn out and
dejected by the strain of writing a long sequence of poems is
suddenly consoled by remembering how his famous prede-
cessor Lucian had his future celebrity revealed to him in a
dream. But the early poem which has been most widely ad-
mired is 'Waiting For The Barbarians', a dialogue between two
figures living in a city and civilization so severely in decline that
only a new barbarism promises anything in which to take
comfort. As so often in Cavafy, the hopes and expectations of
his figures are prey to a defeat that leaves them bereft of
remedy, as in the famous final lines:

Now what's going to happen to us without barbarians?
These people were a kind of solution.

A different kind of solution, less immediately attractive but of
more lasting benefit, is offered in the poem 'Ithaka', which uses
the story of the *Odyssey* to remind us that the journey and not the
arrival matters, even though understanding will have to be
postponed until the moment of landfall. Cavafy himself took no
such journey, or at least not in real terms; he remained in
Alexandria, obeying his own injunction in the poem 'The
City':

Don't hope for things elsewhere:
there's no ship for you, no road.
Now that you've wasted your life here, in this small corner,
you've destroyed it everywhere in the world.

In spite of this apparently intransigent pessimism Cavafy
found that there were two ways of taking imaginary journeys
which would permit a kind of creativity to flourish in the face of
destruction. The first was to reinvent his own past; the second to

invent a much more remote, and almost always fictional past.
The former strategy reaches a kind of perfection in a love lyric
of 1914, 'Long Ago':

I'd like to speak of this memory,
but it's so faded now – as though nothing's left –
because it was so long ago, in my adolescent years.

A skin as though of jasmine . . .
that August evening – was it August? –
I can still recall the eyes: blue, I think they were . . .
Ah yes, blue: a sapphire blue.

This has a universality that some of the more explicitly
homosexual poems, with their obsessive concentration on lips
and limbs and young Adonises, cannot hope to have. The
hesitations and the final decision to solace oneself with a
consoling and possibly misremembered detail are handled
with an exemplary tact and delicacy. The poems of Cavafy's
imaginary past – usually set between 200 BC and AD 600 in
the cities of Magna Graecia, especially Alexandria and
Antioch – are much less intimate. But these fictional creations
have the miraculous realism that only the very best historical
fiction can achieve, especially when the figures are allowed to
speak without any apparent authorial intervention. The diffi-
culty with these poems (of which 'Myris: Alexandria, AD 340'
is perhaps the finest) is that the unmediated recovery of the
past impedes the 'understanding' that Cavafy is intent on
inculcating. More assimilable are those poems in which he
impersonally and ironically directs our understanding, such as
'Orophernis':

His end must have been recorded somewhere only to be lost;
or maybe history passed over it
and rightly didn't bother to notice
anything so trivial.

Confronted with such lacunae, the act of imagining came to
have a special value for Cavafy, as 'Kaisarion' suggests:

Because so little
is known about you from history
I could fashion you more freely in my mind.

Like the painter in his poem 'Pictured' Cavafy was evidently, at moments like this, 'recovering through art from the effort of creating it'.

'The true artist', he wrote in the 1890s, 'writes in serenity of soul.' Yet his own soul was evidently quite the opposite of serene when he recalled to mind the ephemeral liaisons and 'sterile loves' of his personal life. He was, however, necessarily more detached from the *personae* whose fates he dispassionately – somewhat in the manner of the epitaphs in *The Greek Anthology* (one of his favourite books) – recorded:

So boasted Aimilianos Monai.
One wonders if he ever made that suit of armour.
Anyway, he didn't wear it long.
At the age of twenty-seven, he died in Sicily.

('Aimilianos Monai, Alexandrian, AD 628–55')

With real historical personages Cavafy was less detached, though even in the above example the icy and implacable tone is actually an index of fierce involvement. This is notably the case in the poems about Anna Komnina and Julian the Apostate, though for most readers the Caesar of 'The Ides Of March' and the Nero of 'Nero's Deadline' have the added attraction of familiarity. Nero, like Caesar, has come close to having his fortune told:

Nero wasn't worried at all when he heard
what the Delphic Oracle had to say:
'Beware the age of seventy-three'.
Plenty of time to enjoy himself.
He's thirty . . .

But the last three lines of the poem bring the oracular utterance into focus, and ominously close to fact:

So much for Nero. And in Spain Galba
secretly musters and drills his army –
Galba, now in his seventy-third year.

Cavafy reserves a special place of honour for those who can

see more than one step in front of them, though he is careful
not to endorse the use they may be tempted to make of such an
advantage. His view of mankind, whether individual or collect-
ive, almost always tends towards the view that man is either
passively self-deluded or actively deceitful or both at once. It is
not so much his vision which is compassionate as his tone; he
hardly ever seems to raise his voice above a whisper. This was
presumably a consequence of the 'long patience' which, for
him, was essential for the completion of a poem, and which
obviously conditioned the slight bulk of his work. 'The im-
mediate impression,' he told his friend, 'is never a starting-
point for work. The impression has got to falsify itself with time,
without my having to falsify it.'

Most commentators, and most modern Greek poets, regard
Cavafy as the most important poet in the language since the
days of classical Greece. George Seferis planned to write a study
of his work which he never completed, and was profoundly
influenced by his use of *personae*; Yannis Ritsos has written a
touching poem in his memory. He has been particularly in-
fluential on poets who, like Zbigniew Herbert in Poland and
Joseph Brodsky before he left Russia, have been forced by a
politically oppressive climate to 'act' in the way that the self-
confessedly timid Cavafy was unable to do. As an exponent
of counter-eloquence he naturally appealed to Montale.
Cavafy rarely makes an immediate impact on the reader who
expects a poet to indulge him with resonant and readily mem-
orable lines; his poems have to be read with something of the
'long patience' by means of which they were composed. There
is much to be said, having done so, for taking all his work as
essentially one poem, as George Seferis suggested. Out of
preferences and circumstances which can only be described as
marginal, in a language that has not formed part of the main-
stream of European literature for two thousand years, Cavafy
has evidently come to be thought of in all quarters as an
essential part of the fabric of modern poetry, though it is
difficult to believe that the poet himself would have been much
appeased by his widespread posthumous fame. It is his capacity
to disquiet us, and the manner in which he seems to have

effectively disappeared into the circumscribed orbit of his poems, which makes memorable one of the most disorientating of modern *oeuvres*.

Stefan George (1868–1933)

Born near Bingen in the Rhineland, where he spent his child-
hood. Completed a classical education at Darmstadt in 1888.
Subsequently devoted himself to the study of Romance lan-
guages in French Switzerland and in Paris, and pursued similar
studies at the University of Berlin. Frequently in Paris, where
he was a member of the Symbolist circle gathered around
Mallarmé. Travelled very extensively, to London, Belgium,
Copenhagen, Vienna, Central Spain and Italy. Left Germany
after 1914 only for vacations in the Swiss Alps until he went into
voluntary exile in the year of his death, refusing the honours
and awards offered him by the Nazi authorities. Founded the
journal *Blätter für die Kunst* in 1892, which he conceived and
often composed single-handedly for the next twenty-seven
years. Throughout his life engaged in creating and recreating,
after defections, a circle of ascetic aesthetes of like mind.
Profoundly moved by the death of a fifteen-year-old boy in
1902, whom he called Maximin and whom he saw as a figure
playing a similar role in his life to that played by Beatrice in
Dante's. A writer whose reputation has declined since the
beginning of the century, though clearly the most considerable
native German poet between the death of Goethe and the early
poems of Gottfried Benn. One of the great creative translators,
notably of Shakespeare's *Sonnets*, Baudelaire's *Les Fleurs du Mal*
and sections of Dante's *Divine Comedy*.

One of the shrewdest assessments of the genius of Stefan George
appeared shortly after the publication of George's seventh
collection of poems (*The Seventh Ring*, 1907), in a Budapest
literary journal:

[George's poems are] constructed entirely from the inside, purely lyrically, without any adventure or event. The only events they show are reflexes of the soul; the soul's enrichment, but not the source of the riches; the going astray, not the possible point of arrival; the torment of parting, but not what it might have meant to walk side by side with another; the tempestuous joy of a great meeting, but not whether the meeting led to an organic union; only the sweet melancholy of recollection and the intellectual ecstasy, full of a bitter joy, which is born of the contemplation of transience. And loneliness, much loneliness and solitary journeying.

It is a rhapsodic passage, a product of its time, a time when George was regarded in intellectual circles as the most significant German poet of his day. But it may come as something of a surprise to learn that the critic in question was Georg Lukács, later to become world-famous for ideas quite alien to George's as one of the pillars of Marxist literary criticism and the author of a classic study in dialectics, *History And Class Consciousness*. Lukács's essay on George was published in Germany in a book of 1911 called *The Soul And Its Forms* (recently translated into English as *Soul And Form*), a book whose very title has a Georgean ring, for the whole of George's endeavour in poetry was to find the appropriate forms for what he experienced in his soul, and thereby to inculcate a rebirth of spiritual values in the life of his time. George accomplished the first of these aims by means of a theory and practice which are nowadays admired more for their rigour than for their beauty; with hindsight it is clear that the second of these aims was beyond him. For George's tyrannical attitude towards his raw materials extended to his treatment of those supposed to be the beneficiaries of his idealism. His contempt for the vulgar was exercised in a void of his own making; for the vulgar had little intention, and even less opportunity, of reading him. The 'solitary journeying' of which Lukács spoke was both willed and involuntary, and not even Lukács's youthful enthusiasm for 'The New Solitude And Its Poetry' (the title of his essay) can in fact disguise the difficulties he is experiencing in trying to defend it against its detractors, of whom he himself was soon to be one. George took the essentially French doctrine of 'art for art's sake' about as seriously as it is possible to take it; the annual publication which he master-minded for twenty-seven years, between 1892 and 1919, was appropriately titled *Leaves For Art's Sake* (*Blätter für die Kunst*). He collected around him, in his notorious circle, not so much disciples (as Mallarmé may be said to have done) as acolytes; insurrections within the confines of the circle were put down with something like the ruthlessness of a dictator. Many at the time, and more since, have felt that there was something inhuman about George's recommendation of extreme spiritual purity, withdrawal into the most ivory of towers and artificial cultivation of self-serving myths. All of these proved a catastrophic godsend to the Nazis, who misread George much as they misread Nietzsche, the realm of spiritual discourse being effectively a closed book to them; but George's proto-Nazi ideas are much less readily dispersed than Nietzsche's, or rather the quality of his work does not encourage such a dispersal to the degree that Nietzsche's writings do. George is an unfashionable figure even in his native Germany; to find a figure of indisputable magnitude recommending him one must go back to Mallarmé (whose premature death spared him some of the more extreme examples of George's genius) and to Hofmannsthal (who praised the 'spiritual and intellectual discipline' that George applied to 'the general degradation and confusion' but whose own genius was much more flexible). There is a nice touch in André Gide's journal for 1908 where the French writer speaks of admiring George's poetry 'each time I manage to understand it' and of the way George expressed himself 'without self-satisfaction, but with an evident awareness of his evident superiority'.

If a line is to be drawn between poets of historical and intrinsic interest, George should probably be placed, despite a number of very beautiful poems, in the category of the former. Whether he was the 'glorious German and European phenomenon' that Hofmannsthal thought him is doubtful; but he was certainly a phenomenon and he possessed a pan-European potential that greater writers have had to make shift without. While still a child George invented a secret language and a mythical kingdom over which he ruled; in a sense his mature life was but an extension of these. He was a formidable linguist as a young man; having been taught Greek, Latin and French at school, he taught himself Italian and Norwegian (the latter so as to read Ibsen in the original), spent some time in London to improve his English and to become 'more and more cosmopolitan', and was sufficiently doubtful of the expressive possibilities of German to speak and write, during his brief period of attendance at the University of Berlin (where he studied Romance Languages and Literatures), mainly in French and Spanish and in a curious 'Lingua Romana' which combined features of Latin, Spanish and German. When he began to publish collections of his poetry it was in an idiosyncratic German of uncapitalized nouns and minimal punctuation, buttressed by the very stylized typography and ornate design features of the privately published limited edition. The net effect of this ambitious but excessive aestheticism was to put up, in George's own words, 'barbed wire to keep out the uninitiated'. In the event the desire to make converts naturally prevailed, and George collected together his first three slim volumes (*Hymns*, 1890; *Pilgrimages*, 1891; and *Algabal*, 1892) into one trade edition. In *Hymns* the solitary and solipsistic poet can find companionship only when the Muse consents to visit him, inspiring his lips to utterance as in the 'Initiation' poem which opens the volume. The mood is inevitably sombre, for the kisses they exchange are brief and phantasmal, and the poet is left to meditate on the enforced separations which spell the defeat of his poetic aspirations. The collection *Pilgrimages* represents an attempt to escape from a spiritual condition in which he had become voluntarily imprisoned. But, as the inscription to the volume makes clear, the hope of finding a companion suffering from kindred misfortunes was cruelly disappointed:

So I fared forth
And became a stranger,
And sought for someone
To share my sorrow
And there was no-one.

It was George's sense of having been 'banished from lands which are my birthright' which prompted this quest for 'true domains'. And yet, despite his renewed determination to tranquillize his despair, the prevailing mood in this second collection is heavily nostalgic; George is almost overwhelmed by his poignant memories of his 'Journies Of Long Ago'. His despair is most impressively and economically rendered in the final poem of *Pilgrimages* ('The Clasp'), in which he is forced to acknowledge that he has failed to make his poetry 'a smooth and solid band of cold iron'. This poem also prefigures the exotic and exalted atmosphere of the subsequent collection *Algabal*. But the decadent world of the *Algabal* poems only exacerbated the tensions within him to breaking point. Algabal's contempt for the mob is excessive even by Georgean standards, and the sterility of his subterranean kingdom is a permanent reminder of the purposelessness of the power he wields. The morbidity is alleviated only in the final stanza of the final poem in the collection ('Augury'), where the flight of white swallows is a promise of liberation from a wilderness of mirror-images. It is no surprise to learn that in the attempt to go even further 'beyond good and evil' than Nietzsche had tried to do George was actually brought to 'the great desolation' of his first profound emotional crisis, and forced to reconstruct his spiritual position.

George's preface for the public printing of his next volume epitomizes the collection's transitional character. For although he stresses that the poems are 'not intended as reflections of any particular epoch of history' and that they simply 'mirror a soul which has temporarily taken refuge in other areas and regions', he is also at pains to remind his readership that in every age there is 'a spirit which shapes and integrates what is alien and past' in transferring it to the contemporary reality. The cumbersome title of this volume – *The Books Of Eclogues And Eulogies, Of Legends And Lays, And Of The Hanging Gardens* (1895) – is an indication of George's attempt to widen the focus of his pilgrimage to take account of pastoral antiquity, medieval Europe and the Orient. And there is a new purity of vision in this collection, as Hofmannsthal was one of the first of its critics to realize. In an essay on the volume he stressed the 'innate sovereignty' of the self-possession achieved most memorably by the Oriental monarch in the third section. After the 'citron, ambergris and spice' of Algabal's world it is a relief to encounter the earthenware jug of the strategically important first poem of all; and the 'eulogies', addressed to George's personal friends, suggest he had at last found some companionship. In the first poem in 'The Book Of The Hanging Gardens', indeed, George suggests that he has finally discovered a means of access to the 'land which as a child you called your own'; he even feels empowered to make the faculty of song into a redemptive agent for all his previous regrets. This idea is most compellingly embodied, however, in the fifteen very beautiful settings for piano and voice composed by Schoenberg in 1908–9 to texts from this section of George's collection. Schoenberg, a much more revolutionary and influential genius than George, considered *The Book Of the Hanging Gardens* an important landmark on his path towards atonalism and numbered the fifteen settings opus 15, an act that the fastidious George (in his later years somewhat obsessed with numerology) would have been the first to applaud.

The fifth, sixth and seventh of George's nine collections of poetry – *The Year Of The Soul* (1897), *The Tapestry Of Life* (1903) and *The Seventh Ring* (1907) – are usually regarded as the apex of George's carefully constructed poetic career. They certainly offer the most immediate proof of the claim he made in 1894 that 'the worth of poetry is decided not by its meaning (otherwise it would be wisdom, instruction), but by its form'. *The Year Of The Soul*, which Mallarmé considered 'excellent, because all intimate poetry is enacted within the pageant of some ideal year', is written almost exclusively in quatrains, as is *The Tapestry Of Life*; *The Seventh Ring* consists of seven subdivisions circling symmetrically around the central fourth section. It is evident, however, that the value of these poems cannot be divorced from the meanings they inevitably contain, difficult as it may be (as André Gide's journal reminds us) to articulate that meaning in any other form than that employed by George. The opening cycle of *The Year Of The Soul*, for example, is one of George's most compelling renderings of the 'soul-landscape' made popular by the French Symbolists: the external details of the landscape and the inner world of the sensibility are here represented in reciprocal relationship, one with another. The most famous of these poems is the lyric 'Enter the park reputed dead', of which almost all the subtle music is lost in translation, though something of its form and message may survive:

Enter the park reputed dead and see:
The shimmer of remote and blithesome shores
And unexpected blue of the pure clouds
Which shed their lights on ponds and mottled paths.

There gather the deep yellow and smooth grey
Of birch and boxwood in the gentle breeze;
The late rose blooms have yet to wither quite;
Choose, kiss and weave with them a garland.

And these last asters do not disregard,
The mauve around the tendrils of wild vine;
Entwine all that is left of this life's green
With your autumnal vision's gentle hands.

This poem perfectly exemplifies what Lukács calls the 'reflexes of the soul'; it is built on self-addressed imperatives which the reader cannot help but regard as invitations to do likewise. The mood is very much one of 'bitter joy ... born of the contemplation of transience' in Lukács's words; it is, as George states, an 'autumnal vision', mellow, mature, with uncircumscribed contours. This new-found maturity is reflected in the 'Superscriptions' of the second cycle of *The Year Of The Soul*, though George's assumption of the roles of martyr and prophet makes them seem somewhat dry. The 'Mournful Dances' that follow are much more attractive, and magically illustrate Lukács's point that 'the new lyric poetry makes its own music, it is text and sound, melody and accompaniment all at the same time'; these are poems which transposition into any other language would almost certainly wreck.

The Tapestry Of Life opens with a twenty-four poem 'Prelude' which constitutes a kind of *ars poetica*; it is here that George's celebrated commitment to 'Hellas, our eternal love' will be found. And here also that he places his enterprise under the beneficent aegis of an angel. This angel is not, like Rilke's Angels in the *Duino Elegies*, a messenger from the 'Eternal Orders'; it is a spirit whom George has summoned up from within his own soul. George can never, in fact, be fully absolved from the criticism that he is excessively self-absorbed. His one serious attempt to go decisively beyond himself occurred when he was led to place his poetry under the protection of a figure designed to play a role similar to that performed by Beatrice in Dante's *Divine Comedy*: the boy-god Maximin. Maximin evolved, like Beatrice, from a real person called Maximilian whose early death was interpreted by George as confirmation that he was one of 'those whom the gods love'. But it was *George's* love that prompted the Maximin poems, and George's love that they celebrate. And his essentially myth-opoeic conception was protected by none of the ironies that modern poets of a similar cast of mind have employed in order to remain accessible and acceptable. Maximin remains much more important for George than he is able to make him for the reader; he is deified in a manner that makes his incarnation seem insubstantial and his Messiah-like propensities distinctly dubious.

The post-Maximin poetry of *The Star Of The Covenant* (1913) presents a George whose missionary spirit and harshly doctrinaire manner make the beauty and complexity of much of the pre-Maximin poetry seem very much a thing of the past. Easily his weakest book, *The Star Of The Covenant* became popular with German soldiers on the Western Front during the Great War largely because of its militaristic sentiments and rhythms. In effect, like the Nazis later, the soldiers transformed George's spiritual recommendations into practical manuals of self-help, and oriented them towards a physical world to which they never were adapted. The very fact that George could have been so misinterpreted may stand as something of a judgement on the ideas themselves. Much more attractive is George's last collection, *The Kingdom Come* of 1928, the exquisite songs that provide a framing structure and the powerful long poems on themes from Goethe and Hölderlin stand out from the mass of George's later poetry as significant utterances irrespective of their basis in Georgean ideology.

It was George's practice, rather than his theory and ideology, which proved influential upon poets of an Expressionist temperament on either side of the First World War; a decade later Lukács could have found many more examples of 'The New Solitude And Its Poetry'. And for all his limitations, George remains an important figure historically, his most beautiful poems demanding inclusion in any good anthology of modern European poetry. It is, however, doubtful if George will ever regain the fame he once enjoyed, and it now seems fitting to approach his poetry, however musical it may be intrinsically, by way of Schoenberg's many marvellous settings of this austere and unfashionable figure.

Christian Morgenstern
(1871–1914)

Born in Munich, the only son of a landscape painter and tubercular mother, whose malady he inherited. Tutored privately and at secondary school in Breslau. For a time a student of economics and politics at Breslau University, where he began to develop an intellectual humanitarianism. Estranged from his father in 1895, soon after his father's third marriage and a disagreement over money. Translated several plays of Ibsen's into German, and became friendly with Ibsen during his time in Scandinavia. Travelled extensively in Italy and Switzerland; resident thereafter primarily in Berlin. Famous from 1905 for his *Galgenlieder*, though he considered his serious, philosophical and mystical verse much more important. Became a member in 1909 of the Anthroposophical Society of Rudolf Steiner, whom he had heard lecture in Berlin and whom he followed on his lecture tours throughout Europe. Married in 1910, the year in which his health took a decisive turn for the worse. Largely resident in Swiss sanatoria in his last years, he died in private quarters near Merano at the age of forty-three, by which time his comic poems had sold in tens of thousands.

Morgenstern's reputation rests, uniquely among poets of distinction, on a body of work which falls squarely into a category that flouts all attempts to make sense of it: Nonsense poetry. So considerable is his achievement in this genre that it is customary to place him above even Lewis Carroll and Edward Lear, although by virtue of writing in German and not English his audience has been much smaller than theirs in global terms. *A e* with Lear and Carroll, however, the fact that we can speak of considerable achievements in the field of Nonsense is more important than any attempt to compose an order of merit. Conditioned as we are to believe that the practice of poetry is a serious, and even solemn matter, there is a natural tendency to disparage those whose primary intention seems to be to turn it into a game played for its own sake. And yet the pleasure given to masses of readers by the game's most accomplished performers suggests that to write significant Nonsense requires quite as much genius as poetry which is plainly not Nonsensical. It is certainly a relief to read good Nonsense when all 'serious' poetry, as Eliot (himself an able Nonsense poet) suggested, has tended to be difficult. But great Nonsense writing like Morgenstern's involves much more than the dexterity and skill which ensure proficiency in a pastime; however much he may have aimed primarily to delight a group of friends, he was also seeking to instruct. Only the means employed to achieve an end distinguishes the Nonsense writer from the writer of Sense. Even the fact that the former *must* defamiliarize the familiar is only to make a rule of what the latter (and never more wholeheartedly than in modern literature) inevitably and habitually does. The anti-poetry of Dada and the 'transsense' experiments of Russian Futurism are simply two of the more notable reminders that G. K. Chesterton's claim, at the turn of the century, that Nonsense would be the literature of the future was as much a case of prophecy as of paradox. Yet neither Dada nor Futurism can claim to have had such a widespread appeal as the *Gallows Songs* of Christian Morgenstern, beside which they look highbrow and pretentious.

Morgenstern was both more and less than a Nonsense poet. At high school he studied the bizarre universal language Volapuk and invented a secret language of his own; his early intellectual passion for Schopenhauer and Nietzsche led him to read the classic mystical writings of East and West; unable to complete university because of the consumption which finally killed him, he spent a period in Scandinavia translating novels by Knut Hamsun, Strindberg's *Inferno* and six plays of Ibsen; at regular intervals he published verse of a mystical character, which impressed Rilke among others; and in his later years, falling under the spell of Rudolf Steiner's Anthroposophy and convinced that Steiner's 'spiritual purity' made him a 'great leader', he remained an ardent convert until his death. Morgenstern considered the Nonsense poetry which brought him fame to be 'minor work', much less important than the poetry in which, primarily but not exclusively under the influence of Steiner, he explored the faith expressed in one of his aphorisms: 'There is only one progress, progress in love, which leads to divine bliss.' However, the limpid simplicity of his 'serious' poetry would not have been sufficient to keep his name alive outside the circle of those of a similarly mystical disposition; it lacks the universal appeal of great mystical writing. It seems appropriate, indeed, that the essence of the Morgenstern that matters should have been advertised in the titles of his first two published volumes: *In Fancy's Castle: A Cycle Of Humorous-Fantastic Poems* (1895) and *Horatius Travestitus (Horace Travestied): A Student Prank* (1897).

Morgenstern had found in Nietzsche an idea which he considered neither the philosopher nor the decadent Romantic poets had continued to believe in: '[the] child in the human being is the everlasting creative power' was Morgenstern's way of expressing it. His fondness for the fantastic stemmed from his desire to maintain the restorative properties of a childlike vision, the very opposite of his own incurable ill-health. Like other Nonsense poets, Morgenstern was fascinated, as a child might be, by the notion of imaginary animals, animals at once alien and familiar, more rational and yet more irrational than real human beings. These animals provided a natural focus for a mind hostile to the increasing materialism of his age and intent on demonstrating the possibility of the impossible. Some of Morgenstern's animals possess human characteristics, like the shilly-shallying snail whose thoughts peter out, the ram struck by lightning who wonders why he has been thus singled out by fate, and the gloomy donkey who lives happily with his wife after proposing a suicide pact. Others, like the housefly who, on his own planet, catches humans in fly-paper, treat mankind the way they have been treated, but with a finer sense of propriety. The most remarkable are those which go far beyond human capabilities: the Tortortoise who, having never been born, can never die; the Nosobeam, who walks around on his noses. Faced with such creatures, and others like them, man had better, in Morgenstern's view, learn to treat them generously, for his rapacity threatens their continued existence. This is plainly spelled-out (!) in the splendid 'Ant-ology', which shows how the Gig-ant has been reduced to a Tweleph-ant, thence to an Eleph-ant and finally to a Ten-ant. To recognize the advantages animals have over man is infinitely more profitable, Morgenstern suggests, than to diminish them. It actually offers us the opportunity of establishing some kind of rapport with them, as in the case of the seagulls whose M-shaped wings suggest they must all be called Emma:

O humankind, you'll never fly
The way the seagulls do.
So if your name is Emma
Be glad they look like you.

To be human in Morgenstern's universe is to be the prey of petty and trivial irritations like one Paul Schrimm who has a snuffle which ruins his weekend, or like the people at a railway station annoyed by a vagrant farmyard hen getting under their feet. Humanity is, however, infinitely resourceful in coming to terms with its tribulations, as the poems about Palmström and his friend von Korf indicate. Palmström suggests to a nightingale whose song is keeping him awake that the bird should become a fish and thereby impress its paramour; he is obviously oblivious to its Romantic (if not its romantic) possibilities. And yet in another poem he behaves like any self-respecting Romantic poet would, retiring from the clamour of the world into his own soliloquies. Some of his schemes are more obviously designed to benefit mankind at large, however, notably the clock which speeds up or slows down as its owner wishes. And when confronted by indisputable evidence that one of his fellows has, as we should say, 'thrown in the towel', he retrieves the towel and hopes that one day its owner will be reunited with it. Despite Palmström's passion for art –

he finds beauty in upside-down pictures and will not use a handkerchief whose embroidery has summoned up a landscape to blow his nose – he is not entirely self-absorbed. Neither is von Korf, although his more scientific inventions are of very dubious utility. It is true that his joke with a punchline which only takes effect much later provides pleasure for those who were bored by it at the time. And *his* clock actually goes one better than Palmström's and stops time completely. But his ability to turn the brightest day into night would seem to be of profit only to those business men who are going to exploit his invention. And the strategy by which he can shorten a book of any length seems a very equivocal one; it would help to reduce loads of learned lumber, but it would make the brief poem in which it is featured disappear. Von Korf is at his most attractive when he receives an official (and officious) inquiry from the police as to his personal circumstances; since he does not exist in conventional reality at all, he cannot oblige them, though he is sufficiently diplomatic to tell them that his inability to do so vexes him quite as much as it will them. Von Korf is at least marginally more *engagé* than Palmström's female equivalent, Palma Kunkel, who is of such a retiring disposition that even to have her name mentioned in a poem makes her feel she has taken on too clear a definition.

Morgenstern, as will be clear from the example of von Korf's dealings with the police, is perfectly adept at making Nonsense into social comment. The two poems about the housemaid Cecily confirm this. Obsessed with order (as perhaps only a Nonsense poet could really be) Cecily cannot get her mistress's windows really clean without removing them altogether; and though her mistress is delighted to begin with, she soon gives Cecily the sack. Later practitioners of what we have come to think of as the Absurd have made similar capital out of their seemingly nonsensical labours. But few of them can match Morgenstern's deftness of touch, which makes one go on reading him purely for the delight he generates. It is interesting, in this connection, that Morgenstern should have been at once the victim of the 'crisis of language' which afflicted all the great

Modernist poets, and one of its most appealing beneficiaries. In his posthumously published aphorisms he strikes what has since become a familiar note in modern literature: 'I suddenly realize that the complete arbitrariness of our language is but a part of the arbitrariness of our world in general.' But Morgenstern is not crippled by this realization; he turns it to his advantage. The civil war in the Kingdom of Punctuation provides him with a perspective on war in general; the werewolf who cannot understand the mysteries of the heavily inflected German language provides a focus for a useful reminder of how the cases decline. Morgenstern was extremely concerned that his language games should not provide a pabulum for the learned in the way that Mauthner's great *Critique Of Language* had done and Wittgenstein's writings would do. But presumably he would not have been averse to interpretations which remained within the boundaries of common sense.

One of the primary functions of Nonsense may indeed be to take us beyond common sense as we normally exercise it, only to invite us finally to employ the faculty more imaginatively. This is certainly one way of reading Morgenstern's 'Nightsong Of The Fish', which he jokingly described as 'the profoundest German poem'. This makes its point with an economy which is in some ways very un-German and a decorum which would have been alien to the later Dadaists:

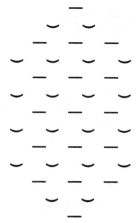

In accordance with the fact that fish are dumb creatures, the poem is wordless, dependent solely on visual patterns. But the patterns speak volumes, for the typography has organized them into the shape of a fish (as if they were stars in a constellation) and the scuds and horizontal lines suggest the closed eyes and mouths of creatures asleep. The poem is at once as rudimentary as a child's drawing and as sophisticated as a picture by Paul Klee. Its rhythm confirms that it is indeed a song, but a song without words, a tribute to the harmony which only the non-verbal arts can hope to achieve. Uniquely among Morgenstern's poems, it removes all language barriers, as music and painting do; as *avant-garde* as one could wish for, it is also as ancient as a hieroglyphic inscription. But to speak of it at any length, other than to whet the appetite of those who have yet to discover Morgenstern, is plainly to confess oneself more nonsensical than the author who 'wrote' it, no doubt an appropriate fate for anyone who ventures into the world of Nonsense.

Paul Valéry (1871–1945)

Born in Sète into a family of Venetian and Corsican origin. Educated at the *lycée* in Montpellier, where he took an interest in art and in classical civilization. Studied law at the age of seventeen, though he was primarily interested in mathematics, physics and music. Deeply influenced by Mallarmé, whom he met for the first time in Paris in 1891. His early poetry, which remained uncollected until 1920, was published in literary periodicals. Abandoned poetry, primarily in despair of emulating Mallarmé, in Genoa in 1892. Concentrated on severely intellectual pursuits for the next twenty years, during which time he was employed by several commercial companies. Married an intimate friend of Mallarmé's daughter in 1900 and became a private secretary to a businessman, thereby gaining security and sufficient leisure to pursue his studies. Inspired to return to poetry when André Gide approached him in 1912 asking for permission to reprint his early poems. Became famous overnight in 1917 on the publication of his longest and most difficult poem, *La Jeune Parque*, and consolidated his renown with the publication in 1922 of his collection *Charmes*. Devoted much of the last twenty-five years of his life to writing prose and prose poems, and to the speculative pages of his posthumously published notebooks. Elected to the French Academy in 1927 and appointed to the Chair of Poetry at the Collège de France in 1937. In bad odour with the authorities in Vichy France during the Second World War. Died soon after the Liberation of France, by which time he was one of the most respected of all modern European literary figures. His writings have been very influential on contemporary French intellectual life. A writer to whom the Nobel Prize, which he never won, might appropriately have been awarded.

Of all the late nineteenth- and early twentieth-century poets to seek relief from a decadent Romanticism in the time-honoured virtues of Classicism, Valéry was the most meticulous and stringent in the demands he made of himself and his technique. With unparalleled *force majeure* and a rarely equalled mastery of verbal cadences, Valéry was able to solve with apparent ease the technical difficulties which he deliberately placed in his own path in order that each utterance should seem a necessary and inevitable one. By dint of the 'obstinate rigour' that he admired in Leonardo da Vinci (whose motto it was), Valéry attempted to evolve a method which, in its precision, would yield nothing to the abstract science of mathematics and give rise to a poetry as solid as architecture and as sonorous as music. The rigour consisted in subjecting his sensibility and, above all, his mental processes to an intellectual analysis more demanding than any other modern poet has seen fit to engage in, of which his inexhaustible notebooks are the permanent record. In one notebook entry he describes himself as 'terribly *centred*', though the sheer bulk and remorselessness of his self-scrutiny might tempt a detractor to call him terribly *self*-centred. For although Valéry's speculation ranged very widely it was usually conducted in a manner that can make his scope seem rather narrower than the 'universal geniuses' of the past. The act of thinking was paramount for Valéry, but his consciousness was orientated inwards rather than outwards. He transformed the external world into a significant object of perception by colouring it with his own inner conceptions; he could never be content with mere observation until it had been elevated to the level of ideas. Valéry's prose writings provide a less forbidding access to the turbulent drama of the quest for a 'pure poetry' than is sometimes the case with his almost too perfect poems, the product of a quite remarkably painstaking attention to detail. But there remains something forbidding, even in the notebooks, in the way Valéry was unable to escape for any length of time from the imprisoning vicious circle of his private concerns. He is likely to prove a much more seminal figure than the Mallarmé he idolized, partly because he wrote more; but those for whom purity and cerebration are of less importance are likely to find sterility as well as greatness, and weaknesses consequent upon his very strengths in the writings of Valéry. 'It is he who will remain for posterity,' wrote T. S. Eliot in a commemorative essay, 'the representative poet, the symbol of the poet, of the first half of the twentieth century – not Yeats, not Rilke, not anyone else.' But Valéry is really in many ways an extremely unrepresentative figure, and it seems probable that his posterity may be more easily numbered than in the case of either of the other two poets referred to by Eliot.

Valéry's early poetry – which remained uncollected until he published his *Album Of Old Verse* in 1920 – was, not unnaturally, derivative, with the careful but brittle precision of the Parnassians enveloped in the mysteriousness of Mallarmé, whose explorations of the 'azure' had captivated Valéry. The poem 'Valvins' is a tacit acknowledgement of Valéry's debt to Mallarmé, though the master himself rightly perceived an original voice – not fully foregrounded, but implicit – in these remarkable juvenilia, a 'distinct fire' (the title of one of the weaker poems) informing the *fin de siècle* motifs of dancers, sleeping women and mythological heroines. This is certainly true in the case of the famous sonnet to Helen of 1891, which portrays the world's most famous *femme fatale* emerging, like any number of Valéry's later *personae*, from the 'grottoes' of a death-like sleep to greet the 'clear song' of oarsmen and the 'sculptured arms' of figureheads. With hindsight it is possible to see that the distinctively *fin de siècle* complex of languor and precision, coldness and passion, is actually less important than the exclamatory opening, which makes the speaker's self-discovery dependent on her awareness of the 'azure'. This gives the poem a currency, in view of Valéry's later and more mature approaches to self-discovery, which 'Narcissus Speaks' (a 'pastoral symphony in the classical style' as Valéry called it, a poem which had itself grown out of a sonnet) does not possess. Most of this 'old verse', as Valéry disparagingly called it, is less ambitious than 'Narcissus Speaks', but more successful, and marginally more accessible than the Mallarméan sonnets which inspired it. 'Orpheus', for example, records the desire to unite music and architecture in an ideal act of construction without any of the complex embellishments that Valéry later gave this theme.

But for the invitation to collect his early verse, it seems possible that Valéry's greatest poems might never have been written, for in the winter of 1892 – under the pressure of an unrequited passion, a night of Mediterranean storm in Genoa, and a despair at ever emulating Mallarmé – Valéry followed the example of Rimbaud (whom he had also been deeply moved by) and in great anguish of spirit abandoned poetry in favour of abstract thought. The two great prose works of this period are the writings brought together as *Monsieur Teste* (begun in 1894) and the *Introduction To The Method Of Leonardo da Vinci* of 1895, to which Valéry added a critical appendix twenty-five years later. These are best regarded, despite their intrinsic merits, as introductions to the method of Paul Valéry, establishing as they do certain models of behaviour and intellectual activity to which the poet, though increasingly aware of the impossibility of realizing them, ever afterwards aspired. Teste and Leonardo are purely contemplative consciousnesses, the first of whom 'differs as little as could be wished from nothingness' and the second of whom manifests his 'unqualified refusal to be anything whatsoever'. Valéry was later to admit that his twenty years of poetic silence were not without the frustrations and uncertainties naturally consequent upon such an extreme intellectualist stance, which was actually less nihilistic than the above quotations suggest. But it was only in 1912, when Gide suggested he should prepare a volume of his poetry to be published, that he began to see how the two activities which most mattered to him – poetry and abstract thought – might be made less mutually exclusive than he had previously thought them. And in confronting the Helen of his early sonnet, who is on the point of weeping, Valéry found the germ of what was to become the opening of the poem that in 1917, after 'four years of toil', made him famous overnight: *La Jeune Parque.*

La Jeune Parque is Valéry's longest, most ambitious and most difficult poem. It is implacably resistant to paraphrase, concerned as it is with what the poet called 'a succession of psychological substitutions' of quite dazzling complexity and concentration. The most succinctly accurate description of what 'takes place' in the poem – even 'takes place' seems too substantial a verb to use, since nothing can be said to happen in the accepted sense – is Valéry's own; he called it 'the *transformation of a consciousness* in the course of one night'. This description does little to suggest the dramatic and manifold oscillations of mood which occupy the space between the weeping of the first three lines and the fire of the sun with which it ends. Through the medium of the young Fate who gives the poem its title Valéry is objectifying the competing tensions in himself between thinking and feeling, self-discovery and oblivion, perfected absolutes and an irremediably imperfect mortality. *La Jeune Parque* is, in other words, at once a critique of Valéry's pre-crisis poetry and at the same time a kind of programmatic poem outlining the absolute or 'pure' poetry which reached its slightly less formidable apotheosis in the 1922 collection *Charms*. Yet it is pre-eminently a poem about its own creation, 'an artificial fabric that took on a natural kind of growth' in Valéry's subsequent estimation. As an example of the 'deliberate hesitation between sound and meaning' which for Valéry was the distinguishing feature of the ideal poetry he wished to write, *La Jeune Parque* has no rivals in Valéry's later verse, although there are critics of it who (like Eliot faced with *Paradise Lost*) have occasionally found more sound than sense in this most musical of poems. Perhaps no one could truly claim to have unravelled all the serpentine transitions of a work which Valéry described as having 'the solidity as well as the ambiguity of an object'. As an exercise in tightrope-walking, it was unrepeatable and was not repeated. But even the less ambitious poems that followed it seem to stand in the shadow of this dauntingly abstract yet sensually passionate masterpiece. As Valéry admitted afterwards, its composition made the writing of the subsequent *Charms* a much less demanding activity, in which the strain of writing poetry at all seems to have been almost completely diffused.

Valéry compared *La Jeune Parque* to a recitative for solo contralto voice; indeed, allowing for differences of spirit between the two works, the piece of music it most resembles is Schoenberg's first great atonal masterpiece, the monodrama for soprano and orchestra *Erwartung*. The *Charms*, however, as their title implies, are most likely to cast a spell on the reader, for they are more modest, like *lieder*. Yet Valéry's epigraph to the collection – *deducere carmen* (to deduce the song) – is a reminder that, despite their smaller compass, they are products of equally stringent intellection. Just as Valéry claimed to have started out in *La Jeune Parque* from 'the language itself' (a distinctly Mallarméan idea) so he stressed that the *Charms* were a 'collection of prosodic experiments'. They certainly called upon him to perform prodigies of complex versification, but they are much less demanding for the reader who cares to follow Valéry's habit of 'driving self-awareness to the capture of its sensibility'. Most of them portray a more serene and unblemished mood than the young Fate is ever mistress of, although the injunction in the last poem – 'Calm, calm, stay calm!' – is a reminder that turmoil has been present. This famous poem ('Palm') compares the amplitude of the palm tree with the mind of a poet whose spirit has been visited by an angelic figure full of grace who has brought him sustenance, and it is arguably the most beautiful poem in the collection, although 'Canticle Of The Columns' and 'Silhouette Of A Serpent' are also very fine. All three of these poems indicate that Valéry's poetics of impersonality does not preclude a kind of intimacy between the poet and the reader, but rather actively encourages it. Valéry spent a good deal of time pondering the paradox whereby poetry became 'something that restores what was not given' and, partly as a result of so often re-reading himself – the early 'Narcissus Speaks', for example, is here refined into the much better poem 'Fragments Of The Narcissus' – came to believe that poetry must 'listen to its reader'. Much of Valéry's prose writing is devoted to articulating the ideal circumstances under which such a collaboration might take place, and it must be admitted that very little of Valéry's best poetry will make much impression on a reader who prefers a more passive role.

This is even true of the most famous of all Valéry's poems, 'The Graveyard By The Sea', the least typical of the *Charms*, though Valéry insisted that it, too, originated in an attempt to solve a specific technical problem. Its density and gravity communicate immediately to a reader baffled by *La Jeune Parque*, although like its great predecessor it situates its protagonist 'between the void and the pure event'. Perhaps this is because it is not so much a drama of self-discovery as a meditation on mortality, inspired by the cemetery overlooking the harbour of the Mediterranean town of Sète, where Valéry was born and is buried. In the face of the most eloquent and irrefutable evidence of human mortality, the poem rejects (like the epigraph from Pindar which stands at the head of it) humanity's pretension to an immortal life comparable to that enjoyed by the blue Mediterranean water. At the heart of a 'motionless midday', translucent and tranquil, the human figure confronts and comes to terms with its inevitable imperfections and in an exclamatory and violent climax abolishes the image of the sea as a classical temple (with which the poem has begun) in favour of a recognition that the sea is never so static, however it may appear. A less familiar expression of the same idea occurs in the prose poems 'Seas' and 'Regarding The Sea' which date from the decade after *Charms* and which have had to wait for the *Collected Works* to begin to be seen as something more than the mere 'odds and ends' which Valéry was content to consider them during his lifetime.

Some of the most immediately appealing verse poems of Valéry were either not included in *Charms*, like 'Hour' and 'Equinox', or date from after 1922, among which 'Snow' and the 'Twelve Poems' posthumously published are particularly fine. The prose poems of his later years, though much more abstract than those of Baudelaire, are less cloying and less impenetrable than those of Mallarmé and deserve to be more widely-known. Valéry's last great utterance was actually in the genre of prose poetry, in a work begun in 1921 but only finished a few months before his death: 'The Angel'. The situation is similar to that adumbrated by the 'mystic without God' Monsieur Teste, but the mood is much more one of plenitude than of vacuum. The poem is in the preferred dialogue form of Valéry's last twenty years (his other dialogues are to be found in volume four of the Bollingen *Collected Works*) but is much the most economical and memorable of Valéry's 'exercises' (as he liked to call all his writing) in this mode. And it ends with a paradox that is a peculiarly appropriate description of Valéry's whole enterprise: 'And throughout an eternity, he did not cease to know, and not to understand.' However, despite the benevolence of the angel figure that the 'he' of this poem encounters, it is possible to argue that Valéry never investigated the world beyond himself with sufficient vigour to make the act of knowing and the act of understanding one and the same thing. Insofar as there was nothing to short-circuit the act of thinking, there were inevitably times when – as in a remarkable undated quatrain poem – he could record only a misery and weariness analogous to that which (as we know from his correspondence after the abandonment of poetry in 1892) his self-imposed rigours had condemned him to:

It is true. I am gloomy. And miserably
Tired of myself, and tired of these gloomy dawns
In which the soul smokes, dreams and sifts its shadows.
. . . I feel the fatigue of an angel weighing on me.

The writings of Valéry, taken as a whole, are the reflection of a mind which, like Coleridge's, is at its most attractive when it seems to be implicated in a drama which is as much a matter of failure as of success. For all Valéry's greatness as a poet, his poetry can take on more attractively human proportions if it is read in the light of the more expansive prose writings which provide such a full record of the splendours and miseries of the quest for pure poetry.

Hugo von Hofmannsthal
(1874–1929)

Born in Vienna of prosperous and cultured parents. Became famous in Viennese intellectual circles at the age of sixteen for the flawless poems he published under the pen name 'Loris'. Studied Romance languages and literatures. Met Stefan George in 1891 and corresponded with him until 1906, when their friendship became strained. Suffered a painful intellectual crisis at the turn of the century, after which he wrote almost no poetry. Commenced a sometimes difficult relationship with the composer Richard Strauss in 1906, devoting much of his energy thereafter to the provision of libretti in perhaps the most famous of collaborations between literary and musical giants. Composed chamber plays of a decadent Symbolist kind before 1900, but later became involved with the world of the public theatre and throughout the rest of his life, having taken up residence in the palace at Rodaun near Vienna, sought to inculcate a humanistic and pan-European culture, often adapting the works of others in a manner which has been much misunderstood. Instrumental with Max Reinhardt and others in founding the now famous Salzburg Festival in 1920. Died suddenly of a heart attack whilst preparing to attend the funeral of his son, who had committed suicide. Wrongly assumed to be a rather marginal figure in the English-speaking world, and yet to be accorded the recognition that other luminaries of turn-of-the-century Vienna have subsequently enjoyed.

'Be absolute for death', the disguised Duke counsels the imprisoned Claudio in Act 3 of Shakespeare's darkest and most

profound comedy, *Measure For Measure*, set in an imaginary
Vienna where values are in flux; 'thou'rt death's fool', he
continues, reminding Claudio that he has 'nor youth, nor age,/
But as it were an after-dinner's sleep/Dreaming on both'. In
Hofmannsthal's Vienna, three centuries later, the dream of life
and the horizon of death were juxtaposed in an even more
ambiguous manner, as the composition and reception of
Hofmannsthal's most characteristic early work, the verse play
Death And The Fool of 1892, abundantly illustrates. The play
owes something to the mysterious Symbolist dramas of Maeter-
linck much admired at the time, but even more to the traditions
of the medieval morality play upon which Shakespeare himself
had drawn. Hofmannsthal's Claudio, more prominent than
Shakespeare's, is locked in combat with the Death he fears,
with no providential Duke to offer him the standard Christian
consolation; there is no system of belief to which he can appeal
in order to make his tribulations meaningful. The play is
representative of its epoch; in the years leading up to the First
World War the old and crumbling imperial capital was much
possessed with death and dreams. Claudio's one consolation,
which he belatedly recognizes as such, is that life is a dream
from which, at the point of death, man awakens into a trans-
cendent and absolute life. Hofmannsthal's play expresses a
religious notion within a context which signally lacks a reli-
gious dimension; it is the product of a very sophisticated culture
in which art matters more than religion. Yet Claudio's es-
sentially aesthetic attitude to life is made to look very vul-
nerable; the play exposes ideas of 'art for art's sake' as painfully
inadequate. In a manner akin to Freud's enterprises in psycho-
pathology it discloses depths that an outwardly pious but
inwardly perverse society had strategically chosen to ignore;
Hofmannsthal, like Freud, is intent on the pathological
because he wishes ultimately to restore health. It says much for
the *Zeitgeist* that the play was widely regarded as contributing
to the malaise rather than a remedy for it. But *Death And The
Fool* leaves itself open to misconstruction, as much of
Hofmannsthal's later writing also does. And with hindsight
Hofmannsthal seems not so much 'someone who contained the

whole age', as was said of him when he was only twenty, but
rather someone fated to experience the tensions of the age
without finally transcending them.

   Hofmannsthal's early verse plays are essentially undramatic;
the poet himself described them as 'lyrical'. And the lyrical vein
in Hofmannsthal proved to be only one of many modes he
adopted to inculcate ideas of wholeness and integration. By the
age of twenty-five, having written some of the most flawless
lyric poems in the German language, he had become con-
vinced that lyric poetry, like the aestheticism which had con-
ferred on it a privileged status, required the admixture of more
mundane and more accessible forms to reach the society from
which it had taken its materials, not least the very language it
employed. Thereafter Hofmannsthal concerned himself with
finding something with a more immediately retroactive pur-
chase upon reality than mere words on a page, however beauti-
ful: the stage play and the libretto that required a composer
and an opera house to make it meaningful. The difficulties
Hofmannsthal experienced in transforming his unprece-
dentedly precocious lyric talent into narrative, dramatic and
mythological one are recorded and, as it were, psychoana-
lyzed, in the only one of his works to have gained much
currency in the English-speaking world: the guardedly con-
fessional *Letter Of Lord Chandos* of 1902. This seems at first glance
analogous to many more openly personal statements, made by
poets of all kinds and conditions, to the effect that words
alienate us from what they are supposed to designate, that (in
Hofmannsthal's own words) they have 'pushed themselves in
front of things'. But beneath this 'word-scepticism', as it has
been called, there remains visible in the *Letter Of Lord Chandos*
the faith which has provoked it and which will ultimately
outlast it, the quasi-mystical idea of 'the whole of existence as
one great unit'. Chandos is, as Hofmannsthal tells us, 'a mystic
without a mystique'; but Chandos's private experience does
not invalidate the mystique. His letter, as its even and some-
times serene tone suggests, is not just a crisis-document but the
record of a crisis conquered. In the lectures and literary criti-
cism of the post-Chandos years Hofmannsthal was not, signifi-

cantly, recommending Rimbaud (who had abandoned lyric poetry in a quite different spirit from Hofmannsthal), but rather Shakespeare and Balzac, and recommending them as writers who had kept faith with the idea of 'the whole of existence as one great unit'. This upward curve is in fact anticipated by Chandos himself at the end of his now famous letter. In 1911–12 Hofmannsthal was moved to reaffirm this faith in the ambivalently naturalistic mode of the philosophical narrative or fable; but he was unable to complete *Andreas* to his own satisfaction. Only in the fragmentary notes towards it is it clear that Andreas, who has begun as 'two halves which gape asunder', is intended to feel, after all the mysterious experiences he has undergone, 'as if the two halves of his being ... were coming together again'. Among the quotations from other writers which add to the interest of these fragments is an aphorism from the German Romantic poet Novalis: 'the destruction of the law of contradiction is the supreme task of the higher logic'. Hofmannsthal quotes this aphorism without comment but with evident approval; like Novalis, he envisages the higher logic as one in which what offers itself to our reason as contradiction is transformed into an integrated whole by our imaginations. But Novalis's higher logician was pre-eminently the lyric poet in his role as verbal magician; Hofmannsthal, having abandoned lyric poetry, was seeking a still higher logic, in which the lyric poet was subsumed in the 'symbolic man'. In the last two decades of his life he was concerned with finding the best form in which to present this 'symbolic man', and two of his most interesting attempts are the great comedy *The Man Who Was Difficult* (1918) and the twice-written symbolic drama *The Tower* (1925; 1927). In writing to a friend on the first production of *The Man Who Was Difficult* in 1921 Hofmannsthal stressed that it should be seen in terms of his previous attempts at resolution, though not necessarily as a solution to the problems it raised:

It is concerned with the problem which has often tormented and oppressed me (already present in *Death And The Fool*), most acutely in the *Letter Of Lord Chandos* ...: how does the solitary individual come to commit himself to society through language, indeed, how does he come to be inextricably connected with society through language whether he likes it or not? And also: how can the man who speaks act, when to speak is to understand, and to understand is to be incapable of action?

Ironically enough, *The Man Who Was Difficult* seems to have been upstaged, for English readers, by Robert Musil's novel *The Man Without Qualities*, in which similar problems are rehearsed at much greater length. And since neither version of *The Tower* is frequently performed on stages outside Austria, it is very difficult for an English reader to address, and seek to answer, the questions Hofmannsthal is raising.

In the absence of regular performances of Hofmannsthal's plays, his ideas have enjoyed a kind of currency from his collaboration with Richard Strauss: *Der Rosenkavalier*, *Ariadne auf Naxos* and *Die Frau ohne Schatten* are all established classics of the opera repertory. But equally compelling and quite as satisfying are the early lyric poems which prove beyond all doubt that, to quote Hofmannsthal's words of 1921, 'to speak is to understand'. In a poem written when he was only twenty-two, 'Inscription', Hofmannsthal addresses, with all the authority of an aged sage, the writers of his time:

Do not neglect the one task which is yours
Which, though it frighten you, is all your own.
No other can disclose life's mystery
And chaos quickly will condemn your craft.

Hofmannsthal's conception of the writer's 'task' is elaborated in an epigram written two years later, 'The Art Of Poetry', in more personal terms: 'This art is awesome: I spin a thread out of my flesh/And this thread is no less surely the wing whereby I fly through the air'. Another epigram warns that the words which have formed in the poet's mouth must exert a pressure on the universe outside the poet, otherwise the pressure of the universe upon him will render them null and void. The universe in question is plainly not simply the world of the present; it is comprised of everything that has ever existed. 'Whenever we open our mouths,' Hofmannsthal wrote in an essay of 1894, 'ten thousand dead speak through us.' This is poetically rendered in one of his most memorable poems, 'Many, truly': the poet's activity is here shown to be much more than the 'slender flame and narrow lyre' of his own life; there are many destinies woven besides his, and all of them are interwoven with his. Hofmannsthal's conception of the poet is of a figure who mediates between the starry heights and the lower depths, the seated majesties on high and the 'roots of tangled life'. The impersonal manner he adopts to express this truth makes it seem axiomatic, individually and collectively true. But the frame of reference is cultural and psychological rather than narrowly social or political; Hofmannsthal the lyric poet, like Freud the psychoanalyst, is intent on exploring the lower depths which our unconscious articulates in the turbulent world of our dreams. One such dream is dramatized in the splendid poem 'Experience', in which Hofmannsthal demonstrates (more economically than in *Death And The Fool*, composed at about the same time) that the idea of death offers us a means of access to, and a disclosure of, our origins. By the end of this poem the figure who has experienced a dreamlike death by drowning and succumbed to its 'melancholy music' has been granted a vision of himself as a child; he stands finally upon the shore watching the guttering candle in his bedroom. And yet a higher spiritual force – here imaged as a vessel whose yellow sails recall the candle – transports him from the scene; this force is at once the source of and the solace for the 'nameless homesickness for life' which this figure, like Claudio, has had disclosed to him by his dream. Hofmannsthal frequently employs the image of the child, and often places him beside the water which is a traditional symbol of life's passage through time. In the poem 'World Secret' (which is partially grounded upon the ancient wisdom that truth is to be found at the bottom of a well and partially based upon the modern Freudian wisdom that it is also to be found in the Unconscious), Hofmannsthal stresses that the poet who remains a child may express the truth without contaminating its mystery. There is a poignant note in the novel *Andreas* in which Hofmannsthal expresses a similar idea: 'to die reconciled to one's childhood'. And the poem 'A Boy' dramatizes how the heedless child must grow up into the adult poet, penetrate the mystery of life and accept the heavy responsibility of disseminating it. Like the protagonist of 'The Youth In The Landscape', this figure must recognize, in the manner of a Christian steward, that perfect service is perfect freedom, and that satisfaction is to be found only by going beyond one's own personal experience. 'A Dream Of The Higher Magic', which concerns a modern follower of the mystic Paracelsus and which obviously invites comparison with Novalis's 'higher logic', confirms that the poet's inner intoxications must be directed outwards, that the writing hand must form part of a permanent dialogue.

Hofmannsthal the lyric poet utters truths of a traditional kind in traditional forms; in 1924 he told Richard Strauss: 'the individual can produce nothing of lasting value unless it be linked to tradition'. The traditional form to which he was particularly attracted in his early years was *terza rima*, with a final line completing the formal rhyme pattern and, as it were, exemplifying the fact that all destinies are interwoven one with another. Three of Hofmannsthal's *terza rima* poems are concerned with the question of man's evanescence and mutability. The first reaffirms the burden of 'Many, truly', that the poet's ancestors are as close to him as his own hair; the second presents, like 'A Boy', the growth from childhood to maturity; the third, which begins with Shakespeare's 'We are such stuff as dreams are made on' confirms (again like 'Many, truly') the close relationship between dreams and the innermost life of things. 'And three are one,' this third poem aptly concludes, 'a man, a thing, a dream.' Hofmannsthal's other great *terza rima* poem is 'Ballad Of The Outer Life', where the first four tercets present the stunned response to man's fate of one who remains outside it and therefore cannot be consoled. In the next seven lines the figure rouses himself from his torpidity and, by asking unanswerable questions, engages more actively with man's plight. Only in the last three lines does a tentative affirmation emerge:

Yet he who utters 'evening' may speak volumes,
From which word gravity and grieving ooze
Like honey out of hollow honeycombs.

The mood of these lines is perhaps gloomier than
Hofmannsthal was later prepared to admit; they have the
heaviness of which they speak. The sadness seems to be insepa-
rable from the fact that the man who utters the word 'evening'
is essentially a lyric poet, whereas all of Hofmannsthal's later
activity is devoted to delineating the superior 'symbolic man'
who adds gesture and physical grace to his predecessor's verbal
magic.

Traces of this 'symbolic man' are, however, to be found in
Hofmannsthal's lyrical poems, especially those which deal with
the world of the theatre. These are all occasional poems,
although they transcend the occasion for which they were
written as great occasional poetry unfailingly does. One of the
most memorable is the prefatory poem which Hofmannsthal
wrote for Arthur Schnitzler's play *Anatol*; it invites the audience
to partake of a seductive entertainment in a spirit of heedless
hedonism. The three poems on the deaths of actors whom
Hofmannsthal knew, admired and had worked with are natur-
ally more grave, though even these are leavened by the para-
dox of *Death And The Fool*: that death is simply the final
transformation in careers which, by their very nature, have
involved the continual abandonment of subjective personality
in favour of objective masks. It is instructive to compare the
poem of 1899 'On The Death Of The Actor Herman Müller'
with the 1910 poem 'On The Death Of The Actor Josef Kainz'.
The Müller poem is elegiac, emphasizing the fact that 'his poor
soul walked/Quite unveiled, and saw with a child's eyes', and
only at the end does it become an unequivocal eulogy:

    with firm grasp, like a heavy cloak
He cast life off from him and did not heed
More than the dust upon his mantle's hem
The forms that now were crumbled into naught.

The Kainz poem is reverential, as well it might be, since the
actor has assumed God's role of unmoved mover:

A man unmoved who moved us, one
Who , when we thought him near, was far from us . . .
And messenger of an ineffable deity.

Hofmannsthal's experiments in the tradition of *theatrum mundi* have remained too little known. But the lyric poems in which he took it upon himself to become 'messenger of an ineffable deity' are of such immense authority that anyone reading them is effectively forced to familiarize himself with the rest of his very diverse creation, and to marvel at an *oeuvre* which is the only one in modern German literature to invite, and withstand, comparison with Goethe's.

Rainer Maria Rilke
(1875–1926)

Born in Prague, the son of a retired officer in the Austrian army and a mother who, disappointed of a daughter, treated him as if he were a girl. Of a very refined sensibility from an early age, and deeply scarred by his education at the Military School of St Pölten between 1886 and 1891, where he was frequently in poor health. Studied at the Commercial Academy in Linz until 1892, and then worked for his barrister uncle. Published his first volume of poems in 1894. Studied at the University of Prague in 1895–6, but by 1899 had decided on a career in literature rather than law. Visited Russia with Lou Andreas-Salomé in 1899 and in 1900, where he met Tolstoy; studied Russian history, literature and art on returning to Berlin. Married a young sculptress he had met in the artist's colony near Bremen in 1901. Became secretary to the sculptor Rodin in Paris in 1902–3 and thereafter lived apart from his wife. Remained based in Paris until 1914, though frequently resident for short periods in Scandinavia, Italy, Spain and North Africa, in great distress of spirit for much of the time. Made many friends among the aristocracy, in the castle of one of whom, at Duino near Trieste, he began the sequence of *Elegies* which were completed in 1922. Called up for military service in Vienna in 1915, where his health broke down; given clerical work and finally allowed to return to Munich. Spent his last years in Switzerland, widely regarded as the greatest poet to write in German since the death of Goethe. Died of leukaemia at Valmont, near Montreux.

'Ultimately,' Rilke wrote in a late letter, 'each of us experiences only *one* conflict in life, which constantly reappears under a different guise.' At the risk of grossly oversimplifying a large and very demanding body of work, we may say that the '*one* conflict' which dominated Rilke's life was between the raw material of experience and the shaped artefact of art. 'I do not want,' he told his lifelong confidante Lou Andréas-Salomé in 1903, 'to sunder art from life; I want them, somehow or somewhere, to be of one meaning.' In practice, however, Rilke needed, initially at least, to separate out the domains of art and life and to pledge his support for the former at the expense of the latter. His temperament and upbringing were of a kind that made the solaces of art seem especially attractive as a refuge from and bulwark against emotional deprivations and short-comings; but even in his withdrawn early phase he recognized that he would ultimately have to effect a *rapprochement* between the world at large and the microcosm of the mind. An entry in a diary written during a visit to Tuscany in 1898 shows Rilke rehearsing the possibility of transforming himself from the troubled and agonized figure he knew himself to be, and becoming a kind of originating deity concentrically present in all the aspects of his creation. 'There will be nothing outside [this solitary man]', Rilke wrote; 'for trees and hills, clouds and waves will only be symbols of those realities which He finds within himself'. In later life Rilke was to speak of this solitary figure in more conventional terms as 'the primordial godhead'; but in his earliest conception of any significance it is evident that he was trying to conjure the lineaments of an ideal human being. Having rejected the Catholicism of his childhood, Rilke was reluctant to see this unmoved mover in traditional Christian terms; in the posthumously published *Visions of Christ*, written between 1896 and 1898, he had rejected the divinity of the figure of the incarnate Christ who is central to orthodox piety. Rilke's profoundly spiritual nature was left without an accredited system of belief in which he might place his trust. All of his efforts thereafter were devoted to creating a system of his own to fill the vacuum. Each crucial subsequent experience effectively forced him, however, to make adjustments in what he had tried to render stable and unified. Only in his maturity did Rilke regard the very process of 'transformation', the constant reappearance of a single conflict in multiple manifestations, as an index of the organic wholeness which he had sketched, more in hope than confidence, in his Tuscan diary. Rilke was occupied all his life with experiments and approximations, all the time aware that, like his *alter ego* Malte Laurids Brigge, 'he was an artist, and hated the approximate'.

Rilke ever afterward regarded his two brief visits to Russia (in 1899 and 1900) as a fundamental influence upon his later development; Russia was the first of the many spiritual homes that the vagrant poet encountered in the course of his wanderings. The extent to which the real Russia impinged upon his consciousness may be judged from his correspondence. But the literary works which were prompted by those journeys create an imaginary Russia, the 'holy' Russia of myth and legend. The coyly homiletic and homespun *Stories of God* (1900) represent this imaginary Russia at its most resistible; the poems of *The Book of Hours* (written between 1899 and 1903) – organized around the threefold structure of 'monastic life', 'pilgrimage' and 'sainthood' – have a more attractive urgency and impetus. But there are actually few poems in *The Book of Hours* which obey his self-addressed admonition to 'Be severe and see'; the orientation, especially in the first two subsections, is too introspective for severity to correct Rilke's penchant for diffuseness. More challenging, and more prophetic, was his concurrent composition of the poems collected in 1906 as *The Book of Images*, in which the features of the external world begin to take precedence over the mind's imaginings. And his belated gravitation towards life as it is actually lived was decisively influenced by his taking up residence in Paris and acting in the capacity of secretary to the sculptor Rodin. 'I am learning to see,' Rilke writes at the beginning of *The Notebooks of Malte Laurids Brigge*, begun in Paris in 1904. And later in part one of the *Notebooks* there is a passage which speaks of an 'obstinate man' who 'ever more impatiently, ever more desperately, had sought equivalents among the visible for the inwardly seen'. This obstinate man is never named, though the context makes it clear that it is Ibsen whom Rilke had in mind. It **was** obviously Rodin, however, who was the really 'obstinate man' of Rilke's first years in Paris. In the same year in which he wrote the first of his two monographs on Rodin, 1903, Rilke told Lou Andréas-Salomé that 'life, once it becomes work, can become art'. It was Rodin's devotion to his art, and his rigorous working methods, that offered Rilke something to emulate. The epigraph to the 1903 monograph – Emerson's 'the hero is he who is immovably centred' – encapsulates Rodin's practice as viewed by Rilke. But in transferring Rodin's practice from sculpture to poetry Rilke required a poetic model from whom he might learn more nearly. And there are passages, both in Rilke's correspondence and in the *Notebooks*, which suggest that Baudelaire – the unacknowledged source of the Emerson quotation – provided him with the catalyst he needed. Malte Laurids Brigge, for all his uniquely Rilkean qualities, is a self-divided creature in the Baudelairean mould; and it cannot be merely coincidental that the volume in which Rilke most triumphantly obeys the command to 'be severe and see' – *New Poems* (published in two volumes in 1907 and 1908) – is very largely comprised of poems in the form that Baudelaire also preferred: the sonnet.

Rilke is at his most accessible in these short poems of 1903–8, and the astonishing consistency of the *New Poems* makes any attempt to extricate a canon of indispensable poems virtually impossible. Insofar as titles alone can suggest their richness and range, the following have a kind of representative status: 'The Panther', 'Piano Practice', 'Leda', 'Late Autumn In Venice', 'Spanish Dancer', 'The Departure Of The Prodigal Son'. In all of them Rilke gives the impression that he is more concerned with the nature and essence of the object viewed than with the sensibility of the observer. Yet these apparently impersonal poems are much less severe than they seem at first glance; they are in fact best regarded as intensely vivid dramatizations of the competing claims of 'the visible' and 'the inwardly seen'. Appropriately enough, it is the famous 'Panther' poem, the first of the *New Poems* to be written, which provides us with a phrase that might be applied to any one of its successors: 'the dance of forces round a centre'. And this same poem also establishes that, for all the poet's talk of a new 'objectivity', this centre is to be found in his own heart. It was precisely in the encounter with things outside himself that Rilke came to realize that the centre could only be maintained by constant self-transformation. The idea is most memorably articulated in the final line of one of the most impressive of all the *New Poems*, 'Archaic Torso of Apollo': 'You must change your life'. Rilke's recognition of the need for change did not, however, lessen his admiration for the 'immovably centred' figure. Such a figure, indeed, stands literally and symbolically at the centre of the outstanding poem 'Orpheus. Eurydice. Hermes'. In this version of the famous story Eurydice does not see Orpheus at all, in any meaningful sense; her vision is trained on the inner space of which Rilke's Tuscan diary had spoken. This Eurydice is offered to us as a solitary figure who has rejected the possibility of there being anything outside herself, and who is to be admired for having contained even death within herself. Yet Rilke evidently felt the need to provide a more telling rationale for this apparent narcissism, and two events in close proximity offered him the opportunity of doing so. The first was the death in childbirth of his friend the painter Paula Modersohn-Becker, the second the suicide of the minor poet Count Wolf Graf von Kalcreuth, in whom Rilke saw aspects of his own creative difficulties.

The emotions aroused by the death of the painter are the subject of the 'Requiem For A Friend' of 1907, which conjures up a ghostly figure more retroactive upon the real world than is feasible in Eurydice's self-absorption. The emotions aroused by a fellow poet's suicide are the subject of the 'Requiem For Wolf Graf von Kalcreuth', which represents another attempt to bring the worlds of life and death into a kind of Orphic unity. Both requiems combine elegy and eulogy, and at the conclusion of the second Rilke gives voice to a new and incisive stoicism: 'Who talks of victory? Endurance is everything.' It was Rilke's capacity to endure which enabled him to complete *The Notebooks of Malte Laurids Brigge*, which he had abandoned in despair in 1904; part two is much more affirmative than part one. At the same time, delighted though he was to have survived a protracted period of trial and error, Rilke knew that as a literary work *Malte* was a compromise, a hybrid, and not the covenant 'between our human life and greatest work' (in the words of the conclusion to 'Requiem For A Friend') for which he had striven. The life and art he had hoped to keep together as a creating and created unity had insisted, largely because of his having weighted the scales in favour of objectivity, on separating out into incommensurables.

Despite its disjointedness *Malte* remains Rilke's most precise formulation of his creative difficulties, and an indispensable sourcebook for his very idiosyncratic views on childhood, 'intransitive love', death, and nun-like women. Yet, as so often with Rilke, art had not so much exorcized as exercised the tensions in his spiritual life. In 1912, whilst staying at the castle of Duino near Trieste, Rilke's distress issued in a question which was only to be answered after he had experienced even greater dereliction of spirit than he had endured during the *Malte* period: 'Who, if I cried out, would hear me among the angelic orders?' He had begun to doubt the beneficence of acts of seeing which threatened to turn him into a passive and disinterested spectator of his own misfortune. As the poem 'Turning-point' of 1914 states as unequivocally as its compressed language permits, 'the work of sight' (the subject of the *New Poems*) needed to be supplemented by renewed 'heartwork on the imprisoned impressions within you'. Rilke carried out extensive 'heartwork' in such superb poems of 1914 as 'The Spanish Trilogy', 'Lament' and 'To Hölderlin' – the great influence on him at this time. And there is evidence in a poem like 'The Great Night' that Rilke was intent on conjuring a new kind of authority figure, with none of the human fallibility which had alienated him from Rodin. In 'The Great Night', Night is being asked to play a role similar to that obscurely attributed to it in the mystical traditions of Greek Orphic religions. The mood and stance anticipate those developed at greater length and with much greater complexity in the more familiar *Duino Elegies*, although the ideas are essentially the same as those adumbrated in Rilke's Tuscan diary:

>   then was it, O highest,
> That you felt it no shame to know me. Your breath

Went over me. So that your
Severe and all-embracing smile passed into me.

It is clear that in this conception the notionally visible is
being stamped with visibility in the inner space of the poet. But
alongside this Rilke also developed certain ideas about audi-
bility first suggested in the Rodin monograph in the familiar
claim that the artist must 'listen to inner depths'. This 'listen-
ing' led Rilke to a new awareness of the power of music, an art
form of which he had previously been suspicious, because it had
seemed too 'approximate'. By 1918, it seems, music had
become a force that could unite all his concerns over the
previous twenty years:

Music: breathing of statues. Perhaps:
stillness of pictures, Speech, where speech
ends, time
standing vertical in the paths of diminishing hearts.
Feelings towards ... ? Ah, transformation
of feelings into ... audible landscape!
Stranger: music. Space that's outgrown us,
heartspace.

This is only one of many examples of the 'fragmentary' poetry
(as the poet himself called it) which occupied him in the years
after he had asked the overwhelming question of Duino. But as
this example shows, Rilke was by this time writing in a manner
that posed formidable problems for any reader not conversant
with his earlier work. More and more he turned to his volumi-
nous correspondence to offer himself as the ideal commentator
on his own conceptions, continually reinterpreting what he
took his whole career to mean. Even so, there are times when
the harassed modern reader may be left wishing, like Byron
faced with Coleridge, that Rilke would explain his explana-
tion, for his discursive writing, as was perhaps inevitable in one
so determined to forge a unity, is virtually a species of prose
poetry.

In the elegies begun at Duino and finished a decade later at
the Château de Muzot in Switzerland Rilke addressed the
question of unity and multiplicity more trenchantly and more
rigorously than he had ever done before, perfecting a kind of

analysis that would leave its mysteries intact, and insinuate
rather than disclose its significance for mortal man. In an essay
of 1913 ('The Young Poet') Rilke had spoken of how the great
poet, like some latter-day Jacob, must endure and withstand
the overwhelming and mysterious 'assault of his god', and in
the years between the inception and the completion of the
Elegies he had often wrestled with refractory and intractable
material, doubtful of his victory. Almost half of what we know
as the *Elegies* existed as 'fragmentary' poetry before he suffered,
in the February of 1922, the final 'assault' which permitted him
to complete and refine the sequence, an assault which brought
with it the unforeseen adjunct of the fifty-five *Sonnets To
Orpheus*. 'One often finds oneself,' he told a correspondent in
1920, 'at variance with the external demeanour of a language
and intent on its innermost life ... a language grasped in its
speech-seed'; just how much at variance he had been is reflec-
ted in the 'fragmentary' poems, where some of the seed falls on
stony ground. But the *Elegies*, despite their origins in disparate
fragments, impress one as organic utterance, utterance that
preserves the freshness and enigmatic vitality of 'a language
grasped in its speech-seed'. They are immensely demanding
poems for precisely this reason, and they depend for their
success upon a reader's active involvement in the metaphysical
issues they raise. It is not uncommon to find the marginally
more manageable, but much more variable, *Sonnets To Orpheus*
preferred to the *Elegies* on the grounds that their burden is more
readily apprehended. But whereas the numerous sonnets in the
New Poems volumes chart 'the dance of forces round a centre',
the *Sonnets To Orpheus*, concerned with 'the dance of forces'
though they are, occasionally manifest a pedestrian earnestness
that is a direct consequence of Rilke's desire to be understood.
It is no accident that critics of Rilke very often turn to the
Sonnets to find quotations that will elucidate his whole career.

In both sequences one may legitimately feel that 'Exposure
on the mountains of the heart' (in the words of another famous
'fragmentary' poem) has led the poet to breathe a more
rarefied air than any common reader could possibly inhabit for
very long; the agonies and ecstasies, elations and desolations,

are unrelievedly lofty. But the nervous energy in these poems, and especially in the *Elegies*, compels one to persevere in the scrutiny of them, and quickens one's perception of their moments of illumination and disclosure. One such moment occurs midway through the ninth elegy:

> Are we perhaps here, simply to say: House,
> Bridge, Fountain, Door, Vessel, Fruittree, Window, –
> at most: column, tower ... but to say,
> O to say them, understand me, as the things themselves
> never thought so intensely to be.

This embodies, as well as discoursing upon, the 'speech-seeds' out of which all human utterance (and especially poetry) is born, and it liberates Rilke to express one of his most fundamental insights at the beginning of the next verse paragraph:

> *Here* is the time of the speakable, *here* its homeland.
> Speak and proclaim. More than ever
> things fall away, that we can live with, for
> what occupies their place is a deed without image.

A similar gravity appropriately informs the last lines of the tenth and final elegy:

> ... if they were to waken, the endlessly dead, a symbol in us,
> look, they would point perhaps at the catkins of the empty
> hazels, the hanging ones, or
> bring to mind the rain which falls in the spring on the dark earth.
>
> And we, who think of happiness
> *arising*, would then feel
> what almost surprises us
> when what is happy *falls*.

The idea of falling, which is common to both these passages and a motif found elsewhere in the *Elegies*, can be traced back to Rilke's lovely 'Autumn' poem in *The Book of Images*; once again, as there, the idea is that man cannot fall endlessly without the prospect of a supreme being. Indeed these ideas of inner space and interpenetration are, despite the oblique language in which they are expressed, the culmination of what first found memorable utterance in his Tuscan diary. The consis-

tency of Rilke's concerns can be seen in the famous letter of
interpretation that he wrote to the Polish translator of the
Elegies, where his early ideas about the 'solitary man' underpin
the complex and paradoxical language of his later years, now
generalized to describe the spiritual condition of a multitude of
such solitary men:

> The earth has no alternative but to become invisible – *in* us …
> *in* us alone can there be accomplished this intimate and continual
> transmutation of the visible and an invisible no longer dependent
> upon being visible and tangible, as our own destiny continually
> *grows at the same time* MORE PRESENT AND INVISIBLE in us.

What holds Rilke's refractory materials together is his deter-
mination, made explicit in the ninth elegy, that the heart and
tongue should continue, in the face of all that might prompt
them to lament, to issue in songs of praise. This, as the *Sonnets To
Orpheus* confirms, is the 'task' of 'heartwork': to offer intima-
tions of continuity and consolation. Uttered in the hieratic
language which might have originated in a supreme being (in
the *Elegies* the Angel, and in the *Sonnets* the great unifier of the
Greek Orphic religions), these poems are actually orientated
towards humanity; Rilke stands between the transcendent and
the terrestrial worlds, interpreting the former to the latter. It
becomes easy to see why he had needed to reject the divinity of
Christ; it created a vacuum which he himself could occupy.
And even if he was unable, on his own admission, to make the
perfect world of the gods fully intelligible to the fallen world of
mankind, he was nevertheless justified in feeling that, after
years of solitary suffering, he had come as near to making art
and life of one meaning as it was possible to do. Only detailed
and expert commentary can make out a coherent case for the
success or failure of such an extraordinary enterprise, but even
if one occupies, like most readers, an uncertain middle ground,
the *Elegies* and the *Sonnets* are plainly prodigious sequences and,
together with the *New Poems*, clearly establish Rilke as the
greatest German poet since the death of Goethe.

In a letter on the death of Marcel Proust, in December of
1922, Rilke spoke of 'the perfect tact of his analysis, which

pitches on no particular thing, playfully releases the very thing it seemed to cling to and still, with almost unsurpassable precision, everywhere admits and makes allowances for the ultimate mysteries'. This brilliant description of Proust is even more applicable to the Rilke of the *Elegies* and *Sonnets*, though his tact is perhaps less perfect and he is certainly less precise. Perhaps this is why the sublime grandeur of Rilke's most ambitious poetry has been more often admired than imitated. It was, for example, what Rilke stood for, as much as what he had actually achieved, that made the Russian poets Pasternak and Tsvetaeva think of themselves as his acolytes. In a letter of 1907 Rilke spoke of 'how much art is a matter of conscience' and no modern poet has been more conscientious than him in pursuit of art. There have inevitably been those, like the young Bertolt Brecht, who have found in his poetry 'the sentimental element of a worn-out bourgeoisie with which I refuse to have anything to do'. But English readers in particular have found him less sterile than Mallarmé and more human than Valéry, in fact the only great European poet to emerge unscathed from the comparison, which the magnitude of their respective *oeuvres* makes almost inevitable, with Baudelaire.

Antonio Machado (1875–1939)

Born in the ducal palace in Seville; his father was an inter-
nationally famous scholar of folklore. Deeply influenced by the
education he received at the Free Institute in Madrid from
1883 onwards. Produced a series of short satirical sketches and
became fascinated by the world of the theatre. In 1899 went
with his brother, also a poet, to Paris, where they worked as
translators for a publishing house and made many literary
contacts with writers of the Symbolist milieu. Returned to Paris
in 1902 as Vice-Consul for Guatemala. Published his first
collection of *Solitudes* in 1903 which was enthusiastically re-
ceived and publicly acknowledged by Unamuno. In 1906 he
took the necessary examinations to be able to teach French in
Spanish secondary schools and was appointed to a post in Soria,
north-east of Madrid in 1907, the year of the revised and
expanded edition of *Solitudes*. There encountered the fourteen
year-old Leonor whom he married two years later. During
study leave in Paris in 1911 he heard Bergson lecture and
discovered that his wife was suffering from advanced turbercu-
losis. Profoundly and permanently affected by the loss of his
wife in 1912. Moved to Baeza in a depressed condition. There
began a systematic study of philosophy which culminated in
1918 with the award of a doctorate from the University of
Madrid. Began teaching in Segovia in the autumn of 1919, and
wrote mainly in prose thereafter, although he collaborated
with his brother on a series of plays in the 1920s. In 1926 he met
a married woman with whom he carried on an intimate and
clandestine relationship and with whom he corresponded for
some years. Elected to the Spanish Academy in 1927.
Published *Juan de Mairena*, a quasi-philosophical investigation,

in 1936. Evacuated with his mother to Barcelona as the Nationalists, whom his brother had joined, began to dominate the Republicans he had supported in the Spanish Civil War. Finally fled to the fishing village of Collioure over the French border, from where he could still see Spain, and died of pneumonia, his mother dying three days later. Posthumously cited in the award of the Nobel Prize to Jiménez and now placed above Jiménez as the greatest of modern Spanish poets.

In a letter of 1904 addressed to his friend and mentor Miguel de Unamuno (later to acquire international fame as the Existentialist theologian of *The Tragic Sense Of Life*) Machado wrote: 'Nothing is more foolish than to think, as certain French poets seem to have done, that mystery can be an aesthetic element . . . Beauty resides not so much in mystery as in the desire to penetrate it'. Machado's disavowal of the widely influential Symbolist doctrines of 'art for art's sake' could not have been more clearly formulated; his own stress was to fall on art for truth's sake and on the need for mankind in general to scrutinize and to participate in the mysteries that lay closest to hand and were available to all. Late in life, masquerading as the 'apocryphal professor' Juan de Mairena, Machado reaffirmed his earlier conviction that 'a few true words' were worth more than a lot of obscure ones and stressed that the poet must be 'a simple stenographer of the spoken word'. This image of the poet as stenographer may strike one at first glance as unduly passive, though in fact Machado was anything but a mere reflector of the *status quo*; he was a man with a distinctly sceptical temperament in search of something in which to believe. His purpose, as expressed by Juan de Mairena, was to 'induce people to recontemplate the already contemplated, to unknow the already known, and to doubt what they already regard as doubtful: for that is the only way we can begin to believe in anything'. One of the primary casualties of such a strategy was Mallarmé's ideal of poetry as a 'trembling of the veil', for which Machado substituted a no less tenuous, but in some ways more commonsensical, view of the 'already contemplated' question of appearance and reality:

> If we doubt the whole world of appearance and regard it as the veil
> of Maya concealing from our sight the domain of absolute reality, it
> can hardly matter much if the veil should one day be rent, revealing
> absolute reality to us. Could we be sure that the reality thus
> discovered was not in fact another veil, destined in its turn to be
> rent and to reveal yet more veils? . . . No one can prevent us taking
> the opposite view – namely, that the veils of appearance, multiplied
> to infinity though they may be, in fact veil nothing; that there is
> nothing behind the appearance waiting to reveal itself; that the
> only permanent reality finally is appearance itself.

For those familiar with the figure of Don Quixote and with Calderón's famous play *Life Is A Dream* this seems a quintessentially Spanish approach to the problem, though both its substance and its tone had been fuelled by Machado's studies in sceptical traditions transcending national barriers. But to characterize his position is less important than to see what he made of it, and in this respect it is clear that it permitted him, in a manner almost unique among poets of comparable temperament, to hold two contradictory beliefs ('faith in the word' and 'faith in the void') in perfect suspension, and that it effectively protected him from anything so sterile and traumatic as the self-induced crises endured by Mallarmé, Valéry, Hofmannsthal and Rilke. It is difficult to imagine any of these more famous figures being satisfied with Machado's straightforward definition of poetry as 'Man's dialogue with time' and none of them would have wholeheartedly endorsed his belief, symptomatically expressed in an essay on Gustávo Adolfo Bécquer, that a pure poetry must necessarily be a transparent poetry. Yet it is precisely Machado's 'transparent' language which enables a reader to enjoy an intimacy with him that the great French and German poets sometimes seem content to dispense with. Machado's suspicion of the French tradition of intimate writing surfaces in *Juan de Mairena*: 'concerning intimate diaries', the professor asks, 'was there ever anything less intimate?' But this shrewd judgement virtually requires us to adjust to the fact that it is a shared intimacy, and not a private one, that we enjoy with Machado, a natural corollary of what

Mairena calls 'heterogeneity of being', which the *journal intime* necessarily finds it difficult to accomodate.

Machado's emphasis on heterogeneity only became fore-grounded in his later writings, although even in his first collection of poems (*Solitudes*, 1903) it is possible to find suggestions of heterogeneity in the title alone. It is more profitable, however, to see these early poems as explorations of impulses too private to generate or to justify the impersonal ideas expounded in his mature writings. On Machado's own admission (in the preface to the revised and expanded edition of 1907) these poems originated in and reflected 'a deep palpitation of the soul', and of a quite individual soul at that. Influenced though he evidently was by Verlaine, by Heine's *Book of Songs* and by Bécquer above all, Machado's *Solitudes* are entirely his own; their individuality is even more obvious if they are placed beside the most famous book of *Solitudes* in Spanish poetry, the complex Baroque masterpieces of the seventeenth-century poet Góngora, whose revival in 1927 Machado viewed with disquiet. There is nothing Baroque or elaborate about Machado's early poems; he makes no pretension to eloquence and is content to record the bare facts of situations. In 'Childhood Memory', for example, he recalls the unadorned reality of his schooldays and prefigures his life as a humble schoolteacher who would never satisfy his ambition to hold a university teaching post in philosophy:

A cold and gloomy afternoon
of winter. The pupils
study. Monotony
of rain on windows.

The dismal prospect of meaningless recurrence which the rain summons up is rendered dramatically in the very structure of this poem, which ends with the verbatim repetition of this initial stanza. The world of dreams is naturally much more meaningful than a reality grown so torpid. But Machado does not withdraw into a world of private fantasy; his aim is to lay bare the fundamental structures upon which a tenuous reality subsists. 'I go', as he says in one of the most famous of the

Solitudes, 'dreaming roads/of afternoon'. This is a much less self-absorbed poetry than it seems at first glance, even if the reader does occasionally feel – perhaps rightly, in view of Mairena's later stress on the importance of being a 'listener' – that he is overhearing a soliloquy.

Machado presents real places and real emotions in dream terms, without them thereby losing their solidity. The scenario is at once empirical and metaphysical. The characteristic situation is one in which the poet, having negotiated a 'labyrinth of streets', finds himself standing alone in a deserted plaza or park, confronting a marble fountain with which he engages – constantly reminded by the action of water on stone of time's erosion – in dialogue. His silent inner world is repeatedly disturbed by sounds from without, the cries of children that remind him of his youth, the noise of his own footsteps leading him unerringly towards death. The mood is sombre, but not unreservedly gloomy. By asking questions of the recurrent features of the external world that he encounters, the poet learns the kind of wisdom which confinement within his own sensibility could never have offered. Only in the sub-section 'Galleries' is Machado close to being trapped 'in the deep/mirror of my dreams', and even here he is subject to visitations which prevent him from becoming self-regarding. In adjacent poems he is visited by a demonic figure with an 'iron hand' who shows him the infernal regions and by an angelic intercessor with an 'amicable hand' who promises redemption. The intrinsic disadvantage of the dreamstate, however, is that its projections are so fleeting and ephemeral that the poet is naturally moved to ask whether it can possibly possess the properties of more substantial things:

Are the anvils and crucibles of your soul
labouring only for the dust and the wind?
                    (*Solitudes*, LXXVIII)

Machado would like to believe, as another poem (**LXXIX**) illustrates, that 'Of your whole memory, only/the illustrious gift of evoking dreams is worth anything.' But one of the miscella-

neous poems which conclude *Solitudes* makes even this seem a
dream:

Decipherment of harmony
assayed by an inexpert hand.

Disgust. Cacophony
of the endless piano
which as a child I listened to,
dreaming – of what I don't know,

of something that would not occur,
all that had already passed.

(Solitudes, XCIII)

In his second volume of poems (*Fields of Castile*, first pub-
lished in 1912), Machado sloughed off the dream world and
directed his investigations outwards, having found in the high
and arid plains of the Castilian *meseta* an external landscape
which matched his altered mood. In a famous stanza of the
'Portrait' with which *Fields of Castile* opens, it is activity rather
than contemplation which is stressed, and a new vigour is
evident:

Am I classic or romantic? I don't know. Let me leave
my verse the way a captain does his sword:
famous for the virile hand that brandished it,
not valued for the learned craft of the blacksmith.

A similar note is struck in the poem 'The Iberian God':

My heart awaits
the Iberian man with the strong hand
who will carve on the Castilian oak-tree
the dry God of the brown land.

In the 'cold and arid' land of Soria Machado became such a
man, although his strength was tested almost to breaking-point
by the illness and premature death of his young wife. Typical of
his strength, and the product of his need to be at once austere
and emotional, is the manner in which he expresses, in 'To A
Withered Elm', his hope of her survival without intruding any
personal details:

before you are uprooted by the whirlwind
and broken by the white sierras' blast;
before the rivers thrust you to the sea
through valleys and ravines,
I want, elm, to record
the grace of your green branch.
My heart hopes
also, stretching towards light and life,
for another spring miracle.

The miracle did not occur, and the loss of his wife cast its
shadow over his whole life thereafter. It gave a new meaning to
his favourite lines from the fifteenth-century poet Jorge
Manrique – 'Our lives are rivers/which flow into the sea/of
death', the inspiration for the poem 'Gloss' in *Solitudes*. As a
famous quatrain from this period indicates, it seemed to
Machado as if his own life had also ended:

Lord, you wrenched from me what I most loved.
Hear once more, O God, my heart cry out.
Your will was done, Lord, contrary to mine.
We are one now, Lord, my heart and the sea.

This is a poem with the spontaneous anguish of a lamentation,
and is a deeply moving outcry. But much more characteristic of
Machado, and quite as moving in its own way, is 'To José
Maria Palacio', in which the poet asks his friend to visit the
cemetery in which his wife's body has been laid and strives to
take consolation from the fact that the landscape will continu-
ally renew itself:

    Palacio, good friend,
have the nightingales returned to the banks of the river?
At the time of the first lilies
and of the first roses in the gardens,
on a blue afternoon, go up the Espino,
the high Espino, where her country is.

In the years after the death of his wife Machado primarily
sought consolation in the study of philosophy; the great eclogue
'Poem Of A Day' records the sceptical and yet positive spirit
with which he applied himself to the subject. With hindsight it

is clear that Juan de Mairena's later dictum that 'what is specifically human is man's conviction of death' – an idea of fundamental importance to a generation of Existentialist philosophers – originated in Machado's experiences at this time. Yet instead of hungering for immortality like his friend Unamuno, Machado patiently reconstructed a doctrine of consolation which would not disguise the fact of man's inevitable mortality. The preface to the second edition of *Fields of Castile* (published in 1917) is in fact anything but morbid and, typical of the Machado who had suffered a severe personal loss, is addressed to mankind in general: our task, prior to the oblivion which awaits us in the sea of death, is 'to weave the threads that we are given, to dream our dream, to live'.

The threads woven by Machado in his later poetry and in the prose of Juan de Mairena are fundamentally impersonal and metaphysical in a mode which first manifests itself in the 'Proverbs And Songs' in the second edition of *Fields of Castile*. Yet Machado's speculations are never dry; in the terms offered by Proverb XXXV we may say that by retaining 'the consciousness of the visionary' Machado ensured that every fish that fell into the net remained alive, unlike those brought to land by the fisherman. In the *New Songs* of 1917–30, and especially in the poem-sequence 'Galleries', he wrote with a spare precision which makes even the reticent earlier collections look garrulous; but his 'few true words' are always instinct with the inflexions of an emotional voice:

> In the bare poplar
> the unperturbed grave crows in silence
> stand like black, cold notes
> inscribed on the stave of February ...
> In the silence sounds
> the Pythagorean lyre,
> the rainbow in the light, the light which fills
> my futile stereoscope.
> My eyes have been blinded
> by Heraclitean fire.
> For a second the world is
> blind, transparent, empty, flown.

The poet's presence is here reduced to a minimum; 'it is not', as some lines in the second group of 'Proverbs And Songs' reminds us, 'the fundamental I/the poet seeks/but the essential you'. Each of these gnomic inscriptions becomes potentially an instrument wherewith to pierce 'the heart of time', none more so than that which states 'Today is always yet'. As if in confirmation of his early letter to Unamuno, Machado is unwavering in his 'desire to penetrate the mystery'. Only in his very last collections does he generate as many mysteries as the Symbolist poets, and even in *From An Apocryphal Songbook* and *Complementaries* he is only taking the logical step enjoined by his conviction that man's 'heterogeneity of being' is its own salvation. Here he employs the *personae* which he had first developed in his prose, but unlike the 'heteronyms' of Fernando Pessoa they do not appear – except perhaps in the hallucinatory 'Memories From Dream, Fever, And Fitful Sleep' – to have provoked a crisis of identity in Machado.

The last poems of Machado are characteristically addresssed to someone: to Guiomar (a woman with whom he conducted a clandestine and doomed liaison), to 'the Great Zero' (the only deity in whom he could meaningfully believe) and, in 'The Gardens Of The Poet', to his contemporary Jiménez, a poem in which he returns to the origins of his inspiration and to the scenario of *Solitudes*:

And the solitary hours pass,
and already the fountains, in the full moon,
are breathing in the marble, singing,
and through all the air the sound of water only.

This poem has all the 'calm magnificence' that Machado found supremely embodied in the paintings of Velásquez, though very little of the magic of the original can survive transplantation into English. This is one reason, perhaps, why Machado has yet to be accorded the kind of recognition in the English-speaking world that would be commensurate with his greatness. Without disguising the fact that (as Juan de Mairena reminds us) 'we live in essential impurity', Machado wrote a pure poetry without the complex cerebral aspects to be found in those French poets who made purity a principle. His commitment, unlike theirs, was to 'the language of Everyman'. Of the many fine writers to have come to prominence in what has effectively been a second Golden Age of Spanish Literature, Machado is the most universal, whether as poet or as unprofessional philosopher.

Guillaume Apollinaire
(1880–1918)

Born in Rome; the illegitimate son of Angelica de Kostrowitz-sky and an unknown father, probably an officer in the Italian army. Educated in Monte Carlo, Cannes and Nice. First achieved notoriety in a small town in the Belgian Ardennes, where he and his brother failed to pay a hotel bill. After a period in Paris he took up a post as tutor in French to a German family in Honnef-on-Rhine, where he met an English gover-ness, Annie Playden, whom he afterwards pursued to London, though unable and perhaps unwilling to pursue her to America, whither she finally fled to evade his ardour. Returned to Paris, where he quickly became the leading apologist for the independent and experimental painters of the first decade of the century, with all of whom he was on friendly terms. Wrote several pornographic pot-boilers to keep himself in funds, and took the painter Marie Larencin as his mistress. Wrote what are generally considered his greatest poems in the period 1903–11, the year *Alcools* was first published. Came before the magis-trates again for his part in the theft of the *Mona Lisa* from the Louvre, for which he was placed in the Santé prison for a few days before being discharged. Began to write poetry of a more experimental kind, influenced by the painters he knew, which was collected in the volume *Calligrammes* published just before his death. Trained for the artillery in Nîmes, where he fell in love with an aristocratic woman he knew as 'Lou', and after-wards with a woman he met on the train between Nice and Marseilles. Received a headwound on the Western Front which hastened his death. Married in the last year of his life. Died in Saint-Germain, Paris, where Picasso's statue in his memory is to be found.

Apollinaire is the first modern European poet to whom the much-abused term avant-garde can be meaningfully applied. Of the great French nineteenth-century poets one might say that they were constrained by certain time-honoured conventions (with the obvious exceptions of Mallarmé's *A Dice Throw* and Rimbaud's *Illuminations*) even as they appeared to push back the bounds of convention; they were evolutionary rather than revolutionary. Apollinaire himself shrewdly observed of Baudelaire that the most powerful of them, the 'painter of modern life' *par excellence*, 'scarcely participates in that modern spirit which stems from him'. It was Apollinaire who was to explore the consequences of the admonition with which Rimbaud had ended his career: 'one must be absolutely modern'. To be 'modern' was the motive force of Apollinaire's artistic activity and its *raison d'être*, and his close association with, and recommendations of, the painters who shared this belief in the period leading up to the First World War has made Apollinaire seem one of the central figures through whom the turbulent and multifaceted conceptions of 'modernism' were fated to pass. In a famous lecture which he gave a year before his death Apollinaire analysed in an exemplary manner the impulses behind what he characteristically called 'the new spirit'. Beside other more obviously rigorous poetics, this new spirit, with its emphasis on liberty, equality and the creation of a permanently marvellous reality available to anyone prepared to open their eyes and see, may seem little more than an extempore effusion, a manifestation of what is in need of demonstration. And yet the lecture offers virtually a compendium of all that can be said about 'the new' and even, as when Apollinaire speaks of it as 'an order and a duty', about what has since been aptly called 'the tradition of the new'. As befits an avant-gardist, Apollinaire is combative and aggressive, especially when identifying, with reference to past achievements, what the new spirit is not: '*It is not a decorative art. Nor is it an impressionist art.*' A similar energy is present in the words which delineate, without ever actually defining, what the new spirit is: 'encyclopaedic', 'synthetic', 'multiple', 'divine' and – the least sublime of the adjectives, and a tacit acknowledgement that it is really inimical to the sublime – 'surprising'. 'The least fact,' Apollinaire suggests, 'is for a poet the postulate, the point of departure for an unknown immensity where the fires of joy flame up in multiple meanings'. As this fire imagery suggests, and as other remarks in the lecture make explicit, the poet's task is conceived of as one of turning base metal into gold, without any attempt to emulate Baudelairean grandeur of manner; the transformations accomplished by the poet are regarded as the same as those attempted by the ancient alchemists (with whom Mallarmé had also compared himself), except that they are no longer conceived of as the esoteric preserve of a secretive and privileged minority. The only aspect of the lecture which suggests that Apollinaire does not have his finger upon the pulse of his epoch is when he determines that 'the new spirit' is distinctly French and cannot afford to be cosmopolitan. Coming from a man who was born in Rome, with a mother of Polish origin, who until taking up residence in Paris answered to a German Christian name, and who derived his pen-name from Greek and Latin, this is likely to strike a contemporary reader as distinctly odd, especially given his close acquaintance with writers and painters from all over Europe who had come to Paris to practice their art. But this peculiar stipulation perhaps reflects the poet's embattled attempt, epitomized by his enlistment in the French Army in 1916, to cast off the indeterminancy of his origins and the vagrancy of his adolescence and to become indisputably French.

Apollinaire's excited and utopian tone in the lecture 'The New Spirit And The Poets' expresses a very powerful strain of ebullience in his nature, which is also reflected in his notoriety as a practical joker. But there was a deep vein of melancholy in Apollinaire which his ebullience was designed to conceal. The 'fires of joy' are not the only fires to burn in his most famous and best-loved volume of poetry, the celebrated *Alcools* published in 1911. The collection contains many descents into the more infernal regions of misery. This is particularly true of the poems written in the Ardennes at the turn of the century, the brief 'Farewell' (with its 'dead' autumn and its twice-repeated injunction to a loved one to 'Remember', a typically Apollinairean request) and the much longer and much more esoteric poems 'Merlin And The Old Woman', 'The Thief' and 'The Hermit'. 'The Hermit' ends abjectly:

For I want nothing more except to close
My eyes

This is almost the only simple and straightforward utterance in these three confused and confusing poems, which were much more important for Apollinaire – as allegorical experiments in finding out what he was and might become – than they could ever be even for the devotee of his poetry. Yet certain details – the dream of an eternal life in the last line of the Merlin Poem, and the references to Orpheus in 'The Thief' – point forward to the mature poetry. The same is true of the poems written during his period in the Rhineland, out of which came the most famous of all his writings, 'The Song Of The Ill-loved'. 'Rhenish Nights', for example, concerns a glass of wine whose inflammable contents explode 'like a clatter of laughter', the laughter which made Apollinaire such a popular *flâneur* and practical joker, and a genuinely funny poet in the later *Calligrams*. 'Autumn Rhénane', by contrast, is much more mournful, like his other poems on the same season – 'Sign', 'Sick Autumn', 'Autumn' and 'The Crocuses'. The morbid autumnal mood is relieved only by the distant murmurs that the poet hears, which include a peasant humming a lovesong and a singing cowherd. The 'new spirit' of which Apollinaire was later to speak is here very much secondary to his delicate appropriation of what the ancient writers would have called an eclogue.

It was in the poems inspired by an English governess (Annie Playden), whom he had followed from the Rhineland to London and whose flight to America he provoked, that Apollinaire first gave voice to his very complex personality in an unforgettable way: 'The Emigrant From Landor Road' and 'The Song Of The Ill-Loved'. The first is a poem of farewell, whose protagonist is about to fare forth on an unruly ocean. The second is also a poem of farewell and of journeying, though the journey is essentially a mental one through the times of pleasure and pain conjured up by a disturbed imagination. Beginning on a misty evening in London, this dazzling sequence of metamorphoses ends on a Parisian Sunday through which the poet wanders, 'lacking the heart to die'. Too abrasive to be a city eclogue, the poem nevertheless manages to exorcize the wounds that being 'ill-loved' has opened up, and to end on an almost positive note, with the poet claiming – as in his last major poem 'The Pretty Redhead' – to have acquired a kind of wisdom. In the five-line preface which Apollinaire added in 1909, he even stresses (more strongly perhaps than the poem will support) that

> if my love in the guise
> Of the fair Phoenix dies one evening
> The morning sees its rebirth

In his lecture on 'The New Spirit', Apollinaire spoke of how an alchemical poetry could awaken mankind to its intrinsic divinity, and activate 'that endless rebirth by which we live'. Such a view also commits mankind, though the poet is careful not to stress this, to endless deaths out of which we may be reborn. In an essay of 1908 ('The Three Plastic Virtues') Apollinaire says: 'Our imagination is touched above all by the creation and by the end of the world.' The dynamism of Apollinaire's poetry derives primarily from the way in which he gives equal weight, either successively or simultaneously, to beginnings and endings. By dislocating more dramatically than his predecessors the idea of time as a sequential line, Apollinaire became more and more adept at '[taking in] past, present and future at a single glance', as the 1908 essay suggests the painter must do. This ultimately led him, in the volume *Calligrams*, to a poetry of 'simultaneism' which makes even 'The Song Of The Ill-Loved' look experimentally timid. But none of the poems in *Alcools*, not even those of the period 1908–12 (where the volume's greatest masterpieces are to be found), goes quite this far. The six outstanding long poems in the volume ('The Voyager', 'The Brazier', 'The Betrothal', 'Cortège', 'Vendémiaire' and 'Zone') are noticeably more discontinuous, however, and much less narrative than 'The Song Of

The Ill-Loved'. The fragmentary utterances create an in-
stability of mood which is slightly less marked in the famous
'Song' because of its formal and regular stanzas. At the same
time each of the six poems is carefully orchestrated to make one
mood dominant over all the others. 'The Voyager', for ex-
ample, in some ways the least ambitious, is primarily elegiac,
like the early 'Farewell' and 'The Emigrant From Landor
Road'; the dominant word is the familiar Apollinaire impera-
tive 'Remember'. The only wisdom he can here lay claim to is
that 'life is uncertain'. 'Cortège' also decides in favour of the
'glimmering past', although in this poem (as later in 'Zone')
Apollinaire is attempting to achieve the higher wisdom of
'knowing at last who I am'. Here, taking up a motif first found
in the early Rhineland poems, Apollinaire concludes that he is
part of the stream of time, a passer-by made up of 'all those who
arrived and were not myself'. This to some extent anticipates
the exclamatory and much more positive 'Vendémiaire',
where his personality becomes co-extensive with the universe
and his own voice is subsumed by the hymn of praise to Paris
which the cities of France are singing. And both 'The Brazier'
and 'The Betrothal' are fundamentally affirmative poems. In
'The Betrothal' (the details of which are partially clarified by
the much simpler 'Poem Read At André Salmon's Wedding')
Apollinaire takes courage from the redemptive myth of the
Phoenix; the dominant image here is the flaming sun, the origin
of what the lecture calls 'the fires of joy'. In 'The Brazier', the
poet flings the deadheads of the past into the flames and hymns
a new earthly paradise; his audience is seen as a flock perpetu-
ally nourished – as was certainly not the case in the early
eclogues – by the song of a shepherd. 'The Brazier' ends with
the suggestion that reality is a spectacle whose enigmatic
features should not be subjected to a narrowly rationalist desire
for knowledge. It is not surprising, therefore, that 'Zone' –
much the most famous of these six very complex poems – should
begin with the image of the Eiffel Tower as a shepherdess and
end with an enigmatic image of a beheaded sun about which no
two commentators seem to be in agreement.

'Zone', the first poem in *Alcools*, was the last to be written, and its treatment of the facts of Apollinaire's life prefigures the 'simultaneism' of his subsequent poems. And yet the way in which it ends virtually obliges the reader of Apollinaire to contrast it with the conclusion of 'Vendémiaire', which is presumed to precede it. At the end of 'Vendémiaire' the poet is on his way home to Auteuil on the outskirts of Paris, and stands transfixed in an ecstasy akin to drunkenness, with an insatiable thirst which can only be quenched by a new day dawning. In 'Zone', by contrast, far from being the 'gullet' of Paris, the poet seems to be drowning in the whirlpool of his memories. 'Weary of this ancient world' and striving to transcend 'the decline of beauty', the images of the past float before him in snapshot fragments that illuminate his plight but do nothing to solace it. The twofold farewell with which the poem ends has a vale-dictory quality which suggests that the poet, though weary of it, has not quite schooled himself of attachment to the 'ancient world'. It is as if Apollinaire has realized that, like the down-and-outs who inhabit the *zone* outside Paris proper, he too in future will have to exist outside all conventions, to make the solitary voyage of the extreme avant-gardist. The beheaded sun may be a modern analogue of the dismembered Orpheus, or it may be a contraction of what Apollinaire dramatizes at somewhat excessive length in the prose piece *The Poet Assassi-nated*. If it is taken to be emblematic of his natural concern at the destruction which seems an inseparable part of the 'new spirit', it may prefigure a letter from the last year of his life, in which he told a friend:

I have never destroyed, on the contrary I attempted to reconstruct ... I wanted only to annex new domains for art and literature, but without ever refusing to acknowledge the merits of the true masterpieces of the past.

Despite 'Zone', Apollinaire – encouraged by the experi-mental painters in his circle – approached the 'new spirit' in a mood of confidence, although it was only later – in the days of Surrealism (a word he himself was the first to use) – that his wilder experiments outside poetry (the prose piece 'Oneirocriti-cism' and the play *The Breasts Of Tiresias*, for example) gained much currency. 'I like the young painters,' Apollinaire said in a lecture, 'because I love light more than anything.' In the volume *Calligrams* (published in 1918) it is as if each line is a separate object upon which the light of the poet's glance has fallen. This makes some poems, 'The Windows' and 'Monday Rue Christine' for instance, seem so random as to be impossible to 'read'. The logical development of such a technique was to distort the typographical surface into shapes which could be read at a glance. This 'music of forms' (as Apollinaire calls it in the poem 'A Phantom Of Clouds') may seem like experiment for the sake of experiment, but the best of these picture-poems are a subtle way of giving new life to old ideas. This is particularly obvious in the poem which demonstrates visually that the poet's heart is an upside-down flame, and again in 'The Little Car', which is inevitably heading for Paris, the centre of the poet's universe. But it is even clearer in those poems which do not form pictorial shapes, such as 'The Musician Of Saint-Merry' (where the poet is once again in the role of passer-by, listening to the 'pastoral music' of a contemporary Orpheus) and 'The Hills' (where Apollinaire admits 'I am the flute upon which I play'). The mood of the *Calligrams* is much more uniform than that of *Alcools*, and much more optimistic; even in the trenches of the First World War (where he received a serious head wound which hastened his death) it was the marvels of war that mattered most to Apollinaire – the rockets which lit up the night, the 'flowers of the cannonade'.

On returning from the front and rejoining a somewhat shaken aesthetic avant-garde, Apollinaire did not cease to commend the 'new domains' to which he was wholeheartedly committed. But Apollinaire's last poems lack the magic of his pre-war utterances. The 1917 sequence of love poems 'Vitam Impendere Amori' is something of a recovery, although it shows him once again remodelling motifs by which he had been haunted for over a decade. Even his last poem, 'The Pretty Redhead', is nothing like so powerful as the great poems of *Alcools*. 'The Pretty Redhead' is at once a *cri de coeur* and a programmatic apologia on behalf of the 'new spirit'. In what the poet calls 'the long quarrel between tradition and invention' he is plainly on the side of the latter, but loath to be cut off entirely from the former. Some of the more radical of the present-day avant-garde might take exception to the way Apollinaire asks to be pitied by those he has outraged; the extreme traditionalist might consider him to be too abject and wheedling. In any case, since the death of Apollinaire in 1918 the 'quarrel' he was seeking to end through tolerance and peaceful co-existence has been exacerbated and polarized. If there is to be a permanent and influential avant-garde 'The Pretty Redhead' will continually be on the mouths of those proposing it, even though it deserves to be considered as more than a charmingly phrased piece of propaganda. And even if the idea of an avant-garde were finally to disappear, Apollinaire's status as the most approachable of all the poets who attempted to embody the 'new spirit' in the early years of this century is not likely to be very significantly threatened.

Aleksandr Blok (1880–1921)

Born in St Petersburg; his father was the Professor of Public Law at Warsaw University, his mother the daughter of the Rector of St Petersburg University. Lived with his mother and her family after the early divorce of his parents. At his happiest on his mother's family estate in the country at Shakhmatovo, to which he ever afterwards repaired at times of stress. Passionately fond of literature and theatre from an early age. Became involved with an older woman whilst on holiday at Bad Nauheim, and indulged his sexual impulses in Petersburg brothels, where he contracted the syphilis which was to shorten his life and cause difficulties in his marriage. Underwent a mystical experience at the turn of the century which afterwards led him and other literary figures to identify his wife as the earthly embodiment of the biblical Divine Sophia. Much distressed by the triangular relationship developing between himself, his wife and Andrei Biely, who challenged him to an abortive duel. Politically active in the unsuccessful revolution of 1905, and thereafter a cultural critic of the split between the intelligentsia and the people. Wrote experimental plays in the aftermath of the revolution, and became enamoured of the first of the two actresses who distracted him from the shortcomings of his marriage. Deeply upset by the death of his wife's child by another man. Visited Italy with his wife in 1909, a journey which inspired some of his greatest poems; went on holiday with her in Brittany in 1913. Served behind the Russian lines in 1916 and was employed by the authorities in Petrograd at the time of the 1917 Revolution, which he had welcomed enthusiastically. In declining health during his last years, and generally concerned by the cultural condition of Russia in the years after the Revolution. Made his last great public speech in 1921 on the subject of the poet Pushkin. Died of a combination of ailments in Petrograd, mourned by all the figures of the literary world in the city, a legend in his own lifetime and since his death regarded as the greatest Russian poet after Pushkin.

It was Blok's fate or, as he himself came to think of it, his 'mission', to be at once the hero and the victim of what a fellow-poet called 'the last act of the tragedy of estrangement between the people and the intelligentsia' played out in Russia in the first twenty years of this century. The profound self-divisions from which Blok suffered have come to seem emblematic of his country's political and cultural history and take on a predomi-nantly tragic character in the light of his passionate but ul-timately vain attempts to 'make whole what is divided'. Blok inherited from the diverse strains of nineteenth-century poetry a conception of the poet as the privileged cup-bearer of neces-sary remedies, but softened the separatist elements in the conception by seeing the poet as a man of the people, a specially gifted representative of those with no voice to speak for themselves who might find succour and inspiration in his utterances. He began his enterprise, as his origins in the highest echelons of the intelligentsia made almost inevitable, in a some-what elitist spirit, although like all the great Russian writers he was never a mere aesthete. He saw aesthetic issues as indices of, and conditioned by, religious, political and in the widest sense cultural questions to which the poet, by vitrtue of his infinitely resourceful soul, could provide fundamental answers. Against the French tendency to think of the Symbolist poet as possessor of a secret knowledge Blok saw Symbolism as justified prim-arily by its recommendation and promotion of actual and radi-cal change in the real world. Even in his short-lived phase as a 'lyric' poet he believed that 'mutually contradictory experiences recreated with equanimity' would 'smash a hole in dead matter'. Unlike many later populist poets, however, he was not, as this quotation reveals, a materialist; there was a very pronounced religious component in his complex make-up. For

Blok the poet's soul was the stage on which a Christ-like combination of the roles of suffering servant, sacrificial victim and redemptive agent was re-enacted. His abiding hope was for an apocalypse like that spoken of in the Book of Revelation, in which there would be a 'new heaven' and a 'new earth' and, most important of all, a 'new man' to inhabit them. He welcomed the Revolution as such an apocalypse, and was inevitably disappointed. As late as 1919 he claimed that he had 'not lost faith that the chaos will form itself into sounds', but by then he himself had, tragically and symptomatically, subsided into silence.

Blok possessed the mystic's faith in the oneness of all things; but his temperament and personality express in almost equal measure the conviction of the *poète maudit* (or 'hooligan' in Blok's own terms) that things are irremediably estranged from one another. The more his Promethean enterprise insisted on rising upwards the more it became enmeshed in vicious spirals downwards. This volatile and self-destructive dynamism is clear even in the poems of his first phase, where he places his trust in a figure of intercession derived eclectically from the Book of Proverbs, from Dante's Beatrice, from the icons of the Orthodox church and from the poems of Vladimir Solovyov.

Blok's temperament led him, in the company of his acolytes, to equate this figure with the woman he loved and later married. In the Hegelian terms which Blok was perfectly familiar with, this constituted a kind of *thesis*, and he wrote upwards of a thousand poems, with astonishing speed and facility, in embattled defence of it. These poems, the *Verses about the Beautiful Lady* (1904) – few of which are translated or translatable – represent Blok at his most immature, although they contain almost all the seeds of his later work. By 1905, however, as he proclaimed in the poem which now stands at the head of volume two of his *Collected Poems*, the Beautiful Lady was 'gone beyond recall'; his infidelities, his venereal condition, and above all perhaps, the confusions inherent in his coterie's elevation of his wife to divine status, had damaged his marriage irreparably. In the void created by the absence of the Beautiful Lady Blok placed his feet more firmly upon the earth, 'my vulgar, healthy planet' as he had called it in the days before her appearance, and wrote his extraordinary experimental drama *The Puppet Show* (1906). This brilliant piece of 'anatomical theatre' effectively inaugurated an *antithetical* phase, in which the white magic of the Beautiful Lady was subverted by the demonic and self-divided tensions within the poet himself. As early as 1904 Blok had decided that it would be more effective to 'go to work with a dagger like Bryusov, like Vrubel' and the first casualty of this aggressive stance was the reverential and esoteric mood of the first phase. In this new phase the poet's soul is openly, though still mysteriously, laid bare to the public gaze; 'my own life', in Blok's words, 'has itself become art'. This new dispensation was no more realistic or naturalistic than the old; but the juxtaposition of heterogeneous elements made it – within its inevitably subjective restrictions – more impersonal and objective. The tutelary female spirit of this phase was the 'devilish alloy of many worlds' about whom Blok wrote most memorably in a poem and a play that are virtually contemporary with *The Puppet Show*: the Stranger.

Blok's return to earth, to 'the terrible world' as he later called it, made him a great tragic poet and a great public poet. The public poetry was stimulated by the abortive revolution of 1905 and includes such masterpieces as the two poems 'Rus' and 'Russia', the poems of Petersburg grouped under the title 'The City', the 1907 cycle 'The Motherland' and the sequence of 1908 describing the Russian triumph over the Tartars 'On the Field of Kulikovo'. The essays 'Nature and Culture' and 'The People and the Intelligentsia' and such plays as *The King in the Square* and *The Song of Fate* offered Blok an extra dimension in which to provide a sword and shield for those prepared to listen to him. More grimly, but no less ecstatically, than Joyce's Stephen Dedalus, Blok too said 'Welcome, O Life!' and sought to 'forge in the smithy of [his] soul the uncreated conscience of [his] race'. But it is inevitably the more private creations of Blok's soul which have most poignancy for a non-Russian audience: the beggar of the long poem 'The Night Violet', the 'unresurrected Christ' of 'You Went Away', the crucified poet of 'When In The Wet And Rusty Foliage', the figure beaten upon by blizzards in the cycle 'The Snow Mask'. At the head of his play *The Song of Fate* Blok had placed the Christian dictum that 'he who would save his soul must lose it', and in poems like 'The Second Christening' (1907) deliverance seems possible only through the perdition he so ardently craved. In less gloomy vein, as for example in the poem 'On Death' (also dated 1907), Blok could admonish his heart to be a Virgil-like guide in his passage through an *Inferno*. But this attempt at detachment, at observing death with a smile, remained vulnerable to his sensual longings, as in the last line of 'On Death':

To sing songs! And to listen to the wind in the world!

The poetry of Blok's middle period is characterized by a tension between 'the will to die' (which he associated with the intelligentsia in an essay of 1908) and the 'will to live' (which he associated with the people). It was not, however, from the *in vino veritas* atmosphere of the poem 'The Stranger', but from the intelligentsia, and specifically from the theatrical milieu which so fascinated him, that Blok elected to encounter an actual incarnation of the Stranger and to experience the equivocal salvation that this dark-haired 'snow-maiden' seemed to offer. Although Blok's love for the actress Volokhova was no less turbulent than his love for his wife, it gave rise to a much more sharply defined poetry than had been possible during the period of partial submission to the Beautiful Lady. The exotic and rich colours of Blok's first phase were abandoned in favour of a much harsher chiaroscuro, and the poetic freedom he had previously sought to find in basically conventional forms (in verse, if not in drama) became possible through their abandonment. One of the first poems in which Blok's new manner manifested itself was the famous 'She Came In From The Frost' of 1908. The dry and laconic conclusion to this poem is one of Blok's most memorable expressions of the 'equanimity' that he believed the ideal lyric poet must possess, although it is a troubled equanimity, quite without serenity:

I was annoyed most of all because
It was not us, but the pigeons who were kissing,
And that the times of Paolo and Francesca were over for ever.

In the spring of 1909, accompanied by his wife, Blok satisfied a desire he had first felt three years before and visited '[the Russian artist's] other motherland – Europe, and Italy in particular'. The poems written during his Italian journey are amongst his very finest, none more so than that written in the place where Dante, the creator of Paolo and Francesca, lies buried: 'Ravenna'. Blok's Symbolist belief that there was no distinction between life and death and that 'we are links in a single chain' found almost perfect expression in this beautiful and subtle poem, which begins with the city sleeping 'like an infant .../In the arms of a somnolent eternity' and ends with the poet, having conquered his elegiac strain, receiving maternal solace from Ravenna's most timeless inhabitant:

The vine-hung wastes,
Houses and people – all are graves.
Only the stately Latin inscribed in bronze
Rings on the tombstones like a trumpet.

Only in the gaze intent and tranquil
Of Ravenna's maidens a sadness
For the unreturning sea
Flickers forth momentarily.

Only by night, bending over the valleys
Taking stock of the centuries to come,
Dante's ghost with its aquiline profile,
Sings to us of the *Vita Nuova*.

There is a similar equanimity in a second poem on the tombs of Ravenna, and again in 'The Girl From Spoleto', whose glance is no less riveting than the gaze of the girls of Ravenna. Blok even conjures a life-force out of Venice, the archetypal city of death. Only Florence provoked his wrath. But the poems which he placed at the end of his 'Italian Verses' restore a modicum of tranquillity. For although 'Annunciation', 'Assumption' and the 'Epitaph for Fra Filippo Lippi' take cognizance of death, they place their ultimate emphasis upon birth into immortality.

Blok's more positive mood did not last long. By October of the same year he was writing, in Dante's *terza rima*, his terrible

'Song Of Hell'. And in the same 'late autumn' he wrote a deeply moving poem about a drunken sailor left behind by his ship, who sleeps in the snow beside the empty anchorage. Unlike the tranquil sleep of Ravenna, this sleep represents a recrudescence of the desire for oblivion which Blok never permanently conquered. Yet when the death of his father in the winter of 1909 inspired him to begin his ultimately unfinished autobiographical poem 'Retribution', Blok reaffirmed in the prologue his faith that there was no end and no beginning to life, and in the conclusion – emphasizing the need to emerge from the 'iron' nineteenth century and to place oneself in the care of a maternal figure – demonstrated that the most ordinary things in life could disclose their beauty. The prologue even makes mention of a 'clear and steady gaze' reminiscent of those which Blok had seen in Ravenna. However, his inability to finish 'Retribution' suggests that he was unable to sustain such a gaze, and that his subsequent reversion to the 'will to die', most memorably expressed in the 'Dances Of Death' of 1912–14, was inevitable.

The 'Dances Of Death' were partially anticipated by two famous poems of 1910: 'A Voice From The Chorus' and 'The Steps Of The Commendatore'. In the latter, one of his greatest poems, Blok dramatizes his attachment to death and to eternal life in the context of the retribution which is the culmination of the Don Juan myth. But in the 'Dances Of Death' the intimations of eternal life have utterly receded, and nowhere more powerfully than in the famous two stanza poem which so perfectly enacts its own theme of pointless and changeless recurrence:

Night, a street, a lamp, a chemist's shop,
A dim and senseless light.
If you live twenty years or more –
It will not change. There's no way out.

You'll die – begin again from the beginning,
And all will be repeated as before:
Night, frozen ripples on the canal,
A chemist's shop, a street, a lamp.

In these same depressed years Blok's faith in the redemptive powers of art came under its sternest threat, as 'To The Muse' (1912) and 'The Artist' (1913) demonstrate. The latter is a particularly intriguing example of Blok's fear that the exercise of artifice must irreparably contaminate the original and mysterious inspiration which has lifted the artist out of the boredom of calendar time. The artist's attempt to understand what is happening to him is concentrated in four unanswered questions, whose familiar imagery unequivocally identifies the artist as Blok himself:

A wind from the sea? Or heavenly birds
Among the leaves? Does time stand still?
Have the apple trees of May scattered
Their snowy blossom? An angel flying past?

The poem ends, however, with the poet cast back upon his own suffering, helplessly awaiting the next occurrence of a kindred confrontation with the 'spirit of music'.

As early as 1907 Blok had told Biely that his soul was like a sentry that must stand watch and never leave its post. Standing watch had now become synonymous for Blok with listening for the 'spirit of music'. In the 'Carmen' cycle of 1914 (inspired by another actress with whom Blok had fallen in love) Blok records his discovery of what the last poem in the cycle calls 'a single melody of joy and sorrow'. In 'The Nightingale Garden' of 1915 (written while on holiday in Brittany with his wife) the possibility of experiencing a paradise on earth is once again entertained. In his moods of gloom, as in 'The Vulture' of 1916, he could still be mesmerized by the circularity he had postulated in the 'Dances Of Death'. But he was by this time permanently on the alert for the sound of the October Revolution of 1917. And when it came it not only suggested itself to him as 'a terrific din'; it also gave rise to his most noisy poem: 'The Twelve'.

Blok's 'Twelve' depends almost entirely on the sudden changes of tone and subtleties of rhythm of the original Russian. And even Russians have not been able to agree on its meaning, in particular the meaning of the Christ figure with which it ends. Blok himself was uncertain about this final touch, as if half-aware that he might have 'acceded to a kind of uncontrollable mystical reflex. But all the available evidence suggests that Blok intended a spiritual, rather than a specific, meaning for his most puzzling and most often-interpreted symbol. And since his whole career had been devoted to demonstrating the artist's apocalyptic powers in the world of the spirit, it does not seem unreasonable to see this figure as an oblique self-portrait. Blok's last imitation of Christ places him firmly in the vanguard, as Blok himself had been. And it could be said of his Christ as of Blok himself that 'he finds his expression as he consumes himself in life'.

Juan Ramón Jiménez
(1881–1958)

Born in Moguer, Andalusia, the son of a rich wine producer and a cultured, indulgent mother. Sent to the Jesuit school near Cádiz at the age of eleven, where he read very widely but was often unhappy. Studied art in Seville, returning to Moguer in ill-health in 1897. In Madrid in 1900, where he met Rubén Darío. Recovered from a nervous breakdown aggravated by the death of his father in a Bordeaux sanatorium in 1901. Lived in Madrid from 1901 to 1905 and in Moguer from 1905 to 1912, years of delicate health, great seclusion and solitude. In Madrid from 1912 to 1916, where he met his future wife. Travelled with her to New York in 1916, returning to Madrid, where they lived for the next twenty years. Regarded by the younger poets as the doyen of modern Spanish literature despite his sometimes abrasive behaviour. Spanish Republic's Cultural Emissary to America in 1936. Resident in Puerto Rico and Cuba from 1936 to 1939. Lived in Miami from 1939 to 1942, where he lectured at the University. From 1942 to 1951 lived in Washington, DC and in Maryland, where he lectured at the University. Lecture tour of Argentina and Uruguay in 1948. In Puerto Rico from 1951 to 1958, where he lectured at the University. Awarded the Nobel prize for Literature in 1956, and deeply saddened by the death of his wife soon after the announcement.

Jiménez became an international celebrity two years before his death on the award to him of the 1956 Nobel Prize for Literature, although in the last twenty years it has become usual to prefer his great contemporary Machado. Jiménez had already achieved classic status in Spain by the mid-1920s, as Alberti's memoirs indicate:

> Never was a Spanish poet more beloved and respected by such a sparkling generation of poets, [Alberti is referring to the so-called 'generation of '27', to which he, Lorca and Guillén belonged], utterly convinced, as they were, of the freshness and purity of the spring where they went to quench their thirst.

However his subsequent relations with this 'sparkling' generation were such as to make him more respected than beloved, partly because of his severe and sometimes curmudgeonly criticism of them both as poets and as people, and partly because of his refusal to join them in celebrating the three-hundredth anniversary of the birth of Góngora – the origin of the label 'generation of '27'. Jiménez's suspicion of 'Góngorism' derived from his fear that it would lead to excesses of the kind he associated with his erstwhile *maître* Rubén Darío, the Nicaraguan who had enlivened a largely moribund Spanish poetry with innovations of essentially French origin. Before Darío's death in 1916 Jiménez had begun a 'purification' of his own early work, thereafter going to extraordinary lengths to retrieve, to revise and even to destroy it. This 'purification' (the origin of Neruda's subsequent call for an 'impure' poetry) took a form similar to that practised by Yeats at about the same time, and it transformed Jiménez, much as it transformed Yeats, from an exceptionally gifted but somewhat conventional turn-of-the-century figure into a more recognizably 'modern' one. Jiménez did not, however, break with the past in a violently radical or avant-garde manner; it was more a matter of what Eliot would later call 'tradition and the individual talent'. Instead of disavowing his early Symbolist leanings, Jiménez set out to deepen them by going back to what he took to be the origins of Symbolism. Having begun in the 'impressionistic' manner of Verlaine and the Spanish poet Bécquer (sometimes called the Verlaine of Spain), Jiménez by-passed the then-unfashionable Góngora and rooted himself in the great Christian tradition of mystical writing represented by such contemplative writers as Thomas à Kempis and St John of the

Cross. He was also, like Yeats before him, deeply impressed by the non-Christian poetry of the now almost forgotten Rabindranath Tagore, which he and his wife translated. The 'generation of '27' were more interested in poetry than mysticism, like the generations that followed them. The 'universal Andalusian' Jiménez was therefore left with only the 'immense minority' of posterity to look to for unbiased appraisal of his merits.

The poetry of Jiménez is best seen against the background which he sought to emerge from. Aware that Mallarmé's desire to create 'The "Great Work"', as our ancestors the alchemists used to call it' had come to grief in the ultimately sterile problem of The Book, Jiménez grounded his Work (*Obra*) in religion and ethics rather than pure aesthetics. It is symptomatic of Jiménez's stance that in his most famous single poem, the lyric of 1917 in which he asks 'Intelligence' to give him 'the exact name of things', we should find him addressing something quite other than what we normally understand by the world 'intelligence'. For Jiménez's Intelligence is akin to divine Intelligence and is presumed to possess similar powers; it is a metaphysical principle rather than a faculty. Despite describing the lyric poet as 'a mystic without a necessary God' and thus inviting a confusion with Valéry's 'godless mystic' Monsieur Teste, Jiménez actually devoted most of his post-'purification' labour to showing how necessary a God was to him, so that in later life he could justly claim: 'my whole progress in poetry was a progress towards God'. The detractors of Jiménez, many of whom had little reason to feel kindly disposed towards him, made much of the fact that this 'progress towards God' was in reality a progress towards his own inflated ego. And many contemporary readers have also found it difficult to accept Jiménez's later poetry, where his 'God desiring and desired' seems more dependent on him than, as one might expect (although it is a characteristic of certain types of negative mystic), the other way round. It is nonetheless curious that the widespread interest in humanist and Existentialist theologies should not have made Jiménez into a more fashionable figure. In the case of other comparable poets, such as Rilke or Wallace

Stevens, it sometimes seems as if the very imperfection of the
syntheses they attempted constitutes one of the great attrac-
tions of reading them. But a similar licence has not often been
extended to Jiménez.

Jiménez published no less than seventeen collections of
poetry between the ages of nineteen and thirty-six, none of
which show him at his best except in isolated instances. Many
of the titles identify them as products of their epoch: *Violet Souls,
Water Lilies, Sad Airs, Far Gardens, Pastorals* etc. There are,
however, individual early poems like the following which offer
relief from the poet's persistent and ultimately cloying
sentimentality:

The afternoon roads
Become one road at night.

By it I must go to you,
Love, securely hidden.

By it I must go to you,
As the light on the mountain,
As the breeze from the sea,
As the fragrance of flowers.

The simplicity of such a poem, reinforced by a music inevitably
lost in translation, seems to require little in the way of 'puri-
fication'. But it is evident from a poem on the same subject
('Love', in the collection *The Pensive Brow* of 1911–12) that
Jiménez felt the need to make his outlines a little less nebu-
lous. In this later poem Jiménez is more concerned with proving
his faith that pure love must necessarily be eternal than with
dramatizing it; the 'purification' seems to have become as much
a matter of content as of form. He was later led to speak of
Góngora and Darío as examples of poets who insisted, wrongly
in his opinion, on giving poetry 'a determined form'. However,
before breaking through into the largely free verse of his later
poetry, he schooled himself in the most demanding and 'deter-
mined' of poetic forms: the sonnet. The *Spiritual Sonnets* of
1914–15 show Jiménez at his most technically perfect, although
their 'spiritual' orientation saves them from being merely

beautiful. One of them, addressed 'To My Soul', interestingly prefigures his later tendency to make his 'interior' world the model of a divine one:

Your rose will be the pattern of all roses,
Your ear – of harmony, your thoughts –
Of radiance, your vigilance – of stars.

The patterned form of the sonnet appropriately mirrors the pattern which the poet is intent on perceiving, and it provides a sharp focus for the potentially infinite attributes of the soul. These attributes, which might in isolation have remained somewhat abstract, served cumulatively in the *Spiritual Sonnets* to delineate, if not to define, the soul's vitally active role in the creative enterprise of fashioning a world. Jiménez could not have failed to note the frequency of the word 'soul' in Paul Verlaine, his favourite French poet. But his own conception of it took him progressively further from Verlaine's languor in the direction of the World-Soul of Neo-Platonist philosophy. 'I am, was, and will be a Platonist', Jiménez wrote to Luis Cernuda in 1943, with an intellectual vigour and spiritual confidence quite foreign to Verlaine. For Jiménez to have constructed a kind of Platonism out of the melancholia which was an almost crippling accompaniment to his first decade as a poet is at once an index of how desperate he had been to find a system of belief and of how determinedly he would continue to affirm it, even at the cost of repeating himself.

In 1914 Jiménez published the first version of a work in poetic prose which made no mention of Plato but concentrated rather on his childhood relationship with a donkey, *Platero And I*. It has since become one of the most popular books in the whole of Spanish literature, and despite its occasionally elegiac tone – it is subtitled 'an Andalusian elegy' – is profoundly affirmative. Jiménez wrote it during the period of his greatest solitude, and its curative properties must have been considerable. But the cure was consolidated by the central emotional event in Jiménez's life, his marriage in 1916. This inspired one of his most famous collections of poems, with the unprepossessing but significant title, *Diary Of A Recently Married Poet*.

Jiménez here proves the exception to the 'rule' that good husbands make bad poets by resisting the temptation to treat the subject domestically. His concern is with the cosmic implications:

I plucked your petals off as if you were a rose
So as to see your soul.
And did not see it.

      But everywhere –
Horizons of earths and seas –
Everything was filled, even
To the infinite, by an essence
Immense and alive.

Too much has perhaps been made of Jiménez's tendency towards abstraction, which is a common complaint against poetry which is concerned with 'essence'. What he was actually seeking to do was to make the concrete and the abstract, the terrestrial and the celestial, indivisible. 'There is no more than one orbit for all things and all men', he wrote just before his death, 'the orbit of time in space. And the orbit of poetry is that of life itself, man and world'.

Of the volumes published after the *Diary – Eternities, Rock And Sky, Beauty* and *Poetry (In Verse)* – only the title of the second suggests that it is concerned with what we would normally call 'life itself'. But Jiménez's conception of 'life itself' was not bounded, as it is for most of us, by a narrow empiricism. 'I think that this world is our only world', he wrote towards the end of his life, 'but why should we not try to make our consciousness contain the infinite universe if it can?' A conflict between the knowledge that man must die (perhaps the root cause of his recurrent psychosomatic illnesses) and the faith that man is infinite and immortal runs through all Jiménez's later work. In an attempt to resolve this conflict Jiménez primarily had recourse to the paradoxical notion of a 'dynamic ecstasy' in which man could be and not-be at once. This he reinforced by his own version of Nietzsche's myth of Eternal Recurrence. Only at the end of his life, however, did he achieve something like the synthesis he had been seeking. Perhaps his very commitment to the passing moment of 'life itself' prevented him discovering it sooner. 'I live, free,/ in the centre/of my self', Jiménez writes in a poem from the volume *Eternities*; but the famous 'I Am Not I' (from the same volume) suggests the opposite, as does 'Zenith' (from the collection *Beauty*):

I shall not be I, death,
until you are one with my life
and so complete me ...

The 'definitive' qualities of death were clearly as attractive to Jiménez as the indefinite properties of life; one of the most powerful expressions of this in the whole of Jiménez's work is an elegy for a nephew killed in the Spanish Civil War. It was in an effort to achieve such clear definition that he had purified the sentimental and nostalgic elements from his early writing, and had devoted himself to what a poem in *Rock And Sky* calls 'all present truth'. But despite his commitment to 'present truth' he suffered from a kind of nostalgia for the future, most memorably dramatized in the late poem 'Fortunate Creature'. Like the Existentialist philosophers (whom he often anticipates and resembles), Jiménez knew man to be an unfortunate creature incapable, except perhaps through poetry, of an eternal recurrence of the kind which the natural world annually accomplishes. In seeking a salvation through poetry, which could embody such a recurrence in refrains or variations within and between poems, he was inevitably accused of an aestheticism as sterile in its own way as that which he himself associated with Mallarmé. But there is nothing in Mallarmé which gives one quite the same feeling of plenitude as the late poems of Jiménez, particularly those in *The Total Season* (1946) and *Animal Of Death* (1949). Although some of the rhetoric that survived his attempts at 'purification' has contributed to him becoming an unfashionable poet (indeed much less fashionable than Mallarmé is at present), Jiménez must be adjudged to have achieved, in many if by no means all of his very numerous poems, the immortality and timelessness he was always in search of.

Umberto Saba (1883–1957)

Born Umberto Poli in Trieste, the son of a Jewish mother and a
Christian father who abandoned the family two years later.
Trained in a vocational school for clerical work, though he had
early decided to be a writer. Wandered restlessly through
Northern Italy from 1902 onwards. In 1907 met the seamstress
whom he was to marry a year later. Served as an inspector of
airfields in the First World War, and after the war became an
antiquarian bookdealer in Trieste, buying a shop which
guaranteed him a steady income. Suffered from psychological
disturbances in the 1920s and underwent psychoanalysis in
1929, becoming for a time a doctrinaire Freudian. Harassed by
the Fascist authorities and forced to close his shop during the
Second World War; protected by Montale during his stay in
Florence. Displeased by the critical neglect he encountered in
the post-war years, which prompted him to write a commen-
tary on his own poems. Died in Gorizia, near Trieste.

Although he wrote a poetry of potentially much wider appeal
than his contemporaries Ungaretti and Montale, Saba re-
mained little known outside Italy during his lifetime, and
frequently ignored by the Italian literary establishment. In
the absence of the critical attention he rightly believed to be
his due Saba offered in his *History and Chronicle of the
'Canzoniere'* (1948) his own assessment of a body of work
which, beside the extravagance of d'Annunzio on the one hand
and the experiments of the 'Hermeticists' on the other, was
bound to seem, in the poet's bitterly sardonic description,
'peripheral and backward'. No one who has read the best of

Saba would describe it in such terms, though the description serves to remind us that, like his friend the novelist Svevo, Saba was born in the most 'peripheral' of the cities of Northern Italy – Trieste – and felt that to have been born in Trieste in 1883 was like 'being born somewhere else in 1850'. Saba's attachment to Trieste was lifelong, broken only by his *Wanderjahre* of 1902–7 (after he had abandoned a business career), his conscription into the army in 1908, his army service during the First World War, and the exile forced on him by Fascist persecution during the Second World War. It was Trieste, its 'backward' qualities in a way epitomized by the poet deciding to become an antiquarian bookseller, which provided the appropriate backdrop for a life 'relatively poor in external events but rich, at times excruciatingly so, in emotions and inner resonances', and nowhere more so than in the great poems of 1910–12 which Saba collected under the title *Trieste And A Lady*. In a manifesto intended to prepare the way for *Trieste And A Lady* Saba explicitly rejected the operatic artifice of d'Annunzio and praised the manner in which Manzoni had contrived 'never to say a word that did not perfectly correspond with his vision'. Saba himself was convinced that 'to keep oneself pure and honest' and 'to resist all seduction' were much more important than any 'uncontrollable desire to be original'; he emphatically stressed the 'long discipline' essential to the disclosure of one's 'authentic being'. In the decade previous to *Trieste And A Lady* he was primarily concerned with schooling himself away from those poets who had mattered most to him in his Triestine backwater, Leopardi and Petrarch. The original title of his first important collection underlines this: 'With My Own Eyes'. Yet it was from Petrarch that Saba took the title for his first *Collected Poems* in 1921, the *Canzoniere* which he spent the rest of his life adding to.

Saba's early poetry was much revised between its first publication and its appearance in his first *Collected Poems*. In one case at least – the long and rather diffuse poem to his mother which he described in 1948 as his first truly original poem – Saba had finally to admit defeat and allow the poem's imperfections to stand. Yet there is much in this poem which confirms his belief (recorded in another early poem 'Meditation') that 'all my strength is in this: to look and to listen'. The stance is less that of a spectator than it might appear. It is clear, however, that his military experience made him a more obviously active participant in his own vision, as is suggested by the famous conclusion to a poem from the 'Military Verses' of 1908:

And my own eyes see the earth today
as I believe no other artist has ever seen it.
Like the animals see it perhaps.

It is this humble and simple vision which makes the most distinctive and celebrated of Saba's early poems – 'The Goat' and 'To My Wife' – so powerful. The former places the poet in a position where his strength is shown to be not so much a matter of listening, as of responding, participating in a universal condition which the tethered and bleating goat has made him conscious of:

That steady blast was brother
to my grief. And I responded, first of all
in fun, and then because grief is forever,
has one voice and does not vary.

The final lines of the poem confirm this insight, offering not so much a reminder of Saba's Jewishness as a Franciscan affirmation of a life lived in common by men and animals:

In a goat with semitic face
I heard lamenting all other ills,
all other lives.

Saba's poem to his wife, which she not unnaturally found unflattering at first, has a similarly powerful simplicity. Written 'as others would recite a prayer' (as the *History* puts it), the poem offers a portrait of his wife as a farmyard pullet, a pregnant heifer, a faithful bitch, a frightened rabbit, a swallow returning in springtime, a thrifty ant and, finally, 'all the females/ of the peaceful animals, close to God'. This is certainly one of the few great modern poems of married love, tender without the sentimentality that mars other poems of Saba's, especially the autobiographical 'Little Berto' poems of 1929–31.

Saba's wife remains a dominant figure in *Trieste And A Lady*. But here her beauty has become sorrowful, as the first poem in the collection ('Autumn') makes clear. Saba's honesty compels him to admit (appropriately enough in the poem called 'My Wife') that he himself is the cause of this, but also to assert that he will not allow his loved one to share the 'dumb sadness' which is increasingly oppressing him. A decade later, in the third poem of the sonnet sequence 'Autobiography', Saba ascribed his increasingly traumatized condition (significantly improved only by psychoanalytic treatment in 1930) to the survival in himself of the quarrel between his Jewish mother and the Gentile father who, in leaving her, had left him fatherless as an infant. But the origins of the claustrophobia which is so marked in *Trieste And A Lady* have yet to be quite so clearly delineated. What is clear in the earlier collection is that Saba is suffering from an 'Amorous Melancholy', which will not yet permit him to seek satisfaction from women other than his wife. Saba turns for relief from this condition to the other major presence announced in the title of the collection, the city of Trieste itself. But the grace she bestows is as 'bad-tempered' as the poet who wanders around her in search of salvation. In 'Three Streets', for example, he is compelled to visit the Jewish cemetery, only to find that his dead ancestors are now 'all alike in heart and faces'; in 'Trieste' he finds the 'air of home' is 'a strange air, a tormenting air'. Only when he can transcend his solitude and see himself as one of those who 'come and go/ from tavern to home or brothel' ('Old Town') can he content himself with anything like the discovery made in 'The Goat', that solace is to be found in the humblest and most timeless things. It is tempting to characterize these very powerful poems as examples of 'The Serene Desperation' which provided Saba with the title for the poems 1913–15 that come next in the *Canzoniere*. In fact all Saba's best poems written before the outbreak of the First World War occupy a curious middle-ground between the extremes of serenity and desperation, none more so, for example, than 'The Cobbler'. Here, with his

characteristic blend of intransigence and guilt, Saba confronts
the consequences of 'making new old souls' (his 'classicism' as
he liked to think of it), especially insofar as they affect the
material and spiritual derivations of his marriage:

> She, who once was love, does not sing today,
> nor smile, and her only word's
> a curse; the fatigue's so great
>
> and not enough to nourish a family.

Saba's return to formal structures in 'The Cobbler' – later
consolidated by the sonnet sequence 'Autobiography' – gives
the poem a less vulnerable appearance than, say, 'The Goat'.
But it would be as wrong to expect only serenity in Saba's
formal writing as to expect only 'Light and Airy Things' in the
1920 collection of that name. For these 'things that by their
lightness wander . . . through and above the heaviness of life' (as
Saba describes them in his *History*), bring him as much pain as
pleasure. Not surprisingly, he is left – as in the poem about the
little boy who has lost his balloon over the roof of the Stock
Exchange – wondering about what Eliot called, in a less
mercantile context, the 'profit and loss'. And it is typical of
Saba that in the 'Young Girls' collection of 1925 he should
remain permanently aware that the objects of his sexual
fantasies ('light and airy things' in their way) will become, with
the passage of time, mothers 'hardened with anxieties' like his
wife and his own mother previously, that their youthful heed-
lessness will not ultimately protect them from the 'Moribund
Heart' which stands at the head of the next sub-section of the
Canzoniere.

It is part of the unfolding drama of the *Canzoniere* that Saba
should follow the cloying eroticism of the 'Young Girls' section
(in which Saba is, in fantasy at least, a vagabond like his father)
with the 'death-wish' poetry of 'Moribund Heart', which ends
with a deeply moving poem to his dead mother. One can
hardly help but read these poems in the light of Saba's sub-
sequent psychoanalysis; no doubt it is symptomatic that the
first and last poems in 'Moribund Heart' – both of which
involve him in a reappraisal of his origins – should be concerned

with the interpretation of dreams. The first poem ('Sonnet Of Paradise') locates 'all the sweetness that there is in life' in the small white house of his childhood, where he spent most of the first four years of his life, being looked after by a nurse while his mother went to work. The poem ends, however, on the word 'farewell', and there are other poems ('My Nurse's House', for example) in which Saba unequivocally indicates that he regards this as a paradise permanently lost. And yet the poem to his dead mother treats of a kind of paradise regained, with the poet longing 'to return to the darkness of the maternal womb', thereby becoming, as she has become, 'a stain born of earth,/which reabsorbs the earth and nullifies'. This is the obverse of the 'ancient hunger' of the great poem 'Longing', which dramatizes the poet's unconquerable libido. But it also connects with the poet's frustrated desire:

>   to go out
> of myself, to live the life
> of all,
> to be like all
> men of all
> days.

('Suburb')

The prayer to his mother indicates that it is death, however, and not life, that he is really longing for.

Saba's longest poem, 'Man' (1928), is an attempt to join his own life to 'the life of all' which, as 'Suburb' shows, he cannot join. But the attempt seems uncharacteristically programmatic, and is much less convincing than Saba's reversion to the poetry of the divided self in 'Preludes and Fugues' (1928–9). Here, even though the disparate voices of the fugues cannot quite be integrated, Saba seems to have become less tormented, more stoical. If it is not quite the harmony envisaged in the 'Prelude', it at least prepares the way for the post-psychoanalytic poetry of Saba's last years. In 'Prelude and Fugues' Saba's quest for a refuge from the world (which surfaces again at the end of the seventh fugue) is finally abandoned, and he begins to seek instead for what the title poem of the collection

'Words' calls 'a corner . . ./in the world'. His aim thereafter was to 'mirror the heart of man' with a new language, 'naked and stunned'. And in his late poems he comes closer than ever before to being 'pure and honest', to achieving the classicism he so often spoke of. In late Saba it is no longer his own origins which compel him into utterance; it is the origins of every man – the Mediterranean world, and in particular the figure of Ulysses (hero of another inhabitant of Trieste, James Joyce). And yet by virtue of assimilating this figure, this 'pilgrim of the world', to the image of journeying that he inevitably associated with his father Saba clearly effected a reintegration of his dislocated origins, which his Freudian psychoanalysis had prepared the ground for.

Saba's later poetry is completely purified of his early attraction for 'light and airy things'. His past, in a Fascist Italy, is 'all in ruins' ('I Had', 1944), and yet the 'brokenhearted love of life' of which the second 'Ulysses' poem speaks is always reasserting itself, thanks to the humble things which always restored Saba to a modicum of contentment. Saba's final judgement of his own career was that he had 'written . . . in vain,/for the birds and a friend, in a sad time,/in my sad Italian'. And the so-called 'Epigraph' – really an epitaph – which ends the *Canzoniere* is utterly desolate:

Alive I spoke to a dead people.
Dead I refuse the laurel and beg oblivion.

But the total effect of the *Canzoniere* is too variegated to be considered merely pessimistic. What it does record are the splendours and miseries in the life of a man as exceptional as any other great poet, who nevertheless requires one to respond to him, as he would have wished, as one of us, as an ordinary man.

Dino Campana (1885–1932)

Born in Marradi, near Florence, the son of a schoolteacher
father and an eccentric mother. Studied Latin and Greek and
became fluent in French, German and English. Enrolled in the
Faculty of Chemistry of the University of Bologna in 1903, and
studied chemistry there and at Florence until 1906. Sailed for
Argentina in 1907, where he worked as gaucho, miner, stoker,
fireman, musician and wandered restlessly. Returned to Italy
via Odessa, Rotterdam, Paris, and Basle and often imprisoned
on grounds of vagrancy; placed in an asylum in 1909. Aber-
rantly pursued pharmaceutical studies in Genoa, Bologna and
Florence. Wrote the *Orphic Songs*, which were to make him
famous, in a few weeks in 1913. Submitted them to the editor
Soffici who lost the manuscript. Rewrote them from memory
in the spring of 1914. Called up by the army and declared
mentally unbalanced. Remained for the last fourteen years of
his life, during which time he wrote no poetry, in a mental
asylum near Florence, where he died.

Only two modern Italian poets, Giuseppe Ungaretti and
Eugenio Montale, have had a profound impact throughout
Europe; a third, Salvatore Quasimodo, was catapulted into
prominence by the much-disputed decision to make him the
recipient of a Nobel Prize. But modern Italian poetry is much
richer than the received idea of it allows for, and one of those
who make it so is Dino Campana. His poetry is plainly not of the
same magnitude as Ungaretti's or Montale's; its dimensions, in
every sense of the word, remain somewhat narrow. He only saw
one small collection of his poems through the press, the *Orphic*

Songs of 1914, a collection which editors before and after his death have expanded to the best of their ability. After a history of restless and neurotic behaviour Campana spent the last fourteen years of his life in a mental asylum, during which he wrote nothing of significance. His mental instability is evident in even his most accomplished poems and leaves his fragments fragmentary indeed. His emotional range as a poet is inevitably somewhat circumscribed; it is understandable, therefore, that an eminent French critic should have suggested that, whilst Campana may be a considerable figure in the history of Italian lyric poetry, he is of little consequence outside Italy, and especially vulnerable to comparisons with Rimbaud, whom he seems at first glance to resemble. But to compare Campana with Rimbaud is at best tendentious and at worst irrelevant, and since the history of Italian lyric poetry numbers several figures of the greatest consequence in European literature, this judgement is itself vulnerable to attack.

Campana requires us to regard him as an 'Orphic' poet without much provision, outside the turbulent world of the poems themselves, of what he understood by Orphism. His prose 'Observations' suggest that the heterodox cults of Orphic Greek religions had very little to do with his conception: 'Italy', he wrote with unconcealed distaste, 'is as it always was: theological'. He was, however, fascinated by the German culture of the nineteenth century, and he must have been familiar with Novalis's quasi-Orphic claim that poetry was 'the one true absolute reality' and that the poet's calling was 'to fashion the earth'. In Rimbaud's *A Season In Hell* the desire to 'possess truth in one soul and one body' is predicated upon a similar belief. And neither Rimbaud nor the writers and painters of German Expressionism would have found much to quarrel with in Campana's observation that 'Art is expression. This ought to imply reality.' Recognizing that mysticism was an 'ulterior phase' within the history of attempts to see 'life as a whole', Campana appears to have regarded an expressive aestheticism as its most intrinsic manifestation. At the time of Campana's maturity as a poet, the French painter Robert Delaunay was producing his own art with a similar set of beliefs and describing it as 'Orphic'. And both Campana and Delaunay became practised exponents of the art of eroding substantial forms and replacing them with areas of colour intended to act as indices of spiritual values. The consequences of Campana's Orphism are in fact much more accessible than the intellectual affiliations whereby he came to commit himself to it.

In Campana's version of the Orpheus myth the poet participates without reserve in the rites he is initiating and participates so totally that he is effectively in a permanent state of ecstasy, whether painful or pleasurable. His own active will is virtually non-existent, or in abeyance; he is the medium through which events come into temporary and turbulent being, the crucible of unpredictable and dislocated metamorphoses. As in the case of a spiritualist medium, however, Campana is dependent upon a source of wisdom of superior authority. And, like many poets of a distinctively *fin de siècle* cast of mind, the authority figure for Campana was a mysterious female. Something more than a mere Muse (though she performs this role quite adequately) and something less than an Earth Mother (though in one poem at least, 'Barbaric Sword', she is indistinguishable from such a deity), Campana's mysterious female is best understood in terms of pre-existent literary and artistic models: the figures of Beatrice and Francesca in Dante's *Divine Comedy*; the androgynous creatures in Leonardo da Vinci's 'Mona Lisa' and 'The Virgin Of The Rocks'; the ambivalent Michelangelo statue 'Night' in the Medici chapel in Florence. This last seems to have exerted a particular fascination on Campana, no doubt because traditional Orphism explains the origin of the universe as the consequence of the mating of Eros and Night. The very mention of Eros, however, is a reminder that this creature of intercession between the finite and infinite worlds has a disquieting tendency to transform herself, for so many 'decadent' writers, from vestal virgin into prostitute, as if suffering from the same dualism of spirit and matter that has compelled her acolytes to call her into being. Campana's Chimera, as he called her, possessed familiar features: a pallid face, an enigmatic sphinx-like smile, black hair, red lips and a statuesqueness belying her chimerical appearance. And whatever form she took, the poet was entirely at her mercy for good or ill, except insofar as he could believe that his verbal and incantatory magic had conjured her into being.

She makes her first appearance in the *Orphic Songs* in the extraordinary prose poem 'Night' which opens the volume, where she displays almost all the characteristics, benign and malevolent, that are her hallmark. 'Night', Campana's most prolonged 'descent and return' *à la* Orpheus, recalls the 'soul-scapes' of Baudelaire's 'Paris Spleen' and Rimbaud's season in hell, and some of its language prefigures Futurist and Surrealist practice, though it is more restrained and articulated than this might suggest. It does not, however, possess the clarity of the very beautiful 'Nocturnes' which Campana placed immediately after it. Two of these ('The Chimera' and 'Autumnal Garden') are particularly fine and a third ('The Window') is a splendid example of the effects that Campana's unique poetic 'stammer' can achieve. 'The Chimera' dramatizes the 'nocturnal' poet's uncertain apprehension of a 'queen of melody' who controls and ratifies his Orphism, ashen of face but with a line of blood at the centre of her sinuous lips. Repetitively, as if spelling out an incantation, the poet simultaneously acknowledges his dependence on her and the fact that he does not and perhaps never can know her. The rhapsodic conclusion has all the urgency of an Orpheus who suspects his Eurydice is irretrievably lost but whose voice nevertheless continues to invoke her:

I look at the white rocks the mute fountains of the winds
And the immobility of firmaments
And the swollen banks that go away weeping
And the shadows of human labour bent on the cold hills
And still through tender skies remote clear shadows running
And still I call you call you Chimera

'Autumnal Garden', set in the Boboli Gardens in Florence, is also concerned with the conjuration of this spectral and mysterious female figure. In the sunset, the poet's senses (especially the senses of smell and hearing) seem to have revived and reconstituted something meaningful and immortal. As in the prose poem 'Night' the poet's self seems to have atomized and become consubstantial with the elements surrounding it. If it comes as something of a surprise to encounter in the final line a personal pronoun indicative of his existence as a separate individual – 'She appears to me, present' – the line ultimately suggests that the poet can only truly exist in the presence of the lady. Even then it remains unclear whether this 'final saluta-tion' (as Campana has earlier called it) has successfully invoked the lady or whether she remains a mere chimera of his sensibility.

'The Window' strikes an equally ambiguous note, this time in a metropolitan context rather than a pastoral one. By the end of this sunset poem the 'red wound' of the evening and the 'burning seal' of the poet's heart penetrated by the shaft of light through the window are indistinguishable. The poem ends with an oracular utterance which at first glance seems utterly pessimistic:

At the heart of the evening there is
Always a red wound languishing.

The evening has shimmered, however, with intimations of an epiphany; the very fact that Campana is insistently asking 'Who has lit a candle in front of the statue of the Madonna of the Bridge?' makes it reasonable to assume that it must have been the poet himself. There is a similar question in the prose poem 'Night' (a question which, being addressed to deaf mutes, is necessarily left unanswered) which suggests that the bridge on which the Madonna stands is more a metaphorical one than a literal one: 'What bridge have we raised to the infinite, that everything here seems the shadow of eternity?' Both these questions are typical of the uncertainties inherent in Campana's Orphism, though it is clear from an entry in the diary 'Mount Verna' (where everything once more takes place under the aegis of an enigmatic female figure) that when Campana felt himself 'raised to the infinite' he could cast off his despair:

... from my childhood a liturgical voice resounded in slow and moving prayer: and you from that sacred rhythm moved by me

arose, already anxious for the vast plains, for remote miraculous
destinies: my hope is aroused on the infinity of plain or sea sensing
the flicker of a breath of grace.

Campana was perpetually in quest of this grace. And it is
the poems which express the essence of the city of Genoa
which are most marked by it. 'I yearn for/Mist and silence in
a great port' Campana wrote in the sonnet 'Simple Poem'.
In 'Genoa' he appears to have found the tranquillity he was
looking for:

At the port lies the ship
In the twilight which glimmers
Through masts quiet with the fruits of light

But it is typical of the extreme volatility of Campana's poetry
that these lines should follow close upon a passage in which all
control seems to have been yielded up to the words themselves,
where contour is lost entirely and the red of the streetlamps and
the white of the vision of Grace are left to fight it out between
themselves. Clearly Genoa was not without its more morbid
aspects for Campana, even if it did become his favoured loca-
tion for the state of grace he was in search of. The same could be
said of the poetic impulse itself, which Campana subjected to
analysis in three related fragmentary poems. In one of them,
perhaps his clearest programmatic account of what an Orphic
poetry might achieve, the 'living soul of things' is concen-
trated finally in the very name Genoa, which is intoned three
times in the last line as if in imitation of a magical invocation.
The riot of colour leading up to this conclusion seems to stem
directly from, and in response to, the poet's desperate cry in the
middle of the poem ('O poetry be a beacon to me'). It is not
clear what part the poet's will plays in this instance. But in the
analogous fragment 'O poetry you will return no more' the
poet's own will has completely atrophied; only the 'sacred
brown eyes' of his familiar Chimera can transform his 'furious
aridity' into 'catastrophic ardour'. And in a third related
fragment ('O poetry poetry poetry') the mood is even darker,
for here the poet's admonition to poetry to 'rise up' from the
terrestrial to the celestial world is drowned by the all-too-

human noises which break in upon his potentially creative
silence.

In accordance with the tradition that it was the beauty of his
verbal music which made the mythical figure Orpheus the
archetypal poet-magician, Campana made his Orphic poetry
aspire to the condition of music, and even his most coherent and
dislocated pieces are remarkably melodious. Yet, paradoxi-
cally, Campana is at his most attractive when he is on the verge
of silence, when his words are at their most diaphanous. The
stammer that betokens a frenzied yearning for impossible ideals
is also employed by Campana for moods of quietude, as in the
lovely conclusion to the fragmentary 'Images Of The Journey
And The Mountain':

Behold the night: and behold watching over me
Lights and lights: and me far off and solitary:
Quiet the harvest, towards infinity
(Quiet the spirit) mute lyrics go
Into the night: into the night: I listen: solitary
Shadow who returns, who had disappeared . . .

None of Campana's excursions into the genre of 'mute lyric' are
more captivating than the four poems for Sibilla Aleramo,
which defy translation and yet are among the greatest Italian
love poems. 'In a moment' conjures extraordinary richness
from its apparent poverty:

In a moment
The roses are withered
The petals fallen
Because I could not forget the roses
We sought them together
We found some roses
They were her roses they were my roses
We called this journey love
We made roses with our blood and tears
That shone for a moment in the morning sun
We made them vanish beneath the sun among the brambles
The roses which were not our roses
My roses her roses

P.S. And so we forgot the roses

This is obviously about as far as the idea of 'mute lyric' can be taken if it is to remain eloquent. And in another of these love lyrics Campana pursues a more conventional eloquence, as if intent on conquering his unique capacity to be hypnotized by his own imaginings:

I loved you in the city where on solitary
Streets the enfeebled footstep rests
Where tender peace that rains
At evening turns the unsated unrepentant heart
Towards an ambiguous spring in violet
Distances above a pallid sky.

It is difficult to believe, on reading these poems, that the best of Campana can continue to remain of little consequence outside Italy, however incoherent the more extreme examples of his Orphism may be.

Gottfried Benn (1886–1956)

Born near Berlin, the eldest son of a Protestant priest and a
French Swiss governess. Received a classical education at
boarding school and briefly studied theology and philology at
the universities of Marburg and Berlin. Thereafter became a
medical student and gained a doctorate in medicine in the year
his first book of poems (*Morgue*, 1912) was published. Fell in
love with the poetess Else Lasker-Schüler. Married an actress
in 1914. Witnessed the execution of Edith Cavell in an official
capacity and at the end of the war became a specialist in skin
and venereal complaints. Lived a solitary life after the death of
his wife in 1922, though an intimate friend of the widow of the
dramatist Wedekind. Wholeheartedly embraced the Nazi ide-
ology in 1933, condemning those who had fled Germany, but
within a short time found himself unacceptable to the new
régime, and forced to go into 'inner emigration'. Married his
second wife in 1938; she committed suicide as the Red Army
approached Berlin in 1945. First published after the war in
Switzerland, because he was *persona non grata* in the Germany of
the reconstruction. Later partially rehabilitated in Germany;
gave a famous lecture, 'The Problem of Lyric Poetry', at the
University of Marburg in 1951. Received many honours in
Berlin on his seventieth birthday, though continuing after his
death to be a controversial figure by virtue of his extreme
political stance in the 1930s. Widely regarded notwithstanding
as the most important native German poet of the twentieth
century.

Whilst none of this century's experimental poets has avoided arousing controversy only Gottfried Benn can claim the distinction of having been called 'a pig by the Nazis, a swine by the Communists, a spiritual prostitute by the democrats, a renegade by the émigrés and a pathological nihilist by the religious'. This bitter self-portrait goes some way towards identifying the exceptionally solitary place Benn occupies in the history of the poetry of the last hundred years. Some critics, prompted by Benn's lifelong commitment to what he called 'the World of Expression', have spoken of him as an Expressionist. But even his Expressionism was of a distinctly non-conformist kind. As one critic has written: 'The expressionist is preoccupied with man and his fate in a world about to disintegrate. He is a humanist before, a pacifist during and a socialist after the [First World] War'. Benn was certainly preoccupied with the fate of man in a disintegrating world. But his scorn for the humanist-pacifist-socialist configuration could not have been more total. Despite a belated attempt to suggest that 'modern man does not think nihilistically', Benn's position before, during and after both the World Wars was as nearly nihilist as it is possible to be.

Benn's major problem was to keep his nihilism sufficiently flexible to permit himself movement within its boundaries. In the early stories about his *alter ego* Dr Rönne, he stressed the anguish of a belief in nothing: 'There is nothing solid behind my eyes any more ... The cortex that was holding me up has crumbled' ('Brains', 1914). Benn could only counter the disintegrative implications of such a stance by strenuously asserting, after Nietzsche, that art was the 'last metaphysical activity within European nihilism' and by insistently proclaiming: 'that which lives is something other than that which thinks'. In the dramatic sketch 'Ithaca' of 1914 Dr Rönne's awareness of these truths leads him to dream of reactivating a primeval Mediterranean world of Dionysiac ecstasy. To achieve it, he must stand outside himself (the root meaning of the word 'ecstasy'):

if only I could return to the state of being of a grassy field, sand dotted with flowers, a vast meadow. With the earth carrying everything to you on warm or cool waves. No forehead left. A state of being lived.

Benn could never, however, fully attain a state of being in which there was 'no forehead left'. By 1933 he was even telling Heinrich Mann that nihilism was not so much an anguish as a pleasure insofar as 'in the intellect man possesses a marvellous agent of self-destruction'. There was certainly something almost self-destructive about Benn's decision in 1933 to throw in his lot with Hitler, and to suggest that those writers who had emigrated were indulging a 'private hobby'. This notorious and unforgivable utterance left Benn quite without sympathizers when he had incurred the displeasure of the new régime and been forced into 'inner emigration'. Even when, in his rehabilitation after the war, his 'Double Life' (as he came to think of it) took on a representative status for those similarly attracted and repelled by National Socialism, the extreme aestheticism that was the only meaningful and respectable attitude for this thoroughgoing nihilist left Benn effectively as isolated as he had always been. For to have condoned his aesthetic position would have been an implicit acceptance of his political position; he had, after all, almost perfectly exemplified Walter Benjamin's contention that the 'pure' aesthete must inevitably gravitate towards the impure politics of fascism. Benn remained untroubled by this. His belief (as expressed in a novella of 1947, 'The Ptolomean') that 'only vision, the style of seeing' can be important for the man who wishes to express the 'All in Nothingness' was unshaken. Since he did not believe that the 'way of the intellectualist' had been compromised by the unintellectual Nazis, he – and humanity with him, so far as he was concerned – was left with the primary and original problem of 'what you make of your nihilism' still unsolved.

What Benn made of his nihilism in his first collection of poems (*Morgue*, 1912) was a scalpel much blunter than those he had seen demonstrated in his anatomy classes as a medical student. Although a number of critics have discerned in these poems, as an implied corrective to their apparently overwhelming cynicism, a sympathy for the mostly dead bodies they are concerned with, the sympathy seems to be exercised in a kind of vacuum. It only becomes impressive at the end of the typically statemental 'Man And Woman Walk Through The Cancer Ward', where the moribund are on the point of release into death:

Here swells the earth about each bed.
Flesh levels into land. Heat passes away.
Sap starts to trickle. Earth calls.

Benn's poems of the metropolis (like 'Night Café') are equally sardonic, though slightly less inhuman. The protagonists, though hardly attractive and still implacably anatomized (in a manner reminiscent of the drawings of George Grosz), are at least alive, even if – as in 'Express Train' – the signs of life are indistinguishable from the signs of lust, or – as in 'Underground Train' – the overwhelming desire is for

                    a dying
into the sea's deep delivering azure.

None of them, however, satisfy Benn's quest for a redemptive form to justify the artistic expression of his nihilism anything like so well as the two 'Songs' of 1913, which anticipate Dr Rönne's desire to attain a primitive mindlessness. In *Morgue* the only salvation (if it can be called such) is to become dust in the earth. The 'Songs', however, envisage a meaningful regression to the Dionysiac world of the Mediterranean, as the last line of the second song suggests:

All is shore. The sea calls ceaselessly –

Benn had demonstrated, in his important but essentially programmatic poem 'The Young Hebbel' (1913) how 'hewing the form out of the marble block' of one's forehead must be combined with uncovering the 'Godheavens' and 'Manearths' buried in the blood, and though the 'Songs' are models of intellectual rigour, they seem not so much cerebral poems as poems of the sensibility.

The same is true of Benn's finest early poems, all of which

were published in the otherwise all too aptly titled collection *Flesh* (1917). In them Benn remains imprisoned in his alienation and isolation, but he is at least able to give vent, as in the excellent 'Poplar', to the 'insignia of cries' that crown his forehead. The insistent imperatives of the famous 'Caryatid' poem are another index of his need to cry out and thereby to conjure the blue Mediterranean world out of the marble block. The conclusion of 'Caryatid' is, however, deeply elegiac, shot through with the recognition that such a world is blossoming for the last time. And only in the magisterial 'Icarus' of 1915 does the 'deforeheaded' world which Dr Rönne dreamed of – an absolute unity in which the brain would be atomized – seem a real possibility. In the absence of such an absolute, the poet can only regard his individuality, Spengler-fashion, as 'a late mood of Nature and therefore fugitive'. The 'I' deprived of absolute unity (which Benn calls 'the late I') is the subject of a very powerful poem of 1921 which seems to make the achievement of such a state even more remote; it presents what Benn described to a correspondent as 'a solitary I, self-installed and knowing only itself', a point nicely dramatized by making 'I' the last word of the poem and 'the last I' the last line. What Benn is really intent on here – as the virtual disappearance thereafter of the never very prominent first-person pronoun indicates – is developing a kind of 'heroic' nihilism in which the Kantian division between subject and object (which Benn believed did not obtain in the Classical world) is transcended by a higher 'totalized' integration.

Benn's temporary commitment to National Socialism must be seen as a corollary of his belief in the 'totalized' work of art. Interestingly, his notorious affirmation of state collectivism in 1933 had been preceded by at least a decade of exploration into the 'collective unconsciousness' recoverable from the world of myth. The totalized work of art, like the totalized state, required a 'heroic', almost mythical, individual to bring it into being. Aesthetically, this could only be the poet in the guise of Orpheus; politically, it must have seemed as if it could only be Hitler. Benn believed that only extreme introversion could lead the poet to rediscover the 'Orphic cells' lying dormant in him.

But as the 1925 poem 'The Singer' shows, his own introversion was not conducted egocentrically. He countered the Romantic emphasis on the dream of the poet with the more objective 'dream of the poem'. As he became ever more convinced that life was indeed the 'inferior illusion' of which a poem of 1936 spoke, so form became ever more clearly 'the faith and the deed'. However when National Socialism revealed its true colours, Benn was left – as another poem of 1936 shows ('Whoever Is Alone') – with only the heroically suffering poet to rely on. And it was at this time that he developed the notion of the 'static' poem. This paradoxical form, designed by Benn as a modern equivalent of the peculiar stillness of classical art, became his preferred mode until the early 1950s, when he again felt the need to shock as in *Morgue* and *Flesh*. Conceived against the background of dynamism which Benn took to be basic to the Expressionist ideal, this 'static' poetry offered him the optimum means of access to the ecstatic condition which would be at once the perfect release from, and the perfect expression of, the nihilism he had always professed.

The 'form-furthering dominion of the void', as Benn called it, was to be achieved by a regression to the undifferentiated flux of the blood and the sea, the 'thalassal regression' of a poem of 1927. But the apprehension of this primeval chaos and its embodiment in the poem could not in themselves be chaotic. This is clear when one places the 'Little Aster' poem of the *Morgue* collection beside the 'Asters' poem of 1936. The latter has the crystalline quality of Benn's other autumnal poems (of which the 1948 poem 'September' is perhaps the finest), with all the brashness of the early poem eradicated. In such 'static' poems as this Benn's answer to the problem of 'what one makes of one's nihilism' took on a distinctly mystical character; the sense of decay and decline is tempered by intimations of time-lessness. These moments of illumination remain elegiac because, as in the famous 'A Word' of 1948, they cannot decisively banish the 'empty space' and the darkness which surround the poet. It does not surprise one to learn that Benn's favourite quotation from the Bible was from the Lamentations of Jeremiah: 'God has walled me in, so that I cannot escape.'

But his own lamentations, with the obvious exception of poems like 'The Death Of Orpheus' (which deals with the suicide of his second wife in 1945) do not exclude the possibility of temporary escape, even if it is only into the formal imprisonment of the poem.

Benn's attempts at writing an 'absolute' poetry, at once 'drunken' and 'cerebral', were by no means uniformly successful. Vary his nihilism as he might, his position did not permit him any permanent relief from the vicious circles of his own consciousness. His absolutist temperament had led him in the 1920 essay 'The Modern I' to propose his own case as exemplary, definitive and representative. But whilst there is a strong solipsistic strain in modern literature, it is simply not the case that, to be 'modern', one must believe Benn's dictum that 'there are no people anymore, but on the contrary only the I always'. Such a belief inevitably affected his rare attempts to be a public poet. The poem of 1943 in which he belatedly castigates the Nazi régime is powerful; but it is never the public poem it might have been and is aptly titled – as many of Benn's poems might be – 'Monologue'. Even those love poems addressed to a 'you' figure suggest a poet in soliloquy with himself. But if Benn's poetry suffers, when taken as a whole, from its narrowness of range, he certainly showed himself adept at making a virtue of what was, for him, a necessity, as in an exceptionally fine lyric from 1927:

See the stars, the fangs
of light and sky and sea,
what shepherd songs
they drive before them, fading,
you also, who invoked voices
and described your circle,
follow the silent steps
downwards of the messenger of night.

When you have emptied out
the words and myths, you must depart,
a new cohort of gods
you will not see again,
nor their Euphrates throne

and writing on the wall –
shed, Myrmidon,
the dark wine over the land.

Howsoever the hours were called,
torment and tears of being,
all blossoms in the lapsing out
of this nocturnal wine,
and silently the Aeon streams away,
scarcely a sliver of shore left:
then give the crown and dream
and gods back to the messenger.

As this poem shows, the audience for Benn's poetry could never, even under ideal conditions, become a large one. Though he was fond of quoting Flaubert's 'I am a mystic and believe in nothing', his mysticism is of a peculiarly German kind, and best understood within the speculative traditions of German poetry and philosophy since the beginning of the nineteenth century; in this respect he is more Romantic then Classical. None of the great modern German poets can be rendered into the non-Germanic languages (or even English) with ease. But Benn's syntax and neologisms pose the kind of intractable and virtually unresolvable problems that suggest his poetry may never be permanently retrieved from the conditions of isolation in which it was written, at least so far as Europe as a whole is concerned.

Georg Trakl (1887–1914)

Born in Salzburg, the son of a Protestant businessman. Hyper-
sensitive to the point of hysteria as a child. Of great physical
stamina as a young man, though addicted to alcohol and
narcotics. Trained as a dispensing chemist, a profession which
offered him optimum access to drugs; attended Vienna Uni-
versity betweeen 1908 and 1910. Presumed to have had an
incestuous relationship with his sister, who shot herself in 1917.
Briefly an apothecary in Salzburg; in 1912 worked at the
garrison hospital in Innsbrück. In the summer of 1914 received
financial support from the philosopher Wittgenstein. Served as
a medical lieutenant on the Galician front, where he attempted
to commit suicide. Hospitalized in Krakow where he died from
an overdose of drugs.

In a celebrated chapter of *The Phenomenology Of The Spirit*
(1807), describing the turmoil experienced by the 'unhappy'
consciousness, Hegel speaks of such a consciousness inhabiting
a 'giddy world of perpetually self-creating disorder'. Of the
many modern poets whose sufferings are prefigured by Hegel
the Austrian poet Georg Trakl seems unhappier than most;
his 'giddy world' was not one made meaningful by the
Absolute Spirit of which Hegel had spoken. Trakl, on his own
admission, suffered the agonies of 'an uninterruptedly precari-
ous and in all things despairing nature'. In a letter to the
Viennese satirist Karl Kraus, who admired his poetry, he spoke
of moods of 'frantic intoxication and criminal melancholy'.
Nowhere was the atmosphere of intoxication and melancholy
which prevailed at the turn of the century more dynamic than

in imperial Vienna, although Trakl's drug-addiction and his tortured sexual life, dominated by incestuous feelings towards his sister, are no doubt best regarded as the outward manifestation of an inner spiritual malaise that he might have experienced anywhere. His one recourse was to confront this malaise, to address the 'internal chaos of rhythms and images' from which he suffered, and to try to give this chaos a determinate shape and coherence by writing poetry. In a letter to his sister Trakl described how withdrawal into this unruly world could nevertheless provide a bulwark or refuge against the nightmare reality by which he was otherwise encompassed:

It must, I think, be dreadful always to live like this, in full consciousness of those animal instincts which promote the continuance of life through time. I have felt in myself the most terrifying possibilities, reached out for them, tasted them, and heard the demons howl in my blood, the thousand devils whose thorns drive the flesh frantic. What an appalling nightmare! But it is done with! This vision of reality has now once more been swallowed up in nothingness, these things are far away, their voices farther still, and again, all animated ear that I am, I lie in wait for the melodies which are within me and my wingèd eye dreams its pictures once again, which are more beautiful than all reality. I am at one with myself, I am my own world, my whole, beautiful world, full of unending melody.

Trakl's ability to conquer his divided nature, as recorded in this letter, has not been inherited by those who have attempted to make sense of his poetry. His meaning has been more often disputed, at least since his rediscovery in 1946, than that of almost any other modern poet, and no general consensus has emerged. It is some comfort to learn that the young Wittgenstein, clearly one of the great intellects of the century, was similarly perplexed: 'I do not understand his poetry,' he wrote, 'but its *tone* delights me. It is the tone of a man of real genius.' Since for most readers Trakl's tone is quite as mysterious as his meaning, one might be forgiven for thinking that Wittgenstein was reacting primarily to the laconic abstraction in Trakl that he himself was to become famous for; though it is salutary to be reminded that it is quite legitimate to take delight in things that we do not understand. Confronted, however, by an enigma, it is a natural reaction to seek the key whereby it might be forced to disclose its significance. And in Trakl one does not have to look far for the key, or what looks like one; he concentrates obsessively on an astonishingly limited number of motifs and images, creating thereby a fractured network of relationships in which certain words and phrases reappear in more or less accessible combinations. This 'repetition compulsion', in Freudian terms, may simply be an index of Trakl's neurotic temperament. But it seems more likely to be the strategy of a man intent on uttering a definitive truth which is perpetually eluding him. In this sense Heidegger's suggestion that Trakl's slim *oeuvre* is essentially one poem seems a sound one, although the definition of that one poem still presents a problem. As for the psychological implications of Trakl's strategy, they are perhaps most fruitfully analysed by his contemporary Rilke:

What life exhales is continually retroactive again upon life – an existence which attempts to unburden itself, burdens itself instead with the intensified expression of all that is unbearable to it, remains encompassed by the very distresses which it has apparently dispelled and transcended, and is more at their mercy than if it had never blossomed and consolidated itself in lyrical consciousness.

Trakl would surely have recognized his own plight in Rilke's words; but he would not have needed to accept Rilke's notion that if he had been a painter or a musician he would have survived. For as the letter to his sister makes clear, he saw music and painting as constitutive elements of his poetic world, and it is the musical and pictorial qualities of his work which are likely to make the greatest impact on a reader encountering it for the first time.

Trakl is one of the most musical of modern German poets, although the way in which he gives weight, density and voluptuary sweetness to his decomposing world is inevitably the first casualty of attempts to translate him. His images, however, the product of that 'wingèd eye' of which he speaks in the letter to his sister, are more readily transportable, even if the way in

which they act to de-stabilize what we customarily call reality
makes his eye seem wingèd indeed. The mysterious 'soul land-
scapes' of the French Symbolist poets are nothing like so
strange or fragmented as the inner world of Trakl. The third of
the 'Rosary Songs' ('Amen') is typical:

The decayed one gliding through the rotting room;
Shadows on yellow tapestries; the ivory sadness
Of our hands is vaulted in dark mirrors.

Through fingers that have died the brown beads run.
In the silence
The blue cornflower eyes of an angel open.

Blue the evening also;
The hour of our extinction, shadow of Azrael
Which makes a small brown garden darker.

'The decayed one' reads like a periphrasis for the poet him-
self; Trakl's other poems, which hardly ever contain the
word 'I', suggest that this deeply self-divided man preferred
his presence to be inferred from his idiosyncrasies of presen-
tation. But the plural forms in the remainder of the poem
suggest that this decayed one is representative of all mankind.
The figure, or figures, moves in the first stanza like a ghost
through an ornate room that mirrors his distress. In the
second stanza the figure or figures have died, and movement
is transferred to the rosary beads and the eyes of the angel;
as if brought back to life by this movement, the figure becomes
aware in the final stanza of the world beyond the room,
reposes for a moment in contentment at the blueness of the
evening (blue being almost always used by Trakl to mean some-
thing positive) and finally records other spectral movements,
analogous to those with which the poem has opened, move-
ments which revive his awareness of the horizon of death.
In the last line the shadow of the Angel of Death of occult
Hebrew tradition – compare the 'Azrael' Symphony of Josef
Suk – is given an active purchase upon the external world
which the poet has characteristically denied himself. Trakl's
other proper names – Elis, Helian, Sebastian and the
mysterious Elai (which may be nothing more than a cry of

lamentation) – also seem to have been modelled on Biblical or saintly figures: Helian, for example, is very close to the German word for Saviour, and the poem 'Helian' makes unmistakable allusions to the story of Christ's passion. The presence of an angel and of rosary beads, together with the title 'Amen', consolidate the feeling that Trakl is concerned with the fundamentally religious issues of death, judgement, intercession, and transcendence. Another of Trakl's letters may be relevant in this connection:

I yearn for the day when the soul can and will no longer dwell in the poisoning miseries of the body, to which it bequeaths these configurations of mockery, filth and decay, all too evidently mirror-images of a godless and cursed century.

'God,' Trakl continues, 'only a small spark of true joy – and man would thrive; Love – and man would be redeemed.' This leaves open the question of whether man is to blame for departing from God, or God for departing from man; but the question of who is to blame was evidently, for Trakl, less important than the fact that they are definitely separate from one another. A longing for transcendence must, it would seem, have been one of the predisposing causes of his suicide; at all events it fuelled his obsessive articulation of what, for want of a better word, we may call 'visionary' poetry. Trakl appears to have disorganized his sensibility in the radical manner proposed by Rimbaud in the famous letter to Paul Démeny, though whether he did so systematically (as Rimbaud suggested) we may legitimately doubt. Trakl certainly never possessed Rimbaud's reckless, and ultimately misplaced confidence that the 'visionary' poet could actually bring new worlds into being.

Trakl's scepticism was not, however, so total as to prevent him from hypothesizing, and occasionally experiencing, the state of beatitude to which the 'visionary' poet must naturally aspire. At the end of one of his most eloquent poems, 'Song Of The Departed', Trakl consoles himself with images of apotheosis:

Out of black minutes of madness, then, the patient sufferer

Always awakes more lustrous at the petrified threshold,
And the cool blue and the glimmering inclination of autumn,
The silent house and the forest legends,
Proportion and precept and the moonpaths of the departed
Embrace him with power.

To rise above the 'black minutes of madness' to which he
was exceptionally prone, Trakl retired within the narrow
confines of his own imaginary world, conjuring ephemeral
solace from the fragments and figments he found there. Yet
for an exceptionally introspective poet Trakl unquestionably
gives the impression of having confronted the fundamental
issues raised by man's knowledge that he must die. His
hunger for death seems to have stemmed directly from his
need to experience the eternal life promised by the scriptures.
In his last year of life, faced with the appalling horror of the
Eastern Front, Trakl seems to have wavered in his faith that
eternity was the only alternative to an unacceptable reality;
'Lament', for example, presents eternity as a kind of predator:

Sleep and death, the darkening eagles
Swoop round this head the livelong night:
The icy wave of all eternity
Would swallow up the golden image
Of mankind. His purple flesh
Is shattered on awful reefs.
And the dark voice
Laments across the sea.
Sister of tempestuous sadness,
Look, an anxious boat subsides
Beneath stars,
The silent countenance of night.

Enigmatic though 'Lament' may be, it has a momentum and
authority which compel us to recognize that it is not his own
fate but the fate of mankind at large that Trakl is concerned
with. Slightly less terse, though actually more ambiguous, are
the last seven lines of Trakl's last poem, written in the Polish
town where he was dealing with war casualties whose suffer-
ings he could not relieve:

Under the golden twigs of night and stars
The sister's shadow glimmers through the silent copse,
Greeting the ghosts of heroes, bleeding heads;
And the dark flutes of autumn sound imperceptibly in the reeds.
O prouder sorrow! You bronze altars,
The spirit's flame is fed today by a more mighty pain,
The unborn grandsons.
('Grodek')

Of the many difficulties raised by these lines the last words
are particularly perplexing; is Trakl, as elsewhere, confirming
the ancient wisdom that 'never to have been born is best'?
Or is he lamenting the fact that the dead soldiers have
been prevented from initiating a lineage, and thus obliquely
dramatizing his own feelings of sterility? Trakl referred to
himself as only partially and belatedly born, and as so often with
his poems the evidence points disconcertingly in two quite
different ways. 'Grodek' has gained considerable currency by
virtue of being Trakl's last poem, written just previous to
what can only be presumed to have been a deliberate attempt
on his own life. But the fact that he died soon after writing
it is almost as much of a hindrance as a help, especially if he
killed himself by accident rather than design.

Trakl ought, given his refractory and enigmatic surface, to
be a permanent source of irritation to the reader, yet his
habits seem endemic rather than wilful, and despite con-
centrating on a very limited number of elements he is hardly
ever strident. He has inevitably been a source of great fascin-
ation to practising poets; he gives the impression of someone
pushing back the boundaries of what can be expressed in
language. It is something of an irony, therefore, that the Witt-
genstein who so delighted in him should have concluded his
first classic work, the *Tractatus*, with the proposition that
'what we cannot speak of, we must consign to silence'. Trakl's
work, however obscure it may be, seems to have been com-
posed in quite a different spirit, as if it were precisely the
things about which we cannot speak which benefit from being
treated in poetic terms.

Fernando Pessoa (1888–1935)

Born in Lisbon, the son of a theatre critic who died whilst he was still a child. Educated in Durban, South Africa, where his stepfather was Portuguese Consul, first at a convent school, then at a grammar school. After a distinguished school career, during which poetry (especially English poetry) became his abiding interest, he briefly attended Lisbon University. Spent the rest of his life as a translator for various commercial companies in Lisbon. Wrote a considerable amount of programmatic criticism in ephemeral literary journals, and mixed with avant-garde and broadly Futurist elements in the Portuguese capital. Gained official recognition as a poet only in the last year of his life, when he published his first volume of poetry in Portuguese; it won him a prize instituted by the Secretariat of National Propaganda. Posthumously famous for the 'heteronymic' figures he developed from 1903 onwards, of which there are no less than nineteen in the prose and poetry he left among his papers, though only three are of paramount importance. Preferred casual employment because it left him time to concentrate on his literary and philosophical interests. Formed close relationships only with the immediate members of his family, with the exception of a typist whom he courted unsuccessfully in 1920. Drank excessively in later life in the bars of his native city, which he hardly ever left, and died there of cirrhosis of the liver at the age of forty-seven. Already regarded as the greatest Portuguese poet since Camoẽs, and likely to grow in stature as more of his voluminous writing becomes more generally available.

*

'The artist,' wrote Baudelaire in his essay 'Of The Essence Of Laughter', 'is an artist only on condition ... that he is ignorant of none of the phenomena of his dual nature'; it was a way of trying to control the volatile vicious circle in which his dual nature moved. But many twentieth-century poets have possessed not so much dual as multiple natures, any or all of which provided the basis for utterance: Hofmannsthal, for example, who moved from lyric poetry to symbolic drama by way of opera libretti and narrative prose, or Antonio Machado, who developed in later life a system of complementary *personae*. 'Would you say,' wrote Machado in *Juan de Mairena* (1936), 'that a man can carry no more than one poet within himself? The opposite would be much more unlikely: that he carried within himself only one.' In 1935, unknown outside his native Portugal, Fernando Pessoa, the most multiple of all modern poets, died of cirrhosis of the liver, leaving his largely posthumous audience to admire the poetic justice whereby in his case name – Pessoa derives from the Latin word *persona* – and fame were so aptly correlated. For Pessoa wrote under as many aliases as Stendhal or Kierkegaard, and not only wrote poetry in Portuguese, but also in French and in English; his last English poem, indeed, dates from only a fortnight before his death. Of the names under which Pessoa wrote poetry, four have become generally known: Alberto Caeiro, Ricardo Reis, Alvaro de Campos and, less remarkably, Fernando Pessoa. These 'heteronyms' (to use Pessoa's own word for them) are not so much 'complementaries' in Machado's sense of the term, but rather testaments to their progenitor's extreme propensity to disbelieve his own existence; they are the reflection, or multiple refractions, of a figure more anxious and less traditional than Machado. Whether they were designed to combat a fear of insanity which oppressed Pessoa from adolescence onwards, or whether they were involuntary projections of a man who in the year of his death admitted 'ever since I was a child, I have tended to create around me a fictitious world' is much less clear. However, what is clear is that this quartet of strange bedfellows should not be misconstrued as evidence of Pessoa's insincerity; in a letter written within a few months of the 'triumphal day' in 1914 which he subsequently regarded as the point of origin for his three most important heteronyms Pessoa wrote: '[my poetry] is written *dramatically*, but is sincere (in my grave sense of the word), just as what King Lear says is sincere, who is not Shakespeare but a creation of his'. He struck a similar note in a letter written shortly before his death: 'Behind the involuntary masks of the poet, the thinker and whatever else, I am essentially a *dramatist*'. Since Pessoa never proved himself adept as a playwright, the contention must obviously be read metaphorically, as must Octavio Paz's suggestion that Caeiro, Reis and de Campos are characters from an unwritten novel. But since each of the heteronyms develops a personality quite distinct from any of the others, there is inevitably a real sense in which, in reading Pessoa, one is witnessing a network of tensions, predominantly tragic in character, of the kind characteristically developed by a dramatic work.

Some years previous to the 'triumphal' day of 1914 Pessoa wrote in a private journal that he had 'attained a pliancy and a reach which enable me to assume any emotion I desire and enter at will into any state of mind'. The remark is ecstatic in the strict sense; it describes how the poet was able to stand outside himself by the unaided manipulation of his faculties. But the first casualty of such a stance was naturally 'Fernando Pessoa'; as the poet himself admitted, the heteronyms were 'the reaction of Fernando Pessoa to his non-existence'. The principal catalyst for this reaction was Alberto Caeiro, the dominant figure or 'master' and to some extent the progenitor of all the other three major heteronyms. Caeiro is the most metaphysical of the four; one cannot help but be reminded of Machado's claim that 'the great poets are defeated metaphysicians'. But Caeiro wills his own defeat as metaphysician; he is always offering metaphysical insights, and then denying them their claim to be considered metaphysical. In poem XXIV of the sequence 'The Keeper Of Sheep' (written in 1914) Caeiro calls this 'an apprenticeship in unlearning', and the whole sequence shows him intent on contributing to the long and respectable tradition of learned ignorance. In poem V, for example, he states categorically that 'The only inner meaning of things/Is their having no sort of inner meaning'. In the terms offered by German phenomenology (with which Pessoa is presumed to have been familiar) we might say that things have existence but no being. As poem XXVI states, a flower and a fruit have 'colour and form/And existence only'. 'Things', as poem XXVII puts it, 'do not have name or personality'. In this respect all names are merely tokens:

Beauty is the name of something which does not exist
Which I give to things in exchange for the pleasure they give me.

(XXVI)

Or, to put it another way, 'what we see of things are the things' (XXIV). In practice, however, this is an almost impossible doctrine to sustain; the very same poem records how difficult it is 'to be just oneself and not see anything but the visible'. For the visible encourages one to think of the invisible and leads one unerringly towards fundamentally mystical speculation. 'My mysticism,' writes Caeiro in poem XXX, 'is not to try to know./It is to live and not think about it.' Caeiro, as will be clear, is actually of far too sceptical a nature to believe his own theories; in poem XXVII he writes: 'In Nature alone the divine, and she is not divine.' This is plainly the product of a faith contaminated by the thinking that has been wished away. And in one of the last poems of this sequence Caeiro cannot in fact resist placing some metaphysical weight upon his avowedly shaky metaphysical foundations and displacing the traditional deity from his scriptural position as universal benefactor of mankind. In poem XLVI Caeiro prides himself on being 'The Argonaut of true feelings' who brings 'to the Universe a new Universe,/ For to the Universe I bring – itself.' This muted pride is at once both justified and unjustified: Caeiro has actually demystified accepted sanctions without in fact benefiting anyone but himself. Perhaps this is one reason why the number of poems attributed to Caeiro diminishes sharply after 1920.

And a decade later Pessoa exposed Caeiro, in 'The Shepherd In Love' poems, to a turbulence from which his peculiar stance ought by rights to have ensured him exemption. It seems probable that Pessoa found Caeiro's position increasingly untenable, and perhaps it is symptomatic that there should even be signs of discomfiture in the basically tranquil first poem which stands at the head of 'The Keeper Of Sheep'.

Caeiro's lapidary pastoral mode seems, at first glance, at the furthest possible remove from that of Ricardo Reis, of whom Pessoa said that he wrote 'better than I do, but with a purism which I consider excessive'. Reis strikes even a Portuguese reader as unduly Latinate, and is much the most difficult of the heteronyms to translate. Yet the formality of Reis cannot disguise the points of contact he shares with Caeiro, of whom he is at once the prophet (Pessoa claimed to have used the name as early as 1912) and the disciple. Reis speaks with impersonal authority on the subjects treated idiosyncratically by Caeiro:

Nature is only a surface.
But its surface is deep
And contains everything
If the eyes look carefully.

Reis is more peremptory than Caeiro, as befits his whole-hearted adoption of the Classical requirement that poetry must be useful. The wisdom of Reis is stoically fatalistic and pessimistic, as for example when he decides that 'short days and sleep' are the defining features of any life, or again when he urges 'Do not hope for anything that is not already within you'. The natural grammatical mood for Reis, who is always implacably reminding us that 'Reality/Is always more or less/ Than what we want', is the imperative:

Sit in the sun. Abdicate
And be king of yourself.

Yet despite his quietism, and in a sense because of it, Reis remains intrigued by those godlike figures who are to be admired precisely because (as Caeiro would have liked) 'they do not think their existence'. Reis is especially fascinated by those expatriated deities who 'Make us offend/Against Jupiter and Apollo' (Classical ideals of excellence) by deluding us into believing that there is actually a world beyond this one. And the prime offender in this regard is unequivocally the 'sad Christian God' who would have us believe that Pan is dead, and whose doctrine makes almost inaudible 'the ancient rhythm which belongs to bare feet'. What Reis wishes to stimulate in his readers is the belief that they are themselves exiled deities, and deities who can become once more as gods if they adopt his regimen, and so 'not have/Even the remorse/Of having lived'. Why this should not be as much a delusion as that which other expatriated deities seek to impose is something that can never be properly confronted in this essentially circular argument; Reis even permits himself the luxury of thinking that 'The gods will surely thank us/For being so much like them'. It is entirely characteristic of his position that he should end one poem with the proposition 'who I am and what I was/Are different dreams'. He is particularly vulnerable when he wryly asks the gods to permit him to ask for nothing, or when he seeks, however vainly, an exit from 'the dungeon of being what I am'.

Reis's classicism, which is inevitably a neo-classicism, is quite distinct from the avant-gardism of Alvaro de Campos. Campos has no system of belief that he can repose any confidence in, and the 'terrible cold' from which he is suffering, however physical it may be, needs more than aspirin to cure it. It is precisely a measure of his plight that in one famous poem Campos should juxtapose truth and aspirin as if the former were little more than a trivial pain-killer like the latter. Such desperate remedies actually make little impression on Campos's imprisonment within 'a nothing which hurts'. His imprisonment is very powerfully rendered in a poem which alludes to the story of Narcissus and also to the ancient proverbial notion that truth might be found at the bottom of a well:

How often I have leaned
Over the well I suppose I am

And bleated 'Ah' to hear an echo,
And have not heard more than what I saw . . .

The extremity of Campos's condition is reflected in the way he finds it a 'happy' idea that 'we in this world should be mere pens and ink/With which someone writes'. And yet, despite its desiccating implications, the idea offers marginally more comfort than is possible in the dreadful insomnia which another poem records. The very fact that it is only an idea, however, exposes it as but one more metaphysical aspirin. This is confirmed in the famous long poem 'Tobacconist's' where the cigarette that Campos is smoking is intended to perform a similar role, but cannot prevent the appallingly desolate admission (of particular poignancy in the case of Pessoa):

When I wanted to take off the mask
It was stuck to my face.
When I took it off and saw myself in the mirror
I had already grown old.

Campos's career, which had begun with the Futurist vitalism of the 'Triumphal Ode' of 1914 and which, in the much finer 'Excerpt From An Ode', had conjured a real moon out of all-encompassing Night, reaches its nadir in this extraordinary poem, which is only equalled in intensity by the other late poems in which Campos is dispersed in 'the sound of the rain' and reduced to 'a heap of fragments'.

Pessoa's Portuguese poems in his own name are, like his English ones, very formal, though without the 'purism' of Reis. A winter poem of 1929 actually acknowledges the absurdity of writing 'five quatrains of eight syllables' when his only audience is his own solitude. There are slightly more positive intimations, however, in the famous quatrain poem of 1932 'Autopsychography', a kind of gloss on Shakespeare's 'the truest poetry is the most feigning'. Pessoa *in propria persona* (insofar as the notion has any meaning in this context) is no less aware than Caeiro that 'the words I say are a sound only', and no less aware than Campos that 'I am no one'. Even the Platonic and idealist strain in his love poems is the product of a fantasy compensating wildly for an irremediable solitude. Yet the fact that the poems of 'Fernando Pessoa' are more full of yearning than those of the other heteronyms is significant; for they are the only ones that embody anything resembling a doctrine in which he might believe. In 'Initiation', 'Eros and Psyche' and 'At The Tomb of Christian Rosencreuz' this doctrine is revealed as Rosicrucianism. Certainly the secular history of Portugal, which provided Pessoa with the material for the sequence *Message* – the only volume Pessoa published in Portuguese, in his lifetime – offered no comparable solace. *Message* won for Pessoa, in the year of his death, a prestigious national prize for patriotic poetry, although it deals almost exclusively – as was unavoidable for Pessoa, and an accurate reflection of the historical fate of Portugal – with the heroes of an irretrievably lost empire.

Pessoa is a deeply melancholic figure who, despite his un-heroic stance, may be called a tragic poet; his condition permits of no permanent remedy, only limited and temporary relief. There is a discursive strain in him which is painfully evident in his early sonnets in English (where he sounds like a lame contemporary of Shakespeare), and which survives into his later and most mature writing in a manner that can make him unattractive to some tastes. But his best poems invest this strain with such power that it cannot be dismissed as an excrescence upon a fundamentally lyric talent, no matter which *persona* is presumed to be speaking.

Giuseppe Ungaretti
(1888–1970)

Born in Alexandria of Italian emigrants in a city suburb on the edge of the desert. Attended a school where the lessons were given in French. After a rebellious youth left Egypt for Paris in 1912, visiting Italy for the first time on the way. Enrolled at the Sorbonne as a law student, but pursued his literary and philosophical interests and made many friends among the Parisian avant-garde, and later associated with the Italian Futurists. Fought in the Italian infantry during the First World War and after returning to Paris at the end of the war, where he married, took up residence in Rome in 1921. Culturally attracted by Mussolini and the ideology of Fascism, from both of which he took refuge in the years 1931–35 by lecturing all over Europe on Italian literature. Became Professor of Italian Literature at the University of Sao Paulo, Brazil, in 1936. In 1939 his son died of misdiagnosed appendicitis. Returned to a professorship in Rome in 1942, by which time his importance as a poet was widely recognized. Subsequently devoted much of his energy to translation. Travelled very extensively in his old age, especially after the death of his wife in 1958. Died in Milan after contracting bronchitis on a winter visit to New York.

In the course of his 'Second Discourse on Leopardi', Ungaretti provides the reader of his own poetry with what is effectively a discourse on how best to approach it:

The art of words imposes a radical metamorphosis. If I say: tree – everyone thinks of a tree; but nothing is less like a tree than the

word I pronounce. Perhaps the word was in the first instance
onomatopoeic; but suddenly the metaphor intervened to free it from
any imitation of nature, to make it an expression of human nature,
to adapt it to express surprise, terror, rapture, necessity, affection,
the sacred, remote and close relationships between objects, and the
renewed participation of the subject in those relationships – a
subject in whom there should always be a thirst for knowledge so
that he may constantly transform reality into his own symbol.

The single most resonant word in this complex utterance is
naturally 'symbol'; Ungaretti is obviously thinking in a
manner which bears some resemblance to that of the
proponents and practitioners of French Symbolism, and in
particular to Mallarmé. Elsewhere Ungaretti admits the
profound effect that reading Mallarmé had upon him as a
young man: 'I threw myself at Mallarmé, I read him pas-
sionately and no doubt did not understand him to the letter;
but understanding poetry to the letter matters little: I felt it.'
It is not so much of Mallarmé the poet, however, as Mallarmé
the prose writer that Ungaretti's discourse on Leopardi is
likely to make one think, and especially those writings in
which Mallarmé develops the idea that poetic creation is the
conception of an object in its absence and that poetry is not
a representational art but a means of creating a network of
relationships. Interviewed shortly before his death Ungaretti
described his own work in words that might almost be Mal-
larmé's: 'this poetic is bred of a feeling that one can ... only
grasp things in their most profound reality when they no
longer exist'. And later in the interview Ungaretti classes
himself with Mallarmé and (rather more controversially)
with Leopardi as poets 'for whom things exist only from the
moment they are created' by the poem. The 'act of words' is
not, then, in Ungaretti's view, restricted – as the empiricists
would have us believe – to the designation of things. Like
Mallarmé he believes that 'Things already exist' and that
the 'act of words' is to *re-create* them. This view is very
close, as Ungaretti came to realize, to that branch of modern
philosophy which is called phenomenology, which states that
one can only describe objects by suspending belief in their

existence as objects. And in speaking of the estrangement of words from things Ungaretti is obviously very close to the view developed, under the guise of Lord Chandos, by Hofmannsthal in his 'word-sceptic' phase. But a permanent estrangement between words and things does not form part of Ungaretti's poetics; 'through words', he writes elsewhere, 'objects may rediscover and confirm the sensual truth of reality'. This is something that the super-sensual Mallarmé might have found it difficult to accept; his later poems in fact reflect the difficulties he had in sustaining such a position. But Ungaretti was continually rediscovering and confirming the sensual truth of reality, which is one reason why his poetry, though often very difficult, makes an immediate impact upon a reader in a way that Mallarmé's very rarely does.

Ungaretti is naturally closest to Mallarmé in the years when he read him avidly, though his manner is quite different. The early poem, 'Eternal', for example, which is only two lines long, reads like a gloss upon Mallarmé's remarks about 'the flower absent from all bouquets':

Between one flower plucked and the other given
The inexpressible nullity

A poem of 1916, 'The Buried Harbour', is a similarly Orphic utterance on the subject of nullity and inexpressibility:

The poet descends
then returns to the light with his songs
and scatters them

Of this poetry
there remains for me
that nullity
of inexhaustible secrecy

'We are cut off from our depths,' wrote Ungaretti in an essay on the estrangement of words and things; 'only the secret still counts.' But though his poetry is concerned with secrets, it is not offered to us in a secretive manner. As 'The Buried Harbour' makes clear, he is seeking to restore us to the depths from which we have departed. Like much modern poetry which at first glance seems whimsical, self-indulgent or merely eccentric, Ungaretti's contains an ethical component. In the same essay which deals with how cut off we are from our depths, Ungaretti states: 'Today everything which provided the custom and rhetoric upon which human discourse was founded – all this is untenable; nor is it possible, I believe, to devise a new rhetoric because the falsity of all conventions is instantly recognizable.' In such a climate the poet's task becomes one of conferring a pristine innocence on the words he is using; in early Ungaretti each utterance seems like an unprecedented revelation offering us access to our origins. Though obviously inspired by the Symbolists, Ungaretti is orientated towards clarity rather than mystery. In another poem of 1916, 'Sunset', a subject the Symbolists had been much concerned with, he ruthlessly prunes away their rhetoric, leaving the essential precipitate behind:

The flushed face of sky
awakens oases
in the nomad of love

An almost fetishistic attitude to language like Mallarmé's has here been replaced by what Ungaretti himself called an 'excavation of the word'. The last poem in his first published volume ('Envoi'; *The Buried Harbour*, 1916) describes, and at the same time embodies, Ungaretti's early practice:

When I find
in this silence of mine
a word
it is excavated from my life
like an abyss

Baudelaire and Mallarmé, in their very different ways, had treated the subject of the abyss in a manner consistent with their respective attempts to transcend it; Ungaretti contrives to make it seem physically present, a constitutive element in reality, one of those 'inexpressible nullities' that are never-theless substantial.

Ungaretti reprinted the poems of *The Buried Harbour* as a

subsection within the volume of 1919, *Joy of Shipwrecks* (later revised and republished as simply *Joy* in 1931). The image of shipwreck once again points back to Mallarmé, and beyond him to Leopardi. But in Ungaretti's predecessors there is far less flotsam and jetsam and joy is conspicuous by its absence. Ungaretti's comments on the 'strange' title of his second volume illustrate what kind of joy he is seeking to promote. 'Strange it would be,' he writes, 'if everything were not in fact a shipwreck, if everything were not swept away, suffocated, consumed by time;' but even out of this dark vision of the fleeting moment an affirmation may emerge, a 'joy whose origin may only be consciousness of the presence of death to be exorcized'. Ungaretti's experiences at the front during the First World War (epitomized by the famous poem 'Vigil') had naturally made him hypersensitive to 'the presence of death'. A close friend, whose death is commemorated in the superb 'In Memoriam', had committed suicide. Ungaretti had every reason to be much possessed by death. But there are many poems in *Joy of Shipwrecks* which suggest that death may be exorcized, especially if one is prepared to be shattered and dispersed into the circumambient universe. This is memorably dramatized in the last four lines of a 1916 poem called 'Gully at Night':

Unending time
makes use of me
as a
rustle

The joy of an Ungaretti shipwreck is when it provides him with access to this 'unending time'. And in the fourteen years between his second and third collections he was occupied with this distinctly Ungarettian matter rather than with any reversions to even vaguely Mallarméan material.

Ungaretti had fought in the Italian army, but he had been born and brought up in Alexandria and had lived largely in Paris from 1912 onwards. Only in 1921 did he take up permanent residence in Italy; he was appointed to a government post in Rome. Rome prompted Ungaretti to assimilate his largely cosmopolitan ideas to native traditions, mainly because of its abundant manifestations of the Baroque spirit. Without abandoning the premises of his early work (though he was unduly susceptible to the rhetoric of Mussolini) Ungaretti transformed himself into a neo-Baroque poet. But the transformation was a logical development of his previous 'shipwrecks'; Ungaretti's Baroque is 'a feeling of something shattered', indeed a succession of shipwrecks. He particularly admired the Baroque strategy of developing 'an excess of units in order to give the impression that emptiness has been eliminated'; he had a horror of the void comparable to that of Michelangelo. Ungaretti saw the 'excess of units' in Baroque art and architecture as expressive of 'a kind of purer reality without substance' and regarded it as the form *par excellence* which 'shatters and reconstitutes'. Within these terms it is clear that the 'Hymn to Death' of 1925 (one of the major poems in his third collection, *The Sense of Time*) is a Baroque poem:

Unmindful sister, death,
You will make me the equal of dream
With your kiss.

I shall have your footstep.
I shall walk without leaving an imprint.

The same is true of a poem of 1927, 'Breeze', which has a less expansive manner and indeed recalls the terse Ungaretti of the early poems:

Hearing the sky
a morning sword
and the hill which climbs into its lap
I return to the accustomed harmony

A tired thicket of trees
grips the foot of the incline.

From the network of branches
I see the rebirth of flight.

At this point Ungaretti also grafted a revived Christian element on to what had previously been primarily a matter of aesthetics, the most memorable expression of which is the poem 'Pietà' of 1928. This deeply confessional attempt to arrive at and yet transcend the point 'where is heard/The man alone with himself' oscillates between utterances of abject dereliction ('I am tired of howling soundlessly') and statements of power ('I have peopled the silence with names'). But the burden of the whole poem is concentrated into the final lines of the original version:

My eyes would once again become innocent,
I would see the eternal spring

And, definitively new,
O memory, you would be honest.

'We have to regress,' wrote Ungaretti in the essay 'On Estranged Words', 'to the condition of our original innocence by means of memory: then poetry perhaps may regain its emotional prestige'. In the sequence 'Death Meditated' of 1932 this idea is grounded in a compelling development of the issues of original sin aroused by the Biblical story of Eve and the Fall. But it is evident from this sequence that Ungaretti's Christianity is a complex of negative and positive emotions, and the same is true of the sequence of love poems with which he brings *The Sense of Time* to an end. Casting himself, as he so often does, in the role of desert nomad, Ungaretti includes among them a poem ('Bedouin Song') which is a series of cumulative statements, much more rhetorical than in his early poems, but essentially simple and declarative:

A woman arises and sings
the wind follows her and enchants her
and lays her on the earth
and the true dream seizes her.

This earth is bare
this woman is beloved
this wind is strong
this dream is death.

Ungaretti's fourth collection (*Grief*, 1947) is a very personal outcry of the kind that would have ruined a poem like 'Bedouin Song'. The whole volume is dominated by the emotions aroused by the death, in 1939, of his nine-year-old son. The sequence 'Day By Day' (indicative of Ungaretti's new 'sense of time') is an ambitious attempt to come to terms with this, as is the famous 'You Were Shattered' which begins with the bare Brazilian earth in which his son had been buried. But in some ways the most important poem in the volume is 'Earth', for here 'the silent/Outcry of the dead is louder' than the sound of the wind in the trees which (like the wind of 'Bedouin Song') is the poet's periphrasis for inspiration. It is the ability of the dead to live again, like the Christ in Masaccio's painting of the Crucifixion (the subject of 'The Dead On Mountains') which tempers the poet's grief and which points forward to his next collection, *The Promised Land*. One cannot help but remember Ungaretti's definition of the Baroque as a style which 'shatters and reconstitutes', but in *Grief*, at least, reconstitution is more of a hope than a conviction.

The Promised Land (1950) is by no means as affirmative as its title might lead one to expect. The most ambitious poem in the volume is the exceptionally difficult 'Canzone', which can only really be understood with the help of the poet's own commentaries on it. The much less turbulent 'Variations On Nothing', in which Ungaretti employs the age-old image of time as an hourglass, is a much more moving poem. Ungaretti seems to have come to terms here with a humanity which is intrinsically tragic: 'I know by now,' he writes, 'that the thread of the human/Web must seem to shatter.' In accordance with this is Ungaretti's renewed interest in stories from classical literature of an ostensibly tragic character; for Dido at the hour of sunset and for Palinurus at the hour of hurricane the human web does indeed seem doomed to shatter. In this sense 'the promised land' would appear to be less a benediction than a fate; an unmistakably Stoical element begins here to complicate the troubled Catholicism of the 'Hymns' in *The Sense of Time*. As if to underline the fact that his vision had taken on a darker colouring Ungaretti pub-

lished in the same year as *The Promised Land*, 1950, a trans-
lation of Racine's great tragic drama *Phèdre*.

Ungaretti published three further collections of poetry in his
last twenty years, years in which he was enthusiastically
acclaimed all over the world as one of Italy's two great living
poets. But, as in the case of Montale (whose world fame has
since threatened to eclipse Ungaretti's), it is difficult not to
feel that his later poetry is largely footnotes to the volumes
which had earned him so much justified respect. The 'Short
Monologue' from *A Cry and Landscapes* (1952) is memorable; so
are the 'Last Choruses For The Promised Land' from *The Old
Man's Notebook* (1960); but the early monologues and the
'Choruses Descriptive of Dido's State of Mind' are much more
moving, and much more coherently organized. Like Saba
before him, and Montale after him, Ungaretti began to think
of his poetry as a kind of autobiography; from 1943 onwards
he published his works under the title *Life of a Man*. But the
later poems seem more important to the life of a man than
to his poetry, if one may make a distinction that Ungaretti
himself was intent on abolishing. Taken as a whole, however,
one cannot be in any doubt that, for a poetry preoccupied
with death, Ungaretti's work is life-affirming and life-
enhancing. And to those who would query the presence in it
of fantastic elements, or of elements that seem regressive,
Ungaretti's numerous commentaries provide a cogent de-
fence of his practice, culminating in one of the most pas-
sionate statements of his faith, as exemplified by any one of his
best poems:

There is no artistic product, no identity between intuition and
expression, if fantasy and memory, both of them necessary functions
of intuition, do not become functions of expression.

Pierre Reverdy (1889–1960)

Born in Narbonne, the son of a winegrower. Educated there in *lycées* until 1910. Moved to Paris in 1910 where, on the death of his father, he became wholly dependent on his writing. Enjoyed the respect of the Parisian avant-garde writers and painters, and became editor of the review *Nord–Sud* in 1917. Married and returned to the Catholic faith in 1926, when he took up residence near the Benedictine abbey of Solesmes, living a secluded and ascetic life, though making sporadic visits to Paris. Died in Solesmes. A major influence on French poetry since the Second World War.

In an influential essay on Cubist painting the art critic John Berger has written

[it is] impossible to *confront* the objects of forms in a Cubist work. Not only because of the multiplicity of viewpoints – so that, say, a view of a table from below is combined with a view of the table from above or from the side – but also because the forms portrayed never present themselves as a totality. The totality is the surface of the picture, *which is now the origin and sum of all that one sees.*

The paintings that Berger primarily has in mind are those painted by Georges Braque and Pablo Picasso – often so similar that two quite different personalities seem to have merged into one – in the years 1907–12, the 'moment of Cubism' as he aptly calls it. But these remarks may also be applied to a poet who was instrumental in continuing the moment of Cubism well beyond the years Berger sees as those of 'maximum Cubist achievement' and extending Cubist practice into literature: Pierre Reverdy. To confront Reverdy's poetry is not, of course, strictly speaking impossible; it is not, however, a confrontation in any traditional sense. Once again Berger has admirably expressed what is taking place:

The Cubists created the possibility of art revealing processes ... The content of their art consists of various modes of interaction: the interaction between different aspects of the same event, between empty space and filled space, between structure and movement, between the seer and the thing seen.

Almost any poem by Reverdy will illustrate how disconcerting the realization of these 'modes of interaction' can be. Here, with its processes inevitably reduced by the act of translation, is a famous poem ('Departure') from the collection *The Slates From The Roof* (1918):

The horizon tilts
        The days lengthen
        Voyage
    A heart leaps in a cage
        A bird sings
        It will die
Another door will open
        At the end of the passage
        Where suddenly lit up
        A star
A dark woman
    The lamp of the departing train

'On each slate/which slides from the roof', run the lines which explain the title of the volume in which this poem appears, 'a poem/has been/written'; this slate (or slates), like all the others in the volume, seems perfectly designed to shatter its reader's preconceptions before it even hits the ground, as if detonated in mid-air or in a fragmentary state from the moment it leaves its place of repose and first makes contact with the air.

It is natural to relate a poem like 'Departure' to the practice of the Cubist painters; one cannot but 'look at' it before one attempts to 'read' it. Yet, as Reverdy reminds us in his explanatory gloss, it has been written and not painted; the idiosyncratic typography insists that we regard it as a written communication since its pictorial properties are in fact limited, nothing like so graphically controlled as the 'picture poems' of Apollinaire, for example. The individual words could not be simpler; each line, taken as an individual unit, is a straightforward description or proposition. But none of them, as Berger's analysis points out with respect to the forms of Cubist painting, is a totality; the totality, if there is one, includes the space which encompasses the words or in which the words float. And the two together are 'the origin and sum of all that one sees' or reads. But blank spaces in a poem operate in a different way from their counterparts in painting or, for that matter, in music; they are signs of non-communication to a degree that effectively prevents them being participants in a communication. Especially so, perhaps, when the words they surround are such common ones; for the very familiarity of such words makes one surprised to find them in a poem. It is as if the poet's typewriter has miraculously overheard them being uttered by a passer-by, but has been unable to articulate the context which will make them meaningful. 'So it is,' Mallarmé told a fellow-poet in 1888, 'that the poet disappears (this is unquestionably the great discovery of modern poetry) and the verse itself projects its own passions through its leaps and bounds; and so verse is born, rather than being imposed or brutally thrust upon us by the writer.' Or, as expressed in an essay first published in 1895, 'typography becomes a ritual'. But in Mallarmé the ceremony, however mysterious it may be, is to celebrate an ideal beauty; in Reverdy there is nothing ceremonial and it is reality which is in question. In a book of prose meditations, *The Sackcloth Glove* of 1927, Reverdy describes in a discursive manner what a poem like 'Departure' is content to leave to the ingenious reader:

The poet is in an always difficult and sometimes perilous position,
at the intersection of two planes with very sharp edges which point
in different directions, the plane of dream and the plane of reality.

Reverdy's position is plainly more intractable than that of
his illustrious predecessors; conscious, like Baudelaire, of being
'two people in one, each one of whom observes the other',
terrified, like Mallarmé, of remaining 'fatally imprisoned in
the created work' (and yet equally intent on 'plunging . . . into
the mirror of abysses in order to scrutinize one's own founda-
tions'), Reverdy inhabits an unstable middle ground in which
every position is an interim one except insofar as there are no
events on either side of it to make it so. It is not surprising to
learn, from an interview he gave in 1948, that Reverdy feared
for his sanity; he even went so far as to say that if he had not
written he might well have gone clinically insane. 'By
writing,' he went on, 'I have saved myself'; 'inasmuch as you
write, speak, publish, even if your words make not the slight-
est echo resonate – you are not alone.' The poems, however,
are rarely even as minimally redemptive as these remarks
suggest: the collections published previous to Reverdy's with-
drawal to the Benedictine abbey of Solesmes are studded
with *cris de coeur* like that which almost leaps from the page
of one of the *Poems In Prose* of 1915: 'Lines in my head, nothing
but lines; if I could only order them a little.' 'I could neither
rise nor descend,' wrote Reverdy later. Like his predecessors
he considered the image to be 'a pure creation of the spirit'.
Like those who came after him (especially the Surrealists – in
1924 André Breton described him as 'the greatest living poet')
he regarded the dream as 'a special category of thought'. But
neither images nor dreams could he wholeheartedly believe
in; and his acute sense of absence or non-existence rendered
'the plane of the real' as agonizing as any other. It is the way
in which different planes disclosed themselves to him as in-
commensurable which accounts for the dislocated and
volatile surface of poems like 'Departure'. And the humble
language employed is tantamount to a confession that this
poet has no access to the verbal magic which those before and

after him could lay claim to. In this respect Reverdy is not so much a prophet of the plenitude (puzzling though it may be) of Surrealism as of the minimalist art which has enjoyed such currency since 1945. A comparable, and in some ways equally neglected, figure is the composer Anton Webern.

An individual Reverdy poem looks, and is designed to look, more vulnerable than a single poem by almost anyone else. But by concentrating, perhaps involuntarily, on a limited number of motifs, the particles which remain mysterious in isolation very nearly begin to add up to a world. Annunciations are always being made, but either there is no one there to hear them, or the person who hears them cannot understand them. The very presence of a human being becomes doubtful; one is reminded of John Berger's point that the Cubist painters 'do not illustrate a human or social situation, they posit it'. The virtual replacement of a subjective 'I' by a depersonalized eye means that Reverdy is always, as he says in the aptly-titled 'Myself' (in the 1919 collection *The Guitar Asleep*, a title with obvious Cubist affiliations), 'on the threshold'. His peculiar style is not merely mannerist; it is a reflection of his condition. And as with any condition there are moments of alleviation; in one poem from *The Guitar Asleep*, for example, 'Noises Of Waking', he can actually believe that 'the earth is full'. Even if it is empty the act of writing provides temporary relief; an unusually expansive poem in the collection *Great Nature* (1925) concludes:

And if all that I have seen has deceived me
If there is nothing behind this canvas
but an empty hole
What reassures me a little is that I can always keep myself
    within limits ...
And leave on the earth a faint memory
A gesture of regret
A bitter grimace
        which I had better do

The difficulty for Reverdy – as the longest of these lines ironically reminds us – is that there are really no limits, for he is looking for 'a lost address in the hidden street' and there is no one and nothing (except the intermittent flashes of what he sees) to point him in the right direction. As the opening lines of a famous later poem put it:

The world is my prison
If I am far from what I love

But he cannot help but be some distance from what he might love, and only occasionally is he granted glimpses of an escape from the imprisonment of solitude.

There is a poem in the collection *The Song of the Dead* (1948; with lithographs by Picasso) in which Reverdy says that it is possible to die from remaining too long in the same position; written during the Second World War, it partially reflects Reverdy's agonized reaction to the war, and obviously expresses a truth that those involved in the war would have had no difficulty in substantiating. But there is a sense in which, in poetic terms, Reverdy did precisely this. Although his later poetry is given an increased urgency by the proximity of death, his resources were not such as to permit him much room for movement. As a miniaturist, albeit of the most subtle and exacting kind, he contributed to his own neglect. Although he frequently visited literary Paris from his retreat at Solesmes he did not, and obviously could not, cut a charismatic figure. Yet he was deeply respected, and not only by his countrymen. There is a very moving tribute to Reverdy where one might least expect it, in that section of Pablo Neruda's *Memoirs* designed to demonstrate that 'poetry is an occupation' like any other, a surprising confirmation of the fact that, in the magnetic field of poetry, like poles repel and opposite poles attract, even when one great poet reads his own preconceptions into another. 'Reverdy was a physical poet,' Neruda writes; 'his poetry was like a vein of quartz, subterranean but filled with light.' The images are very apposite, and Neruda's characteristic multiplication of them does nothing to make them less so:

Sometimes it threw off a hard glitter, like the sheen of some black mineral torn with difficulty from its thick covering of earth.

Suddenly it flew out like a spark from a match, or hid in the gallery of its mine, far from the light of day, but faithful to its own truth. Perhaps this truth, which identified the substance of his poetry with nature, this Reverdian tranquillity, this unflagging honesty, gradually paved his way to oblivion. He was eventually taken for granted by others, like a natural phenomenon, a house, river or familiar street that would never change its outward appearance or its place.

This is not just an example of Neruda rhapsodizing upon a theme; it is a genuine attempt to stimulate the reader who has taken Reverdy for granted to a reassessment, and also to create for the reader who has never grappled with him the taste whereby he might be enjoyed. It explains why André Breton's 'greatest living poet' has had nothing like the impact of his contemporary, Apollinaire, and none of the influence of the great nineteenth-century French poets who most influenced him. It characterizes his evanescent properties ('like a spark from a match') and the plight that was behind them ('torn with difficulty'). And even Neruda's heavy emphasis on the material rather than the spiritual elements in Reverdy, inevitable in one of Neruda's materialist inclinations, has a certain justification. For Reverdy, much more dramatically than most other modern poets, requires his reader to confront the raw materials out of which his poetry has been made, the contributory particles towards the never-realized salvation of perfect articulation.

Anna Akhmatova (1889–1966)

Born Anna Gorenko near Odessa, the daughter of a naval engineer, but resident throughout her childhood at Pavlovsk and Tsarskoye Selo near St Petersburg. Began to write poetry after a serious illness in 1899 and read widely in European poetry, being familiar with the French nineteenth-century poets. Met her future husband Nikolai Gumilyov at Christmas 1903. Shared the general concern at the Russian fleet's defeat at Tsushima in 1905, the year in which her parents separated and Gumilyov attempted suicide. Chose the name of her Tartar great-grandmother as *nom de plume* in 1906. Lived in Kiev 1906–7, and studied Law and Latin at the University there. Agreed to marry Gumilyov in 1909 and twice visited Paris with him, where she met the painter Modigliani. Lived in Tsarskoye Selo, her husband frequently abroad, until 1912, when together they visited Switzerland, Italy, Austria and Poland. Highly respected in Petersburg circles before the outbreak of the First World War; ill with tuberculosis in a Helsinki sanatorium during the war. Broke with Gumilyov on the eve of the February Revolution of 1917, and thereafter considered herself as essentially a homeless person. A close friend of Mandelstam's in 1917–8 and after his marriage. Remarried in 1918; separated from her second husband in 1921, the year in which Gumilyov was shot for alleged complicity in an anti-Bolshevik plot. Prevented from publishing her poetry from 1925 to 1940. During the Kirov case of 1934 her son by Gumilyov was arrested. Spent seventeen months attempting to secure his release from a Leningrad prison in 1939–40. Met Tsvetaeva for the first time in Moscow in 1940. Evacuated to Chistopol and

Tashkent in 1941. Suffered renewed harrassment after a meeting with Isaiah Berlin in Moscow in 1945; reunited with her son in 1956. Visited Sicily in 1964, where she was awarded a prize for her poetry. Awarded the honorary degree of Doctor of Letters at Oxford University in 1965. Died of a heart attack in Moscow; buried in Leningrad.

In a prose preface composed long after the events commemorated in her poetic cycle *Requiem* (consisting of poems written between 1935 and 1940) Akhmatova offers what amounts to a description of the poet's role at a time of personal and public calamity, in this case the so-called 'years of Yezhov' during which Stalin's crimes against humanity were associated with the man in charge of his secret police:

During the appalling years of Yezhov I spent seventeen months in the queues outside the prison in Leningrad. One day somebody recognized me. Standing alongside me was a woman with blue lips who naturally did not know who I was and who suddenly awoke from that torpor which afflicted us all and whispered in my ear (all of us there spoke in whispers):
   'Can you describe *this*?'
   And I replied: 'Yes, I can'.
   And then something like the shadow of a smile flickered in what had once been her face.

This preface has the simple authority and power of one who has unselfconsciously accepted that she is the voice of her age, that poetry is only justified in a time of distress if the poet is prepared to bear witness, to fix her eyes unwaveringly upon a common reality, to speak fearlessly and to console to the degree that any consolation is possible for those without hope. The frozen lips of the woman who has asked whether poetry can address appalling realities are relaxed into the ghost of a smile, an index of a happiness which, like that referred to in the last words of Thomas Hardy's *The Mayor of Casterbridge*, could only be 'the occasional episode in a general drama of pain'. The question is one that Akhmatova must often have asked herself, for she had first become famous in pre-Revolutionary Petersburg for her miniature studies, with all the 'vertiginous brevity' that she admired so much in Pushkin, of affairs of the heart which had little to do with the public realities of the century. Perhaps the very disclosure of her name rang a remote bell in the mind of her questioner. And yet in truth there was no reason for the woman to know that she was standing beside one of her country's great poets; between 1922 (when her fifth collection of lyrics was published under the title *Anno Domini*) and 1940 (when a severely censored selection of her work appeared in Leningrad) Akhmatova had become, in the eyes of the authorities, a 'non-person', unable to publish because of the 'reactionary' tendencies of her verse, and persistently harrassed because she had once been married to a poet executed for his supposedly counter-revolutionary sentiments. Like Boris Pasternak, who in a poem of 1928 had stood out against her critics and praised her for maintaining links with Russia's past, and like Osip Mandelstam, who had increasingly come to think of her as a Cassandra-like prophet of impending doom, Akhmatova had been effectively silenced. But out of the years of silence and whispering emerged, against all odds, a voice of unshakable convictions about poetry's need to tell harsh truths, speaking with such power that by the end of her life Akhmatova was everywhere recognized as the leading spokesman for what the Russian people had suffered in the aftermath of Revolution. Acclaimed in 1916 (notably by Marina Tsvetaeva in a sequence of poems in her honour) as the 'Muse of lamentation', Akhmatova had by the end of her life become identified with the lamentations and aspirations of a whole people, as if in confirmation of her friend Mandelstam's prediction (made in the pre-Revolutionary period) that she would become 'a major symbol of Russia's grandeur', though the years of Yezhov and Stalin did all they could to make any talk of grandeur seem out of the question.

Even in the decade or so leading up to the first denunciations of her poetry as irrelevant to revolutionary socialism Akhmatova had spoken on public themes. 'July 1914', for example, is a poem warning of the horrors of pan-European conflict; 'When In Suicidal Anguish' of 1917 confronts the realities of Revolution; 'To The Many', written at a time of the mass exodus from Russia during the Civil War which followed, is an expression of her determination to remain, through thick and thin, 'with my people' (in the words of the famous quatrain at the head of *Requiem*). The *Anno Domini* poems published in 1922 consolidate the impression that her own private sufferings were beginning to seem representative and emblematic of the sufferings all around her. Yet it must be admitted that the bulk of Akhmatova's early poetry was prompted mainly by her volatile personal life, even if she did treat her raw material with something of the timeless and impersonal poignancy of folk-poetry. A painstaking attention to details, either of behaviour or as perceived in the external world, enabled Akhmatova to transform essentially senti- mental subject-matter into *tableaux vivants* and miniature dramas appealing to the sophisticated and the unsophisti- cated in equal measure. In the famous 'Song Of The Last Meeting' of 1911, for example, the focus falls on a confused and bewildered woman struggling vainly to thrust her right hand into a left-hand glove; the activity is an index of her inner feelings of dereliction at the end of a love affair. These feelings are only verbalized later in the poem when the solitary woman engages in conversation with an autumnal tree whose whisperings seem to be soliciting her to join in its death-throes. The last meeting to which the title primarily refers has taken place before the poem begins: the woman and her lover have parted. But the exchange with the tree is also a kind of last meeting: the woman is encountering a tree which cannot live much longer, and she is tempted to regard death as the only release from her emotional con- fusion. Without making her state of mind explicit, Akhmatova concentrates the reader's attention on the 'indif- ferent yellow flame' of candles burning in the 'dark house' which the woman is approaching, and on the cold stone steps which lead to it. The details give weight and solidity to a scenario which is elusive and evanescent, full of nuance like Symbolist poetry and yet quite without any sense of a transcendental mystique as the originating impulse of the poem.

In the poem 'I Wrung My Hands Under My Dark Veil', written eight months earlier, Akhmatova describes the actual moment of separation with equally consummate skill. The 'dark veil' which conceals the woman's hands in this poem plays a role similar to that of the glove in 'Song Of The Last Meeting'; it is at once an object in its own right and a prophetic participant in the drama. The movement of the woman's hands is once again an index of her distress, though it is complemented here by the passionate feeling which prompts her to run after the man in a vain attempt to persuade him to return. However, the detail which really focusses the poem is reserved for the end, as the man addresses the woman, roughly and yet as if with some residual concern for her. From his 'tormented' mouth, which he is trying to crystallize into a smile, come the words ' "Don't stand in the wind" '; once again the impression is of something human and mundane, a scene such as might be played out anywhere at any time in the course of a passionate love affair. What makes Akhmatova such a remarkable love poet is her abiding awareness that man and woman are at their most vulnerable when seeking fulfilment in one another and at their most abject when that fulfilment shows signs of proving perishable. The desperate requests for forgiveness (as in 'Black Road Twisted' and 'Wide And Yellow The Evening Light') are balanced by equally urgent injunctions, when all has failed, not to forget, as in the poem 'Parting'. Aleksandr Blok was moved to criticize the early Akhmatova, though he admired her, because she wrote as if a man were looking at her; 'you should write', he told her, 'as if God were looking at you'. But this famous criticism tells us more about Blok and about Symbolism than it does about Akhmatova; the equally famous description of her as 'half harlot, half nun' is much nearer the mark. In 1946, when she was subjected to renewed attacks on her poetry, this phrase was used by the authorities to indicate that neither her sensuality nor her asceticism conformed to the tenets of Socialist Realism, but she had, of course, by then abandoned the early manner which had first given the phrase its currency.

In the early poems of Akhmatova her faith in the spoken words of a lover (whether an actual or potential one) is always in danger of being disappointed; in 'A Ride', 'In The Evening' and 'The Guest' the garments and the ring she wears seem to be her only defence against total surrender. The written words which originate in the poet's soul are, by contrast, much less likely to be misinterpreted; writing becomes (as in the poems of Akhmatova's protégé, Joseph Brodsky) the symbol of a covenant that no amount of personal misery can significantly alter. In a poem of 1914 she describes a visit she made to Aleksandr Blok, during which his piercing eyes seemed to speak as volubly as any one of his famous poems. But Akhmatova's stress falls finally on the words they exchanged, as if speech between poets were more important than any of the more charismatic and perishable features in their make-up. 'He has eyes,' writes Akhmatova, 'that no one/can forget . . . But I remember what we said.' She does not tell us what passed between them, and some have interpreted her reticence to mean that they spoke of very intimate matters; but the abiding impression is that poetry took precedence over passion, and that only poetry possesses the power to provide a bulwark against time, a memorial that will be proof against ephemerality. Almost all Akhmatova's many poems about poetry and poets (and especially those prompted by her favourite writers Dante, Shakespeare and Pushkin) confirm that, for her, the poet was engaged in making past, present and future a single, indivisible thread to withstand any ravages that might threaten it. In this conception, as in Pasternak's, the poet does not so much inhabit historical time, but exists rather in an extratemporal (and hence eternal) continuum; it is easy enough to see why both Pasternak and Akhmatova should have fallen foul of authorities for whom only a tendentious historicism had much meaning.

Akhmatova's experiences during her years of silence naturally enough consolidated her feelings that to be a poet was to speak as one outside time altogether, although the whisper of the blue-lipped woman in the prison queue in Leningrad is a reminder that this did not betoken withdrawal into a world of private fantasy. The *Requiem* cycle, and all the poetry of her last thirty years, is a pledge of remembrance; the last poem of the cycle is a prayer (which needless to say the Soviet authorities have ignored; they have also forbidden the publication of *Requiem* in Soviet editions of Akhmatova) that if the privilege of a memorial should be vouchsafed her, the only appropriate place for it would be outside the prison where for three hundred hours she stood waiting for news of her son. But the anger and bitterness is finally, as befits the title of the sequence, subsumed in a plea for peace. This plea is echoed in another poem of March 1940, 'Way Of All The Earth', where Akhmatova adopts the guise of a legendary pilgrim, but undertakes a pilgrimage through time as well as space, sustained by the quotation from the Revelation of St John the Divine which acts as an epigraph: 'And the angel swore by him that liveth for ever and ever ... that there should be time no longer.' Akhmatova's paradoxical sense of time is relatively clear in 'Way Of All The Earth'; but it is deeply puzzling in 'Poem Without A Hero', that 'triple-bottomed box' (as she called it) containing memories of pre-Revolutionary Petersburg in mysterious interaction not only with the besieged Leningrad of the Second World War but also with a Russia of post-Stalinist reconstruction. Opinions are divided about the merits of this extraordinary poem, begun in 1940 and worked on obsessively thereafter for upwards of twenty years. It is perhaps best approached by way of the fragmentary sequence of 'Northern Elegies' which were also begun at this time. The first elegy goes back to 'Dostoevsky's Russia' and the epigraphs from Pushkin place it in an even more remote context; the poem is aptly titled 'Prehistory'. In the penultimate poem of the sequence Akhmatova attempts to reaffirm the idea that the poet is the supreme agent of continuity, because only the poet can claim to 'know beginnings and ends/And life after the end'. The last of the 'Northern Elegies' is much less affirmative, however; 'we realize,'

Akhmatova wrote in 1953, 'that we could not contain/this past within the confines of our life'. 'Poem Without A Hero' seems to have been inspired by a desire to test the conviction that continuity and containment were impossible against the belief that poetry could remove the barriers between possibilities and impossibilities. Deeply embedded in a poem which appears to be backward-looking are allusions to a 'Guest from the Future'. This figure seems to combine the retributive aspects of the Commendatore in Mozart's *Don Giovanni* (the source for a famous poem by Blok) and the redemptive properties of a Messiah; perhaps Akhmatova was also thinking of the mysterious figures who, in her early poems, offered her either the covenant of marriage or the covenant of poetry. The conception may strike one as unduly literary for a poet avowedly concerned with life. But in the event she found her life could indeed contain such a figure. She identified this 'Guest from the Future' as Sir Isaiah Berlin, whose visit was made the pretext for renewed attacks on her in 1946. The most moving poems to emerge from the brief meeting with Berlin are the fragments collected as 'Sweetbriar Flowers: From A Burnt Notebook'. As a record of meeting and non-meeting they are almost more poignant than the early love poems, a way of giving voice to the 'unspoken speeches' which were all that was left her after that 'tragic autumn'.

The greatness of Akhmatova's later poetry is that, whilst it is quite as stony as the age she was living through, it nevertheless concerns itself with the residual evidences of flesh and blood ingrained in the marble. In the 'flight of time' (as she habitually thought of it) she could still perceive the sounds of what was past and passing and to come. One cannot help but think of Blok who, at the end of his life, was finally forced to acknowledge that the chaos would not form itself into harmony. Akhmatova was spared the poetically barren years that made Blok's decline into death symbolic as well as actual. But as a poem of 1960 ('Echo') indicates, she was awaiting the eternal life promised by the scriptures in a mood of almost speechless desolation:

Long closed the roads to the past,
And what is the past to me now?
What is to be found there? – Bloodstained flagstones,
Or a bricked-up door,
Or an echo that still refuses
To keep quiet, though I ask it to . . .
The same thing happened to the echo
As with what I carry in my heart.

It was because her heart could not keep quiet that Akhmatova became a symbol of liberation to the post-Stalin generation of poets; she became the classic embodiment of someone who, by speaking in little more than a whisper, could 'unshackle the soul' (in Mandelstam's now famous phrase) of a people who would otherwise have been spiritually as well as physically imprisoned by 'the real, not the calendar Twentieth Century'.

Boris Pasternak (1890–1960)

Born in Moscow; his father was a celebrated painter and his mother a distinguished musician. Took piano lessons with the composer Scriabin, but gave up his ambition to be a composer on discovering that he did not possess perfect pitch. Spent a term in the summer of 1912 at the University of Marburg studying philosophy under Hermann Cohen before returning home by way of Italy. Joined the group of Futurist poets who gathered around Mayakovsky and composed several prose works before and after the Revolution of 1917, in which he took no active political part. Divorced his first wife and remarried in 1930. Made friends with the Georgian poets who were to perish during Stalin's purges and translated them into Russian. Began to make translations of Shakespeare and other writers as his own creative spirit increasingly proved anathema to the authorities in the 1930s. Profoundly moved by the suicide of Marina Tsvetaeva in 1941, with whom he had corresponded during her years of emigration. Repudiated what he took to be the stylistic excesses of his early work and strove for a greater simplicity of utterance in poetry. In 1946 began a liaison with Olga Ivinskaya which was to last until his death and which partially influenced the novel he had begun to think of in the 1930s, *Doctor Zhivago*; awarded the Nobel Prize but not permitted to go to Stockholm to receive it. In poor health and subject to persistent harassment in his last years. Died in the seclusion of his summerhouse in Peredelkino after a succession of heart attacks, in official disgrace.

*

'All his life,' Pasternak wrote of his most famous *alter ego* Yuri Zhivago, 'he had struggled after a language so unpretentious as to enable the reader or hearer to master the content without noticing the means by which it reached him. All his life he had striven to achieve an unnoticeable style, and had been appalled to find how far he still remained from his ideal.' The closest Pasternak himself came to Zhivago's ideal was in the poems which he 'gave' to his hero, and placed at the end of his great novel. But it is possible to interpret even his early poetry – the poetry which made him famous, both inside and outside Russia, long before the world had ever heard of *Doctor Zhivago* – in the light of Zhivago's ideal, difficult and forbidding though it may at first reading seem. In later life, in the autobiographical sketch begun in 1957, Pasternak repudiated all his writing previous to 1940 and criticized it for its 'affected manner'. Yet the affectation, if such it is, should not be thought of as an unnecessary encrustation upon a fundamentally simple poetry, but rather as an unavoidable concomitant of the way in which the young Pasternak responded to stimuli. Pasternak's concern, throughout the fifty years of his writing career, was – more explicitly than with most poets, and yet at the same time less obviously – with 'life', with *zhizn*' (as Russian expresses it, and as Pasternak incorporated it into his poet-doctor's surname). As a poet – and even in prose Pasternak was that above all else, as both his style and his subject matter indicate – he was seeking a language which would embody 'life' in the manner in which life manifested itself, that is to say in an inescapably vibrant and vivid way. But for Pasternak life was plainly a language before human kind had translated it into actual words and phrases. The minutiae of life were inherently poetic, requiring only to be passed through the filament of an individual sensibility to disclose their poetry. Life and poetry were, in Pasternak's conception, synonymous; the figure of the poet was not so much an intermediary between them as a constitutive part of both of them. In this sense, the poet had no personal life, but became a representative figure of all that comprised life as a totality. The massive response to Pasternak's solitary novel, however 'political' or 'sentimental' it may in some quarters have been, suggests that Pasternak's thoughts on the subject of art and life possessed a validity which enjoined acceptance of them, despite (and at the same time because of) the fact that it was he who had thought them.

In an essay of 1922 (titled 'A Few Principles') Pasternak was intent on disabusing the audience of his time of their fascination with what seemed to be becoming, in the excitable years on either side of the Revolution, a kind of model for all art:

The contemporary orthodox is to imagine that poetry is like a fountain, whereas it is actually a sponge. The orthodoxy has determined that art should gush forth, whereas what it should do is absorb and become saturated.

The young Pasternak had actually been close to the well-springs of this 'orthodoxy'; his first two volumes of poetry, *A Twin In The Clouds* (1912) and *Over The Barriers* (1914), were published under the Futurist auspices from which – mainly as a result of what he justifiably considered a decline in the quality of Mayakovsky's poetry – he was later to dissociate himself. In his temporary allegiance to Futurism, however, he had none of the hard-line Futurist contempt for works of the past. Indeed, as the autobiographical *Safe Conduct* (1931) would later make explicit, it was precisely the way that the past – and particularly the poetry of Rilke – had joined itself to his present and predestined his future which gave him the confidence to propose the poet as a universal figure of continuity. Late in life Pasternak told one inquirer that his writing career had been a matter of translating and diversifying Rilkean attitudes and originality did not enter into it. The position is an extreme one, and overstated, for the young Pasternak was actually applying a Rilkean model to a sensibility of a very individual, and even idiosyncratic, kind. It was Rilke's impersonality, his concern with objects and with the objectivity of perceptions, that most impressed him. But to the idea that poetry was a uniquely absorbent medium

he gave his own personal inflexions. Reflecting on two poems
in his first volume of poetry, Pasternak later said: 'I wanted
one poem to contain the city of Venice, the other to contain
the Brestlitovsk railway station.' This presupposes a poetic
method more absorbent than any that has yet been de-
veloped, though it is interesting to note that the stress should
fall, as later with Zhivago, on content, on poetry as a con-
tainer. Many of Pasternak's early critics were quick to point
out that such a stress also had repercussions on formal mat-
ters, although the poems in the first two volumes seem to pay
scant heed to form as it is normally conceived. Neither of
the two poems to which Pasternak refers – nor those to
which, with appropriate substitutions, the remark could also
be applied ('Marburg', 'February' and 'Spring', for example)
– can really be considered successful, even in the heavily re-
vised later versions in which Pasternak tried to make them
so. Deprived of any controlling metaphor by a welter of
metonymies, they offer not so much substantial wholes as
scattered fragments. Unlike the stable and coherent poems of
Rilke, they are diffuse, and therefore lack the 'power' which,
by the time of *Safe Conduct*, Pasternak insisted great art must
possess. It was only in the volumes written during the great
collective trauma of 1917–23 – *My Sister Life: the summer of
1917* (published in 1922) and *Themes And Variations* (1923) –
that Pasternak harnessed this power, and without abandon-
ing the idea that the poet was a sounding-board against which
mundane and everyday phenomena – especially those taking
place, apparently without any external agency, in the natural
world – vibrated and made themselves manifest. Pasternak's
feverish intensity in these years, which also saw the writing
of his magnificent unfinished novella 'The Childhood of
Lyuvers' (1918), had found the necessary focus that would
make sense of a world in which the barriers between mind
and matter – still largely operative in the two early collec-
tions – had been dissolved. The notion remained central to
Pasternak's poetics, as is clear from a passage in chapter
fourteen of *Doctor Zhivago:*

The ascendancy is no longer with the artist or the state of mind which he is trying to express, but with language, his instrument of expression. Language, the home and dwelling of beauty and meaning, itself begins to think and speak for man and turns wholly into music, not in the sense of outward, audible sounds but by virtue of the power and momentum of its inward flow. Then, like the current of a mighty river polishing stones and turning wheels by its very movement, the flow of speech creates in passing, by the force of its own laws, rhyme and rhythm and countless other forms and formations, still more important and until now undiscovered, unconsidered and unnamed.

The references to 'music' and to 'inward flow' in this passage give it a Symbolist aspect; the idea that language can speak for itself is certainly Symbolist in origin. But, as an epitaph in *My Sister Life* and an essay of 1944 confirm, it was not the enclosed and hermetic Symbolism of Mallarmé that Pasternak wished to emulate; it was the spontaneity and the timbre of a speaking voice which he had found in the poetry of Paul Verlaine. The idea of an almost demonic possession – which the *Zhivago* passage dramatizes very clearly – is perhaps better regarded as Romantic in origin; the dedication of *My Sister Life* to Lermontov (combined with the first poem in the volume, ('In Memory Of *The Demon*') epitomize the Romantic strain in Pasternak. *My Sister Life* was, however, independent of both Romanticism and Symbolism; he had blended two traditions and given the alloy a flexibility not present in either of them, a flexibility which epitomized the idea that the reciprocation between mind and matter was to be seen as a dynamic one. 'Life,' as he wrote in *Safe Conduct*, 'opens up for me only in the place where the reader is inclined to balance accounts.' Not unnaturally, the reader of the poems in *My Sister Life* and *Themes And Variations* (especially in English translation, which cannot even capture their pictorial quality particularly well) finds himself perplexed by the multiplicity of ways in which life opens up for the poet. Only perhaps in those poems inspired by the poet's passion for a particular woman – a recurrent stimulus for Pasternak's best writing later on (*A Tale* [*The Last Summer*], 1929; the Marburg section of *Safe Conduct*; the volume *Second Birth*, 1932; and of course *Zhivago* itself) – does the reader feel himself on something resembling firm ground. Repeated rereading, however, discloses what Marina Tsvetaeva found in *My Sister Life* on its first publication: 'an unbroken chain of first things'. The poet's concern for the primal genesis of things and feelings is such as to actually give one the impression that one is present at the origin of a world. In a manner resembling that of the Post-Impressionist and *pointilliste* painters (and in some ways resembling the compositions of Scriabin, under whom the young Pasternak had studied), 'life' is recorded with a volatile and pristine exactness, as if the doors of perception, in Blake's famous phrase, had been truly cleansed. There is a moment in chapter thirteen of *Doctor Zhivago* when the poet suddenly realizes the transformational power of his mistress Lara, crediting her with 'the gift of speech and hearing granted to inarticulate life'. And it is this same 'inarticulate' life, often with its inarticulacy only just on the point of being dispersed, which crystallizes into memorable utterance in Pasternak's poetry of 1917–23. Whether the subject is (as in 'Thunder, Instantaneous Forever') the seasonal change so marked in the Russian climate, or (as in the sequence 'The Break') the turbulent emotions generated by lovers separating, the poetry seems to be creating, out of its own independent materials, an irresistible and passionate energy.

The almost pantheistic qualities of *My Sister Life* and *Themes And Variations* were gradually replaced by more orthodoxly Christian sentiments in the later Pasternak, although according to the poet himself he was actually at his most orthodox in the period 1910–12. The transition is particularly clear in the imagery of 'second birth' ascribed to the traumatic last year of Mayakovsky in part three of *Safe Conduct*. As often in Pasternak (though one might scan *Safe Conduct* in vain for anything explicit on the subject) it had a personal basis: he had dissolved his first marriage and married again. *Second Birth* (1932) contains poems both elegiac and affirmatory, a reflection of Pasternak's uncertainty as he stood at one of the many crossroads in his life. But its primary importance with respect to his poetic development is that it prefigures the later manner of simplicity which the poet came to prize above all other qualities. Pasternak had prepared the ground for this in the years 1923–30 when he had made an ill-advised excursion into more epic modes. *The Sublime Malady, 1905, Lieutenant Schmidt* and the unfinished *Spektorsky* appealed to many who, like Gorky, had found the poet's early manner very difficult, but they have not stood the test of time with the same resilience as the more daunting poems. At the same time they were clearly a necessary experiment for a poet who was convinced that impersonal and collective truths needed to be uttered. In Stalin's 1930s such truths were forced underground, and the poet was virtually obliged to become a translator of other poets (of Rilke, of Shakespeare, and of the Georgian poets). And the original poems that he did write were, on Pasternak's own admission, mediocre. Even the volumes *On Early Trains* (1944) and *Vastness Of Earth* (1945) contain only a few poems as memorable as those he had written during the Revolution and its aftermath, usually when poets – as in the case of two poems on the appalling end of Marina Tsvetaeva – or poetry itself – as in the excellent 'Thrushes' poem – is the subject under consideration. 'The world's best creations,' Pasternak had written in *Safe Conduct*, 'those which tell of the most diverse things, in reality describe their own birth.' This is certainly what makes 'Thrushes' so memorable, and it is of course one reason why Pasternak goes into such detail about how Zhivago actually created the poems that are presumed to be his.

'It's gone past. You'll understand it later', the poem 'We're Few' (from *My Sister Life*) reminds us; in early Pasternak the need to understand is less pressing than the need to record what is flying past. The later poems, however, show Pasternak to have become as much concerned with understanding as with recording fleeting phenomena. In 'The Earth' for example, Pasternak sees himself as a kind of guardian whose vocation it is to ensure that

The distances should not lose heart
And that beyond the suburbs
The earth not feel lonely.

The motifs are not new – spring floods, snowstorms, summer thunder, encounters and separations. But 'life' has come to mean more than a passive recording of natural events; it has become imbued with an active purpose, a gift of one's self to others, an assumption into common humanity. This is why the figure of the incarnate and resurrected Christ is never far from the poet's mind. In 'Hamlet', indeed, the first and most famous of the *Zhivago* poems, the *Angst*-ridden hero of Shakespeare's play – which Pasternak considered a drama of 'duty and self-denial' becomes someone who accepts 'the order of the acts' and who can therefore speak the words of Christ in the Garden of Gethsemane with perfect decorum. It is part of the same drama that the last of Zhivago's poems should bear the title 'Gethsemane'; Pasternak must have known that, in the furore aroused by the publication abroad of his novel (and the Nobel prize which followed), he would have to play a similarly sacrificial role and be publicly vilified. In stylistic terms he had found sacrifice – the removal of those obstacles – to be a means of attaining that purity of utterance which, increasingly in his later years, made him think of the art and craft of poetry as irresistibly redemptive. By depending less on what he had called, at various times, improvisation' and 'extemporization', and more on the self-denial which he had always believed to be necessary, Pasternak made his later poetry even more inclusive than it had previously been, so that in fact – for all Zhivago's despair at ever achieving it – one is fully enabled to 'master the content without noticing the means', however dependent the impact of the former may be on the subtlety of the latter. 'Before me,' wrote Marina Tsvetaeva in 1922, 'is Life.'

Though she did not live to read the later poetry – having died in circumstances which grieved Pasternak for the rest of his life, feeling as he did that he should have done more to help her – it is difficult to believe that she would have wished, on seeing the poems 'given' (as if in confirmation of the spirit of giving they speak of) to Zhivago, to alter one word of her encomium.

Osip Mandelstam (1891–1938)

Born in Warsaw, the son of an eccentric leather manufacturer steeped in German and Jewish culture and a cultured mother who was fond of music. Grew up in St Petersburg, where he was educated at the distinguished Tenishev school and received a classical education. Visited Paris in 1907, where he became interested in the French Symbolist poets. Studied Old French Literature at Heidelberg University in 1910, during which year he made two visits to Italy and spent some time at the Sorbonne. A student of Romance and German philology at St Petersburg University in 1911. Famous in Petersburg literary circles after the publication of his first volume *Stone* (1913), reprinted three years later. Employed by the authorities in Moscow in 1918; in 1919 in Kiev, where he met his wife. Briefly arrested in Feodosia during the confusion of the Civil War; jailed in Georgia on suspicion of being a Bolshevik spy. Returned to Petrograd, then briefly in Moscow, having reunited with his wife in Kiev. In Tiflis in the Caucasus for six months. Employed as a translator on returning to Leningrad. Resident in Tsarskoye Selo with his wife and Anna Akhmatova from 1925 onwards, with summer spells in the Crimea. Accused of plagiarism in 1928. Journeyed to Armenia in 1930–31. Wrote a poem in denunciation of Stalin in 1934, news of which reached the authorities through the agency of an informer. Arrested and interrogated in 1934; exiled for three years to Voronezh. Arrested on 1 May 1938 and never seen again. Presumed to have died of ill-health or been murdered by camp guards in Vladivostok in December of the same year.

*

Within the last decade or so, prompted by the appalling disclosures in the widow's memoirs, the audience for Mandelstam has grown to the degree where this once-neglected figure threatens to dwarf all but a handful of the very gifted Russian poets of his generation. Mandelstam has become known in the West as the poet who died because he had written an anti-Stalin poem at a time when Stalin was beginning to purge the Soviet Union of elements known or suspected to be weakening its internal security. But Mandelstam's fate was effectively sealed when he failed to respond in the manner the authorities expected to the years of Revolution and Civil War, and neither his mandarin early poetry nor his oblique critiques of the effects of Bolshevism could have proved acceptable to a régime intent on inculcating a proletarian art of Socialist Realism. In pre-Revolutionary Petersburg Mandelstam was admired by the intelligentsia; after the Revolution the State-controlled publishing houses placed obstacles in his path which only good fortune and influential friends enabled him to circumvent. From 1928 onwards he was to all intents and purposes silenced; one of the great modern exponents of 'the living word' was forced to entrust his writings to flimsy school exercise books and to the memories of his friends. The survival of Mandelstam's later poetry is one of the literary miracles of the century, the cardinal modern confirmation that the pen is mightier than the sword.

The events of Mandelstam's life predispose one to an admiration of his poetry; but he is certainly one of the most difficult of modern poets, and translation of his work poses formidable problems. This is precisely because of his commitment to 'the living word', which he analysed in an essay published in 1921:

Is the thing really the master of the word? The word is Psyche. The living word does not designate an object, but freely chooses for its dwelling-place, as it were, some objective significance, material thing, or beloved body. And the word wanders freely around the thing, like the soul around an abandoned, but not forgotten, body.

This stress on the creative function of language is reminiscent of the Symbolist claim that words have the power to displace the objects they are usually presumed to describe, and early Mandelstam is in fact best regarded as Symbolist poetry. But he came to suspect the way in which the Symbolists had left man without a 'dwelling-place' in their restless quest to correlate real and ideal worlds. In his own words:

The Russian Symbolists discovered ... the primordial, image-bearing nature of the word. But they sealed up all images, all words, designating them as exclusively for liturgical use. An extremely awkward situation resulted: no one could move, or stand up, or sit down. You could no longer eat at a table because it was no longer simply a table. You could no longer light a lamp because it might signify unhappiness later.

Mandelstam's 'living word' is not, like the 'liturgical' word of the Symbolist poet, in competition with reality, but commensurate with it, the 'ensouling' agent, as we might call it, of what is physically present to the senses. 'Only reality,' in another of the poet's formulations, 'can bring to life a new reality.' The theoretical position is relatively simple; but the practical application of it involved a distortion of what the naïve realist would call reality. One of the best descriptions of what actually happens in a typical Mandelstam poem (especially of the pre-Revolutionary period) is this subtle analysis by his sometime friend and fellow-poet Gyorgy Ivanov:

Least of all can one call Mandelstam an impressionist who reproduces directly and without selectivity, without any rational associations, those visual spots which are the first and as yet unrealized impressions of outer objects. At first glance the details selected may seem accidental and nugatory; but in the creative imagination of the poet their significance is immeasurably exaggerated; a trifle grows, as if in a purposely distorted grotesqueness, to fantastic proportions; at the same time the perspectival relationship between large and insignificant objects disappears; in the projection the remote and the near-at-hand seem of equal dimensions. But by means of this deliberate distortion and fantastic exaggeration a previously unsuspected particularity becomes expressive and characteristic of the subject matter being presented.

Mandelstam's words, one might add, adhere so closely to the impulses which have prompted them into being that they seem to pulse with a life of their own independent of their creator. 'Inimical to all that is personal', as he professed himself to be, he wrote, at least until the last years of his life, as daunting an 'impersonal' poetry as any of the modern poets who have adopted such a stance for the purposes of creative expression.

Mandelstam's first collection of poems appeared in 1913; he had first of all intended to call the volume *Seashell*, but altered it to *Stone*, which is actually more appropriate in the revised, expanded and definitive version of 1916. For the earliest poems of Mandelstam have an oddly weightless quality about them; they are as 'guarded' and 'voiceless' as the falling fruit which, in the very first poem, fails to disturb the silence of the forest. Verlaine's celebrated injunction to the effect that nuance mattered more than contour can rarely have been more rigorously obeyed; Mandelstam seems to be trembling on the verge of speechlessness. The most famous example of this is the poem 'Silentium' which entirely conforms to the Symbolist dictum that the primordial unity of the world can only be expressed in a form which attempts to imitate the music of the spheres:

Remain foam, Aphrodite,
and let the word become music,
and heart deny division
fused in the origins of life.

A miasmal dreamworld, shot through with sudden and inexplicable illuminations, is all that remains available to a poet of this persuasion. But repeated recourse to a Mallarmé-like world of voids and absences only exacerbates the condition it is designed to relieve:

What use is this wounded bird sadness?
The earth's dead and silent.

Someone has stolen the bells
From the mist-bound belfry,

And bereft and dumb
Stands the lofty air,
A white, vacant tower
Of haze and muteness.

                  (*Stone*, xxi)

Some tranquillity is restored in the adjacent poems in which
Mandelstam surrenders any claim to possessing a personality
and vests authority – like the Novalis of *Hymns To The Night* –
in a superior and mysteriously consoling power which re-
creates 'the origins of life'. But real vigour only becomes
present when Mandelstam begins to question the funda-
mentally Symbolist assumptions upon which these early
poems depend. An entirely new mood, a riposte to the
Symbolist mystique of 'correspondence' between the mun-
dane and the sublime, is present in poem XXXI:

No, it isn't the moon, but the face of a clock
which lights up for me – and am I to blame
if the pallid stars strike me as milky?

It is in the poems of *Stone* for which Mandelstam provided
titles (and especially 'Santa Sophia', 'Notre Dame', 'Peters-
burg Stanzas' and 'The Admiralty Building') that he
decisively counters his residual idealism. Here he sets himself
the task of creating beauty out of intrinsically weighty objects
in which the hand of the artisan is everywhere manifest. 'The
Admiralty Building' is a particularly good illustration of
Ivanov's suggestion that Mandelstam has an almost micro-
scopic purchase upon particulars. For the poem presents one
of the familiar landmarks of Petersburg in the light of biblical
and classical emblems awakened in his mind by its domina-
tion of the space it occupies. Resembling a Greek acropolis
and the Old Testament ark of the covenant between God and
man, it appears to open up for him 'all the seas of the world'
and all its culture also. In subsequent poems he begins to
voyage upon these seas, in one poem assuming the guise of the
biblical Joseph (of which Osip is a Russian equivalent) and

then, in a succession of poems, becoming a reincarnation of the Roman poet Ovid, banished into exile on the shores of the Black Sea. The somewhat derivative complexity of the early poems is replaced here by a uniquely Mandelstamian combination of concerns, nowhere more effective than in poem LXXVIII, where the poet tries to assuage his insomnia by reading Homer, reaffirms Dante's belief that the world is moved by love, laments his own lovelessness and records his fear of the slow approach of thunder which culminated in the Revolution. Together with the even more allusive final poem of *Stone* ('I shall not see the famous *Phèdre*'), this poem prefigures the second of Mandelstam's collections, where the Ovidian complex of love lyric, elegiac lament, literature and politics is foregrounded in the very title: *Tristia* (1922).

Tristia is, as its title implies, full of sad things; it is Mandelstam at his most tragic. And despite its Latin title it is Greek tragic figures that are most in Mandelstam's mind. The volume contains numerous references to Odysseus, Antigone, Penelope, Helen, Eurydice and – perhaps the most important and prominent of all – Persephone. Many of the poems in the volume are, as these classical allusions might suggest, addressed to particular women of Mandelstam's acquaintance; three poems describe his brief relationship with the poet Marina Tsvetaeva and three of the finest register his mixed feelings at the breakdown of his passionate liaison with the actress Olga Arbenina, which seems to have posed the severest threat to his marriage. Obviously the emblematic figures of literature and mythology were employed to give his private feelings the protection of an impersonal stance, though the very gravity of the language marks them out as *cris de coeur*. One of the Arbenina poems, however, the finest ('Because I could not keep your hands', written in December 1920), is imbued with a gloom which describes more than the dereliction at the end of love-affair; behind its multiple disguises a passionate lament for a Russia sliding into Civil War is readily discernible. Though it may not immediately appear so, *Tristia* is an outcry provoked by the public drama and massive upheaval of the Revolution and its aftermath. The 'we' of the famous poems 'We shall die in transparent Petropolis' and 'We shall meet again in Petersburg' is inclusive of everyone in the city, unable to lift the heavy weight which lies like a stone upon a Petersburg in the grip of a more than merely literal winter. The ark of the Admiralty Building which, in *Stone*, had prompted the poet to sail the seas is now unequivocally in the process of going down in shipwreck. 'Petropolis', with its ironic connotations of order and polity, has become a kind of underworld, like that to which Persephone was suddenly transported. The star or fire which might betoken a covenant of continuity is impossibly distant; it is, as the title for a poem written shortly after the Revolution tells us, 'The Twilight of Freedom'. The mood is valedictory; the poet is steeling himself to learn 'the science of goodbyes' and, risking arrest and execution if he speaks in a more accessible manner, he becomes the purveyor of a 'dark truth'. A new kind of speechlessness, quite different from the insubstantial pageants of the early poems in *Stone*, is present here, as in the very grave poem 'I have forgotten the word I wished to utter', which ends with the Stygian gloom of lips frozen by black ice. 'Silentium' describes a Mandelstam primarily concerned with private difficulties of creative expression; 'I have forgotten the word' is much more profound, for the word he would like to utter is a consolatory one, and there are no meaningful consolations to be dredged from a city hell-bent on uprooting its cultural heritage and destroying itself in the process. Under such conditions he must content himself with the 'blessed senseless word' of 'We shall meet again', a pale reflection of God's word which makes the act of benediction seem at once heroic and absurd. This word may be nothing more than the sand which, at the end of one of the poems to Tsvetaeva, passes from hand to hand and is dispersed, or the falling fruit (reminiscent of the first poem of *Stone*) which is referred to in the poem 'A Ring of Shades'. Yet this latter poem stresses that to 'throw a name' – a recurrent Mandelstam periphrasis for writing – into the ring of shadows which encompasses his friends and his city is the only meaningful act, however meaningless it may seem.

Mandelstam vigorously combated his gloom by seeing himself as an agent of continuity between the old and the new; he was crafting, by hand (like Penelope with her embroidery), something that might defy the ravages of an anarchic time. 'The Age', one of the many poems which show Mandelstam assuming (like Akhmatova later) the mantle of public spokesman for the epoch, suggests that the modern Orpheus must imitate his ancient avatar, survive his dismemberment and continue to play his oaken flute. The task of glueing together the broken backbone of the age is to be assumed by the poet in his role of sacrificial mediator. The largely passive poet of *Stone* has completely disappeared; but he now has to face up to the fact that he is at once more active and more helpless. He has 'human lips/Which have nothing to say' by way of consolation; what he actually says is not so much said by him as 'dug out of the ground like grains of petrified wheat'. This excavatory activity, echoed many times in Mandelstam's later poems and prose works, will have to be continued beyond the duration of a merely seasonal winter; the New Year poem of 1924 speaks grimly of the 'tyrant century' that is beginning. The years of Revolution and Civil War worked a decisive change in Mandelstam's sensibility: in *Stone* he seems content to craft glittering jewels and watch the stream of time passing in the hope that he will soon transcend time altogether; in the poems of the eight years after *Stone* he is attempting to hold the very fabric of time together, however much it insists on tearing itself apart. One of the great statements of this latter attitude is 'The Slate Ode' of 1924 where Mandelstam wishes to make 'the firm notation of a moment', an elemental utterance, with the agent of continuity his own hand, thrust 'into the flint path .../as into a wound', to staunch the blood being senselessly split on all sides.

'Poetry,' wrote Mandelstam in an essay published in 1921, 'is the plough which cultivates the soil of time so that its abyssal strata, its black earth, may appear on the surface.' His widow's memoirs, in their own way, perform a similar function of disclosing the 'abyssal strata' of the times they lived through. But between 1924 and 1930 Mandelstam seems to have doubted his ability to write poetry in the face of the worsening crises of his country, and turned to prose, evidently with some reluctance, as the medium whereby his message might be heeded. A brief return to Leningrad in the winter of 1930 enabled him to once more find his voice in verse, though by comparison with the elaborate poems written previously, the voice is more broken and more terse. In 1922, thinking no doubt of his earliest poems, Mandelstam wrote 'there's no comparison between/how the blood used to whisper/and how it whispers now'; but the same might be said of the difference between the later poems and those of the early 1920s. Even so, as we might expect of a poet so concerned with continuity, there are intimations of the later manner in the poems written in the aftermath of Revolution. A winter poem of 1922 describes how 'the snow eats to the eyes to the quick'; in the years of exile in Voronezh this image completely loses any metaphorical status it may have had. In this same poem of 1922 Mandelstam's sole possessions are, as later in Voronezh, 'a clay pot/And the twittering of the stars in my thin ears'. 'I shall love my poor earth', he had promised in poem IV of *Stone*, where he begs to be granted a childlike vision; in Voronezh, where it was all that he had, he confirmed the accuracy of his prophecy and his prayer was answered. In conditions of dreadful privation his extraordinarily alert sensibility was always ready to record whatever signs of renewal were presented to it. This enabled him, as in the great poem 'Black Earth' (a virtual periphrasis for poetry, as the essay of 1921 demonstrates), to find the kind of freedom that his poetics of 'the living word' had been designed to locate, but which had been occasionally encrusted by difficult allusions and hybrid purposes. There is a single-mindedness about the later Mandelstam that enables the poetry to function with the implacable efficiency of the plough to which he had compared it. As a means of tilling the soil of time, it became a tool without peer. Like a Roman elegist, in conditions utterly remote from anything resembling what we should regard as a 'dwelling-place', he continued to hymn the virtues of the hearth and of the household gods. Reduced to what the 'Stanzas' of 1935 call 'my last weapon', he wrote with uncanny and remorseless vigour, with something of the 'iron tenderness' that he found in Rembrandt's painting 'The Crucifixion' in the Voronezh museum, almost the only evidence of high culture he could find in the circumstances. In the winter of 1936–7 he was extraordinarily prolific, confirming that, in his own words, 'under the ice the leads go on blackening'.

The Voronezh poems are the words of a man reduced almost to a whisper, aware that he is addressing a posterity he cannot hope to know. There is a poem in *Stone* which describes how the pattern created by breathing on a frosty window can never be erased; in the unconstricted world of the Voronezh steppes to breathe became as much an act of life as an act of art. The Mandelstam of *Stone* and *Tristia* is a very impressive poet indeed, though even experts on the subject tend to disagree about his precise meaning; his obliqueness can be forbidding, as is typical of a poet who possessed what T. S. Eliot called 'the historical sense' to a degree that Eliot himself might have found it difficult to equal. But there is nothing more moving, more lapidary and sad, and yet at the same time so full of consolatory vigour, than the poetry Mandelstam scribbled in his school exercise books, of which these lines must serve as a summary of their style, mood and message:

I shall not fall silent nor numb the agony,
But I shall write what I am free to write,
And by yoking to my voice ten oxen
Will move my hand in darkness like a plough
And fall with the full heaviness of harvest.

César Vallejo (1892–1938)

Born in Santiago de Chuco, Peru, of mixed Spanish and
Indian origin. Enjoyed a contented rural middle class child-
hood as the youngest of eleven children; brought up in an
atmosphere of religious piety. Briefly studied medicine at the
University of Lima in 1911; in 1912 worked as an assistant
cashier on a sugar plantation, an experience which awakened
in him a sympathy for the exploited workers. Studied Law
and Literature at the University of Trujillo from 1913 to
1917, supporting himself by teaching. Graduated with a
dissertation on 'Romanticism in Castilian Poetry'. Associ-
ated with avant-garde literary elements in Trujillo and
involved in a number of relationships with women, the
break-up of one of which prompted him to leave Trujillo.
Profoundly upset by the death of his mother in 1918. A
student and schoolteacher in Lima in 1918–19. Imprisoned
for four months as an innocent bystander at riots in San-
tiago in 1920, and released with charges unproved, an ex-
perience which influenced the poems collected in *Trilce*
(1922). Disappointed by the cold reaction to *Trilce*, he left
Peru for Europe in 1923. Settled in Paris in cheap hotels,
knowing little French and very poor. Operated on for an
internal haemorrhage in the autumn of 1924. Supported him-
self by writing journalism in the next few years. Became
deeply interested in Marxism in 1927–8. Visited Russia after
a serious illness in 1928 and again in 1929. Married in 1929.
Several times arrested in Paris and expelled for his political
affiliations in 1930. Moved to Madrid, where he and his wife
endured great hardship. Wrote primarily in prose between
1930 and 1932. Joined the Spanish Communist party and

made a third trip to Russia in 1931. Resident in Paris from 1932 to 1937, acquiring a permit on condition that he engage in no political activity. Wrote a great deal of the poetry posthumously published by his wife. Twice visited Republican Spain in 1936 and 1937. Died suddenly in Paris of an intestinal complaint possibly aggravated by the malaria he had previously contracted.

Probably the most inventively experimental poet in a period of unparalleled experiment, the Peruvian César Vallejo is a posthumous beneficiary of the worldwide growth of interest in the literature of Latin America. In a poetry even more 'impure' than that written by his friend Pablo Neruda – so impure, it would seem, that some Spanish critics have failed even to recognize it as poetry – Vallejo subjected his medium to a series of unprecedentedly volatile stress-fractures, which at times amount to nothing less than a total revaluation of the conventional relationship between words and what they designate. Vallejo is probably – with the exception of Mallarmé at the other and purer end of the spectrum – the most difficult major poet in an age of difficult poetry, sometimes effectively incomprehensible even for those who are fully conversant with his very idiosyncratic Spanish. He is at his most difficult in his most famous single volume, *Trilce* (1922), which contains seventy-seven poems of immense and often rebarbative power, only a handful of which yield up their secrets at all readily. He is even difficult in the poems which his widow (misguidedly it now seems) called *Human Poems*, written in the last fifteen years of his life, which – despite a certain amount of textual unreliability – are perhaps his most abiding achievement. The moving sequence of fifteen poems written at the end of his life in support of the Republican cause in the Spanish Civil War (first printed by Republican soldiers during the war) is the only work of Vallejo's that is readily accessible, and even here there are dislocations that one does not normally associate with a great public *cri de coeur*.

Comparison of Vallejo's *Spain, Let This Cup Pass From Me* with
Neruda's 'Spain In The Heart' or with the Civil War poems
of Rafael Alberti reveals how exceptionally intransigent
Vallejo was in the pursuit of a kind of utterance which, with-
out ceasing to be poetry, disdained the accepted poetic strate-
gies utterly, and in a manner quite different from that of other
Marxist poets.

Vallejo's origins were not so prohibitively poor that they
prevented him attending university, where he wrote a disser-
tation on 'Romanticism In Castilian Poetry'. However he
had to support himself, then as later, by teaching and by
journalism, and when he left Peru for good in 1923 – weary
of a repressive political régime which had imposed on him
an undeserved four-month prison sentence – his fifteen years
in Paris – broken only by short periods in Spain and Russia
– were a time of great hardship, tempered only by contacts
with other writers and artists, the temporary fame which
followed the publication of a prose work (*Russia In 1931*), and
a liaison with the woman he later married. Vallejo's sym-
pathy for the wretched of the earth was based on his justified
sense of oneness with them, memorably recorded in the most
famous of the poems in which he foresaw his own death
('Black Stone On A White Stone'):

César Vallejo is dead, they beat him
all of them, without him doing anything to them.

Vallejo actually died of a mysterious intestinal ailment, much
as this poem had predicted, 'in Paris on a day of heavy rain'.
But ironically or symbolically, according to one's predis-
positions, his death did not take place on one of those Thurs-
days to which he had so often, as in this poem, referred, but
on Good Friday, as if in confirmation of the modern idea that
the poet is inevitably a scapegoat.

The American poet and translator Robert Bly has des-
cribed Vallejo's first volume, *The Black Heralds* (printed in
1919) as 'the greatest single collection of poems I have ever

read'. The sheer difficulty of later Vallejo does indeed make one grateful for the comparatively straightforward disclosures of *The Black Heralds*. And the title poem, the first of the seventy-two that comprise the whole, establishes a mood which, in everything except its lack of complexity, dominates the whole *oeuvre* of Vallejo. Here the poet exclaims his help-less ignorance at the origin of the brutal blows which life inflicts on man, but suggests that God's hatred is the ultimate source and cause of them. Man's fate is to be the passive recipient of the black messengers sent by death, so that he ends up ultimately as no more than 'some loaf left burn-ing at the oven door'. The harshness of Vallejo's vision is even more apparent in 'The Spider' where the disjunction between the spider's head and abdomen and its position on 'a ridge of stone' are plainly symbolic of man's plight. Vallejo oscil-lates in *The Black Heralds* between four slightly different, but related, responses to the God which religion offers as a source of ultimate meaning: pointing a 'god-murdering finger' at him (as in 'The Weary Circles'); empathizing with a God who, like the people he has orphaned, has a pain in his heart ('God'); passing judgement on him (as in the famous 'Verdict' where he suggests that 'God was gravely ill on the day of my birth'); and begging his forgiveness either (as in 'The Eternal Dice') for having stolen his bread or (as in the brilliant and ironic 'Agapé') for not having already died. All these different aspects are subsumed under the conviction that if God had really been man, he would know how to be God. Yet sceptical though he might be about Christ's Incarnation, Vallejo is inevitably sensitive to his Passion; Christ's Passion has be-come, as the strange plural in the third stanza of *The Black Heralds* indicates, a sacrifice which all men have to repeat endlessly. *Agapé* has given way, in Vallejo's case, to the *eros* of 'Forbidden Love', in which 'there is no Our Father' and love itself becomes 'a sinning Christ'. The seeds of the bitterly sexual *Trilce* poems are sown here, and there are poems (like 'The Black Cup') where the sense of evil is almost over-whelming. At this stage, however, Vallejo could still dream, as for example in 'Twilight', of a Mary-like figure, a compound of his Catholic upbringing and his deep affection for the mother he had recently lost. Indeed the only moments in which he can cast off his rancour are those in which he is able to contemplate the domestic harmony of the family. The tender *in memoriam* for his dead brother Miguel is one such moment, and there is another in 'The Distant Footsteps', although in this poem he lodges all the discord in his own heart and imagines himself leaving home in order to preserve its domestic contentment. In one of the finest of the *Trilce* poems (LXI) he pictures himself returning to the house in which 'all are asleep for ever', resting in a repose of death which makes 'everything all right'. And in the prose poem 'No One Now Lives In The House' (in the so-called *Human Poems*), Vallejo explores once again 'that irresistible similarity between a house and a tomb', though careful – as one who was never much comforted by the neatness of an analogy – to distinguish between them. These are poems in which Vallejo manages to regain something of the tranquillity which one or two of the poems in *The Black Heralds* set against the prevailing gloom of the collection as a whole.

There is little tenderness, and no tranquillity, in *Trilce*, where the *triste* element in the neologism comprehensively dominates the *dulce* with which it seems to end. The verbal and typographical surface of this volume bristles with bewildering transpositions and lacunae, which make even the wilder Surrealists look almost ordinary. But this is far from being automatic writing; indeed it is the very artifice of writing which Vallejo is calling attention to. The familiar configuration of love, death and religion in *The Black Heralds* is here turned inside out in a strenuous and unremitting defamiliarization which marks a watershed in modern Latin American writing. One is tempted, in distinguishing *Trilce* from what followed it, to call these poems 'inhuman'. But what Vallejo is concerned with here is an irremediably fallen humanity, imprisoned not only literally (as he himself had been) but also figuratively, embroiled in the pointless vicious

circle of its sexuality. In *Trilce* procreation has become an un-
thinkable absurdity, the continuation of a species which is
doomed. It is possible, as poem X is not alone in suggesting,
that Vallejo is here obliquely confronting a liaison of 1919
which brought him uncomfortably close to the reality of off-
spring and which, under social pressure, he terminated. But
the presence of Vallejo himself in this collection remains am-
biguous, and he hardly even seems to be present in the first
person verbs which the grammar of Spanish permits to stand
without an antecedent pronoun. In *Trilce* the human function
is either dispersed through parts of the body and concentrated
in the sexual organs, or usurped by numbers, scientific words,
neologisms, letters of the alphabet, and words which seem to
mis-spell themselves deliberately. Many of these, and es-
pecially perhaps the latter, seem to invite decipherment in
sexual terms. For at every touch, as later in the *Human Poems*,
the lovers are reduced to 'a pair of poorly plastered sepul-
chres' such as poem XI in *Trilce* speaks of. The 'mute outcry'
of orgasm is transformed, in the weird mirror-writing of poem
XII, into an object of absurdity, with two words collapsed
into one so that the letters which spell out the Spanish word
for death (*muerte*) can be even more clearly seen. Similarly,
in poem XV, the lovers are transformed into material objects,
'two doors that come and go with the wind', and finally into
two words, the same word ('darkness'), facing one another,
but separated forever by the typography which fixes them to
the page:

darkness   to   darkness.

The collection as a whole is orientated towards the sexual act,
the 'mysterious pulse' of poem XLIV, the 'immoral after-
noon' of poem XXX, the 'kitchen with shadows, the squalor
of love' of poem XXVIII, and the habitual images of food
and appetite. The latter are also, however, an oblique index
of the new materialism of Vallejo's vision, which led him to
embrace the ideas of Marxism much as Neruda, from a simi-
larly anguished origin in eroticism, later would.

Each poem of *Trilce*, in its different way, becomes what

poem XXVII calls 'a whole/place for this not knowing where I am'. This 'not knowing', which is reminiscent of the refrain in the first poem of *The Black Heralds*, is conditioned by what is absent, the 'what has arrived and has already gone' of poem XXXIII. In *Trilce* it seems to be both love and the beloved which is absent. In poem XXXIII Vallejo recognizes that this condemns him to a more permanent imprisonment than any government can impose. His role as 'amorous notary' of the body's intimacies (XXXV) therefore seems utterly gratuitous. Insofar as his sadness will permit him, he ends up 'dying with laughter' (LII). The consummate irony of Vallejo finding himself imprisoned in this way is, of course, grounded in the fact that he has in *Trilce* liberated his language in a way that free verse of the more traditional kind almost never does. Vallejo's only recourse, in such a vicious circle, was to broaden his spectrum and to present an arena in the *Human Poems* much wider than the merely sexual.

The locus of the *Human Poems* is only rarely specified, but is plainly Paris. Like Rilke's Malte, but with a good deal less self-absorption, Vallejo confronts here a place of death in which he is paradoxically still alive. (This is even clearer in the title 'Payroll of Bones' which Vallejo apparently wanted to use for some of them). His imprisonment in a Peruvian jail is no longer the most perilous moment in a life which is now threatened by death at every single moment. His own existence now seems immaterial, as in the powerful prose poem 'I Am Going To Speak Of Hope' where he realizes 'I don't suffer this pain as César Vallejo'. With personal survival no longer of primary concern, the act of writing seems even more pointless than it has previously done, especially 'if after so many words/the word doesn't survive'. This helps to account for the poet's ambivalence. Sometimes, as in 'Paris, October 1936', it seems to Vallejo as if he is the only one who has departed from life; at other times, as in 'Today I Like Life Much Less', he dreams of living for ever, if only because he has never been properly born. The paradoxes seem more painful than those of *Trilce*, because more accessible:

O always, never to find the never of so much always!

The residual faith of *The Black Heralds* has by now been utterly shattered by the reality of 'people so wretched that they do not even/have a body', as in a poem which parodies the Beatitudes. 'A Man Watching A Woman' performs a similar parodic critique of the Song of Solomon. But the greatest paradox of these poems is that though Vallejo's 'I' has become a 'not-I', and although 'to express my life I have only my death', the poet can still write, and can even contemplate the composition of a 'Sermon On Barbarism'. The possibility of a religious consolation has receded completely; but the solidarity of being human has at least partially filled up the space, as in the conclusion to the 'Sermon On Death':

at the centre I am, and to the right
also, and to the left, in a similar fashion.

Vallejo's syntax is at its stammering best here. And when it is pain that is at issue, as in one of the untitled late poems, the words take on independent life and seem to force things through to an irresistible conclusion:

Today is Sunday and, therefore,
comes into my head the idea, into my chest the cry
and into my throat, just like a large lump.
Today is Sunday, and it
is ages old; or
it would be, perhaps, Monday, and into my heart the idea
would come,
into my brain, the cry,
and into my throat, a frightening desire to choke
what I now feel,
like a man which I am and have suffered.

It is the experience of suffering, recorded with an almost visceral use of language, which the poetry of Vallejo bears unmistakable and one is tempted to say unparalleled witness to. He is clearly, in spite of the difficulties one sometimes encounters in reading him, one of the few ultra-modern poets whose experiments with language immediately impress one as necessary vehicles of his superficially idiosyncratic, but fundamentally universal vision.

Marina Tsvetaeva (1892–1941)

Born in Moscow, the daughter of an eminent professor and a cultured mother. Wrote poetry in German as well as in Russian as a child. Educated in boarding-schools in Switzerland and Southern Germany; attended lectures at the Sorbonne during a brief residence in Paris; spent the summer of 1910 in Dresden. Deeply influenced by the poet Voloshin and those who gathered at his Crimean residence in Koktebel, where she fell in love with Sergei Efron, whom she married. Gave birth to a precocious daughter in 1912 and later to another daughter who soon died, and to a son. Emotionally involved with Mandelstam in 1915–16. Culturally supported her husband's activities on behalf of the White cause in the Civil War and reunited with him on his evacuation to Prague in 1922. Lived in the Prague suburbs until 1925, during which time she fell in love with another White officer. Reunited with her husband in Paris in 1926. Condemned by the Russian *émigrés* in Paris for defending the poetry of Mayakovsky and thereafter ostracized by them. Corresponded with Rilke and Pasternak. Remained in the vicinity of Paris until 1939, her husband having begun to work for the Soviet secret police and been implicated in the assassination of Trotsky's son. Wrote primarily in prose in the 1930s. Sought relief from a troubled marriage in a number of liaisons, but returned to Russia in 1939 in search of her husband. Encountered hostility on her return to Moscow, where she met Anna Akhmatova for the first time. Engaged in translation in an attempt to support herself. Evacuated from Moscow in 1941 to the provincial town of Elabuga where, friendless and unable to find work, she died by her own hand. Still regarded with suspicion by the Soviet authorities, but otherwise considered the greatest of *émigré* poets and in some quarters the most exceptional poet of the post-Blok generation.

No modern Russian writer had a greater reverence for the act of the poet and the fact of poetry than Marina Tsvetaeva, and none has more vitally confirmed the interchangeability of what have often been separated into 'life' and 'art'. Of the many moments in her work which illustrate her conviction that poetry is the most precious of possessions, one of the most memorable occurs at the end of the ninth of her 'Poems For Blok' (1916–21), inspired by, and written the same day as, Blok's last public reading in Moscow:

So, solitary, like a prisoner,
(Or like a child that chatters in its sleep),

There stood revealed throughout the whole huge hall
The sacred heart of Aleksandr Blok.

For Tsvetaeva, as these lines suggest, poetry was an act of revelation, an act of the heart and soul laid bare. 'The sole target of all poetry', she wrote in an essay, 'is the heart'; and – in a letter to a friend of December 1935, saying much the same in her characteristic 'telegram' style – 'pierced to the quick = the soul'. All Tsvetaeva's thoughts on the subject of poets and poetry indicate that she regarded the person so 'pierced to the quick' as one marked out by destiny for a fate at once tragic and affirmative, as an exemplary figure, like the Pushkin she described as 'a lesson in courage; a lesson in pride; a lesson in fidelity; a lesson in fate; a lesson in loneliness'. Blok and Pushkin were two of the poets whom she invested with symbolic attributes of a distinctively spiritual kind; but she also wrote poems and poetic prose in praise of Akhmatova, Mayakovsky, Pasternak and – the figure she regarded as supreme among European poets of his epoch – Rilke. The combination of courage, pride, fidelity, fate and loneliness was irresistible to her; and she herself manifested these qualities to an exemplary degree. Like the poets she admired, she regarded the poet's task as a sacred one; in explanation of the title of her 1921 collection *Craft* she invoked a line from a minor poet describing poetry as 'my misfortune, my wealth, my sacred craft'. This sacred craft, however, as the mention of misfortune may serve to remind us, was also a sacrificial one; it is symptomatic that the solitary and childlike figure in the Blok poem should surrender himself to his audience in a manner reminiscent of Christ's sacrifice for mankind. One of Tsvetaeva's letters to Pasternak, dated 1927, is interesting in this connection, describing as it does her feelings on having completed a book of lyric poetry:

I am tired of being torn to bits and smashed into pieces like Osiris. Every book of poetry is a book of farewells and dismemberings, with Thomas's finger probing the wound between one poem and the next.

From a conventional and orthodox Christian standpoint such an attitude is obviously (even without the reference to Osiris) tantamount to heresy; in 1919 she wrote 'I am an inexhaustible source of heresies'. But it also reflects a commitment to poetry which, for Tsvetaeva, was of much more fundamental importance than pious observances. And though her language, here as elsewhere, may seem excessive and rhapsodic, it is evident that her ideas on this subject were the product of very considered and very considerable deliberation. This is nowhere more evident than in a prose work published in 1932, the essay 'Art In the Light Of Conscience' which, despite embodying the ecstasies of which it speaks, unfolds with a remarkably rigorous logic. In this essay Tsvetaeva speaks of art as equivalent to nature, and therefore elemental, dynamic, organically creative and destructive; the 'conscience' which most appeals to her is plainly not the one of which morality and religion typically speak. The essay in fact subverts the accepted notions of salvation and damnation in accordance with this initial position. 'Perdition, for the poet,' she writes, 'is the abjuration of the elemental'; in these terms it is a surrender to the artificial and culturally conditioned which would constitute immorality. There are traces of Nietzsche's hubristic 'will to power' and his subtle excursions beyond good and evil in the essay; Tsvetaeva had a profound acquaintance with German literature and philosophy. But she is in fact preparing the ground not for a display of power so much as a surrender of the kind adumbrated in the poem to Blok – a surrender of oneself to a superior power which has demonically possessed its victim. 'To be possessed by the work of one's own hands', writes Tsvetaeva, resolving her dualisms into a single complex, 'is to be held in someone's hands.' The same idea is expressed, albeit more serenely, in Rilke's famous 'Autumn' poem from *The Book of Images* (1906). But Tsvetaeva is here concerned, to a degree which distinguishes her from her mentor, with the question of how the poem can be at once its own reward and a source of spiritual strength to others. There is nothing egotistical about her stress on the apotheosis of the poet; 'there is no such thing', she tells us, 'as a personal creative will.' The Blok poem reminds us that the poet is not so much imprisoned in his sensibility (as a Symbolist, and indeed Rilke, would characteristically be) as bound by his responsibility to his poem and, by extension, to his audience. In the words of 'Art In The Light Of Conscience', the poet is 'bound by someone over into someone's hands'. It is against the background of such a conception of the craft of poetry that we should see Pasternak's verbal epitaph for Tsvetaeva, shortly after she had killed herself, in which he speaks of 'deeds performed out of loyalty to the only country of which she was a citizen: poetry'.

It was in accordance with the views sketched here that Tsvetaeva developed what she called 'a vocabulary and usage belonging to the here-and-now' to express the 'imponderable' soul which is normally hidden behind the mundane. Believing as she did that form and essence were indivisible, she did not wish to practise any of the separations between word and world, and between one world and another, that were the product of the Symbolist epoch. To an even greater degree than Mandelstam, Tsvetaeva was an exponent of 'the living word'; indeed, her words are sometimes so alive and volatile that, especially in poetry but also in prose, she becomes difficult to follow. Leaving out what she considered superfluous connectives, she wrote in a style which has often been compared to that of a telegram. The analogy will not withstand serious scrutiny, but it does serve to convey the extraordinary urgency which is found in all her work, an urgency which stems directly from her deep need to experience 'the bliss of annihilation', as she calls it in 'Art In The Light Of Conscience'. Her urgency derives from her need to surrender herself. 'I give myself to all', she wrote in a poem of 1916; it is the motif of giving which dominates all her poems of that year, especially those in which she gives her 'huge city' Moscow to the Petersburg poets Blok, Akhmatova and Mandelstam. And many of the love poems of 1918 strike the same note, notably the 'Psyche' poems, or this splendid extension of Akhmatova's more guarded studies in chiaroscuro (as found, for example, in her *White Flock* of 1917):

I am a page for your pen.
I accept everything. I am a white page.
I am the guardian of your goods.
I will return them a hundredfold.

I am a village, I am black earth.
To me you are light and the moisture of rain.
You are my Lord, my Master – I
Am black earth and a white page.

It is the manner in which Tsvetaeva gives herself without reserve which distinguishes her from the Akhmatova she so much admired. If Akhmatova may truly be said to be 'half harlot, half nun', Tsvetaeva is wholly harlot. A brief poem of 1920 is typical:

No need to talk to me.
Here are my lips: let us drink.
My hair: to stroke.
My hands: you can kiss them.
– Or else let us sleep.

As Tsvetaeva acknowledged in a poem of the following year, her soul was 'fanatical and ignorant of measure'; it is no accident that a powerful late prose work should celebrate a religious sect of flagellants who were similarly fanatical and extreme. It is precisely as a poet of extremity that Tsvetaeva makes her greatest claim upon us, though her mastery of formal devices (which translations cannot hope to capture) is remarkable and a constant reproach to Soviet detractors of her work who accuse her of undue 'hysterics'. For what most deeply impresses one about Tsvetaeva is her ability to suggest, in the midst of extremity, that she is on the point of conquering it. This is notably the case in one of the 'Psyche' poems of 1918, in which she thinks of herself as reliving the traumatic myth of Psyche, the Greek legend of the turbulent passage of the soul through life. And it is present again in a poem written shortly after:

Words etched in a black sky.
And fine eyes blinded.
And the bed of death not terrible for us.
And the bed of passion not sweet for us.

By sweat – writing, in sweat – pasturing.
We know another fire:
A light flame, which dances above the crown,
An exhalation – of inspiration.

It is typical of Tsvetaeva that she should find no terror in 'the bed of death'. In a poem of 1915 ('I Know The Truth') the prospect of death is viewed with the equanimity of someone seeking relief from the insomnia of living, a theme later brilliantly explored in the 'Insomnia' sequence of 1916. The same motif is present in the 'Verses About Moscow' addressed to Osip Mandelstam, in the last two of which the longing for sleep and the reality of a continuing insomnia are juxtaposed. But Tsvetaeva's equanimity gave way to despair after the defeat of the White Army in the Civil War had forced her and her husband into exile. In 1923 she wrote one of her finest tragic utterances, partially inspired by the execution of Akhmatova's estranged husband, the poet Gumilyov, the almost untranslatable 'Letter':

You don't wait for a letter like this.
You wait for this letter.

A ragged scrap
With the tape round it
Not stuck down. Inside – a scribble.
And happiness. – That's all.

You don't wait for happiness like this.
You wait for the end.
A soldier's salute
And three lead bullets
In the breast. And red eyes.
And nothing else. – That's all.

Happiness – I'm past it.
A flower blown away on the wind.
A square yard
And black gun muzzles.

(A square letter:
Black ink and magic.)
No one's too old
For the sleep of death.

A square letter.

Tsvetaeva's contention that 'every book of poetry is a book of farewells and dismemberings' acquires a special force in the context of her immensely powerful love poetry. Perhaps no modern poet has conveyed more eloquently the dereliction of lovers at the moment of farewell. In 1921, separated from her husband by the Civil War, Tsvetaeva composed the brilliant sequence 'Separation' which shows her at the height of her powers. But even more impressive are two sequences prompted by a brief and passionate liaison in Prague in 1925: 'Poem Of The Mountain' and 'Poem Of The End'. Tsvetaeva's language is at its most heartbreakingly dismembered in these two sequences, of which the second is particularly moving. The climax of this second sequence occurs in the tenth poem, through which the words 'to separate' and 'separation' reverberate like the bells of the 'forty times forty' churches of her native Moscow. Even at what is explicitly 'the point of death' the language is extraordinarily animated; in 'Poem Of The End' it becomes impossible to do otherwise than 'listen to/This flesh more true//Than poems'. Tsvetaeva's passion for a person and for passionately dramatic speech become almost indistinguishable: life has become 'a place where it's not possible to live:/ the Jewish quarter', and 'all poets are Jews'. The sequence generates more turbulence than any other comparable poem, yet once again it is Tsvetaeva's control of volatile emotions which impresses one most. By the end of the sequence one feels that she has once again conjured something positive out of the débâcle, as if the very strength of her anguish is a value in itself. This is nowhere more true than in the last poem of the sequence, where the lovers accomplish something analogous to the intimacy that Tsvetaeva's poem creates between herself and her reader, 'a bond/More intimate/Than lying down together./The very Song of Songs/Yields to our speech'.

'Poem Of The Mountain' and 'Poem Of The End' show Tsvetaeva's poetic speech at its most elemental; her subsequent poetry has tended to be neglected and undervalued. Her folklore epics and the other long poems of the 1920s are too 'Russian', it would seem, ever to find anything like a wide audience. But there are two later sequences of great depth and range, one prompted by the suicide of Mayakovsky in 1930, the other 'For The Czech Lands' oppressed by Hitler. And in a splendid sequence of poems addressed to her writing desk, Tsvetaeva celebrates and laments the pain and pleasure of a commitment to writing in a manner reminiscent of some of Kafka's diary-entries and letters. The concluding lines of 'The Desk' (1934) perfectly encapsulate the courage, pride, fidelity and loneliness which stimulated her whole artistic endeavour:

I shall stand there on the Day of Judgement naked:
With my two wings as protection.

On returning to Russia Tsvetaeva could find no protection in a country purged of dissidents and once more locked in combat with German armies. In Moscow she supported herself at subsistence level by translating, often from languages with which she was unfamiliar. Her husband, whose allegiances were sufficiently elastic for him to have worked for

Stalin's secret police, despite having actively supported the White Army in the Civil War, had been done away with. What was left of her family was dispersed. As German forces encroached still further into Russian territory, Tsvetaeva was evacuated to the provincial town of Elabuga, where she searched vainly for work. In unappeasable distress of spirit, she judged her case to be hopeless, and hanged herself from a beam in the cottage in which she was lodging. The deprivations of her life did not cease with her death; she was buried in an unmarked common grave. The paragraph on the death of Lara from the conclusion to *Doctor Zhivago* is the most memorable description of 'what so often happened in those days'. But the most poignant memorial for Tsvetaeva is to be found in the second of the books in which the late Nadezhda Mandelstam recounts the tragic fate of her husband: 'I know of no fate more tragic than Marina Tsvetaeva's ... I now realize that what she always needed was to experience every emotion to the utmost'. Insofar as it is the peculiar property of great poetry to satisfy comparable needs in its reader, Tsvetaeva must be accounted one of the greatest poets of the present century, more obviously vulnerable than those of a less ecstatic disposition but more triumphantly moving by very virtue of that vulnerability.

Vladimir Mayakovsky
(1893–1930)

Born in Bagdadi, now Mayakovsky, Georgia, the son of a
forester. Grew up speaking Georgian, though taught Russian
at school. Joined the Bolshevik movement in 1908, having
read revolutionary pamphlets as a child. Resident in Moscow
after the death of his father in 1906. Arrested for the first time
in 1908, and twice arrested in 1909, on the second occasion
being sent to Butyrki prison. Entered art school in 1911.
Encountered the avant-garde painter David Burliuk and
became one of the prime movers of the Russian Futurist
movement. Met Lili Brik in 1915, having first courted her
sister Elsa (later married to Louis Aragon) among others.
Lived in Moscow with Lili Brik and her husband from 1915
to 1917; often threatened suicide because of difficulties in his
affair with Lili Brik, despite her complaisant husband. In
Petrograd for the 1917 Revolution. Moved with the Briks to
Moscow on its reinstatement as the capital of the country in
1919, where he became a public performer, film actor and
poster artist. Often quarrelled publicly with the equally flam-
boyant poet Sergei Esenin. Endured periods of separation
from Lili Brik with what little fortitude he could muster, her
husband acting as peacemaker between them. Worked in
advertising and propaganda from 1923 to 1925. Visited
Mexico and North America in 1925, after which time he and
Lili were no longer intimate. In his last years engaged in
demanding lecture tours all over the Soviet Union. Fell in
love with a White *émigré* resident in Paris, whom he wished to
marry; refused an exit visa in 1927. Exhausted, depressed by
public criticism of his poetry, disturbed by the failure of the
First Five Year Plan and emotionally unsatisfied, he shot

himself through the heart in his Moscow flat. In 1935 Stalin was prompted to speak well of him, since when his poetry has been more or less uncritically adulated in the Soviet Union, and therefore often ignored outside it.

The traumas and ultimate tragedy of the life of Mayakovsky have been rehearsed sufficiently often for him to belong, unlike most modern poets, as much to the history of publicity as to the history of poetry. His posthumous fate, indeed, has been to continue to belong to both, the one poet of a prodigiously gifted generation of Russian writers to be canonized by the Soviet authorities, who otherwise sought so strenuously to throttle what we should now call 'dissidents'. Neither Lenin nor Stalin, it appears, cared much for Mayakovsky's verse, and the latter (whose later record suggests that not even a non-suicidal Mayakovsky could have survived for very much longer) needed some prompting before he could see the political and propaganda advantages of nominating him as *the* revolutionary poet *par excellence*. Since 1935 it has been virtual heresy to propose within the Soviet Union that Mayakovsky was *not* the Pushkin of his age, and accordingly his stock has fallen well below that of those poets whom the West sees as having a more secure entitlement to that position: Akhmatova, Pasternak, Mandelstam and Tsvetaeva. Tsvetaeva herself, interestingly enough, treated Mayakovsky no differently from any of the other poets, dead or alive, who were part of her personal pantheon; her passionate and typically undiplomatic defence of him, at a time when most of his best work was behind him, incurred her the intense and acrimonious displeasure of Russian *émigrés* in Paris who had every reason to dislike the state with which they indiscriminately associated him. Tsvetaeva, indeed, treated Mayakovsky much better than his professed antipathy to her work justified, and no doubt we should most of us now transfer her praise of his 'strength of anguish' to her own poetry. But it is within the terms proposed by Tsvetaeva that

Mayakovsky might once again find an uncommitted audience in the West, since neither his strength nor the anguish which inseparably accompanied it have much to do with what successive Soviet governments have tried to make of them.

'We do not need,' wrote Mayakovsky, 'a dead mausoleum of art where dead works are worshipped, but a living factory of the human spirit – in the streets, in the tramlines, in the factories, the workshops, and the homes of the workers.' It was ideas like these which led the young Mayakovsky, already a political activist, to think of art as a weapon of liberation that could be placed in the hands of those suffering under the whip of oppression; his project was nothing less than the demystification of cultural elitism. Culture, conceived of as an organic and evolutionary activity, was to be replaced at a stroke by manufacture, the systematized transformation of raw materials into objects of utility. Art was to surrender its claims, particularly vocal during the Symbolist epoch, to privileged access to the world of transcendent spiritual essences and become unashamedly materialist in accordance with the material needs of man; the appeal was unequivocally to 'the human spirit' rather than to anything so intangible as essences. Its utility was to be self-evidently exemplified in its application to the here-and-now. Its legitimacy was to be established by the fact that it was not a personal expression of feelings but a collective expression of convictions. This 'new spirit' naturally required manifestoes to root itself in the public domain, and the most famous of these was the aggressive document of 1912 ('A Slap In The Face of Public Taste') which recommended 'the throwing overboard of Pushkin, Dostoevsky, Tolstoy and others from the steamship of Modernity'. The stance was radically progressive, and epitomized by the adoption of the term Futurism as a rallying call. As an art form devoted to the production of real change in the world to which it was addressed, it prided itself on its vitalism, though crediting it largely to the circumstances out of which it had arisen. 'The poetry of Futurism,' said Mayakovsky in a speech of 1914, 'is the poetry of the city, of the contemporary city ... Feverishness is what characterizes the tempo of the contemporary world. In the city there are no flowing, measured lines of curvature: angles, fractures, zig-zags are what make up the profile of the city.' Mayakovsky's stress on visual properties is very striking here; he had begun his Moscow career by enrolling as an art student. His early poetry reads like an extension of his first impulses, especially the poem 'Could You?' which epitomizes the aggression and materialism of all the early Futurists:

I splashed some colours from a tumbler
and smeared the map of the drab world with them.
I daubed on a dish of jelly
the slanting cheekbones of an ocean.
I read the summons of newly vocal lips
upon the scales of a tin fish.
And you –
could you perform a nocturne
with just a drainpipe for a flute?

This is plainly an assertion of power, of *force majeure*, of what Tsvetaeva called 'strength'; but there is more than a little admixture of bravado, designed not so much to dare the addressees into emulation of the author as to place him beyond their reach. Mayakovsky's collectivism was spiced with more than a dash of egoism and inevitably gravitated towards a charismatic cult of personality.

Mayakovsky's first city poems are essentially verbal portraits of the metropolis at the moments of maximum transformation: dawn and sunset. The dawn of day is seen as an apocalyptic purifier of the hellish forces unleashed under cover of darkness; Mayakovsky's eye is fixed so implacably upon the objects of his perception that his own agency in animating them is effectively forgotten. This animation of everything from telephones to traffic is reminiscent of another great poet of the city, Dickens, always very popular in Russia; and it is the hallmark of all Mayakovsky's writing. No modern poet has rivalled his ability to render 'the language/the trains are yelling in' and his last long poem is characteristically titled 'At The Top Of My Voice'. But the bellowing Mayakovsky is only one of many; and the many-sidedness of Mayakovsky is nowhere better seen than in the play to which he, accurately rather than egotistically, gave his own name: *Vladimir Mayakovsky: a tragedy* (1913). The stage is populated by multiple Mayakovskies in frenzied juxtaposition one with another, the reflection of the poet's equally strong compulsions towards collectivism and egoism. 'All these cardboard dolls,' wrote an appreciative Russian commentator, 'were his dreams, dreams of a solitary and forgotten human soul, trapped in a chaos of movement.' The point is well made; Mayakovsky's need to multiply himself could never reach a terminal moment of repose; the lines of centrifugal force emanated from an inherently unstable centre, like a dynamo become detached from its fixture. It is significant that the lines which first came into the mind of Pasternak on hearing that Mayakovsky had shot himself should have been: 'I feel/that my "I"/is too small for me./Somebody keeps wanting to burst out of me'. His vitalism had, as its obverse, a desperate need to short circuit the circle within which it moved. As multiple man Mayakovsky felt perfectly justified in equating himself with the incarnate Christ; but his Christ was a suffering servant rather than a redeemer, since his innate materialism did not permit Him to be otherwise. As suffering servant Mayakovsky could see himself as necessary; the poet, he wrote in *Vladimir Mayakovsky: a tragedy*, 'is destined to suffer for all'. But his fear was that his sacrifice was meaningless, and to be 'so large, /and so unnecessary' (as in 'To His Beloved Self The Author Dedicates These Lines' of 1916) was to be crucified without redemption.

Most of Mayakovsky's claim to being 'wherever pain is' can be substantiated by his remarkable love poems, most of which were inspired by Lili, the wife of Osip Brik, with whom he lived more or less tranquilly in a *mènage à trois*. In his love poems Mayakovsky's voice is much more tender than in his rebarbative city poems, but his tenderness is never complacent. This is particularly clear in one of the great love poems in Russian, 'Lili dear! In Lieu Of A Letter' (1916), of which the following lines are especially moving:

If an ox is tired out by hard work –
off he goes
and plunges into cool waters.
Apart from your love,
for me
there is no sea,
and not even tears can wrest me a respite from your love.
If an exhausted elephant craves for rest –
he lies down in the scorched sand like a king.
Apart from your love,
for me
there is no sun,
and I don't know where you are or who you're with.

We might say of this unusually formal writing what Maya-kovsky says in another epistolary poem (the 'Letter From Paris to Comrade Kostov On The Essence And Meaning Of Love' of 1928), that it is 'simple/human/and true'. Or we might appropriate a line from Mayakovsky's great long poem of 1914–15, now a Russian proverb, and think of him as 'irre-proachably tender,/not a man but – a cloud in trousers!' It is certainly Mayakovsky at his least bombastic, and far re-moved from his avowed intention 'always to shine ... no matter what'. He could 'trample/ on the very throat of my own song' in ways that were more than merely destructive.

It was important for Mayakovsky to believe that he had 'erased the distinction/between my face and the faces of other people'; the Soviet authorities have inevitably taken the word for the deed, whilst nevertheless admiring the extravagantly long 'Vladimir Ilyich Lenin' of 1924 which makes its hero seem quite unlike 'other people'. The greatest of Maya-kovsky's long poems is undoubtedly the aptly titled 'Man' of 1916, which is typically volatile but ultimately pessimistic. The only moments of calm envisioned by this 'shadow torn to pieces' occur when, after visiting the 'sterile harmony' of heaven, he dreams of the 'caressing seas of eternity' and begs the vast open spaces to 'take this homeless one/again/to your bosom'. As a redemptive programme for man in general this is plainly not without its shortcomings, and has more to do with Mayakovsky's need to get beyond his age, and beyond time altogether, than with his embodiment of the *Zeitgeist*. As Viktor Shklovsky has said, 'The Revolution gave Mayakovsky new strength and peace of mind'; it provided a rationale for what had previously been gestures in a void. The Mayakovsky who became a 'newspaper poet', screenplay writer and commercial artist is, however, of much more limited appeal. The two and a quarter hours which it took Pasternak to read '150,000,000' (1919) understandably did nothing to convince him that it was anything other than 'uncreative' beside the earlier writings. Mayakovsky's proud boast that 'no one is the author of this my poem' can unfortunately be turned on its head; in his best work he is very definitely the only possible author. The poem on Brooklyn Bridge, inspired by his visit to America, attractive insofar as the poet has at last found something larger than himself, is much inferior to poems by Walt Whitman and Hart Crane. One of the most successful of the later poems is 'To Sergei Esenin' (1926), about the composition of which Mayakovsky writes most interestingly in his brief poetry manual 'How Verses Are Made'. But although it is a perfect illustration of how 'you must calculate how the printed text will be received *as* a printed text' – more so, perhaps, than some of the better-known experiments of William Carlos Williams – the poem's primary interest consists in the fact that Mayakovsky is mildly reprimanding the poet Esenin for a suicide which he himself was only four years away from.

Mayakovsky would have enjoyed the ironic component in the myth-making that has transformed him into the Pushkin of Soviet Russia. In a sense he almost predicted it; one of his late fragments shows him oscillating between a desire to be understood by his contemporaries and a fear that he may never be. In this respect he has certainly 'passed by my native land/

like a slanting rain', whatever those of a Socialist Realist persuasion may think of him. He has hardly received his due outside of Russia either, however, which ought to prompt readers to ignore his official Soviet status and to follow his own advice in the poem 'About That': 'Make me live again!'

Jorge Guillén (born 1893)

Born in Valladolid, and educated there until 1909. Studied in Fribourg, Switzerland from 1909 to 1911. Studied philosophy and literature in Madrid from 1911 to 1913 and spent a year in Germany after graduating. Lecturer in Spanish at the Sorbonne between 1917 and 1923; professor of Spanish literature at the University of Murcia from 1925 to 1929. Lecturer in Spanish Literature at the University of Oxford from 1929 to 1931. Professor of Spanish Literature at Seville University 1931–38. Jailed as a political prisoner in Pamplona in 1936; left Spain in 1938. Professor of Spanish at American universities from 1940 to 1957. Death of his first wife in 1949. Professor of Poetry at Harvard 1957–8, where he gave the Charles Eliot Norton lectures. Married for a second time in 1961. Largely resident in Europe after leaving America, and currently living in Malaga. A recipient of almost every major international academic and public award except the Nobel Prize, and recognized throughout Europe and North America as Spain's greatest living poet.

'During the nineteenth century', wrote Guillén in a book based on lectures given at Harvard in 1957–8, 'more than one writer was to wrestle with that problem which is so false: which is preferable, life or art? These words designate two distinct moments in close interdependence.' This is Guillén the critic, indeed Guillén the professor, speaking; but so close is the interdependence between his many activities that it is also an oblique statement of the poetics on which, over sixty years, Guillén has based his practice as a poet. In countering ideas of 'art for art's sake' Guillén does not revert to the opposite pole of 'art for life's sake'; he is quite as opposed to poets of a self-destructively vitalist tendency as to those of a world-dissolving aesthetic tendency. 'Interdependence' is his watchword; in another lecture he speaks of 'the requisite of great poetry: everything is related to everything else'. This does not, despite appearances, require the poet to be god; 'if there is to be poetry,' he says, in what looks truistical but is intended as a mild critique of some modern practices, 'it will have to be human'. The very fact that he tends to speak of 'poetry' rather than 'the poet' is an index of his distaste for anything resembling a cult of personality; discussing the poetry of Góngora, for example, he says 'Of the subject himself we know only what the glorified object tells us.' What agent, we are naturally led to inquire, glorifies the object? And Guillén's answer is: language. In this respect he is ostensibly inscribing his own enterprise within the poetics of Symbolism as articulated by Mallarmé; but he restores a dimension that Mallarmé, along with much else, wished to eliminate. He is happy enough to quote Mallarmé's famous 'It is not with ideas, my dear Degas, that poetry is made; it is with words'. But Mallarmé's severity is naturally anathema to a poet basing his own enterprise on ideas of interdependence: 'a word in a poem', comes Guillén's gentle reproof, 'is also an idea'. This explains why he should so admire the way in which, in St John of the Cross, 'the poet has acted along with the thinker'; Guillén believes, surely rightly, that the separation of thought and feeling will make the poet gravitate towards allegory and obscurity. Poetry, if it is to be human, must be 'intelligible sound' appealing to the mind and to the sensibility equally; in another formulation, where once again both elements are to be stressed, it is 'creative contemplation'. Guillén effectively corrects his penchant for Symbolism by returning to the Romantic notions out of which such ideas grew; when he speaks of poetry as 'a procreation half sought, half autonomous' we might almost be listening to Wordsworth or Coleridge. But any Romantic diffusion or vagueness is alien to him; he prizes 'exact language' and is suspicious of sublimity because rhetoric and eloquence threaten to disrupt the coherence of the enterprise and its essentially humble status. Only exactitude can temper the afflatus which inspires the poet to utterance; insofar as he is exact and exacting he cannot be a mystic visionary or a mere dreamer. As human being he is a creature of space and time, and poetry, or the individual poem, is similarly spatial and temporal. To quote once more from his exemplary analysis of St John of the Cross: '[it] is not a past already concluded that the poet reconstructs ... nothing in the poems is alien to the burning actuality which here and now – within the compass of the poem – sets forth its present acts of love'. Creation, whether of the world or of the poem, is conceived of as an act of love; Guillén, on his own admission, has never become estranged from his Christian upbringing. And though it might seem heresy to propose that the poet inhabits a continuous present such as orthodox Christianity attributes to its God, it is obviously only during 'creative contemplation' that he does so, and even there he is subject to restraints that God cannot be presumed to labour under.

If it seems dry and pedantic to begin the study of Guillén with his poetics, the profit which accrues is actually very considerable; it saves one from misapprehensions. He has often been taken to be the Spanish equivalent of Paul Valéry and therefore an exponent of 'pure poetry'. Guillén has indeed praised Valéry as 'a model of exemplary elevation of subject matter and of exemplary rigour of style' and he is probably the best translator of Valéry in any language. In giving the title *Cántico* (*Canticle*) to his gradually enlarged collection of poems (first published in 1928, and extended in 1936, 1945 and 1950) he appeared to have been influenced by one of the finest of Valéry's *Charms*, the 'Canticle Of The Columns'. But he must always have been unsympathetic to Valéry's stress on the 'manufacture' of poetry, and the same goes for Valéry's emphasis on the elimination of impurities. 'I am not pure in anything,' he writes in a poem in the volume *Clamour* (1963), 'And least of all in poetry.' The difference between the two poets has been very well defined by Octavio Paz:

Valéry's is a dialogue with himself; *Cántico* is 'the dialogue between man and creation'. Guillén's transparency reflects the world; his writing is a perpetual will towards incarnation.

It is precisely this will towards incarnation which gives Guillén a religious dimension that Valéry lacks; the impulse to call his first collection *Cántico* was not in emulation of Valéry, but rather an echo of the 'Spiritual Canticle' of St John of the Cross. *Cántico* was written, as its subtitle reminds us, 'In Praise Of Living', in the faith that – in the words of its most famous and most misunderstood line – 'The world is well/Made'. Since Guillén's poetry is also astonishingly well made, his critics were quick to reproach him for a utopian optimism out of kilter with a predominantly tragic age. The poet's reply to such criticisms occurs in a poem ('From Contact To Act') in his third collection *Homage* (1967): 'The human world will never be well made.' This conviction obviously precluded a 'retreat into the inner life' such as Valéry had undertaken; for Guillén, 'the "I" is imprisoned in something infinitely superior to itself' and only liberates itself when it experiences 'the fundamental emotion of wonder'. A more profitable parallel, then, would be with the late poetry of T. S. Eliot, whom Guillén has often quoted with approval; for Guillén, like the Eliot of 'Marina', is in quest of 'a grace dissolved in place' in the fullest sense of the phrase. In a preface specially written for the first English translation of a selection from *Cántico*, he stressed that his subject matter was 'drawn from a number of actual experiences, rooted in time and place', at the same time as emphasizing that they were only points of departure towards the place of the poem that made sense of them. It is this 'reality', and not the quantity surveying of 'realism', which makes Guillén so much more than a mere landscape poet. Even in the poems written after *Cántico*, which more often reveal their precise points of origin, Guillén's world remains essentially the same wherever he happens to encounter it, whether in Spain, or Italy, or Denmark, or America. And, clearly, *whenever* he happens to encounter it, the similarities are more important than the dissimilarities; it is typical of Guillén to treat his own poetry, in his most recent selection for an English-speaking audience, in thematic rather than developmental terms, as if it all existed in a kind of permanent present, and the differences between earlier and later poems did not matter.

It is the present which concerns Guillén, and his favoured tense is naturally the present indicative. But it is not, as some critics have felt, a timeless present; as Guillén himself has warned us, 'the present is never free: it has a past and goes towards the future'. Guillén has perhaps paid the price here for the sheer solidity of his intimations of plenitude, clarity and integrity, although the subtle architecture of his poems is designed to reveal the disorder from which these intimations have sprung. He is the opposite of a static poet; this is clear in any number of short poems which, without foregrounding their virtuosity, stand revealed as a single sentence. It is best to think of Guillén, as he sees himself, as a poet of 'imminence', one of the words – typically enough a substantive – which he habitually uses. The paradisial May of the beautiful 'Garden In The Middle', for example, is moving without haste towards June; the perception of 'some man/In his serene moment' is a prelude to the realization that at another time the moment will be 'recomposed' to disclose 'the discordant world round about'. Similarly, although the long poem 'The Concert' – a reflection of Guillén's passion for music – begins with the hope of 'A world/Where I begin to breathe with all/My harmonious silences', it is only at the end that 'Absolute harmony in human air' is actually achieved. Guillén's triumph is the supremely difficult one of playing variations on a single theme, and he achieves this by giving a quite remarkable precision to whatever stanza form he elects to use. The reciprocation between word and world is dramatic and total, and exemplifies the complex truth of Guillén's apparently simple claim that 'Cántico is an act of attention'.

Since Guillén has been persistently presumed to be an exponent of 'pure poetry', it is only natural that he should also have been thought to be cerebral and bloodless. But he is much less so than Valéry, and as he openly says in part four of his magnificent 'Salvation Of Spring': 'The flesh expresses more.' This is an explicitly sexual poem of perfect delicacy; it recognizes the unsustainable ecstasy of the sexual spasm without doubting the perfection of love. The same is true of another excellent long poem 'Ring', where the sexual climax becomes an index of 'Delight in being' and everything becomes subservient for a moment to the 'potency of an astonished cry'. It is with such an 'astonished cry' – 'O absolute Present!' – that the famous short poem 'Nude' ends, with the gradual crystallization of a body, recognized as such only in the last stanza, and suddenly revealed to be feminine. The body here, as in that most delicate of single quatrain poems 'Love Sleeping', is in repose, and the stanza form is a reflection of this repose. It is out of this repose, this 'just monotony', that the exclamation at the end emerges, justifying the attribution to the body of a 'prodigious/Plenty of presence'. A quieter revelation informs 'Love Sleeping', where the insomniac man is suddenly encircled by his lover's arms and consoled by the realization that 'Your dream involved me, I felt myself dreamed'.

The epigraph to section four of *Cántico*, a quotation from Lope de Vega, reminds us that the poetry of Guillén is 'a real essence demanding to be touched' and far removed from 'weary philosophy'. But it is precisely because the touching agent is the soul that Guillén's poetry seems philosophical in a wider sense. 'How watchful the soul!' Guillén exclaims in 'Cradle, Roses, Balcony'; but the soul is not merely a spectator, as the conclusion to 'The Hoped For' confirms. Guillén's characteristic discovery of 'plenitude' is here achieved by a soul which ('without losing/The body') conquers the 'aching vacuity' which has been threatening it. The more obviously physical 'Ring' poem is built on similarly metaphysical foundations, with the soul succouring the flesh and lifting it beyond its momentary 'delight in being' to a transcendent 'delight of delights'. The soul does not exist in isolation; as the poem 'Portent' shows, it remains 'invisible' until it finds itself 'among things'. These 'things' are often non-human, but not exclusively so. Indeed, in the very moving poem 'More Life', it is the poet's own son who brings into being, and clarifies, his father's soul. Similarly, in the poem 'Invocation', it is the 'naked mouth' of a beloved which enables the poet's soul to 'unfold its form'. Guillén's unique sensitivity to 'imminence', especially clear in 'Invocation', is a corollary of his notion that the soul is keeping vigil, like a sentry, over our dreams ('World Understood', i). It is clear that he sees the soul as the source and origin of the poet's never ending 'adventure': to recreate the world in words. The images of rebirth which stud the whole of *Cántico* are at once descriptive and mimetic, a reflection of the dawns and springs which take place outside the poet and yet inaugurate kindred dawns and springs within him.

Guillén is not, then, the 'still life' poet he is so often taken to be; the poem in *Cántico* called 'Unstill Life' confirms this. But it is even clearer in the volumes beyond *Cántico*, in *Clamour* (with its explicit orientation towards the 'time of history') and in *Homage*. Like *Cántico*, these volumes are committed to the idea expressed in a poem from *Homage*, that 'the earth is a great adventure'. They are, however, much less laconic and taut than the *Cántico* poems, *Clamour* especially. The 'concrete wonders' of *Cántico* have given way to more malleable forms. But there has not been any loss of power, as a comparison of 'The Story With No End' (a poem in *Homage* addressed to his son) with the famous 'More Life' of *Cántico* reveals. *Clamour* actually contains some of his greatest love poems. The quality of these two later collections, together with the 'other poems' which Guillén has recently added to them, consolidates what *Cántico* had already proved: that it was possible for a great poet to breathe 'our air' (*Our Air* is Guillén's new title for his 'one work') and to make his poetry an irresistible invitation to his readers to do likewise. Of the poets of Spain's 'generation of '27' – so called because of their desire to celebrate the tercentenary of Góngora's birth – Lorca is likely to remain the most popular; Guillén has described his friend as 'Spain's only great tragic poet since Calderón'. But of those who survived the Spanish Civil War and continued to practise their craft in exile Guillén has certainly made the most profound impact on the world at large, in the quiet, gradual, uncharismatic manner he would have preferred.

Paul Éluard (1895–1952)

Born Eugène Grindel in Saint-Denis of lower middle class parents, and educated in Paris. Suffered from tuberculosis and spent the years 1912–14 in a sanatorium at Davos, where he met his future wife. Fought on the Western Front during the First World War. Married in 1917. A close associate of André Breton's, with whom he founded the Surrealist movement after the war. Suddenly left Paris in 1924 because of difficulties in his marriage, spending eight months in South America, Australia and the Far East. Separated from his wife, who later married the painter Salvador Dalí, in 1930; remarried in 1934. Supported the Republican cause in the Spanish Civil War and renewed his early allegiance to the Communist party, an act which led to estrangement between him and Breton. In hiding during the Second World War, having joined the Resistance in 1942. Death of his second wife in 1946. Internationally famous after the war, and invited to visit Italy, Yugoslavia, Greece and Poland. Married for a third time in 1951. Died in Paris of a heart attack.

In a programme note for the 1917 production of *Parade* Apollinaire praised the ballet for its 'surrealism' and expressed the hope that this collaborative venture – concocted by Picasso, Diaghilev, Cocteau and Erik Satie – would be 'the point of departure for a series of manifestations of that New Spirit which ... promises to modify the arts and the conduct of life from top to bottom'. Rarely can such an inherently ephemeral publication have contained such a prophetic statement; but Apollinaire did not live to see his prophecy fulfilled. In the event it was left to an even more vocal apologist, 'one of the centres of gravity of our time' (in the words of Octavio Paz), to be the chief spokesman for Surrealism: André Breton. Breton led by example; his novel *Nadja* (1928) is one of the most successful of all Surrealist literary works. But he naturally made most impact with the theoretical statements describing the nature and aims of the Surrealist movement – the First (1924) and Second (1929) Manifestoes of Surrealism. In the second manifesto, for example, Breton spoke of a 'total recuperation of our psychic forces by a means which is none other than a vertiginous descent within ourselves' and proceeded to show that Surrealism was an experiment designed to determine the psychic point which would guarantee such a recuperation:

Everything induces one to believe that there exists a certain point in the mind where life and death, the real and the imaginary, the past and the future, the communicable and the incommunicable, the sublime and the mundane, cease to be perceived as contradictory.

The idea was much less new than it appeared; over a century before the German Romantic poet and mystic Novalis had suggested that the destruction of the law of contradiction would be 'the supreme task of the higher logic' of poetry. But Breton did not pride himself on his originality. In fact he delighted in demonstrating that Surrealism always had existed and always would do so. What he had done was to extend, in a manner anticipated by Apollinaire's reference to 'the conduct of life', the 'higher logic' from the purely literary sphere in which it had originated to life as it is lived. Surrealism thus became virtually synonymous with reality, except insofar as it had to combat a reality inimical to it. In this respect it required a strategy whereby the party of opposition might come to power. And Breton found the model for such a strategy in the life and writings of Arthur Rimbaud. Two works of Rimbaud's had a particularly profound effect on him: the now famous letter to Paul Démeny in which Rimbaud speaks of a 'systematic disorganization of all the senses' as an essential preliminary for the 'visionary' poet, and *A Season In Hell*, which stresses that 'Love must be reinvented' and which ends with Rimbaud on the point of possessing 'truth in one soul and one body'. Surrealist activity – and Breton's stress (like Rimbaud's) fell quite as much upon the performative aspects as upon the introspective 'descent' – was largely fuelled by the determination to make Rimbaud's idealism bear fruit in practice. And, since the Surrealists viewed differentials as improperly perceived manifestations of a higher unity, collaboration – like that which had given rise to the ballet *Parade* – was actively encouraged. The most important of the many who either collaborated with Breton or sympathized with his aims was the figure whose secession from the movement effectively precipitated its fragmentation: Paul Éluard.

If there is little agreement as to whether Dalí or Magritte should be considered the most considerable Surrealist painter, there is a general consensus that Éluard is the finest of the many poets who joined the movement. Significantly perhaps, his early poems show that he was a Surrealist in all but name long before Breton's first manifesto. With hindsight it is clear that his early poems – the best of which are included in the selection he made from his many volumes, by which he is generally known – prefigure the distinctively Surrealist exaltation of love, desire, freedom and the subconscious. In the 1918 *Poems For The Peace* Éluard added the socio-political dimension which was once again to become important to him during the Second World War and the years which led up to it. But the first really experimental poems of Éluard's are the eleven *haiku* of the collection *To Live Here* (1920), their very brevity a dramatic illustration of the 'dumb speech' to which the poet refers in the pivotal poem of the sequence. And the subsequent prose poems of *The Necessities of Life and the Consequences of Dreams* (1921) are similarly terse. Of the poems in this volume which we should now unhesitatingly designate 'surreal' 'Laziness' is one of the most eerie and disconcerting:

I threw my lamp into the garden to see day
and I went to sleep. The noise shifted everything
outside. My ears sleep. The light knocks on the door.

As a 'disorganization of all the senses' this is more extreme
than anything in Rimbaud, though it is very difficult to say
what is 'systematic' about it. The Surrealists were really not
interested in systems; having taken *A Season In Hell* to be an ex-
tempore work they felt justified in recommending 'pure
psychic acts of automatism'. A great deal of very poor, and
anything but pure, poetry had significance conferred on it
simply because it was the product of automatic writing. But
Éluard's verse did not become merely anarchic; he was care-
ful to keep (in the words of the poem 'Eye Of The Deaf' from
the 1921 collection) 'the thoughts of my head fastened to the
hands of my activity'.

Éluard's poetry is dominated by the awareness that love
must be reinvented perpetually, not just once and for all; des-
pite his fundamental optimism, he was a prey to moments
of acute desolation in which love and brotherhood were
threatened by the inescapable evidences of human frailty.
One of the *152 Proverbs* written in collaboration with Benjamin
Péret illustrates, if it is Éluard's, how the positive and negative
aspects of love were of equal significance to him: 'it is better
to die of love than to love without regrets'. Love, for Éluard,
embodied the dynamism of death and rebirth. The title of his
1924 volume (which Picasso had found in St Teresa of
Ávila, and which lost its religious meaning on its adoption by
Éluard) is significant in this respect: *Dying Of Not Dying*.
Éluard described this collection as 'my last book' and the day
before it was published left Paris in a Rimbaud-like attempt
to leave literature behind; his first marriage had run into diffi-
culties owing to his wife's infidelity with the painter Max
Ernst. But *Dying Of Not Dying* contains many of his most
memorable poems, notably the lyric which has achieved con-
siderable currency in Samuel Beckett's remarkable trans-
lation ('Lady Love'):

She is standing on my lids
And her hair is in my hair

She has the colour of my eye
She has the body of my hand
In my shade she is engulfed
As a stone against the sky

She will never close her eyes
And she does not let me sleep
And her dreams in the bright day
Make the suns evaporate
And me laugh cry and laugh
Speak when I have nothing to say

'Love,' as Éluard came to realize in 'Out Of Sight In The
Direction Of My Body' (which Beckett also translated), 'is
man unfinished'. And to reflect this the poetry inspired by
love (the bulk of Éluard's *oeuvre*) must also be 'unfinished'; it
must be demonstrably a matter of the process rather than the
product, the 'mirror of a moment' in the words of a title from
the volume *Capital Of Pain* (1926):

What the hand has grasped disdains even to take the form of the hand,
What has been understood exists no longer,
The bird is confounded with the breeze,
The sky with its truth,
The man with his reality.

Capital Of Pain is a very turbulent volume, nowhere more so
than in the greatest of Éluard's prose poems, the long 'Nights
Together', which ends with him hoping to sublimate his erotic
confusions in a more general love of mankind: 'perhaps I shall
take the side of beings different from the one I invented. What
good will I be to them?' He restored his equilibrium by
learning to love love itself rather than any specific loved one,
and by making love the basis of his ideas on the subject of
political freedom. In 1926 he joined the Communist Party
and began to 'take the side of beings different from the one I
invented.' But Éluard's political poetry is much inferior to
that of Mayakovsky, or Brecht, or Neruda, or Yannis Ritsos;
he ceased to sing and began to shout. In the years before war
broke out he wrote a number of fine love poems and many
mediocre political ones. His cause was always Surrealism

rather than Marxism, even if his populist tendencies did lead to disagreements with, and ultimately separation from André Breton. And one of his most valuable efforts on behalf of Surrealism was his collection of Surrealist and pre-Surrealist *obiter dicta*, where he showed himself to be a supremely good anthologist. Only when he joined the French Resistance did he find a real struggle to which his ideas were perfectly adapted, and with the poem 'Liberty' of 1942 he achieved a massive audience throughout France, the first Surrealist that the French had really taken to their hearts. Here at least Surrealism was not in competition with reality, as was inevitable in the days when the Surrealists were beginning to become notorious, but equivalent with it. Breton had proclaimed as much at its inception, but the sheer strangeness of the language in which he and the other Surrealists had tried to demonstrate the fact had inevitably made it difficult for those who saw reality differently to be convinced by them.

Éluard's renewed vigour during the war years was confirmed by the publication in 1946 of *Uninterrupted Poetry*. This is a kind of Surrealist equivalent of what the much-despised Realist writers would have called 'a slice of life', beginning and ending *in medias res* as if it were only a selection of what might be said. The title poem opens with a mass of random attributive adjectives designed to embody a pre-creative chaos against which the relative clarity of the rest of the poem may figure. These suspended juxtapositions are a crude exemplification of the principle of identity elaborated in more subtle strategies later in the poem. Having spoken in various roles throughout the poem, Éluard concentrates his energies in the conclusion on an attempt to make the lover and the beloved an index of universal human brotherhood. The living stand revealed at the end as beneficiaries of the 'conquered liberty' which the poem has actively embodied. But the living can only be beneficiaries if they are actually involved in the real world; Éluard's Surrealism remained from start to finish profoundly activist, in accord with the first principles of the movement.

It was Éluard's conviction that a poet could only be

described as inspired in the sense that he inspired others; the 'descent within ourselves' proposed by Breton was transformed by Éluard into an activity in which mankind was collectively involved. But despite widespread admiration for the manner in which he made his poetry 'uninterrupted' there were many voices raised against it. In an essay of 1949, for example, Eugenio Montale offered cogent reasons why purely Surrealist poetry ran the risk of leaving its reader much as it found him:

> At best it is sustained by a mechanical association of ideas. The reader has to create the poetry for himself; the author has not chosen for him, has not willed something for him, he has limited himself to providing the possibility of poetry. This is a great deal in itself, but not enough to remain with us after the reading.

The point is well-made; even the most forbiddingly difficult and complex modern poetry that is non-Surrealist in inspiration lives longer in the mind than the best Surrealist poems. Novalis's dream of a higher logic in which the law of contradiction might be transcended depends upon the poet exerting a strict control over his materials, on his not departing too far from the procedures of the logician whose function he is assuming; to impose such a control remained foreign to the whole spirit of Surrealism. The watchword was 'surprise', as in the later poems of Apollinaire; but the poetics of surprise are vulnerable to the very processes of change and erosion which they are intended to reflect. Éluard came as near as any poet could come to realizing the project of a genuinely 'uninterrupted' poetry and he invariably delights a sympathetic and selective reader of his work. But his primary function was to inspire others, and it is in those who passed through a Surrealist or quasi-Surrealist phase – Paz, Ritsos, Popa, Bonnefoy – that we should look for the enduring achievements which this profoundly influential, but peculiarly musclebound, movement generated.

Eugenio Montale (1896–1981)

Born in Genoa, the youngest son of a businessman. Deeply
impressed by the landscape of the Ligurian coast, where his
formative years were spent. Called up for military service in
1917, after which he abandoned his first ambition to be an
opera singer and began to write the poems of *Ossi di Seppia*
which were to make him famous. Moved to Florence in
1927, where he worked for a publisher and was appointed
director of a library. Considered his twenty years in Florence
the most important so far as his cultural development was
concerned, though his non-alignment with the Fascist
authorities caused him to lose his job and to be viewed with
suspicion. Supported himself by translation during the war
years and shielded the poet Saba from Fascist persecution.
Turned to journalism after the war, moving in 1948 to Milan,
where he was given a regular column in the *Corriere della
Sera*. Began to paint in watercolour in 1946 during his wife's
illness in a sanatorium. Travelled widely throughout Europe
and the Middle East in the immediate post-war period; a
regular first-nighter at La Scala for many years. Inter-
nationally known before the Second World War, but especi-
ally highly regarded at home and abroad in the years since the
war. Deeply distressed by the death of his wife in 1963, and
thereafter increasingly solitary. Made a senator for life in
1968. A trenchant critic of modern culture in his journalism
and in his prose writings; an accomplished translator, especi-
ally of English poetry.

In an essay on T. S. Eliot published in 1947 Montale spoke of how the Anglo-American poet had been brought 'back to the centre' by an 'internal gravitation' purified of any tendency towards narcissism: 'his conversion', Montale writes, 'was not due to looking in a mirror'. The essay was written at a time when Montale himself, ever-conscious of the 'internal gravitation' of his own sensibility, felt most powerfully the need for a comparable 'conversion'. However, Montale was temperamentally unable to accept the way the 'exemplary' Eliot – Anglo-Catholic, royalist and classicist – had chosen to go 'back to the centre'; the position occupied by this greatest of modern Italian poets was the more troubled, more Existentialist, more vacillating one of being between the centre and the circumference. In post-war Europe this has come to seem as 'exemplary' in its own way as anything that Montale found in Eliot, and it led – belatedly but justifiably – to Montale being awarded the 1975 Nobel Prize. But it deprived Montale of access to the security that might have followed a 'conversion'. His desire, as he himself admitted, had always been to 'interrogate life': 'I have knocked desperately [on the doors of the impossible] like one who awaits an answer'. He accordingly chose none of the answers that have dominated twentieth-century Italy: Catholicism, Communism, Fascism. And although he believed that 'the earthly adventure of a man must have some sort of meaning' he became more and more convinced that 'life has a significance which eludes us'. Without turning his back on life, which in his opinion no true poet could ever do, he came to the conclusion that 'the art which best reflects its time cannot live unless it escapes from its time'. The artists he favoured were therefore those who, from their own isolation, 'echo the fatal isolation of each one of us', but who nonetheless communicate, who 'remain on the alert', who 'keep their eyes open'. The poet, in Montale's view, 'needs a truth which talks of that which unites man to other men, without denying all that separates and makes him unique'; in this sense he was justified in seeing poetry as 'more a means of knowledge than of representation'. But the knowledge he was able to impart was conditioned by his overwhelming sense of dislocation:

'since I have felt completely out of harmony with the reality surrounding me ever since my birth, this same disharmony was necessarily my source of inspiration'.

Montale's most celebrated expressions of 'disharmony' are to be found in his first collection *Cuttlefish Bones*, first published in 1925 and reprinted three years later with five formidable new poems added. In 'Intentions' (an 'imaginary interview' of 1946) he describes the volume in terms of a quest that had failed:

I wanted my words to adhere more closely to what I was expressing than was the case with other poets I knew. I seemed to be living under a glass bell, and yet I felt myself close to something essential. A thin veil, a mere thread divided me from that definitive *quid*. Absolute expression would have meant the tearing of that veil, the breaking of that thread: an explosion, the end of the illusion of the world as representation. But such an end was unattainable . . .

The sense of someone living 'under a glass bell' is indeed very strong in *Cuttlefish Bones*. As one untitled poem puts it: 'Above the graffitied wall/which shades a few seats/the arch of the sky seems/finite'. The long and complex 'Chrysalis' poem (one of those added to the second edition) strikes a similar note:

we shall go forward without dislodging
a single stone in the great wall;
and perhaps everything is fixed, everything written,
and we shall not see rising out of the road
freedom, the miracle,
the single fact that was not necessary.

If this is indeed the case, the poet's only recourse, as expressed in the most famous line of this collection, is 'following a wall/ with sharp shards of glass on top of it'. Yet this deterministic vision is not narrowly solipsistic; the stimulus towards utterance repeatedly originates in the world outside the self. This is notably the case in the sequence 'Mediterranean', where Montale makes his most ambitious and conventionally eloquent attempt to be 'vast and various/and hold as one' like the 'ancient one' on whose shore he spent the summers of his childhood. He is in search, as one of these poems shows, of a 'brotherly heart' which will temper what is elsewhere called 'the evil of living'; and if the quest fails, it clearly represents an advance on the private solution recorded in the poem 'Perhaps One Morning'. In this latter poem a 'miracle' (a 'tearing of [the] veil' in the terms of the imaginary interview) takes place; but the poet seems content to hug his 'secret' to himself. The only brotherly aspect of such a gesture is that 'those who do not turn' have been spared from seeing the vision of the void that the tearing of the veil has disclosed. Montale later claimed that 'the miracle is as obvious as the necessity', but it hardly seems so in *Cuttlefish Bones*. 'The world exists', as 'Wind And Flags' reminds us, and transcendence of the world seems to involve its immolation and disappearance. It is a pessimistic vision, clearly enough influenced by the philosophy of Schopenhauer. But like that philosophy it permits what Montale (in 'House On The Sea') calls a 'miserly hope'. 'House On The Sea' is an elegiac poem of farewell at the end of a love affair, in which Montale experiences exactly the kind of threshold situation which is emblematic of being 'close to something essential' that is 'unattainable':

I think that for most there is no salvation
but someone may subvert each plan,
cross over, recover the self he wanted.

'House On The Sea' is one of the poems added to the second edition of *Cuttlefish Bones*, and even if these were also written, as Montale suggests, 'with clenched teeth and often without the calm and detachment that many believe essential for the creative act', they are manifestly among the greatest poems he ever wrote. The most famous of them is 'Arsenio', where the poet's *alter ego* suffers a 'delirium of immobility' during a sudden Mediterranean storm of the kind that had decisively reorientated the career of the young Paul Valéry. This annihilating storm leaves Arsenio fixed in 'a frozen multitude of dead' like those encountered by Dante in the *Inferno*, haunted by intimations of something that has been irrevocably swept away:

and should a gesture brush you, a word
fall beside you, that perhaps, Arsenio,
in the hour which melts, is the sign of a
strangled life which rose for you, and the wind
carries it off with the ashes of the stars.

Out of this desperate melancholy Montale conjured, in the
poems 'Delta' and 'Meeting', the first manifestation of a
potentially redemptive figure, a Beatrice who might intercede
for him after his descent into the infernal regions. It may or
may not be coincidental that, as his letters to the novelist
Svevo show, it was at about this time that he met the woman
who was to become his wife. 'I know nothing about you', he
writes in 'Delta', 'except the mute/message which sustains me
on the way'. It is into her care that he is ready to surrender
himself at the end of 'Meeting':

> Pray for me
> when I descend another way
> than a city street,
> in the red-black air, before the swarm
> of the living; that I feel you at my side; that I
> descend without cowardice.

The poems of Montale's second collection (*Occasions*, 1939)
chart the consequences of such a surrender and the various
hells to be endured if any kind of salvation is to supervene.

Montale suggests in the imaginary interview that he was
seeking in his second collection to resolve 'the dualism be-
tween lyricism and exegesis' which for him had compromised
his first collection. His new aim was 'to express the object and
to say nothing about the stimulus for the occasion', thereby
'immersing the reader *in medias res*'. However, many of the
more expansive poems in *Occasions* ('Dora Markus, i', 'The
Shorewatcher's House', 'Low Tide' and 'Stanzas', for
example) are recognizably like those which mix lyricism and
exegesis in *Cuttlefish Bones*. 'Dora Markus, i' describes the
poet's parting from a kind of existential heroine who survives
catastrophe by placing her faith in trivial but effective
talismans; 'Stanzas' treats of the more sublime but less effec-

tive talismans of the great modern poets against whom
Montale would wish his own enterprise to be judged.
Temperamentally unable to place his trust in either the
mundane or the transcendent palliatives offered by these
companions, he is left, as in 'The Shorewatcher's House'
(perhaps the finest of this group of poems), utterly bereft and
bewildered, immersed in a turmoil of uncertainties, equally
unsure of who or what remains and of who or what has
departed.

In the sequence 'Motets' (composed between 1923 and
1938) it is the reader who is most likely to find himself be-
wildered, for Montale is here at his most terse and enigmatic,
and saying next to nothing about the 'stimulus for the
occasion'. The notion that the poet can still cling to the
threads which his memory preserves (which has already been
subjected to intense pressure in 'The Shorewatcher's House')
is effectively abandoned in the 'Motets', where memory seems
to have become defenceless against a reality grown truly
infernal:

> I seek the lost
> sign, the only pledge of grace I had
> from you.
> > And hell is certain.
> > > ('Motets', i)

Yet despite this manifest deterioration in Montale's spiritual
condition, there remain threads for the creative reader to
weave into a pattern. The 'Motets' are full of signs regained
and lost again, a perfect illustration of the line with which
they begin: 'You know it: I must lose you again and cannot'.
None of these signs is more memorable or more puzzling than
that which ends the sixth poem of the sequence:

> The hope of even seeing you again
> was slipping from me;
> and I asked myself if that which encloses
> each sense of you, that screen of images,
> contains the signs of death or of the past
> still in it, distorted and grown fugitive however,
> some glare of *you*:

(at Modena, between the arches,
a liveried servant dragged
two jackals on a leash).

Much of the comparative obscurity of the 'Motets' is attri-
butable to the fact that they were written during the period
which saw the growth of Fascism in Italy; this effectively
forced Montale to mask what his poetry was really saying and
to undertake an 'inner emigration' of the kind that other
poets in the 1930s were also forced to make. Italy's temporary
decline into barbarism provides a backdrop for the un-
mistakable but enigmatic gestures of farewell throughout the
'Motets', which culminate in the last words of the last poem
in the sequence: 'Life which seemed/vast is smaller than your
handkerchief'.

   The poems that follow the 'Motets' in *Occasions* dramatize
Montale's quest for something that he might not have to say
farewell to, though he is now unavoidably aware of the harsh
truth contained in the penultimate motet: 'And time passes'.
It is passing time which dominates 'Times At Bellosguardo',
'Point Of The Mesco', 'Eastbourne' and 'Boats On The
Marne'. In trying, in the second of the 'Dora Markus' poems
(written thirteen years after the first one), to conjure a voice
that does not change, Montale is forced to acknowledge that
'it is late, always later'. Survival (as the poem 'New
Stanzas' suggests) is dependent on developing 'eyes of steel'
appropriate to the worsening political situation; the 'thin
stream of pity and piety' which makes the end of 'News from
Mount Amiata' so memorable is plainly not going to be sus-
taining in the face of the cataclysm ahead.

   During the war Montale published the collection *Finisterre*
in neutral Switzerland; it was later incorporated into what is
best considered his third major collection, *The Storm And Other*
(1956). The first part of this title is taken from the first poem
in *Finisterre*, 'The Storm', which bears an epigraph indicative
of the mood of the collection: 'Princes have no eyes to see great
marvels,/Their hands serve only to persecute us'. Here the
Beatrice-figure of intercession seems to have receded, or to be

present only in glimpses that increase the poet's sense of persecution:

> If only I could hear
> nothing of you, escape the glare
> of your glance. Quite otherwise on earth it is . . .
> prayer is torture and not yet
> among the surging rocks has the bottle
> from the sea reached you. Empty, the wave
> breaks on the promontory, at Finisterre.

('On A Letter Unwritten')

As another poem indicates in its title, the crucial *personae* are now increasingly *separatae:*

> Your shape
> passed here, and paused on the water
> among the grounded lobster-pots, then faded
> like a sigh, dissolved – and there was no
> deluge . . .

('Personae separatae')

Montale has described *Finisterre* in 'Intentions' as his 'Petrarchan experience' which suggests that it was a more secular and more tormenting one than the essentially Dantean experiences, infernal but with at least the prospect of salvation, which had preceded it. It certainly seems as if the 'Christian struggle' referred to in 'News From Mount Amiata' had taken on a different character. Montale himself spoke of the female figure found in *Finisterre* as 'the continuator and symbol of the eternal Christian sacrifice', and one wonders how much the illness of his wife affected this conception. But insofar as Montale's new stress fell on sacrifice, he must have known himself to be openly embracing what the creator of Beatrice (who is not sacrificed), the orthodox Dante, would have condemned as heresy. The nature and extent of this heresy only became clear when *The Storm And Other* was published in 1956.

It is the short poem 'Syria' in the 1956 collection which indicates the direction in which Montale is moving:

The ancients used to say that poetry
is a ladder to God. Perhaps this is not the case
if you read me. But I knew it the day
I found my voice again through you ...

The female figure has here become more important to him
than the God whose representative she might once have been.
And in 'The Garden', with its more characteristic Montalean
insistence on 'I do not know', it is the poet and his muse which
matter, not God. A lessening of tension supervenes, for in
'Voice Arriving With The Coots' this muse tells him that
'Memory is not a sin so long as it is not sterile', which is
virtually a retrospective critique of the experiences drama-
tized in *Occasions*. And the famous 'Eel' poem, one long ser-
pentine sentence, even speaks of 'edens of fertility' that were
signally absent from the harsh landscapes of Montale's earlier
poetry. But just at the point where he seems to be about to
experience a 'conversion', albeit of a much more secular kind
than Eliot's, Montale's habitual scepticism reasserts itself.
Although both of the poems in the 'Provisional Conclusions'
which bring *The Storm And Other* to an end make use of the
image of the rainbow, the biblical sign of God's covenant with
men, neither is truly affirmative. Montale remains 'close to
something essential' but does not quite attain it:

I have risen, I have fallen
into the depths whose epoch is the passing minute –

and once again resound the blows and footsteps
and still I do not know whether I
shall eat or be eaten at the banquet. The suspense is long,
my dream of you is not ended.

The three subsequent collections, in which a garrulous and
casual Montale replaced the reticent and hesitant figure of
the earlier volumes, indicated precisely how unfinished his
dream was doomed to remain. The death of his wife in 1964
prompted him to write poems in which the 'stimulus for the
occasion' (to adopt his own description of *Occasions*) became
remarkably explicit and all pretension to objectivity disap-
peared. Of the poems he wrote after turning sixty these

are certainly the most moving; 'out of the inertia of intimate speech,' Joseph Brodsky has written, 'emerges a private mythology'. Montale himself said: 'I would not dare to speak of the myth of my poetry ... I am a poet who has written a poetic autobiography'. The 'Diary' and 'Notebook' poems, together with the prose pieces in *The Butterfly of Dinard*, confirm this. But the profound dissatisfactions out of which Montale's great poetry sprang seem to have become trivialized into irritations. He simplified his style, like other difficult poets before him; but it is in his difficult poetry that he comes closest to being 'essential'. In his last three volumes he seems to have acquiesced in his failure to find the meaning and the knowledge that he had previously struggled to discover; he became refractory and contingent in ways that were disconcerting rather than illuminating. Montale's claim to distinction depends on the poems of his first three volumes, where he is by general consensus the greatest Italian poet since Leopardi and one of the great Italian poets of all time.

Federico García Lorca
(1898–1936)

Born in Fuentevaqueros, Granada, the eldest son of a rich farmer. Suffered a serious illness soon after his birth which left him with a slight limp. Fascinated by the theatre from an early age. A brilliant musician in both the classical and the folk-song traditions. Educated in Granada and in Madrid, but not of an academic disposition; a close friend of Salvador Dalí and associated with all the leading Spanish literary figures in the capital. Left Spain for New York in the wake of accusations that he was homosexual; spent some time in Cuba. Returned to Granada, where he enthusiastically welcomed the Spanish Republic of 1931. Visited Argentina in 1933 and lived in Madrid. Largely occupied in the writing of plays after the phenomenal success of his *Romancero Gitano* in 1929. Murdered in Granada by Nationalists.

Garcia Lorca is the one modern Spanish poet whose life and work have taken on a symbolic and representative character in the minds of readers throughout the world; so popular has Lorca been that in some quarters his name is considered effectively synonymous with modern poetry in the Spanish language. His exceptionally vivid and vibrant verse has had much to do with his posthumous fame; but it is the manner in which he met his death – murdered by Nationalists during the Spanish Civil War – which has given Lorca an eminence above all the other luminaries of a prodigiously gifted, but tragically dispersed, generation of writers. Amid much which remains unclear, it is evident that the murder of Lorca was conceived and carried out as a political act; yet Lorca cannot, and should not, be described as a political poet. He made no attempt, unlike Brecht for example, to inculcate dogma or to articulate a doctrine whereby others might live; he contented himself with reflecting the way life was and had been lived in the Spanish peninsula for hundreds of years. Lorca is the outstanding exemplar, in modern literature, of a popular 'folk' poet quite as sophisticated as any of the more esoteric writers who characteristically attract specialist attention. Unlike other members of the 'generation of '27' to which he belonged, Lorca was never an intellectual, though one has only to read his 1930 lecture 'The Theory and Function of the *duende*' to realize that his multifaceted creative gifts – he was also a competent painter, a most promising musician and probably the most inventive Spanish dramatist of his time – were not dependent merely upon inspiration and spontaneity. Lorca's famous lecture establishes that inspiration can provide only the raw material of poetry (what Lorca called 'the image') and that inspiration must be supplemented by more deliberative and methodical, if less charismatic, faculties. A friend records Lorca as saying: 'If it's true that I'm a poet by the grace of God – or of the devil – it's because I'm also a poet by the grace of technique and effort.' Despite the innumerable translations of his poetry and the good intentions of many expert commentators, Lorca has continued to be thought of as 'a poet by the grace of God' because the effort he expended and the techniques he employed seem to have been transmuted by a stroke of genius into the kind of elemental utterance which is rare in poetry of any period, and especially rare in the present century.

Lorca's poetic corpus, which is very large (even when his drama is excluded from consideration), offers more immediate rewards than most modern poetry. This is in part because of its intensely vivid presentation of emotions. These qualities are present in his first *Book of Poems* (1921), which is mostly immature and derivative but which contains the seeds of later Lorca. Many of the poems have the question-and-answer structure of the folk ballads they imitate, and even the poems not designated as ballads have a ballad-like propensity to rely on refrains and to return to their point of origin. The structures do not, however, always keep in focus the material which they contain, for Lorca is not simply writing replicas of the old songs but instead attempting to create the compound of 'new themes and old suggestions' which he later spoke of, in connection with his great *Gipsy Ballad Book* (1928), in a letter to Jorge Guillén. The 'new themes' emerge not, as might be expected, in the imagery (which, however strange and striking, can usually be related back to tradition), but rather in the way the imagery is manipulated and moulded. Questioned by the children in the 'Ballad Of The Little Square', the poet acknowledges that 'the fountain and stream/of ancient song' have revealed 'the path/of the poets' to him. But as the 'Ballad Of The Sea-water' demonstrates, Lorca's water imagery can take on very modern lineaments:

The sea
smiles in the distance.
Teeth of foam,
lips of heaven.

This graphic personification is typical of Lorca's first collection, in which dead leaves weep and a solitary poplar strikes at the moon with its 'centenarian hand'. But Lorca supplements it by reversing this anthropomorphic strategy and making human emotions into natural phenomena. At the end of 'Ballad Of A July Day', for example, the poet's heart 'bleeds like a fountain'; in another poem he longs for the 'tranquil passion' of a solitary oak to take root in his 'subsoil'. The vibrancy of the imagery in this first collection is startling but strangely numbing; it is as if Lorca is more the servant than the master of the turbulences, psychological and external, he records. The poem 'Longing' suggests that the poet is primarily in quest of the earthly paradise of a heart in whose love he may find repose. In the absence of such a heart, he can only envy the lower orders of the animal kingdom, the cicada that 'dies drunk with light' and the old lizard which has time to 'admire the stars' as the worms eat him.

Lorca's only consolation for the pain of living is that, as in the almost impersonal 'Landscape' poem, night will come, that the repose of death will ultimately tranquillize human longing. The origins of what will become unforgettably powerful in his famous 'Lament for Ignacio Sánchez Mejías' are clearly visible even in these early and often callow poems.

In the 'Poem Of The Deep Song', which makes the traditional Andalusian *cante jondo* into a vehicle which will bear Lorca's personal misery, the tensions of this first book take on a more crystalline form. Once again it is 'things far away', or the absence of them, which make the whole world seem broken and weeping. And yet it is things near at hand, like the swinging door of a tavern, which make death a permanent feature of the landscape. The very olive trees are 'freighted/ with shrieks'; the whole collection seems to oscillate between the cries of the living and the silence of the dead. In a lecture Lorca expressed his admiration for the way 'a feeling gradually assumes concrete shape' in the *cante jondo* and in this collection, as in the collection of 'Songs' which followed it, Lorca made much more precise what had previously been somewhat diffuse and ephemeral. The heart remains his primary point of reference, but the dagger in it seems more real and more deadly, as in the splendidly terse little poem 'Crossroads'. The sharpening of focus is epitomized by the 'Ballad Of The Little Square', in which Lorca appropriates that most ancient of metaphors, the journey, to express his gloom at the fact that he has no prospect of arrival anywhere.

In the 'Songs' of 1921–4, Lorca's new clarity permitted him a certain impishness, as in poems like 'Half Moon' and 'Pause Of The Clock', or best of all in 'The Dumb Child', where the child searching for his voice does not know that it has been appropriated by the king of the crickets. These dreamlike transformations take place in a context of harsh reality or reflect a state of mind, like that in 'Granada and 1850', in which 'I dream that I do not dream'. The narcissistic elements present in the *Book of Poems* are in the process of being sloughed off; in 'Song Of The Dry Orange-Tree', for example, the tree is seen as an objective correlative of the poet's desire 'to live without seeing myself' and of his prayer to be delivered from 'the torture/of seeing myself without fruit'. The difficult and powerful sonnet 'Adam', a demonstration that Lorca could emulate more intellectual poets when he chose to do so, dramatizes a similar confrontation between sterility (the 'neuter moon of stone') and fertility (the 'tumult of the veins') in a much more impersonal manner. The objectification of the poet's private sexual tensions – which are presumed to have influenced his decision to leave Spain for America in 1930 – is almost total, as it is later in the tragic plays, where the central figure is almost always a woman, like the Eve who has sprung from Adam's rib in this complex and cerebral poem.

Lorca's most respected and most popular volume, the *Gipsy Ballad Book*, (1928) continues this process of objectification, with the poet almost indistinguishable behind the troubadour mask he has donned with such apparent ease. Here Lorca sought, as he told Jorge Guillén, 'to harmonize gipsy myth-ology with everyday reality'. He succeeded to the extent that both the mythology and the reality are now thought of as distinctively Lorca's own. The 'neuter moon of stone' of the sonnet 'Adam' casts its eerie light over the whole collection. It is the moon who steals a child in the famous opening poem, the moon who shines on a dead gipsy-girl at the climax of the matchless 'Somnambular Ballad', the moon who watches unmoved as the repressive forces of the black Civil Guard stalk their traditional enemy the gipsy, and the moon who supervises Amnon's rape of Thamar, which forms the climax to the overwhelming sensuality of the volume. This last poem, together with 'Preciosa And The Wind' and 'The Faithless Wife', is Lorca's most explicit poetic treatment of sexual themes, although the plays deal with similar material, and the quasi-Arabic poems of Lorca's posthumous collection *The Divan Of The Tamarit* approach the same subject-matter in a similar spirit. Even 'The Martyrdom Of Saint Eulalia' is presented in sexual terms, though it ends with the saint hanging – like the gipsy-girl of the 'Somnambular Ballad' – in a frozen waste. All colours except black are bleached from this final scene, which is like the negative of a photograph, and all the verve and energy in this extraordinary volume cannot disguise Lorca's obsession with bitterness and sterility.

In two hexameter poems written before Lorca's trip to New York, he turned first towards the 'Catalan light' of his friend Salvador Dalí and then towards 'the concrete/multitude of lights' of the Eucharist in the hope of finding something to offset the negative emotions by which he had been oppressed. The New York experience, however, as reflected in the posthumously published and controversial *Poet In New York*, was evidently a more profoundly dark night of the soul. It is primarily, though not exclusively, on the strength of this volume that critics have attached the label of 'Surrealist' to Lorca's poetry, though almost all the potent images in the collection can be found in poems dating from well before the first Surrealist manifesto, and obviously Lorca's friendship with Dalí and Buñuel cannot be considered the origin of them all. Even the 'Little Infinite Poem', in which the images seem to transform themselves with the speed and randomness of automatic writing, derives its power from Lorca's ability to generate one image from another and his abiding sense that 'we shall have to graze without repose on the grass of cemeteries', a conviction found everywhere (if not so precisely expressed) in his earlier verse.

Lorca's most famous individual poem is his richly orchestrated elegy of 1935 on the death of his friend the bullfighter Mejías. In the first section of the poem Lorca states, as if stunned, the bare facts of what has happened and the phrase 'at five in the afternoon' operates like the mournful tolling of a memorial bell. In the second section the focus narrows to the dead body of the bullfighter and Lorca's reluctance to confront the unimpeachable evidence of his mortality; here the refrain is the anguished and exclamatory 'I do not want to see it!' By section three Lorca has sufficiently composed himself to become one of the men 'of durable voice' who can withstand the harrowing prospect of death and thus emulate their departed hero:

I do not want them to cover his face with handkerchieves but rather for him to grow accustomed to the death he carries.

And in the fourth and final section of the poem Lorca's lament takes on a more impersonal tone, as he reaffirms the poet's time-honoured task of crafting epitaphs for those who might otherwise be forgotten. These deeply moving lines are predicated upon the fact that the world no longer knows Mejías and the faith that it will know him more deeply from his epitaph:

Much time will pass before is born, if such there be,
so grand an Andalusian, so rich in enterprise.
I sing his elegance with words that groan
and remember a sad breeze through the olive-trees.

This last stanza is, naturally enough, frequently transmogrified into an epitaph for Lorca himself.

The *gacelas* and *casidas* of Lorca's posthumously published *Divan* (or 'Song Book') remain full of longing; again and again the word *quiero* ('I want' or 'I love' according to context, and here almost always the former in the absence of the latter) resounds through these distinctively Moorish verse-forms and themes. In one of the most beautiful *casidas* the poet, having shut his balcony, discovers that 'there is nothing but weeping to be heard'; in another Lorca realizes that, as in the case of Mejías, he has no alternative but to 'look at the heart pierced by the dark bodkin of the water'. In the 'Gacela Of The Dark Death' he expresses his desire: 'to learn a lament that will cleanse me of the earth'. But Lorca's whole *oeuvre* dramatizes, even in its wildest flights of fancy, what it means to be earthbound, and it is the sense of man's temporary residence on earth which makes his lamentations so powerful and irresistible. It seems appropriate that, in one of the late 'Sonnets Of Dark Love' which have survived, he should have spoken of death in terms of a tree with its roots deep in the earth; Lorca's whole enterprise, as the subject-matter of his plays confirms, was to remind mankind of its tragic enslavement to mortality and its need to live vitally, passionately and atavistically.

In a letter of 1926 Lorca told Guillén that 'the poem that pierces the heart like a sword has yet to be made'. But all of his best poetry disproves this, and the tragic circumstances of his death have ensured that, over and above its intrinsic merits, it will continue to do so. There are few modern poets who pierce the heart more keenly than Lorca, and perhaps none can claim to have possessed in equal measure the secrets of that elusive chemistry which enabled him to delight the simple-minded and to command the affection and respect of the learned.

Bertolt Brecht (1898–1956)

Born in Augsburg of bourgeois parents, his father the manag-
ing director of a papermill, his mother the daughter of a civil
servant from the Black Forest. Rebellious at school, he voiced
violently pacifist views on the outbreak of the First World
War and spent most of his time at Munich University in
bohemian activities, beginning his lifetime practice of con-
ducting several amours at once. Acted briefly as an orderly
in a reserve military hospital before becoming involved in the
post-war Communist revolution in Bavaria, where he soon
acquired celebrity as a vagabond balladeer in the clubs and
cafés. Published some vitriolic theatre criticism in local left-
wing newspapers, and commenced the playwriting for which
he is primarily famous. Active in the Berlin theatre from 1924
to 1933, during which time he met the composer Kurt Weill,
with whom he was to collaborate on his first great success,
The Threepenny Opera. Went into exile the day after the Reich-
stag fire of 1933, living in great simplicity in Denmark,
Sweden and Finland. In 1939–40 he emigrated to the USA,
travelling overland through Russia, which he had previously
visited only briefly, though much admired by radical creative
elements there. Expended much fruitless energy on trying to
make films in Hollywood and finally returned to East Berlin
after a typically ironic testament before the Committee on
Un-American Activities. Founded the famous Berliner En-
semble, but often in conflict with the Stalinist East German
authorities. Buried in the old Huguenot cemetery in East
Berlin.

*

Until recently Brecht's plays have been presumed to be his primary contribution to German literature. During and after his fifteen years of exile – begun the day after the Reichstag fire of 1933 – Brecht preferred to be thought of as a dramatist presenting, in as objective and dialectical a manner as possible, the political realities of an exploited proletariat and an exploiting capitalism. Only since his death has it become clear that before, during and after 'the dark times' (as he called them), it was in poetry that he expressed this theme most devastatingly and most economically. In the face of truths which needed to be acknowledged collectively, Brecht was always intent on denying the importance or significance of his own very complex personality. In his 'Epistle On Suicide', for example, written about 1920, he wrote:

It should not seem
As if one had put
Too high a value on oneself.

It now seems as if, in his dealings with others (and notably his numerous mistresses), Brecht experienced some difficulty in living up to this ideal. But as a poet, even in his pre-Marxist-Leninist days, his preferred mode was one in which the general applicability of what he was saying should be seen to take precedence over the fact that it was Bertolt Brecht saying it. A poem presumed to have been written just previous to his leaving Germany reads:

I need no gravestone, but
if you need one for me
I should like it to bear these words:
He made suggestions. We
carried them out.
Such an inscription would
do credit to all of us.

Despite preferring drama as a more immediate agitprop medium, Brecht conceived of poetry as one of the primary means by which the masses could be instructed in the whys and wherefores of transforming reality. And whilst a large amount of his verse must be accounted propaganda in the

pejorative sense, at its best it has the power to make such
a project seem not only necessary but also possible, within
the terms articulated by each particular poem.

As a poet Brecht achieved some fame, and a great deal of
notoriety, on the publication in 1927 of his *Domestic Breviary*,
'intended for the practical use of readers'. As in the case of
another, though much less secular, light which shone in dark-
ness, the darkness comprehended it not. Brecht had at-
tempted to avoid such an outcome by writing poems designed
for 'actual delivery', and including an appendix of his own
accompanying music to encourage their performance. Even
here, in his most obviously 'literary' poetry (heavily influen-
ced by Villon, Rimbaud, Kipling and the Lutheran Bible),
Brecht's genius at making 'low-brow' forms like the ballad
into powerfully expressive instruments is unmistakable. But
these poems are clearly, like the early plays they most re-
semble (*Baal, Drums In The Night,* and *In The Jungle Of
Cities*), more diagnostic than curative, the product of Brecht's
increasing desperation in the face of a Germany beginning,
after defeat in the First World War, to slide into decline.
Brecht is here seeking relief from his despair by imagining
Rimbaud-like escapes on drunken boats, or in the fumes of
tobacco smoke, but he cannot free himself from a horrified
fascination with death in all its forms. Deprived by his atheism
of any religious consolation, and yet to adopt the strategies
of dialectical materialism, Brecht's morbidity was bound up
with his not inconsiderable, indeed headlong, relish at the
widespread evidence of decomposition that he was revealing.
The tensions within Brecht himself gave this early poetry a
tremendous and irresistible magnetism. But his subsequent
analysis of the *Domestic Breviary*, whether or not we accept his
ideological base, is a perfectly legitimate description of the
volume's shortcomings:

Under its wealth of feeling lies a confusion of feeling. Under its
originality of expression lie aspects of collapse. Under the richness of
its subject matter there is an element of aimlessness.

There are many poems in the *Breviary* to which this critique cannot be applied. The great poem on the infanticide Marie Farrar, in which the Villon-like refrain is varied in preparation for the climactic demonstration of the conclusion, is a perfect example of the way in which Brecht casts doubt on (through an 'it seems' or a 'they say') and thus makes more painfully present the unsavoury facts which did not permit her to behave otherwise. A similar sympathy informs Brecht's presentation of the 'hard' life of Hannah Cash, and also his account of the gratuitous murder of his parents by the thirteen-year-old Jacob Apfelböck. But the mood is bitterly pessimistic, with death (the 'man in violet' of 'Report Of A Tick') the only prospect of deliverance, and even death's repose denied in the 'Legend Of The Dead Soldier', the poem that placed Brecht on the Nazi wanted list as early as 1923.

The grotesqueness of the resuscitation of the dead soldier is softened in those poems which, like the 'Ballad Of The Death Of Anna Cloudface' or the famous 'Remembering Marie A.', refer obliquely to Brecht's numerous *amours*. But disguise himself as he may, and soften his manner as he will, Brecht nowhere absolves himself from the harsh and unflattering light he trains on all his subjects, as such poems as 'Utterances Of A Martyr' and 'Observation Before The Photograph Of Therese Meier' indicate. It is out of a prevailing nihilism that Brecht's self-addressed admonitions ('Of Climbing In Trees', 'Of Swimming In Lakes And Rivers') and his marginally more objective attempts to inculcate some rudimentary values ('Ballad On Many Ships', 'Ballad Of Friendship') emerge. But it is clear, in the words of one of the superb 'Psalms' of 1920 that Bert Brecht is 'not doing too well'. There is a brief poem written at about the same time – one of the earliest examples of the 'rhymeless verse with irregular rhythms' that became his favourite form – which is unequivocally gloomy:

I admit it: I
Have no hope.
The blind talk of a way out. I
See.

When the mistakes have been worn out
There sits as ultimate companion
The void in front of us.

Brecht's only recourse, when seeking to dissipate this gloom, was to adopt a new, even lower-brow, plainness, of more immediate 'practical use' than the *Breviary*. This new mode surfaces in the 'Reader For Those Who Live In Cities', which is presumed to have been begun before the *Breviary* was published. These poems were written in the conviction that (as Brecht says in the poem 'The Gordian Knot'), 'not everything which is difficult is useful', that poetry must be a utilitarian act. But in a situation conceived of as a class struggle, mere plainness would have exposed the writer of such a 'Reader' to harassment, and so inevitably some difficulty remains. Brecht is effectively addressing, as Walter Benjamin pointed out, an underground which he wishes to provoke into activity. Direct as the poems are, therefore, they necessarily exemplify to some extent the warning addressed to those who comprise such an underground: 'Cover your tracks'. Only a few of them in fact, use 'the driest words' to 'speak to you simply/Like reality itself', and those which do lack the ironic force of Brecht's most memorable utterances. The few remnants of a transcendental vision which had survived the onslaught of the *Breviary* are nonetheless in the process of being decisively swept away in favour of a thoroughly materialist poetry, with the poet indistinguishable from the artisan and (as 'Song Of The Cut-Price Poets' reminds us) quite as badly paid. Throughout this period of adjustment Brecht remained capable of writing more or less formal sonnets, and he continued to write in this form (notably in a series of sonnets on largely literary subjects) during his exile in Scandinavia. But the vast bulk of his post-*Breviary* poetry was in the more obviously 'unpoetic' form of free verse.

One aspect of the changing character of Brecht's poetry between the *Breviary* and his departure for California in 1941 has been excellently summarized by Walter Benjamin:

In the *Domestic Breviary* landscape occurs above all in the form of a
sky that has been purified, as though washed clean, upon which
delicate clouds appear from time to time, and beneath which
vegetation outlined with a hard pencil may be visible. In *Songs Poems
Choruses* [a collection of 1934] nothing is left of the landscape; it is
covered by the 'wintry snowstorm' that sweeps through this cycle of
poems. In the *Svendborg Poems* it is glimpsed now and again, timid
and pale, so pale that the posts 'put up in the yard for the children's
swing' already count as part of it.

Benjamin's description of the 'German War Primer' (begun
in 1936) – 'these words ... contain the gesture of a slogan
scrawled in haste on a plank fence by a man being pursued'
– gives an even better idea of the conditions which made
such changes inevitable. However, a good deal of the 'public'
poetry which Brecht wrote during this immensely productive
period does seem 'scrawled' rather than written; the best
poems are those in which Brecht records his complex
personal experience of being a refugee. These are never
merely 'personal' poems; as in some of his plays, Brecht can
be extraordinarily adept at appropriating and adapting – for
example in 'The Shoe Of Empedocles' and 'Legend Of The
Origin Of The Book *Tao Te Ching* On Lao-Tzu's Road Into
Exile' – pre-existent material. Even poems in which he con-
fronts himself and his situation directly – 'Why Should My
Name Be Mentioned?', 'Place Of Refuge', 'Spring 1938' and
'1940' – are written with an addressee in mind, in the hope
that there might be someone still listening to him. The best
known of all Brecht's oblique 'self-portraits' is the poem of
1938 ('To Those Born Afterwards', the last of the *Svendborg
Poems* on their original publication), which contains one of
his most riveting utterances:

What times are these, when
To speak of trees is almost a crime
Because it implies silence about so much injustice?

Yet Brecht is quite as much himself when his own presence
is kept to an absolute minimum, as in the prose poetry of
the 'Five Visions', which are impersonal in a manner that

will presumably conspire to keep them less well-known. Free of any doctrinaire contamination, these visionary poems, like 'To Those Born Afterwards' epitomize the difficult achievement of a solitary man talking to mankind in general, and are much finer than the many poems in which Brecht is effectively, if unintentionally, preaching to the converted.

There is nothing in the American poems of 1941–7 to compare with the best of those written during his Scandinavian exile, although there are some excellent reminders of Brecht's devastating sense of humour (applied to everything from cant to Kant), notably, when he decides that Shelley's description of London as Hell would have been altered if he could have seen Los Angeles. When the humour discloses a slight suspicion that all may not be well in the Soviet Union, as in the belated epitaph for Mayakovsky, it is bound to be especially attractive. But it was only in the poems written after Brecht (with an Austrian passport and a West German publisher) had returned to the new state of East Germany and found that all was plainly not well there either, that he regained the power to be both simple and profound. In these he contrived to remain a believer in Hegel's dictum that 'the truth is concrete' and at the same time an exponent of the art represented by the figure on his Oriental silk-screen 'The Doubter'. Not all of the poems Brecht wrote in East Berlin are sufficiently 'Socialist Realist' to have been made available by the authorities. But those which have been published show that Brecht's experience of a Marxist-Leninist reality did not assuage his belief in the necessity of change:

Sad in my youth
Sad later
When will I be happy?
Better be soon.
('Things Change')

This is also the burden of the most famous of the 'Buckow Elegies':

I sit by the side of the road.
The driver changes the wheel.

I do not like where I have come from.
I do not like where I am going to.
Why then do I watch the wheelchange
With impatience?

The psychological complexity of Brecht's dialectical think-
ing is perhaps best seen in the underrated *Tales Of Mr
Keuner*, which he had begun to write in the early 1930s. The
posthumously published *Book Of Twists And Turns* has some-
thing of the same character, being at once enigmatic and crys-
tal clear, depending on the perspective one takes up in
relation to it. 'Here you have someone on whom you can't
rely', he had written of himself in the poem at the end of the
Domestic Breviary ('Of Poor B.B.'); his appearance before the
Committee on Un-American Activities in 1947 is one of many
famous examples that this was indeed the case. But the classic
instance of Brecht's ability to unsettle people is the remark
he made to someone lamenting the fates of those caught up
in Stalin's Great Terror: 'the more innocent they are, the
more they deserve to die'. One would have had to be an
accomplished dialectician to have realized at once that Brecht
meant that only those who really were innocent of plotting
against Stalin deserved to go to their deaths. On this occasion
he was hurriedly shown the door, no doubt consoling himself
that it was his fate to be a social pariah and outcast. This
incident arguably tells us more about Brecht than the im-
mense popularity of *The Threepenny Opera* ever can, although
it is doubtful even in this case whether the millions who enjoy
the *Opera* understand it the way Brecht would have wanted.
There are pitfalls of this kind ahead of anyone who reads
Brecht's poetry, especially that which he wrote as a young
man. And yet insofar as there can be a key which would un-
lock the riddles of Brecht's personality, it is obviously enough
in his poetry that one would begin to look for it, and for all
his accomplishment as a dramatist his poems seem likely to
enjoy a more secure posterity.

Jorge Luis Borges (born 1899)

Born in Buenos Aires into a family of mixed English, Spanish and Portuguese origins. Read widely as a child in his father's very extensive library, though early manifesting the poor eyesight congenital in the Borges family. Educated in Geneva during the First World War, where he was unhappy for much of the time. Learnt Latin, French and German, and was deeply influenced by the great nineteenth-century poetry in the modern languages and by the German philosophical tradition, though all his life passionately interested in English and American literature. Began to write poetry towards the end of the period that he lived in Switzerland; expanded his literary connections in Spain and Majorca in the years 1919–21. Returned to Buenos Aires in the spring of 1921, and wrote poems, essays and criticism in great profusion over the next decade, during which time he was regarded as the leading exponent of Ultraism, a movement deriving from German Expressionism. Wrote mainly in prose for the next twenty years, beginning the *Fictions* for which he subsequently became famous after being seriously ill with septicaemia in 1938–9. Recurrently in love with a series of beautiful and unattainable women during this period. Demoted during the Perón régime from a library appointment to a job as a chicken inspector. Appointed director of the National Library of Argentina after the fall of Perón. Professor of English and American Literature at the University of Buenos Aires in 1957; from this time on increasingly dependent on others as his very poor sight deteriorated into blindness. Internationally famous since 1961, when he won a major literary prize, and since when he has frequently been visiting professor at

American universities and given innumerable interviews. Awarded the honorary degree of Doctor of Letters at Oxford University in 1970. Belatedly and unsuccessfully married in 1967; in 1970 returned to living with his aged mother. Has probably received more academic and public signs of recognition than any other living writer, although his poetry has been largely neglected.

In their introduction to the first of *The Book Of Imaginary Beings* (1957) Borges and his collaborator write: 'We are as ignorant of the meaning of the dragon as we are of the meaning of the universe, but there is something in the dragon's image that appeals to the human imagination ... It is, so to speak, a necessary monster.' It would be neither difficult nor disparaging to say much the same of the first Argentinian writer to have achieved world fame, for Borges himself has very plainly appealed to certain elements basic to the human imagination and in the last twenty years he has come to seem one of the more necessary monsters of modern literature. He has been granted a classic status almost exclusively on the basis of his prose writings, in particular those which we would normally call short stories but which his own terminology compels us to describe as 'fictions'. But the case for Borges – and it is one which does not condemn us to remaining ignorant of his meaning – is greatly enriched by consideration of his poems. There is even a sense in which everything he has written, whether in verse or prose, can be regarded as a fundamentally poetic apprehension of the human condition. 'A passage read as though addressed to the reason,' Borges writes in the introduction to the bilingual *Selected Poems*, 'is prose; read as though addressed to the imagination, it might be poetry.' If this is tantamount to making literature synonymous with poetry, it clearly does not worry Borges overmuch. Of the ostensibly hybrid volume *In Praise Of Darkness* (1969) he writes: 'although the difference between prose and verse seems to me superficial, my wish is that this volume be read as a volume of poems'. He is, indeed, full of nostalgia (as the introduction to *The Gold Of The Tigers* indicates) for a time when 'there can have existed no division between the poetic and the prosaic' and 'everything must have been tinged with magic'. From such a perspective, if he could maintain it, literature would become a species of magic, a sorcery or enchantment contrary to all the principles of reason and inimical to them. But the magician in Borges is permanently waging war with the sceptical and rational intellectual, and it is out of this dynamic tension that he has created a vision at once highly idiosyncratic and surprisingly traditional.

Borges is what philosophers would call an immaterialist and what theologians would call a Gnostic. For him the material world is an emanation of evil, the mistake of a deity who could not remain content with non-being and ever afterwards regretted his error. A hunger for non-being and restoration to the primal unity is an almost unavoidable concomitant of such a view, and death is therefore the natural focus for it; life on earth tends to be seen as a kind of purgatory. But the purgatory may be alleviated, and may take on an expiatory character, if the faculty of the imagination is exercised; it is the only one of man's faculties, Borges would say, which enables him to experience a freedom comparable to that promised by the oblivion out of which he came and to which he must return. What might otherwise induce morbidity and paralysis therefore contains within it the germ of a possible salvation; the mind compensates for the deficiencies of material reality, and the nominally real world is conjured away by one that is less unreal than it appears, indeed more real than what it replaces. The whole operation is, however, extremely vulnerable to the dictates of a common sense which can never be completely silenced; the flight of fancy – nowhere, perhaps, more urgent in Borges than in 'A New Refutation Of Time' (the last essay in *Other Inquisitions*) – characteristically comes to grief in the descent to earth: 'The world, alas, is real; I, alas, am Borges'. It is Borges's recurrent realism that prevents his imaginings from being merely gratuitous and self-indulgent; he is the proponent of a faith towards which he takes up the troubled stance of an agnostic.

The whole of Borges's diverse activity may be summed up by a phrase he used in the preface to his second volume of poetry, *Moon Across The Way* (1925): 'a dialogue between life and death'. However it was death which dominated his thinking initially; life (a word virtually without meaning for him if it does not somehow betoken immortal life) seems to play a somewhat negligible part in the dialogue. In the poem 'Sepulchral Inscription' for example (the first of a number of poems in memory of his great-grandfather, and his ancestors generally), Borges sees death as a liberating force:

He died walled in by implacable exile.
Now he is a handful of dust and glory.

His own life, by contrast, is little more than 'implacable exile', only to be relieved by such few glories as he may perceive or activate through his imaginings:

The light streaks in inventing unclean colours
and with some remorse
at my complicity in its daily resurrection
I search for my house,
amazed and glacial in the white light,
while a bird detains the silence
and the consumed night
lingers in the eyes of the blind.

('Daybreak')

During his adolescent years in Europe Borges had been much impressed by the dominant figures in nineteenth-century German literature and philosophy: by Schopenhauer, Heine, Nietzsche and the Expressionist poets. And 'Daybreak' has a distinctively Expressionist colouring that no amount of revision – one of Borges's ways of 'creating his precursors' where his early poetry is concerned – can entirely eliminate. Reading Walt Whitman, however, provided him with a counterbalance, and something of Whitman's optimism survives in a poem like 'My Whole Life', where the American poet's claim to 'contain multitudes' is echoed in the Argentinian's belief that 'my days and nights are equal in their

poverty and riches to those of God and of all men'. Here the
'remorse' of 'Daybreak' seems to have been banished by an
act of will. It is evident, however, that the young Borges
vacillated between abject misery and a willed ecstasy without
really understanding either. Only in one great poem, 'To
Francisco Lopez Merino' (a poet friend who had committed
suicide) did he find a way of fully expressing his ambivalence.
Troubled by the fact that his words may be bringing his friend
from the non-being he has sought back to the reality he had
wished to evade, 'I think,' Borges writes, 'that perhaps we
may contrive our own deaths with images of our own choos-
ing.' This permits him to think of the poem he is writing as
not so much a profanation as a consecration, an act that –
despite the barriers between them – allows them to enjoy a
kind of camaraderie. It suggests that Borges had at last found
a justification and rationale for poetry. And yet after the
volume containing this poem (*San Martín Copybook*, 1929), he
published no more poetry for fourteen years, and indeed –
apart from the eight poems added to his 1943 reprint of
Poems – did not write any poems that have since seen the light
of day. This followed upon being awarded second prize in
an annual Buenos Aires literary competition, though it seems
unlikely that it was disappointment which was the primary
cause of his effectively abandoning poetry. Perhaps he had
come to think of the poetic act as in some respects com-
parable to the ill-advised creation of the world by an in-
sufficiently omniscient deity; he may also have felt that the
bulk of his early poetry was too private and too confused for
him to continue in the same vein. In the event he turned from
the drama of self-accusation and self-justification so memor-
ably conveyed by the Merino poem to a calm and lucid prose
which would enable him to secrete his own thoughts on
human destiny behind a succession of personae; only the two
very moving prose poems in English (dated 1934) are any-
thing like the *cris de coeur* that his previous 'versifying' (as he
had come to think of it) had tended towards in the previous
decade.

During the traumatic years which bore fruit in his now

internationally famous *Fictions* (first published in 1944), Borges developed the metaphor which will always be primarily associated with him: the labyrinth. As befits someone who later expressed his doubts about the virtues of originality and emphasized his conviction that myth was the beginning and the end of literature, Borges discovered the metaphor in Greek myth rather than in his own mind. The construction of a craftsman (Daedalus), a finite structure containing seemingly infinite variations, to be conquered only by an ingenious hero (Theseus), liberating the creature half-man, half-beast imprisoned at its centre (the Minotaur) by an act of violence – the myth clearly offered Borges the perfect model for a more coherent 'dialogue between life and death'. And having made use of it in his prose he began to see the possibilities it offered for a new kind of formal poetic utterance, quite different in character from the free verse he had previously preferred. Though never specifically invoked, it is the metaphor of the labyrinth which lies behind the ideas of imprisonment and recurrence which make 'The Cyclical Night' (a poem of 1940) one of Borges's most memorable verse utterances. In 'Of Heaven And Hell' (1942) and in the famous 'Conjectural Poem' of 1943 Borges makes the metaphor explicit. This latter poem records how the 'intimate knife' of an assassin enables its protagonist to complete 'the perfect/pattern God knew from the beginning'. But this is obviously something that the living Borges himself, neither Theseus nor Minotaur (although his imagination occasionally permits him to imagine that he is one or the other or, sometimes, both), can never emulate. Instead of the ultimate reality of death, he must remain content with the interim reality of life. Not even art, it seems, can bridge this fundamental gulf. In an essay written in 1950 and called 'The Wall And The Books' Borges tentatively suggests that art can only be concerned with the 'imminence of a revelation which does not occur'.

Many of the poems in Borges's *The Self, The Other* (1960) – his own favourite among his purely poetic volumes, and probably his best – explore the consequences of this sceptical position, notably 'The Golem' and 'The Other Tiger'. The latter bears an epigraph from William Morris reminding us that, whatever form he chooses (or, as he would say, chooses him), Borges is always meditating on the 'craft that createth a semblance'. Reduced to prose, the argument of 'The Other Tiger' demonstrates that the poet can never create in words the contents of his imagination. But read as a poem – and Borges has stressed that it is the spirit in which one reads that matters – the 'semblance' is tantamount to a revelation. Apparently in infinite regress from an absolute reality, Borges nevertheless manages to suggest how a cosmos might be conjured out of chaos, and how brief glimpses of a perfect pattern must serve as icons of the grand design. It is not, in other words, mere aestheticism that leads him to speak of books as 'sacred objects'; as such, they must be presumed to contain truths. 'Art,' as he says in the poem 'Ars Poetica', 'should be like that mirror/Which reveals to us our own face.' The very simplicity of the idea, which is of a very respectable lineage, is indicative of a new confidence in Borges; the tendency to self-absorption which makes for torment in the early poems is here transcended by a much more public and universal vision. The emphasis in later Borges actually falls on revelation rather than defeat, even in poems like 'Matthew XXV:30', where he sees himself as the 'unprofitable servant' of the biblical passage to which the title refers.

The vast majority of the poems in *The Self, The Other* are sonnets, though it is literature rather than love that they celebrate. It was perhaps inevitable that Borges should ultimately have chosen the form which has traditionally offered poets the 'infinite riches in a little room' of which Marlowe's Barabbas speaks. Any number of these sonnets show the 'modest and hidden complexity' which Borges's prose is famous for. But it is their relative simplicity, in an age of difficult poetry, which is their most conspicuous feature. 'Camden 1982', the finest of all Borges's tributes to a literary figure who has mattered more to him than most, is typical in this respect, and characteristically ends on a note of revelation:

The end is not far off. His voice declares:
I am almost gone. But my verses scan
Life and its splendours. I was Walt Whitman.

It is this moment before the end which prompts Borges to similar prodigies in 'Odyssey, Book Twenty Three' and 'Snorri Sturluson (1179–1241)'; and it is in the same spirit that, in the sonnets 'A Poet Of The Thirteenth Century' and 'A Soldier Of Urbina', he hypothesizes the spiritual states of Dante and Cervantes before they had written the works on which their claims to immortality primarily rest. The dialogue between life and death is obviously at its most poignant at such moments; the fundamental mystery is close to being solved. Borges's solution, insofar as one can call it that, is to consider all men as essentially one man and all dualisms as imperfectly apprehended fragments of a total unity. In its essentials it is a beneficent vision, although the fact that Borges has placed, in successive editions of his poetry, this 'apocryphal' two-line poem at the end is a reminder that he should not be interpreted too optimistically:

I, who have been so many men, have never been
The one in whose embraces Matilde Urbach swooned.

(‘Le regret d'Héraclite’)

This also serves to indicate, as many of his interpreters seem to have forgotten, that his supposedly metaphysical thinking has its origins in eminently physical feelings. This is quietly confirmed by the title poem of the 1972 collection, where the gold of 'your hair/which these hands long for' is even more precious than the 'gold of the tigers'.

The famous *Fictions*, for all their brilliance, can sometimes give the impression of a bloodless and cerebral man; the poems, '[springing] from what a particular man feels at a particular time' – Borges's test for 'true poetry', as the foreword to *Selected Poems* shows – almost never do. Borges now enjoys a readership which justifies his Whitmanesque pretension to 'contain multitudes'. But there cannot be a true estimate of his achievement which excludes his poems from consideration. It is difficult to believe that the common reader to whom Borges is primarily addressing himself will continue indefinitely to neglect his poetry, especially when he considers the author's own opinion of it. 'In the long run, perhaps, I shall stand or fall by my poems.'

George Seferis (1900–71)

Born in Smyrna (modern Izmir). Educated in Athens and Paris where he studied Law. Entered the Greek diplomatic service in 1926, and became Acting Consul-General in London from 1931 to 1934. Thereafter served as Greek Consul in Albania, Crete, South Africa, Egypt, England, Italy and in Turkey with the Greek government in exile. Counsellor of the Greek embassy in London from 1951 to 1953; occupied a similar post in Ankara and became Ambassador to the Lebanon between 1953 and 1957. Ambassador in London from 1957 until his retirement in 1962. In 1963 became the first Greek poet to win the Nobel Prize and lived in Athens until his death. Very well acquainted with modern French and English literature, and with the creators of it; influenced by T. S. Eliot, whom he knew, and by Cavafy. Kept an important journal, of which only sections have as yet been published, which suggests that he found certain aspects of diplomatic life irksome.

Seferis first became famous in Greece on the publication in 1935 of a collection (*Mythistorema*) which epitomizes his commitment to a poetry that, without being 'narrative' in the accepted sense, occupies the middle ground between the plots of myth – in this case the Homeric story of Odysseus – and the circumstances of a history described by Seferis as being 'as independent from myself as the characters in a novel'. Surprisingly perhaps, given his career and his early aims, Seferis cannot really be meaningfully described as a public poet. Indeed his public career does not seem to have been a source of much satisfaction to him. In the only section of a lifelong private journal to have been made widely available (*Days of 1945–51*; this also contains the residue of a projected but ultimately unfinished study of Cavafy, which partially accounts for its Cavafian title), Seferis speaks of public life as a jungle in which 'people make you feel as though you were chewing fog'. And in a short poem from the *Book Of Exercises* of 1940 Seferis suggests that a 'bitter smile' is indispensable for the man who has to deal with 'business and clients'. The stance reminds one of another poet who had to deal with business and clients, T. S. Eliot, whom Seferis much admired, and whom it would also be difficult to describe as a public poet. And the analogy with Eliot serves to identify what kind of poet Seferis actually was, for like his English predecessor he did not wish to be thought of as a private poet. Seferis aimed, as a mature poet at least, at the kind of impersonality which English readers inevitably associate with the early theoretical writings of T. S. Eliot.

The mood of his first collection (*Turning Point*, 1931; collecting poems from 1924 onwards) is, however, far from being impersonal; Seferis is plainly afflicted here by a private grief that cannot be kept at arm's length. The title poem of the collection does, it is true, describe how the 'tragic clepsydra' of his verse is relieved from having to express the desiccating passage of time by a kind of privileged Proustian moment 'sent by a hand/I had loved so much' which illuminates the impending darkness. But this is not a turning-point in the sense of initiating an upward curve in the poet's spirits; it is simply a point about which, if only for a second, the world appears to turn. The same is true of the words spoken by a loved one in 'Slowly You Spoke', although here the darkness seems to have fallen more decisively. But no comparable benediction seems possible in the poem 'Automobile'; this is essentially a reminder of how fruitless the bodies of lovers become when they are nothing more than separate branches on the tree of life. And in a poem originating in Poe's *Narrative of Arthur Gordon Pym* ('The Mood Of A Day'), the poet sees himself condemned, having lost a 'love that with one stroke cuts time in two', to a 'monotonous monologue' and a feeble wave of farewell. These early poems establish the mood of gloom which is basic to Seferis's whole output, but they are less convincing than his more impersonal later poetry. Try as he may to synthesize the motifs of these poems into a *logos*, Seferis is left at the end of the volume still waiting for 'the miracle/that opens the heavens'.

It is in the title poem of *The Cistern* (1932) that Seferis first discovers something rooted in the earth which promises, despite its secrecy and silence, and indeed because of them, if not a miracle at least a miraculous serenity. But the epigraph from El Greco suggests that this may be an illusion created by the false perspectives that an artist is dependent on. And the epigraph from Rimbaud which is placed at the head of *Mythistorema* indicates that the comparative security of earth and stones will have to be tested against the experience of an epic journey, or Odyssey, from which only Odysseus will return. Seferis's sense of homelessness (especially painful in the entries in his journal which record his return to his birthplace) seems to have stemmed primarily from the loss of his native Asia Minor to the Turks in 1924, and it was certainly exacerbated by the vagaries of his diplomatic career. But nothing in Seferis's poetry enables us to take relief in the thought that it is only one man's homelessness; it is plainly the universal condition of mankind that he is concerned with. *Mythistorema* is dominated by tragic images: the mutilated hands of the hallucinatory third poem in the sequence, the 'silence, without a drop of water' of the second. And yet Seferis's determination to find some kind of *logos* is not entirely quenched. Poem IV, for example, finds him in the position of reaffirming the Platonic wisdom that

> if the soul
> is to know itself
> it must look
> into a soul.

This 'search for the other life/beyond the statues' (V) is being constantly imperilled in *Mythistorema* by the 'clouded glass'

(VI) of the poet's solipsism. The condition of spirit from which Seferis is suffering is very similar indeed, without at any time seeming merely derivative, to that of Eliot in *The Waste Land*. The 'bodies that no longer know how to love' of poem X are, if possible, even more depressing than those encountered by the Fisher King in his role as Tiresias. At the same time a certain serenity, quite different from the turbulence which brings *The Waste Land* to an end, begins to be felt as the sequence unfolds. Poem XV, for example, is a wonderfully serene meditation on a sleeping woman. And in the last four poems of the sequence Seferis seems to have conquered his feelings of rootlessness. Poem XXI is almost optimistic by comparison with what has preceded it:

the ancient dead have escaped the circle and risen again
and smile in a strange silence.

The reactivating of ancient myth that is basic to *Mythistorema* appears for a moment to have offered the poet a *logos* in which he can believe. However, in two of his most famous poems, both written in October 1935 ('Santorini' and 'Mycenae'), all traces of such a consolation have disappeared. These poems, which are marked by the 'heavy rhythm' of the dances that give them their collective title (*Gymnopaidia*), are not so much poems of rising as poems of sinking. 'Mycenae' in particular offers a melancholy gloss on poem XXI of *Mythistorema*:

Not even the silence is now yours
here where the mill stones have stopped turning.

Seferis's sadness is made to seem inevitable by the impersonal wisdom with which this poem ends:

Sinks whoever raises the great stones.

The concentrated gravity of the *Gymnopaidia* is such as to make Seferis's subsequent collection of poems seem little more than a *Book of Exercises*. And yet the *Book of Exercises* is really a book of changes; the dominant figure is no longer so much Odysseus as the god Proteus. The exercises are very various, with the poet writing some *haiku*, some 'sketches', some prose poems, a 'Letter of Mathios Paskalis' and even one poem 'In The Manner of G. S.' himself. Seferis seems to be hoping that, by virtue of such variety, he may accomplish, or increase his chances of accomplishing, the moment 'when you let your heart and your thought become one' ('Syngrou Avenue, 1930'). But the collection is really too protean for this ever to be a real possibility, and Seferis is left, like 'The Old Man' (a version of Eliot's 'agèd eagle' perhaps), as an 'empty cage that waits/for the hour of fire'. Only in the 'Sketches For A Summer', where the hand of the writer takes on the more beneficient aspect of the clasped hands of lovers, does the poet really seem close to achieving an escape from the 'empty cage' of his own previous achievements.

The somewhat discursive mode which distinguishes the *Book of Exercises* from the more concentrated poems of the period 1933–5 carries over into the first of the three *Logbooks* in which Seferis, once again in the guise of Odysseus, records the events of a continually frustrated homecoming. Many of these poems possess 'something of that voice/at the root of a cry' of which 'Mathios Paskalis Among The Roses' speaks. This is especially true of the poem 'Our Sun' which, like many of the other poems of this period, depends for its full power on the spoken words of someone outside the poet, which rouse him from his solipsistic tendencies. The dry-breasted woman who cries 'Cowards!' to those who have carried off her children to die in battle is here juxtaposed with the messengers who come from the shades to tell the living that they 'don't have time' to live. Bravery, it is suggested in 'The Last Day', consists in recognizing the truth of a wisdom not unlike that of Rilke's, and accepting that

each of us earns his death, his own death, which belongs to no one else
and this game is life.

Seferis shows himself aware in his first *Logbook* (notably at the end of the poem 'Narration') that he is in danger of repeating himself to the point where no one will listen. But he justifies the enterprise on the grounds that his *alter ego*

> doesn't stand for anything
> and I talk to you about him because I can't find
> anything that you're not used to.

As if liberated by this, the four poems which follow ('Morning', 'Les Anges Sont Blancs', 'The Decision To Forget' and the famous 'The King Of Asine') show Seferis beginning to replace his habitual images of darkness with intimations of light and discovery. These are epitomized by the bat which, emerging from the dark into the sunlight in 'The King Of Asine', inspires the poet to believe that he may have touched with his fingers what had been 'only one word in the *Iliad* and that uncertain'. This chance encounter with a kind of *logos* seems to mark a turning point that is rather more than the vicious circles the poet has previously been confined in.

The major poem of the second *Logbook* is the three-part 'Thrush' composed on the island of Poros. *Days of 1945–51* describes this period of Seferis's life in detail, and shows that the serenity which marks the conclusion to the poem (Seferis's 'house by the sea' was called *Galini*, Greek for serenity) only came after Seferis had been exposed to the blinding light of the 'angelic Attic day'. The great affirmation of part three of the poem has the clarity of the light it celebrates. However, without the journal and the letter of interpretation that the poet himself provided, parts of 'Thrush' would come close to being impenetrable. With the aids which Seferis has provided, 'Thrush' stands revealed as another meditation on the story of Odysseus. This Odysseus has not yet reached Ithaca and home, but he has found a kind of home in the palace of Circe. It is Circe and the sensual Elpenor of whom he is dreaming in part one of the poem, and it is these same figures who are at cross purposes in part two. In part three the voices multiply, with Odysseus becoming indistinguishable from Socrates, Antigone and finally Oedipus. Seferis's Eliotic habit of embedding quotations from other writers in his own verses and yet making them appear to be his own, reaches a kind of climax here. The final silence which ends the poem no more belongs to Seferis than at the end of 'Mycenae'. But here it does not seem to matter, for he is looking into what Eliot called 'the heart of light' and receiving the benediction of a mystical experience.

It is the light of another island, Cyprus, which dominates Seferis's third *Logbook*. In this collection he triumphantly accomplishes his desire 'to speak simply, to be granted that grace'. But his prevailing melancholy is never completely dispersed, not even in the poem 'Engomi', where he comes closest to achieving another moment of mystical illumination. Seferis can only briefly see the world as belonging to, and in harmony with, mankind. But the waste land reasserts itself, and the drama of memory and desire continues. In the *Three Secret Poems* published in 1966, Seferis speaks with all the equanimity he can muster of how central the waste land experience has been for him throughout his journeying. And he convinces us, in a language of the utmost simplicity, with the kind of 'grace' he had long hoped for, that the experience – though not in itself constituting a redemption – is a crucial preliminary to being redeemed. Unlike Eliot, Seferis did not undergo a decisive conversion to established religion; it is natural, therefore, that he should come across in his poems as a much more comfortless figure than the later Eliot. It is the unsparing manner in which he analysed his discomforts that has made Seferis second only to Cavafy in the modern Greek poetic pantheon, and the first Greek poet to receive the Nobel prize.

Salvatore Quasimodo
(1901–68)

Born at Modica, Sicily; moved to Messina, where he studied
engineering at the Technical Institute. Resident in Rome
from 1919–26, where he studied at the Polytechnic and began
to read the Greek and Roman lyric poets. Employed by the
Ministry of Public Works in Reggio Calabria from 1926–9.
Resident in Florence after 1929, where he met the novelist
Elio Vittorini. Briefly visited Sardinia in 1934. Lived in
Milan from 1934 onwards; left government service in 1938
and thereafter worked as an editorial secretary. His much-
praised translations of Greek lyrics into Italian appeared in
1940. A professor of Italian Literature in Milan from 1941.
Imprisoned by the authorities for anti-Fascist activities dur-
ing the Second World War. Suffered his first heart attack
whilst visiting Russia; in hospital in Moscow for a consider-
able period. Visited Stockholm to receive the Nobel Prize for
1959. Honorary Doctor of Letters degree from Messina in
1960 and from Oxford in 1967. Travelled very widely
throughout Europe after the award of the Nobel Prize. Died
in Sicily after a succession of heart attacks.

Quasimodo was made internationally famous by the award
of the 1959 Nobel Prize for Literature, the first Italian poet
for fifty years to be thus honoured. Both inside and outside
Italy, however, it was felt that Ungaretti (who was never to
receive it) and Montale (the Nobel Laureate of 1975) had
prior claims. The terms of the Nobel citation – 'poetry which
... expresses the tragic experience of life in our time' – were
interpreted as referring primarily to Quasimodo's attempt,

after the Fascist defeat in the Second World War, to 're-make man' (as a famous essay of 1946 phrases it) through a more *engagé* and accessible style than he had previously employed. Many critics, with some justice, felt this to be less expressive of the man than the elusive and 'hermetic' manner of his pre-war work. The in some ways insensitive, but by no means indefensible, decision of the Nobel committee, together with the typically inadequate citation, had the effect of polarizing opinion about the Sicilian poet to the extent that a just estimate of his work became almost impossible. But it is now clear that, after Ungaretti and Montale, Quasimodo was one of the major Italian poets of his epoch, and that the sum total of his writings – in which his translations (from the Latin and Greek poets, from Shakespeare, and from such moderns as the Rumanian poet Tudor Arghezi) bulk largest – constitutes an exceptionally distinguished contribution to the mainstream of European literature in the present century.

Quasimodo's mid-career concern to 'remake man' stemmed from a feeling of solidarity occasioned by the cataclysm around him at the time of the Second World War. However, his pre-war poetry shows that his first preoccupation – an obviously necessary preliminary to the success of his later venture – was to remake himself. At the age of eighteen Quasimodo had left his native Sicily for the Italian mainland and begun what he came to think of as an 'exile' from his origins. The early poetry is a record of his attempt, stimulated by his study of the Greek and Latin poetry at the origin of Mediterranean civilization, to temper his sense of exile. By choosing words as stark, elemental and weathered as the Sicilian landscape he had left behind Quasimodo strove to combat the self-absorption that was his instinctive defence against dislocation. His most famous early poem, for example, is uttered in the impersonal manner of an epitaph, with a classical terseness and gravity:

Everyone is alone on the heart of the earth
pierced by a ray of sunlight
and it is evening suddenly.

At first sight the poem seems too brief to earn our assent; but it is as piercing as the ray of sunlight of which it speaks. There is an unanswerable finality about it, an index perhaps of the poet's refusal to be comforted, irrespective of what the brief ray of sunlight may illuminate. The other early poems are not usually, however, so absolute as this; the poet is normally dependent on the 'ray of sunlight' or some other stimulus from the natural world to rouse him from his passive torpor. Often, as in 'Deadwater', he is roused from his misery only to be returned to it:

So, as on water memory
extends its rings, my heart;
it moves from one point and then dies:
as if it were your sister, stagnant water.

Yet even this poem is more than a mere vicious circle; the stagnant water provides the poet with a companion for his solitude and instructs him in the mechanics of memory. The same is true of 'Alleyway', where the poet is called back to his childhood but ends with a disabused adult wisdom:

Alleyway: a cross of houses
that are calling quietly to one another,
and do not know it is the fear
of remaining alone in the dark.

These are all poems of loneliness and solitude, and yet the external world is continually offering the poet patterns which will provide temporary consolation. The splendid 'Wind At Tindari', perhaps the finest of Quasimodo's early poems, which could have been merely regressive insofar as the poet's memory is going back to a hilly Sicilian coastline, shows how the poet saves himself from the drift towards death and the *Angst* it occasions by finding inspiration in the natural world. As in the two previous examples, Quasimodo ends by transcending his misery and gaining a kind of private wisdom:

Return serene Tindari;
stir me gentle friend
that I may jut out from a cliff into the sky

and feign fear to those who do not know
what deep wind has searched me out.

Of the four primary elements it is earth, air and water
which provide Quasimodo with his most abiding intimations
of consolation. When they work together , as in the beautiful
spring poem 'Aries', to 'recompose' a grace that the poet
imagines himself to have lost irretrievably, they can even
effect a temporary cure. A similar 'miracle' makes 'Mirror'
an unexpectedly positive poem, although in that poem it is
very clear that the poet has had to strive actively to bring
such a miracle about. As 'Ancient Winter' demonstrates, it
is only his 'desire' for sustenance which can make him into
a living organism once again:

The birds sought the grain
and suddenly were snow;
like words.
A little sun, an angelic halo,
then mist; and the trees,
and us made of air in the morning.

The poet's appetitive relationship with the earth becomes
more explicit sexual in his second collection, *Sunken Oboe*
(1932), but the intimations of rebirth and renewal are no less
fleeting than in the previous volume. A decisive alteration in
attitude had to wait for *Erato And Apollyon* (1936) to manifest
itself. Quasimodo's adoption of mythical personae in this
latter volume is a reflection of his increased determination
to escape from self-absorption and to give his enterprise a
more archetypal resolution. At the same time Erato (the
Greek Muse of lyric poetry) and Apollyon (the destructive
demon of *Revelations*) very clearly reflect the competing
impulses in the poet's heart. 'Song Of Apollyon', for example,
describes the demon's inability to conquer his solitude;
attempting a human and earthly love leaves him grieving,
imprisoned in eternal life. 'In Your Light I Am Wrecked'
is equally gloomy, with Apollyon left at the end 'a man
alone/a single hell'. But in 'Apollyon' Quasimodo begins to
become aware of the potentially beneficial aspects of ship-
wreck. Here the destructive principle finds a human being

prepared to love him; love permits him to assume the ordinary human mortality he has previously been denied. The mood is a paradoxical one of demise and renewal: 'the hour/of full death is born'. The idea is somewhat reminiscent of Conrad's famous 'in the destructive principle immerse'; it certainly seems appropriate that in one of the finest of Quasimodo's many river poems ('The Anapó') an immersion should take place. The immersion permits Apollyon, who carries 'the nuptial seed of death' within him, to emerge as a new Adam, with the 'docile beasts' of a new Paradise around him. In another poem addressed to the same river ('In The Just Human Time'), a similar rebirth is envisaged:

> from your deep blood
> in the just human time
> we shall be born again without pain.

The rebirth is not simply a regression to Sicily, where the river Anapó flows. In a poem about another island ('Sardinia') and a much more familiar mythical figure (the Polyphemus of the *Odyssey*) Quasimodo shows that he is becoming increasingly aware of the comfort of love and, milder than the wind at Tindari, the 'fraternal breeze' that blows, irrespective of where one happens to find oneself. The sense of a crisis overcome is felt throughout the *New Poems* of 1936–42. The orientation shifts from the timeless and transcendent world of myth to the passing moment of the 'just human time'. 'Street In Agrigentum' is representative of the shift. For at the beginning of the poem Quasimodo is primarily concerned with the pre-Socratic Greek philosopher and suicide Empedocles, who lived in the ancient Sicilian town of Agrigentum; but at the end he has found a contemporary living figure to inspire in him what another poem in the volume calls 'a true sign of life'. The landscapes are only rarely Sicilian in *New Poems*; Quasimodo's scenario is now pre-eminently the Northern Italy which he had come to terms with and found beauty in. The mood is no more unreservedly positive than it was unreservedly pessimistic in the earlier collections. In Lucca, in front of Della Quercia's famous statue of Ilaria del Carreto, he is moved to pity the solitary black figure which the passing courting couples disregard. But he does so with a tenderness which makes the poem much more than a mere lament. As in previous poems he turns to water for images of renewal and continuity. By the Lombardy lakes (in 'The Rain Is Already With Us') he is so much a part of the 'just human time' that lamentation is out of the question. In 'On The Banks Of The Lambro' Quasimodo can actually reinforce his acceptance of 'levelling time' by openly acknowledging that he still suffers from a nostalgia for a timeless world in which death would have no part. Whereas in previous collections Quasimodo had a tendency to dwell on the mournful aspects of being alive, here (as, for example, in 'In The Másino Valley') even the lament of the crow heard at evening comes to seem 'a clear/presence ... of life'. In the so-called 'hermetic' poetry the reader had to try to penetrate a secret or hidden wisdom; here it is clearly, as this poem explicity states, 'ingenuous'. A certain secrecy prevails in such poems as 'Delphic Woman' and is also manifest in the recourse to emblematic animals as a point of reference. But these poems of evening and autumn are largely without anguish. Powerless to halt the passage of time, the poet is beginning to develop a kind of stoical *apatheia* which, without being mechanically applied (the world being far too changeable for that to be appropriate), enables him to accept it:

The meagre flower already flies
from the branches. And I await
the patience of its irrevocable flight.

It is in the war poems of *Day After Day* (1947) that the poet is roused from acceptance to engagement. Still seeking 'a sign that goes beyond life' he finds it – as he was always tempted to find it – in 'the soft verses of antiquity' ('19 January 1944'). But where 'death is in flower' (as in 'Letter'), literature seems 'no more/than a game of the blood'. Only if, in a contemporary world that has lost all pretension to culture, someone can 'howl in the silence' ('Snow') is literature redeemed. Quasimodo's most moving 'howl' is 'Milan, August 1943', where all he can say is that 'the city is dead'. But the very fact that, despite extreme provocation, he has not himself given way to death enables him even in wartime to find reminders of life, in the 'gentle beasts' of the plain of Lombardy and at the 'Fortress Of Bergamo Alta':

[rage is] quieted in the green of the young dead
and pity grown remote is almost joy.

This is one of the most subtle of the poems written during the war. Elsewhere, as in 'Man Of My Time', the need to warn, to remind his contemporaries that each and every one of them carry the mark of Cain upon them, takes precedence over any desire to write well, and the poems become strident. Quasimodo was plainly distressed that he could not be the saviour (Salvatore) that his Christian name suggested he might be. In default of this he thought of himself as a composer of epitaphs, as in 'Of Another Lazarus', 'Written, Perhaps, On A Tomb' and the poem for Bice Donetti. These publicly orientated statements were plainly well-intentioned, and part of his programme to 'remake man'. But it is generally agreed that Quasimodo writes best when his personal life provides him with the impulses towards utterance, and only a few poems written between 1945 and 1959 – 'Letter To My Mother' and 'To My Father', for example – can survive comparison with the earlier poems.

The 'balance between the debit and credit' of mankind is more finely articulated in Quasimodo's last collection (*Debit And Credit*, 1967). The volume is dominated by the poet's knowledge that, after a succession of heart attacks, his own life is near its close. For the first time the scenario becomes international as the ailing poet, made famous by his Nobel prize, travels the world. The wisdom he dispenses becomes almost orthodox, expressing the fundamentally Christian, almost Franciscan, message that we must 'live in the midst of the animals' and become 'a multitude of hands seeking out other hands'. The patience which, under wartime conditions, had threatened to turn into helpless rage, returns here and, partly no doubt as a result of the rage that has preceded it, loses its purely contemplative element. Quasimodo is here, for the first time perhaps, successful in his efforts actively to 'trace a possible link/between life and death'. In visiting places of death (Glendalough, Chiswick cemetery and so on) he finds tokens of survival. The concentration on the theme is too intense to be programmatic; Quasimodo repeatedly reminds us that he is speaking with his heart and not his mind. Indeed the last poem in the collection is one of his most heartfelt. Death is so close that the heart seems hardly to be beating. But the poet's patience has actually become an affirmation of life, a vigorous acceptance of all that it means to be human:

> Perhaps I am always dying.
> Yet I listen willingly to the words of life
> that I have never understood ...

It was in poems like this, which were not of course available to the Nobel committee, that Quasimodo expressed most memorably the 'experience of life in our time' which they had predictably credited him with. Despite the shortcomings in a poetic *oeuvre* which always had to make its way against the more obviously compelling poems of Montale and Ungaretti, Quasimodo had earned the right, by the end of his life, to be considered a worthy successor of the Greek and Latin poets he had sought to emulate and had so memorably translated into Italian.

Lucio Piccolo (1901–69)

Born in Palermo of Sicilian nobility of long-standing. A student of Latin, Greek, medieval literature, algebra, philosophy and occultism; greatly impressed by the music of Wagner as a young man and an accomplished amateur violinist. Widely read in English literature as an adolescent; corresponded with W. B. Yeats at the age of twelve. A relative and friend of Lampedusa, who was inspired to write his famous novel *The Leopard* by his cousin's success at the 1954 literary symposium at San Pellegrino, to which Montale had invited him. A virtual recluse before and after this success, living with his sisters in great splendour at Capo di Orlando, near Messina, where he died.

The case of Lucio Piccolo is one of the strangest in the history of modern poetry. He published only three volumes of poetry, containing thirty-seven poems in all, during his lifetime. The first was printed privately when Piccolo was fifty-three and sent, in what appears to have been his solitary gesture towards the Italian mainland and its literary establishment, to Eugenio Montale. Montale has recorded how, a little ruefully, he had to pay excess postage on the parcel in order to redeem it. It was Montale's invitation to Piccolo to attend a literary symposium, together with his subsequent recommendation of Piccolo's volume to a publisher, which ensured the middle-aged Sicilian an audience much larger than he could ever have hoped for or even perhaps wished for. This appears to have inspired Piccolo's cousin Lampedusa to write the solitary novel for which he became posthumously famous throughout the world (*The Leopard*), the manuscript of which was discovered by the novelist Giorgio Bassani.

Piccolo later described himself in a rare interview as 'a very savage spirit' and it is clear that his eccentric personality – on returning to Sicily he once again became virtually a recluse – did not endear him to the literary establishment. Since he was also writing of a 'unique Sicilian world ... on the verge of disappearing' (in the words of the accompanying letter to Montale, which Piccolo afterwards told Sciascia had been written by Lampedusa), and in a poetry he admitted to be 'difficult', no doubt he was content to be judged by posterity if he was to be judged at all. Symptomatic as this is of Piccolo's aristocratic stance, it is also part of what Glauco Cambon has called his 'post-historical consciousness', for both in his poetry and in what little one can glean of his personal life, he seems, as Cambon says, to inhabit 'a world where everything already happened long ago, where history can only regress to folklore, shadow, sorcery'. At the same time Piccolo does write a distinctively modern poetry, irrespective of the term 'Baroque' which he used to describe the four poems which he considered his finest achievements and placed at the head of his first volume. Piccolo's distinction is not, in other words, simply attributable to the fact that he is more 'Baroque' than any other twentieth-century poet has chosen to be; even his 'post-historical consciousness' was not sufficient to make him more than neo-Baroque. As Montale was the first to say, Piccolo is 'truly a poet of our time' insofar as he explores 'the contradiction between a universe changing but concrete, real, and a self, absolute but unreal because it lacks tangibility', a theme he had derived primarily from his reading in the philosophy of Husserl.

Piccolo is the best, indeed almost the only, guide to what he is attempting in his poetry. In an interview he gave towards the end of his life he claimed to have 'dispersed my energies in obstinate study from the very first years of my life' and to have studied everything contrary to his nature 'because I wanted my lyrics to be born from necessity'. Acknowledging his 'extreme subjectivism' and his Mallarmé-like need to 'scrutinize my inner being', Piccolo stressed that he was 'never abstractly symbolic' and that his poetry started 'from earthly roots'. In almost all the cases where the 'earthly roots' of Piccolo's poetry are visible they point to the city of Palermo as of decisive importance in his cultural make-up, and above all the Palermo of his childhood, 'baroque in its life and monuments' and dotted with 'funereal and luxurious' convents. But it is clear that if Piccolo's poetry starts from earthly roots it does not end there, and that a lifetime of obstinate study inspired in him a passion for less terrestrial things. Piccolo evidently indulged this passion in many ways, having 'studied very deeply the Spanish mystics, especially St Teresa', being fully *au fait* with the somewhat ethereal ideas of Husserl, and having conducted occult experiments like the Yeats with whom, as a young man, he had briefly corresponded.

It is because Piccolo treats the terrestrial world in the manner of a mystic, as something to be transcended, that his poetry poses problems for the reader. And yet at the same time what the poetry most often records is the drama of a failed transcendence and Piccolo's subsequent melancholy; in this sense he is always returning us to his 'earthly roots'. The blissful anguish of a St Teresa ('utterly consumed by the great love of God' as she wrote of her ecstasy) is not often available to Piccolo; the rhapsodic strain in him is always being pulled up short (as in the sudden and powerful end to his great 'Sundial' poem in *Baroque Songs*) by a far less florid speech denoting a return to earth. Piccolo's own description of what is happening in this 'noon' poem (flanked on one side by a morning poem, and on the other side by poems of sunset and night) is unmistakably a record of how a modern 'godless' mysticism must come to terms with its own insubstantiality:

Noon is the moment of the greatest expansion of consciousness, in which the 'I' and 'non-I' become one, are indistinguishable. Noon symbolizes this: anguish is finished ... but it's a mistake, because the ray which tells the hour is the noon bell of Palermo Cathedral

... [It tells] the existential tragedy of time, the flight of time which is anguish, and the eternity which is terror.

A critic of seventeenth-century poetry has written: 'Time as creator and destroyer ... is the primary religious experience of the Baroque.' This only requires the substitution of 'existential' for 'religious' to hold true for Piccolo, for his quest for the still point in which anguish is ended is continually being frustrated by an insistently 'Unstill Universe' (the title of one of the nine lyrics he sent to Montale). The fidelity with which Piccolo renders this unstill universe makes his poetry as turbulent and elusive as that of the great Spanish Baroque poet Góngora (whose *Solitudes* Sciascia aptly compares with the solitudes of Piccolo). There are times, indeed, especially in his long poems, when one feels that there is no limit to the images being generated, and so begins to suspect that there is more sound than sense in them. (On being interviewed Piccolo, an accomplished musician, repeatedly described his poetry in precise musical terms.) But the exhaustiveness of his strategies is an index of his desperation, his need to buttress 'fictions' against the threat of a vacuum. The great Argentinian 'fiction-maker' Jorge Luis Borges has written that the Baroque is 'that style which deliberately exhausts (or tries to exhaust) its possibilities and borders on its own caricature' and – though Borges is much more crystalline than Piccolo – this definition explains why the Sicilian poet seems at times to make errors of taste or judgement that a more prolific, or less Baroque, or more mature poet (Piccolo admitted there were elements of immaturity in his work) would not have made.

His confidence in his *Baroque Songs* was not, however, misplaced. Here above all, in the words of the 'Sundial' poem, 'vaults rise of radiant sound/which breaks and recreates an instant', even if all four do end in a mood far removed from radiance. The drama of 'Oratorio For Valverde', for instance, takes place between the initial prayer to dawn to 'cease [its] flight' (which stimulates the poet to a long flight of fancy) and the final prayer of 'invoked souls' to 'let/the torpor of first days descend'. The 'Sundial' poem also begins in this imperative mood with 'nothing but an endless bursting of ephemeral drops', apparently 'inexplicable', though (as the poet's own commentary on it makes clear) only too decipherable. The brief sunset poem 'Scirocco' also generates immense activity but here, too, the poet cannot prevent the vibrant world succumbing to the onset of darkness. And even if in the fourth poem 'night sometimes turns tender' (permitting a 'backwash of vanished life that overflows/the urn of Time'), the 'quiet oil' of the studious poet is finally overwhelmed by 'a darkness more dense [which] seems repose but is fever'. Night, with its ambiguous shapes which 'a quick glance catches,/a fixed stare annihilates' (Piccolo is very Baroque here), appears to offer the optimum time for the poet to 'seek in vain to pin/the changeless tulips/to fluid curtains' (in the words of the eighth of the nine lyrics which accompany the *Baroque Songs*). But there are signs in these very lyrics that he is not blind to the splendours of day. It is at dawn ('on the borders of light') that the poet brings 'an unknown balm,/an oil that mellows things' which 'gives me back the world'. This tempers his melancholy with the confidence that 'the hidden colloquy never stills,/the secret voice never settles'. The first of the nine lyrics ('Unstill Universe') seems to support his confidence:

And the arch of the low door and the step smooth
with too many winters are a fable in the unforeseen
rays of the March sun.

The last of the nine lyrics, however, acknowledges the vanity of the poet's quest and the failure of the Mallarméan ideal of pure poetry. It is finally not light but darkness which offers consolation:

the pure hand draws
on the rain that passes: illusion.
But the staff of the beggar
who awaits his ration of oil
will flower . . .

This flowering staff recurs in the fourth of the six poems

placed between the *Baroque Songs* and the nine lyrics, collectively called *Bosco the Conjurer*. The epigraph to this section speaks of how 'from the vain litigations of our unquiet heart we seek to make a secret of stars and fountains'. And the first poem augurs well, recapturing for a time the period nostalgically and magically retrieved by Lampedusa in *The Leopard*. But in the second half of the poem we encounter the 'terror' that is never far from Piccolo. The second poem warns not so much against nostalgia as against an inaccessible hermeticism. And the third, a prose poem, follows this advice, admitting us into the workshop or crucible of the poet's mind. In the fourth poem Piccolo concentrates on the figures he has magically brought to life but at the same time admits that they are 'phantoms of hours/that don't exist, that never will'. In the last two poems he is deprived of all company and left in bitter solitude; 'even if the lost recovers/its frontiers' he knows that on his brow there is a 'sign/of a melancholy without end'. Montale seems not to have cared much for these poems, but it is clear that they were an important attempt on the part of Piccolo to believe in his own fictions.

The nine poems of *Hide And Seek* (1960) inscribe a similar parabola, with the upward curve of the first four reaching its peak in the prose poem at the centre and then, under the pressure of anguish and anxiety, beginning to curve downwards. All of them are full of what the title poem calls 'forms that invoke and/negate a meaning' but, in 'Anna Perenna' at least, invocation is temporarily more important than negation. In this poem Piccolo brings back to life a Roman goddess to whom sacrifice was offered in order that the cycle of the year might be happily completed. It is one of Piccolo's most difficult and most impressive poems, with the poet's desperation tempered by the knowledge that 'sorrow is the note of a song' and that a flowering staff can make the beggar into a good shepherd: 'the fleeces .../are calm in sleep to the hand'. 'The Oven' continues this feeling of benediction, with its assertion that 'strength can never/diminish in he who listens to the soil'. And 'The Farmhouse' also consolidates it, although the key figure is plainly the poet himself, burning midnight oil so as to 'resume the interrupted tales that will never end'. It is in the night storm of the poem 'Candles' that this refuge begins to be penetrated:

nothing is lost as yet
but someone said once
that one day all will be lost.

By the end of the fifth poem this 'but' (one of Piccolo's favourite words) begins to bulk larger; 'But of the day, of its secret, of the coiffure,/nothing remains'. And even the vicious circle of 'The Days' cannot disguise the fact that they will not return. However, in the beautiful 'Shadows', which concludes *Hide And Seek*, Piccolo manages to be at once disenchanted and hopeful. For his habitual anxiety rises only to subside, and the night is calm.

Of the nine poems of Piccolo's third and final volume (*Plumelia*, 1967), very much the most important is the first, which describes an imaginary ascent of Mount Pellegrino (the mountain of the pilgrim) above Palermo. Here, as at the end of his first volume, Piccolo confronts his withdrawal from the world and makes plain the consequences of a quest for pure poetry. Questioned as to the significance of this poem Piccolo replied:

This fable symbolizes the plight of the poet who has given up everything because of his search for pure poetry and who has isolated himself from other men, thus becoming not a poet but an inflammable puppet made of tow. His own blaze of desire for pure poetry has worn him out, has burnt him up.

The other poems are, not surprisingly, more accessible than is usual with Piccolo. The best of them is perhaps 'The Lost Message', where all his previous turbulence seems to have become stoical acceptance:

in daylight
no verdure is missing from the garden,
no fleeting imprint of a foot
visible. No one
will say who in the hours of sleep
passed by, what message
went by unheeded and was lost.

Piccolo seems to have disappeared from the histories of modern poetry without a trace, like his own lost message. But he had learnt the virtues of what a poem in *Bosco The Conjurer* calls 'quiet waiting' and he will surely rematerialize. It is a testament to the quality of his work, and not simply a reflection of its slight bulk, that Piccolo is one of the few modern Italian poets to have been honoured by a complete translation of his poetry into English.

Attila József (1902–37)

Born in Budapest into a proletarian family. Deeply trauma-
tized by his father's abandonment of the family in 1908. Lived
with foster-parents in Öcsöd from 1910 to 1912; educated in
Budapest and experienced great poverty. Attempted unsuc-
cessfully to commit suicide while still a child; visited Albania
briefly in the summer of 1918. Profoundly depressed by the
death of his mother at Christmas 1919. Studied at the
Gymnasium at Máko. In 1922 his first poems were published.
Prosecuted for blasphemy and acquitted. Enrolled at the
University of Szeged in 1924 and expelled the following year.
Studied French literature at the University of Vienna and
wrote poetry in French in 1926–7. Became a Marxist during
his time in Paris; returned to the University of Budapest in
1927–8. Unsuccessful affair with a girl of good family which
led to him being hospitalized in an asylum for the first time.
Became a member of the illegal Communist Party in 1930;
began to live with the woman who remained his companion
until 1936. Attacked as a Fascist by Stalinist Hungarians in
Moscow in 1931, the year in which he commenced psycho-
analytic treatment. Expelled from the Communist party in
1933. Fell in love with the woman who was his psychoanalyst
in 1935; hospitalized with severe depression and mental in-
stability. Committed suicide by throwing himself under the
wheels of a goods train at Balatonszarszo.

The widespread contemporary interest in the poetry of the
countries once collectively designated *MittelEuropa* has been
one of the few benefits of a political climate of confrontation

between East and West. In a period of more or less constant 'Cold War' between the so-called free world and a manifestly unfree one, poetry has crossed barriers more readily than people. Since none of the languages in question is spoken outside *MittelEuropa* except by *émigrés*, the *rapprochement* has been effected almost exclusively through the medium of translation. And if there have been times when the fact of being a poet of Eastern Europe has taken precedence over the quality of the poetry, the sheer weight of translated material has effectively forced the Western reader to exercise a criterion of excellence, if only to reduce it to manageable proportions. In the case of Hungary five poets have made an impact – Gyula Illyés, Ferenc Juhász, Sandor Weöres, Attila József and Miklós Radnóti. It is ironic, in view of the post-war conditions which have prompted the response, that those to have aroused most interest – József and Radnóti – should have perished in the one case by his own hand before the war and in the other at the hands of the Nazis before the war ended. Unlike Radnóti, József has not been anything like widely enough translated into English for a just estimate of his greatness to be possible. But it is quite clear from what we have that in József Hungary has a poet who, if Hungarian were more widely spoken, would be on everyone's lips as of equal stature with the acknowledged giants of European literature.

In his foreshortened life József experienced the full gamut of personal and public rejection. His father left home when he was three; between five and seven he was with foster parents; at nine he attempted suicide; at fourteen his mother died; before reaching maturity he had been accused of blasphemy in one poem and expelled from university for another; almost all the women he fell in love with failed to reciprocate his affection; he was hospitalized with mental illness; he never lived much above the breadline; and after being a member of the (then illegal) Hungarian Communist Party he was attacked by Stalinist elements in it as a Fascist. On his last birthday József wrote of his gestation as 'a judiciary detention of nine months', of his birth as a sentence of 'lifelong correction in a workhouse', and of his life as a transfer into 'the world of incorrigible criminals'; eight months later he killed himself. Such a profile seems to invite us to compare József with any number of *poètes maudits* in Western Europe; but the social dimension present in the note written on his last birthday marks out the manner in which he differs from them. Cursed with a neurotic and ultimately schizophrenic personality, József located the real cause of all ills in the existing structures of society. He admired both Rimbaud and Blok, and he translated them into Hungarian; but he was aware of their shortcomings, as is plain from a letter written to his sister in 1926: 'Symbolism is nothing. We need to consider everything rationally and analytically.' Of the analytical models available to him in prosecuting this enterprise he was most impressed by what he had found in the sociological writings of Karl Marx, and he developed, in his surprisingly cogent theoretical essays on the relationship between poetry and science, on scientific socialism and on the origins and purpose of creativity, a basically Marxist position on the function of literature. The severity of his attitude, partially prompted no doubt by the confusions of his unstable psychology, is epitomized by his claim that 'things artistically confused are also logically confused'. Even after commencing psychoanalytical treatment, which might have been expected to make him more introspective, he addressed himself to matters of more than merely personal concern: 'the cure of the neurotic', he wrote, 'is none other than to make him aware of his social reality'. All the great poems of the neurotic József, however personal, demonstrate his abiding commitment to the alteration of the social conditions that permit neurosis to occur. In a gesture emblematic of his whole career, József repudiated Nietzsche's *Thus Spake Zarathustra* and recommended the creation of a 'multicellular' man who, by transforming alienation into harmony, would benefit mankind with ideals of brotherhood less separatist than those of the ostracized Zarathustra. Yet he had himself been ostracized, and spoke feelingly when he said that 'the writer rejected by society is of an incomparable moral grandeur'.

What distinguishes József from those who have made similarly extravagant claims is that this belief was at once the stimulus for, and the ratification of, his belief that the poet differed from the ordinary man only in his 'multicellular' potential.

The idea of the 'multicellular' poet creating in his art a cosmos ('a world all of whose points are Archimedean points' in the poet's own words) is given memorable utterance in József's poem 'On The Edge Of The City':

> Words on the poet's lips are a clatter,
> and yet it's he who engineers
> the magics and enchantments of this world;
> he foresees mankind's career,
> constructing harmony within himself;
> as you shall, in the world's sphere.

As these lines make clear, the poet was, for József, an agent of cosmogony like the God of the scriptures, a universal human benefactor. Such a conception obviously involved the abandonment of belief in a transcendent deity:

> I don't believe in God, But if
> there is one, He shouldn't bother with me.
> I shall absolve myself.
> And those who are alive will help.

'We're not', József wrote in 'On The Edge Of The City', 'rolled out of God or Reason':

> we're from iron, coal, oil.
> So you hear, when we're struck, the note
> of all human huan creations, like a violin plucked.

This defiantly secular orientation was designed to supplement his stress on the poet as 'a just man' with his eyes unerringly fixed upon contemporary reality. It was not poetry but justice which mattered to him, as a stanza in his 'Ars Poetica' makes explicit:

> I am a poet, What does poetry
> itself matter to me?

It would not be just if the star were to rise
to the sky from the river of night.

Given this hierarchy among his concerns, even the 'me' ceases
to matter; in the aptly titled poem 'A Just Man' all except one
of the poet's vital organs are shown to be expendable:

I shall step out on to my lips
and my vertebrae can scatter
in all the directions of the globe
because I'll be standing straight
among the crooked bodies of the dead.

Even József's neurotic relationship with his dead mother
and his vagrant father (as reflected in the poem 'Guilt') could
be solaced by the thought that he was 'not the only one'. And
in one of the most powerful of his poems of unrequited love –
the great cry of pain 'It Hurts A Lot' – it is typical of him to
enlist the aid of 'all living things' in his vain attempt to
awaken the heart of his beloved. His belief in human freedom
depended on his sense of the necessity of human interaction,
and on a sense of solidarity that was obviously threatened by
failures in the sexual arena.

József's demystification of traditional sanctions is entirely
of a piece with his profession of the Marxist ideology. Yet he
was much less straightforwardly materialist than many
Marxists have been. 'Only in others can you wash your face,/
it's no use to bathe it in yourself', he wrote in the title poem
of his second volume; it is a sentiment which sounds reassur-
ingly and familiarly collectivist. The next two lines are, how-
ever, concerned with nature and the cosmos:

Become the edge on a little blade of grass
and you'll be greater than the world's axis.

József's need to transcend himself is advertised in the first line
of this poem ('That's not me shouting, it's the earth that
roars') and it is precisely his ability to 'become the edge on a
little blade of grass' which gives his rural poems their
tremendous power. Merging with the natural world as a
refuge from the 'iron world' of capitalism, József could

experience a kind of Pantheist beatitude, as in the last stanza of 'A Tired Man':

Evening ladles out the quiet.
I am a warm slice from its loaf of bread.
The sky is resting, and stars come out
to sit on the river and shine on my head.

A similar tranquillity, sharpened by a sense of loss, informs 'Sleep Quietly Now' and 'A Little Dew' and even in poems where the landscape is less nourishing (the first of the 'Without Hope' poems, for example) it is present:

My heart is perched on nothing's branch,
its small body trembles without a sound.
The stars quietly gather
to gaze, and gaze, from all around.

József's sense of the earth and his ability to 'see with her eyes' ('Sad') makes his poetry both precise and suggestive, as for instance in the last stanza of 'Since You've Been Away' (where 'distant space' takes on human features) and the first lines of 'The Rain Falls' (where the poet accepts that it is 'just doing its job'). He is at his most compelling, however, when, as in 'The Wasteland', the landscape 'revolves/around a farmhouse'. For this enables him – confirming the suggestion made in 'Glassblowers' that the poet is himself a kind of labourer – to concentrate on those who work in the fields. The poem 'Village' actually suggests that the poet's gift of speech is in retroactive relationship with the farming community. In one of the most beautiful evening settings of the many in József's poetry, he hears 'a sound whose only depth is silence' which suddenly crystallizes the sources of his strength and makes sense of his activity:

And as knowledge dawns here, the words
for understanding are already in the air:
'shovel', 'plough'

words because the farmer says them to the sun,
the rain, the land. I use these words
to trust all this to time's care.

As 'The Wasteland' is not alone in showing, József is reviving the classical mode of agrarian pastoral in order to make it into a weapon of devastating critique. 'The blade of a scythe' flashing like lightning at the end of 'Summer', for example, is a reminder to the 'comrades' that they must liberate themselves from oppression. Like the poet of 'Finally' they must 'take sides', because 'time is ripening in the land'. However, unlike many propaganda poets, József does not merely mouthe utopian ideas. His dystopian childhood would not permit it. He remembers his own past ('I was beaten as a small child'), records his present unease ('under my feet the brittle leaves/tossed sleeplessly and moaned/like beaten children'), turns reality into metaphor ('fragile villages .../have fallen from the tree of living rights/like these leaves') and metaphor into reality ('Give birth to a new order'). In the poem from which these quotations are taken ('A Breath Of Air!') József's personal history and Hungary's public history become indistinguishable, for freedom is a surrogate mother, and the alienated proletariat are her children. In perhaps his most successful combination of Marx and Freud, József here effectively reintegrates the originating matrix and gives birth to both himself and to freedom.

In the magnificent poem 'Consciousness' József admits that 'the suffering is deep inside'. But his attention is always concentrated outwards. This is not so as to escape suffering, but rather to experience it fully as part of a process. The orphanhood of the adult ('someone who has/no father and no mother in his heart') is inevitable; but like the train into which he is transformed at the end of the poem – which also illuminates 'Winter Night' and 'Night In The Slums' – the adult can be a light-bringer. The position is not a theoretical one, but an emotional one, or rather it demonstrates that there cannot be division between the heart and the mind (as the last stanza of 'A Breath Of Air!' also shows). It is because József cannot countenance continued division of the kind which he himself was the victim of that he looks at the stars as well as at the earth, at the factory workers as well as at the farmhand, at the soul as well as at the body. In a sense he *socializes* Rimbaud's personal synthesis at the end of *A Season In Hell*. For his 'rebel psalms' (as József called his poems) were evidently written in the knowledge that a personal salvation would be a contradiction in terms. 'Let our souls be free of torment/and our bodies free of vermin' is how József ends his hellish 'Night In The Slums'; the first person plural is characteristic. In the same way the insistent 'you yourself' of 'The Seventh' is clearly intended to create not so much a singular identity as a 'multicellular' one.

It seems appropriate that a poet who believed that 'freedom creates an order in itself and disciplines itself' should have written with equal power in free verse and in the virtual straitjacket of the 'Corona' sonnets (collectively and significantly entitled 'Song Of The Cosmos'). And it is clear, even from the relatively few poems translated into English, that József's imagery is astonishingly consistent in all the many genres he attempted. Charles Tomlinson (in a poem in the collection *Written On Water*) has spoken of József's 'verse grown calm with all it had withstood', a very apt description of such fine late poems as 'No One Can Lift Me' and even the tragic last poem of all ('I Finally Found My Home'). In the latter József decides (as some of his almost uncanny winter poems suggest he was bound to do) that

> winter's best
> for one who finally leaves his hopes
> for a family and a home to others.

He committed suicide in December 1937.

In personal terms, József's suicide must certainly be considered tragic, especially as he elected to kill himself under the wheels of one of the trains he had so often seen as potential light-bringers. But it is typical of József to have left in his last poem his 'hopes' of a heritage to others, especially at a time when – as he says in one of the poems that use his own name for titles – 'his decay was like his country's'. And there is what József would have perhaps called justice in the epigraph from his 'By The Danube' which Tomlinson uses: 'my heart which owes this past a calm future'. For it is inconceivable that future translators will not want to bridge the gap between English and Hungarian with as full as possible a collection of József, to reveal him as the 'European' he claimed to be, and probably the greatest Socialist poet of the present century.

Pablo Neruda (1904–73)

Born Naftali Ricardo Reyes in Parral, Chile, the son of a rail-way worker. Grew up in the wild regions of Southern Chile at Temuco, where he knew the poetess Gabriela Mistral. Adopted the pseudonym Pablo Neruda in October 1920. In 1921 moved to Santiago to study at the Teachers' Institute for a career as professor of French. Achieved overnight fame on the publication in 1924 of *Veinte poemas de amor y una cáncion desperada*. Made Chilean consul in Rangoon, Burma in 1927; consul in Colombo, Ceylon in 1928, in Batavia, Java in 1930 and in Singapore in 1931. First married in 1930. Consul in Buenos Aires in 1933, where he met García Lorca. Consul in Barcelona and Madrid 1934–5. Dismissed from his post by the Nationalists in 1936. Lived in Paris in 1937 and again in 1939. Consul in Mexico 1940; beaten up by Nazis in Cuernavaca. Visited the Peruvian Inca ruins of Macchu Picchu in 1943. Removed from the Chilean Senate in 1948, and forced to go into hiding, crossing the Andes on a horse. Travelled very extensively in Europe and South America in the next four years, returning to Chile in 1952. Settled in later life with his third wife in Valparaíso. Communist Candidate for the Chilean presidency in 1969; stood down to make way for Allende. Ambassador to France 1971, the year in which he won the Nobel Prize. Died twelve days after the military coup which toppled Allende in Santiago. Internationally recognized and the recipient of numerous honours from the 1930s onwards.

Neruda is perhaps the major modern example of a poet with

sufficient vigour and versatility to breathe new life into Walt Whitman's famous line 'I am large. I contain multitudes'. It is as a poet of the multitude, of the lowest common denominator viewed as the highest attainment of the human spirit, that Neruda asks, and indeed requires, his reader to take him. Yet within the multitude the poet himself remains a substantial and important figure; Neruda's aim is the double one adumbrated in the first lines of Whitman's *Leaves of Grass*:

One's-self I sing, a simple separate person,
Yet utter the word Democratic, the word En-Masse.

We encounter in Neruda, as in Whitman, the egotistical sublime of the Romantics turned inside out to reveal the democratic vistas which it has masked, the poet no longer a Promethean and sacrificial figure but simply an ordinary craftsman. It is a natural consequence of such a stance that expression should come to matter more than finesse, and that anything resembling 'art for art's sake' should be shunned. In the *Memoirs* on which he was working at the time of his death we find one of Neruda's most eloquent statements to this effect:

I have always maintained that the writer's task has nothing to do with mystery or magic and that the poet's task, at least, must be a personal effort for the benefit of all. The closest thing to poetry is a loaf of bread or a ceramic dish, or a piece of wood lovingly carved, even if by clumsy hands.

Neruda's, like Whitman's (and unlike Mayakovsky's), is an agrarian vision: poetry which is a kind of cottage industry, restoring the word manufacture to its original meaning – a making by hand. The worth of poetry is to be judged by the contribution it makes to the lives of those who might otherwise ignore it; in Neruda's own words, once again from the *Memoirs*:

We have to disappear into the midst of those we don't know, so that they will suddenly pick up something of ours from the street, from the sand, from the leaves that have fallen for a thousand years in the same forest, and will take up gently the object we made. Only then will we be truly poets. In that object, poetry will live.

Such a view naturally exposed Neruda to the criticism that poetry was something more than propaganda, even if (as Mayakovsky claimed) it could be shown to be 'at its root tendentious'. But here, too, Neruda seems to have understood a much-abused word in its original sense of expansion and enlargement, and to have regarded propaganda as the inevitable consequence of the centrifugal forces generated by the poem. Neruda's poetry is not crystalline but dynamic, participating in the life forces it records. Against the notions of 'pure poetry' which held sway in his youth he urged the claims of a poetry 'as impure as our clothing'; in a memorable apologia written in 1934 he concludes 'to be afraid of "bad taste" is to suffer frostbite'. In the last analysis this impure poetry differs only from that which we associate with 'good taste' in the degree to which it has a palpable design upon us: to cure ills, to warm the blood, to be in the broadest sense therapeutic. But by virtue of flouting accepted canons of taste it may require us to accept things we have been trained to suspect: empty rhetoric, for example. Finesse is ultimately no less at a premium in the kind of poetry written by Neruda than in the tradition which he so strenuously opposes.

Neruda subsequently came to regard his first collection of poems, *Crepusculario* (1923), as 'immature'. Insofar as maturity is equated with 'a personal effort for the benefit of all' the judgement is a just one. But *Crepusculario* is a book of great promise, irrespective of the fact that it deals largely with personal problems. The subtlety of the young Neruda is particularly evident in the most popular poem in the volume, the first of his many fine poems of farewell. 'Farewell' is a celebration of the 'love which loves freedom/in order to love again'. But the celebration is a muted one, haunted by memory ('Together we made/a bend in the road where love passed'), by the absence of any clear itinerary ('I do not know where I am going') and most of all by the frank admission which characterizes much of Neruda's early poetry: 'I am sad. But I am always sad'. As these quotations suggest, the mood of melancholy developed in *Crepusculario* is quite unlike that shrouded in 'mystery' and 'magic' by the French Symbolists;

even the sequence which retells the archetypal Symbolist
tragedy of Pelleas and Melisande has a clarity quite alien to
the murky meditations of Maeterlinck. A similar clarity is to
be found in 'Dark Suburb', a poem which obviously owes a
debt to Baudelaire's poems about city sunsets. The initial
question as to whether life and poetry are mutually exclusive
suggests an active man rather than a contemplative one, and
the last stanza of the poem is plainly a critique of those who
withdraw into themselves:

Here I am, having begun to bud among ruins,
nourished only by miseries
as if weeping were a seed
and I the only furrow of the earth.

The idea is consolidated in another sunset poem ('Here I am
with my poor body ...') which describes a moment of
expanded consciousness in which the poet's miseries are
assuaged by a pantheistic sense of the immensity of the
cosmos; the crepuscular moods identified by the book's title
are far from being unreservedly negative. Indeed the book
ends with a powerful affirmation of the coming of dawn, the
first of those poems in which, as Neruda later said, 'my verses
free themselves of me':

The words came, and my heart,
as uncontainable as dawn,
was atomized in words, delighted in their flight,
and like heroes they escaped and carried it with them,
abandoned and insane, and forgotten beneath them
like a dead bird, under their wings.

Despite the fact that these final words are addressed out-
wards, to the poet's companions in distress, it is clear that
his poetic afflatus is its own reward and therapy. And this is
also the case with the volume which followed, in which his
companions have been reduced to one, a beloved woman
from whom he has parted and whom his 'fugitive' words are
designed to conjure: *Twenty Poems of Love and One Desperate
Song* (1924).

Neruda's 1924 volume, composed without any thought for

'the benefit of all', proved immensely popular; a decade before he explicitly recommended it, 'impure' poetry had shown itself to be equally attractive to the public and to the intelligentsia. These agitatedly sensual poems are imbued with an ecstatic agony which the poet is striving to transcend; but he cannot free himself from the vitalist premises which have directly inspired it. Like the light which envelops the beloved in poem II of the sequence, the flame of love has proved 'mortal' and 'full of sadness', and the poet is almost derelict, bereft of the plenitude which had given his life a purpose. The mood is so hectic that it seems as if clarity must be sacrificed; but because all the attributions stem from and are directed towards a single focus the poems are actually extraordinarily translucent. The vigour of the language belies the poet's dereliction; in the words of poem IX it is 'one wave,/lunar, solar, flaming and freezing, all at once'. We may recall the 'icy fire' of Petrarch. But the poems are much more inflammatory than they are chilling. As the sequence unfolds, the beloved seems to grow at once more remote and more present, and having, as it were, reconstituted her, the poet is left at the end in a position of strength. The turbulence has passed, and simplicity supervenes. The last poem begins 'Tonight I can write the saddest lines' and so it proves in the conclusion:

I no longer love her, it's true, yet perhaps I do love her.
Love is so short, forgetting takes so long.

Because on nights like this I held her in my arms
my soul is unhappy at having lost her.

Though this be the last pain that she causes me
and these the last words I shall write to her.

As the single song of despair confirms, 'it is the hour of departure' in every sense.

Experiment of Infinite Man (1926) is, appropriately, a new departure for Neruda, and avowedly an experiment. But even these fifteen unpunctuated 'cantos' of 'words without grace' are organized around the age-old nucleus of an imagin-

ary voyage. 'I am building here', Neruda wrote – reminding
his readers that the poet is only an artisan – 'a construct of free
matter with my words'. The *Experiment* is certainly a good deal
more 'dispersed' in its language than the final poem of
Crepusculario, which has dispersal for its theme. By virtue of
being less constricted, however, it is also less concentrated. It
is in the poems written between 1925 and 1931 (published in
1933 as *Residence On Earth*) that this new 'dispersed' language
reaches its apotheosis. Here we encounter for the first time the
so-called Surrealist Neruda; but the primary influence is not
so much the Surrealists as the poet whom they made their
patron saint – Rimbaud. In order to construct a habitation
upon the earth Neruda is passing through states of mind that
would not be out of place in Rimbaud's *A Season In Hell*,
especially when (as in part II of the book) they are expressed
in such volatile prose poetry. The 'Gallop Towards Death'
which opens the volume is an index of how Neruda's early
vitalism included a headlong urge towards death amid its
more obviously hedonistic impulses. And the poem 'Ars
Poetica' presents the problems that must be experienced by a
poet of such a pronounced centrifugal capacity when he
begins to look inwards: he is bewildered and bombarded by
a 'swarm of objects'. A monsoon-like rain – many of the poems
were written in the Far East, where Neruda began his con-
sular career – beats remorselessly, 'indefinitely sad' and
'obstinately shapeless' like the poems it provokes. And yet, as
with Rimbaud, behind the turbulence the poet can be seen in
quest of those resources which will permit the dream of
reunification – with native land, with loved one, most of all
with alienated self – to become a reality. In the opening poem
of the second volume of *Residence On Earth* (consisting of poems
written between 1931 and 1935, and published in 1935) an
upward curve begins to be inscribed. Like many of the poems
in the 1933 collection, this initial poem is dominated by
sound. But here, for the first time, it is the sound of 'growth
and degree'. The beautiful 'Barcarole' confirms that Neruda's
new sense of purpose is not misplaced. The pessimistic mood
has not, however, lifted decisively. A domestic contentment

seems as far away as ever, and the famous 'Walking Around' is an admission that his efforts to transcend the gloom have made him exceedingly weary. There are 'so many things that I want to forget', Neruda writes in the penultimate poem of the second *Residence*. But the title of the poem is an implacable reminder that 'There Is No Forgetting'. Many years later, in the huge *Memorial of Isla Negra* of 1964, a similar realization seems to have prompted Neruda to record how many things he was obliged to remember.

Neruda's third *Residence On Earth* (consisting of poems written between 1935 and 1945, and published in 1947) is dominated by the 'Meeting Under New Flags' described in its third subsection; here we encounter his first explicitly political poems, inspired by his espousal of the Republican cause in the Spanish Civil War. A plainness reminiscent of his early love poems returns here, though it is now employed to express ideas of human brotherhood rather than private passion. Many of these 'occasional' poems (especially perhaps 'I Explain Some Things' and 'Song About Some Ruins') will always transcend the occasions which prompted them; they have a gravity and density which make them applicable to many subsequent political conflicts. But, like Brecht, who was similarly impressed by Stalin's Soviet Union before the full facts became known, Neruda wrote many perishable poems on public themes, of which the 'Song to Stalingrad' is typical. The paradox of Neruda's expansive poetics is that some events of public significance are incapable of any further expansion; the task of the poet begins to seem redundant, tautological and thus reductive. Much better than the 'Song to Stalingrad' is a song to his native Chile with a less specific point of origin, in its way prefiguring the famous but controversial volume of 1950, *General Song*.

General Song is probably the most successful of all modern attempts to write epic poetry; it celebrates the expansion of the whole American continent from the primeval slime of 'Some Beasts' to the poet's own present in 'I Am'. But the impulse, as the title acknowledges, is quite as much lyrical as it is epic, so the whole vast edifice seems inherently more unstable than the epics of the classical civilizations. 'In a poem of any length,' as T. S. Eliot pointed out, 'there must be transitions between passages of greater and less intensity.' The crucial word is 'transitions', and in this respect Neruda's practice seems too sporadic. The poem lives in the mind as a sequence of miniature epics which lack the network of cross-reference by which they might properly be linked to one another. The central section, the seventh, is obviously being offered as the seed of the whole enterprise; but is the enterprise truly organic? By general consent the finest part of *General Song* is the second section, the well-known 'Summits of Macchu Picchu'. The 'permanence of stone and word' which Neruda perceived among the Inca dead has, in addition, important resonances for his later poetry. In 'Summits of Macchu Picchu' the 'transitions between passages of greater and less intensity' seem to have been moulded as much by Neruda's intellect as by his sensibility; this cannot be said of other parts of *General Song*. Significantly perhaps, the Macchu Picchu poems were written two years after Neruda had visited the ancient Inca burial place. Even a poet of his prodigious gifts was not generally at his best when writing strictly 'occasional' poems.

During the 1950s, partially stimulated by the prospect of reaching an even larger audience through the columns of a newspaper, Neruda wrote four books of *Elemental Odes*, less elemental than they appear, and odes only in the sense that any casual utterance can be thought of as a song. There are fine poems here, notably the odes to his watch in the night, to his own socks, to the undersea diver and to the fragrance of wood (always one of Neruda's favourite materials). 'To write simply,' said Neruda, 'has been my most difficult task.' Sometimes the difficulties are not conquered, and there are many perishable poems among the odes. But the concentration on particular words of great importance to him (elemental, as we might say) – 'sea' in 'Ode To The Double Autumn', 'earth' in 'Ode To The Girl Gardener', and 'hand' in 'Ode To The Old Poet' – is an index of Neruda's seriousness of purpose. *Estravagario* (1958) – one of the poet's own special favourites among his work – is an exercise in levity by comparison. But if 'the fool' has taken over (as he admits in 'We Are Many') it is a wise folly which emerges. On occasion, as in 'Return To A City' and in the poem addressed to 'The Unhappy One' whom he left there – both of which stem from his period in the Far East – Neruda's gloom actually leaves little room for levity. But when he transcends his own personal experience, or treats his own personal experience as something that has been repeated everywhere by everybody, the genial mood is maintained. Even the openly autobiographical 'Autumn Testament' is predicated on the belief that 'this happens to everybody'. If Neruda's language is no longer, as in the *Experiment* and the first *Residence*, 'dispersed', his personality most certainly is. Properly understood, these poems are no more self-obsessed than Whitman's, though there are many that seem unduly self-indulgent.

As its title implies, *Estravagario* is something of a rag-bag. 'The word En-Masse' in Neruda is by no means always to be preferred to the 'simple separate person'. Even Neruda's 'private' poetry, however, is variable. The anonymously published *Captain's Verses* of 1952 are really rather slight, and the hundred love sonnets of 1959 are much less compelling than the twenty love poems of 1924. Yet these 'houses of fourteen planks' have a certain solidity, as do the 'flinty' utterances in *The Stones Of Chile* (1961). Whilst it is impossible not to experience a feeling of *déjà lu* with respect to the later volumes of Neruda, it is clear that the poet is engaged in rereading himself in order to remake himself. The rereading takes two basic forms and is reflected in the two modes – lyric and epic – to which Neruda was temperamentally attracted. The lyric mode – as represented in *Full Powers* (1962) – moves more and more towards those limits of language where 'it is not necessary to say anything'; the utterance is naturally, therefore, more crystalline than in the early volumes. One poem in *Full Powers* actually describes the strategies which permit a 'white' poetry to be written. The epic mode – as represented by *Memorial of Isla Negra* – is at quite the opposite extreme; here it seems necessary to say absolutely everything, and the mood is much darker, appropriately so given the title. Neruda's autobiographical impulses are so strong here that he becomes, as in his posthumously published *Memoirs*, more interested in what he is saying than in how he is saying it. Though the *Memorial* is in no sense negligible, it is likely, for precisely this reason, to be neglected. As an investigation into origins *The Burning Sword* of 1970, a meditation on the myths of Genesis, may be preferred simply because it is so much less dependent on the facts of one man's life, however extraordinary and compelling that life may have been.

In his last years Neruda saw, and actively participated in, the triumph in his native Chile of the ideals by which he had lived for the previous thirty years; but he also witnessed its tragic aftermath. In 1969 he was chosen by the Central Committee of Chile's Communist Party as its candidate in the forthcoming presidential elections. He was a leading spirit in its transformation into a Popular Unity party. He resigned his candidature in favour of his friend Salvador Állende, and in the following year the party swept to victory at the polls. The public Neruda was at the height of his fame. But the private lyric poet – the author of the superb 'white' poetry of *The Hands Of Day* (1968), *End of the World* (1969) and *Stones of the Sky* (1970) – was a more troubled figure. These are not agonized poems; they seem to possess the very stillness of the stones they celebrate. But Neruda had become more and more conscious of his own mortality, of being 'a transitory man'; he had, as it were, watched the hands of day go round so often that it seemed the end of the world must be at hand. In the event, the darker tones in these lyrics take on the lineaments of prophecy: in 1973 Allende was toppled by a military coup in which he was murdered, and twelve days later Neruda died. The fate of the poet and the fate of the people are very rarely linked by such a tragic concatenation of circumstances. It is almost as if history had conspired to confirm the poet's personal mythology. But Neruda was really a maker of history, not a victim of it, and his poems will live longer than the political beliefs from which they sprang.

In an *oeuvre* which is over three thousand pages long, there are inevitably a number of poems which are expendable, though the quality of writing in the early years, and again in the last three lyric volumes, is astonishingly consistent. For those of a very refined disposition, much of even the best of Neruda will seem vulgar. But to regret the vein of vulgarity in his composition is to wish him other than he was; he had the common touch that only artists of the greatest magnitude seem to possess, and the triviality into which he was sometimes led was really only an inevitable by-product of the vitality and passion with which he consistently reaffirmed the necessity of art and opposed its degeneration into a gratuitous luxury.

René Char (born 1907)

Born in Isle-sur-Sorgue in the Vaucluze, the only son of a manufacturer. Disturbed by the death of his father in 1918 and by a distant relationship with his mother. Educated locally and at Avignon from 1922 to 1925. Began to write poetry during this period, greatly influenced by the poetry of Reverdy. Briefly in North Africa in 1924; later attended the University of Aix-en-Provence. Military service as an artilleryman at Nîmes in 1927–8. Sent some poems to Paul Éluard in 1929 and joined the Surrealists in 1930, remaining a member of the group until 1934, though ever afterward a Surrealist in all but name. Seriously ill with septicaemia in 1936–7; a supporter of the Republican cause in the Spanish Civil War. Fought heroically in the Resistance in Provence during the Second World War. A close friend of the novelist Albert Camus and the philosopher Martin Heidegger. Lives in the South of France, and has gradually emerged since the war as one of the more influential, original and respected of modern French poets.

The novelist Albert Camus and the philosopher Martin Heidegger, both of whom have been regarded as representative of fundamental strains within Existentialism, were each independently of the opinion that René Char was the greatest French poet of the century. But though he has been widely and discriminatingly admired in France Char has had almost no impact in England, and has only recently received the kind of attention in America which might lead to a more general acknowledgement of his importance. The neglect of Char is partially, it would seem, a response to the fact that he is an enigmatic writer, though this hardly distinguishes him from other widely praised modern poets. Char's enigmas are, however, of a kind that make them difficult to categorize; despite the plaudits of Camus and Heidegger, they do not seem to qualify as distinctively Existentialist. Now it is clearly part of Char's purpose to frustrate the desire to reduce his scope by more or less conceptual approaches to his poetry; but even in his semi-discursive writing the reader may be left without a set of keys to unlock the mysteries in which he has been implicated. The reflex reaction, and one partially conditioned by the history of Char's affiliations, is to regard him as a particularly extreme embodiment of the Surrealist revolution which has made so little headway either in Britain or America. Between 1930 and 1934 (the period in which he wrote the aptly-titled *Masterless Mallet*) Char certainly subscribed to the primary tenets of Surrealist doctrine, and he was involved (notably with Éluard) in the typically collaborative enterprises of the movement. However, the epigraph to his first published volume (*Arsenal*, 1929), written before he had made the acquaintance of Éluard, contains a remark which helps to explain his secession from the group: 'a moral suicide could not suffice me'. By its very nature Surrealism does not lend itself to description in static and stable terms: but it is obvious that several of its exponents manifested markedly 'immoralist' tendencies which must have been anathema to Char. The extent to which he was prepared to go beyond the abrogation of moral responsibility associated with the 'ivory tower' is illustrated by his commitment, during the war years, to the cause of the French Resistance, for whom Camus and Éluard also worked. No doubt it was this living proof of what an Existentialist would call *engagement* that first awakened an interest in Char in post-war France.

Despite, or possibly because of his experience of it, Char does not appear to have ever believed that the real world is susceptible of rational explanation; his initial attraction to the irrationalism of the Surrealists would otherwise make little sense. In this respect he may be said to have remained,

despite his secession, faithful to the spirit of Breton's Sur-
realist manifestoes. 'The poet', Char has written, 'is that part
of a man stubbornly opposed to calculated projects'; the
poetry written by someone professing such a belief should
obviously not be regarded as a product but rather conceived
of as contributing to an ongoing process. Char found a more
acute and economical expression of this than any Surrealist
could have offered him in the pre-Socratic Greek philosopher
Heraclitus, whose most celebrated aphoristic proposition
expresses man's inability to step twice into the same river.
There is an echo of Heraclitus's idea in one of the more
immediately accessible of Char's own aphorisms: 'Poetry is,
of all clear waters, the least likely to linger at the reflection of
its bridges.' The very idea of poetry as clear water marks
Char out from most of his contemporaries in a sceptical age,
and this is one reason why he is often spoken of as an exception-
ally affirmative poet by twentieth-century norms. Yet it is
obvious to anyone who reads a word of Char that his poetry
is by no means as translucent as it might be; it is too full of
the eddies and the turbulence which are a consequence of its
refusal to 'linger at the reflection of its bridges'. It is not
irrelevant in this respect that Char should also have been an
exponent of what he calls 'the pulverized poem', the poem
made up of the residual minerals left after the pounding of the
masterless mallet or the erosions caused by the passage of
water over stones. Char has openly acknowledged his fascina-
tion for the 'unapproachable object which shatters in frag-
ments when, having overcome the distance, we are about to
grasp it' – an apt description, his detractors would say, of
what happens to them when confronted by his poetry. How-
ever, for Char this fascination is comparable to that which is
exerted by a loved object: 'the roads which do not promise the
country of their destination,' runs another of Char's
aphorisms, 'are the best-loved roads.' Both these gnomic
aphorisms can be construed affirmatively if one so wishes: but
it is also clear that they contain an elegiac residue, that
they are more than merely affirmative.

Char's stance is too ambivalent to be categorically and

restrictively defined; 'one must,' in another of his formula-
tions, 'be the man of rain and the child of fine weather'. The
position expressed in this latter aphorism is so fluid as to be
scarcely a position at all; it seems more like a literary
equivalent of modern topological mathematics. For if the
aphorism begins in exhortation, it ends in equivocation; and if
it is addressed to the future it is plainly conditioned by the
past. A similar fluidity and suspense are present in one of the
most beguiling utterances in a prose poem ('The Rampart Of
Twigs') from Char's impressive collection of 1950, *The
Matinals*:

> We have lost our way and are dreamless. But there is always a
> candle that dances in our hand. So the shadow we are entering is
> our future sleep foreshortened without ceasing.

This at once prefigures and embodies the truth of a later utter-
ance in the poem: 'I expect nothing *finite*, I am resigned to
sculling between two unequal dimensions.' It is also an
illustration of the dream of 'plentitude' with which the poem
has begun, a plentitude which is plainly unavailable to those
who are not prepared – as some of Char's readers have
evidently not been – to scull between two unequal dimen-
sions. It would be wrong to read Char with the expectation
that he will confine himself, as most of us do, to a world
which can be empirically verified; but equally wrong to sup-
pose that, in going beyond the empirical, Char inhabits a kind
of personal cloud-cuckoo land to which we do not have access.
The climax of 'The Rampart Of Twigs', for example, is a
moment at which it would be difficult, if not impossible, for
most readers to resist being incorporated into Char's sense of
what it is to live and die:

> One must clear the barrier of the worst, run the perilous race, still
> hunt beyond, cut to pieces the iniquitous one, and disappear finally
> without undue fuss. A faint thanks given or received, nothing else.

Even this climax, however, can only impinge deeply if we
yield to the more enigmatic utterances that have preceded
it, and so rid ourselves of the Aristotelian rejoinder to the pre-

Socratics, that a thing cannot at once be itself and something else.

Precisely because he wishes to establish what he calls in a famous verse poem a 'common presence' (the title which he gave to an important anthology of his own work) Char's poetry is full of material that seems, to an English reader, unduly metaphysical or, more precisely, metapoetical. This is especially true of the poems in prose which are so distinctive a feature of Char's *oeuvre* as a whole; among modern French poets only Francis Ponge has more singlemindedly enriched this genre. The prose poem inevitably manifests itself on the page with a less finite circumscription and a more 'common presence' than the verse poem, however uncommon it may be statistically. Yet even the most tranquil of Char's prose poems exhibits the 'dislocating energy' which, as he stresses in a poem of homage to Hölderlin, is constitutive for him of poetry and reality, and also the mediating agent par excellence. There is a very beautiful poem in the collection *Furore And Mystery* which shows how Char makes no distinction between the dislocating energy of his subject-matter and that of his own writing:

We were watching flow in front of us the water growing. Suddenly it wiped out the mountain, shooting itself out of the maternal flanks. It was not a torrent submissive to its destiny but an ineffable animal whose word and substance we became. On the omnipresent arch of its imagination it kept us amorous. What intervention could have restrained us? A quotidian moderation had fled, the dispersed blood was restored to heat. Adopted by the open, pumiced to the point of invisibility, we were a victory which would never end.

('The First Moments')

This poem remains as stubbornly impervious to paraphrase as perhaps any poem may reasonably expect to. Yet it is clear that Char's perception, in the aftermath of war, of the famous fountain in his native Vaucluze – a region which the reader can hardly help but associate with the 'amorous' Petrarch – has provided a kind of solace. In a programmatic preface to *The Matinals*, Char reminds us that the 'relaxed breathing' of a 'temperate slope' is inseparably associated with our 'fiercest fevers'; 'The First Moments' is both relaxed and feverish, a fervent and yet subtle riposte to the philosopher Aristotle, whose rational and tragic view of man is epitomized by his suggestion that a man dies because he cannot join his end to his beginning.

There are, of course, signs, even in this ecstatic poem, of the 'tiny wound' which, as Char's preface to *The Matinals* stresses, can be found in any fabric. And a more recent poem ('Traced On The Abyss') subjects the same landscape to more mysterious and more ominous metamorphoses, or stress-fractures:

In the visionary wound of Vaucluze I watched you suffer. Where, although brought low, you were green water, and yet a road. You passed through death in its disorder. Flower undulating with a sustained secret.

Once again it would be folly to presume that one had fully penetrated Char's meaning, for the briefer he becomes the more elusive he is, as many of his aphorisms demonstrate. He has been insistent that he should not be interpreted too mono-lithically, and he has disabused his readers of the idea that he is simply engaged in a 'return to the source'. He certainly seeks nourishment from his place of origin, but he tends to find consolations only in the most 'disinherited' places. Since the mountainous upland of the Vaucluze only intermittently permits him to find relief, his poetry naturally becomes a per-manent testament to his need to continue walking the roads in quest of it.

Char seems destined to remain, a little like Wallace Stevens, so 'caviare to the general' that he may never enjoy the 'common presence' of more than a handful of devotees. He is perhaps as little understood now as Mallarmé a century ago, and Mallarmé's audience is at present still only a small one. It seems appropriate, therefore, that one of Char's favourite paintings, 'The Prisoner', should be by a painter, Georges de la Tour, who has had to wait several centuries to be rediscovered. Char wrote a prose poem in praise of this painter and this painting which he included in his inspiring wartime notebook, *Leaves Of Hypnos*:

The woman explains, the immured one listens. The words that fall from this terrestrial silhouette ... are essential words, words which bring immediate succour. In the depths of the dungeon, the flickers of candlelight stretch and dilate the features of the seated man ... Better than any dawn whatever, the Word of the woman gives birth to the unexpected.

Thanks to Georges de la Tour who will master the Hitlerian gloom with a dialogue of human beings.

It seems premature to claim, as some have done, that Char is already one of the immortal poets in the French language. But a poem like this clearly contains the terms within which and upon which such a claim might be more generally upheld.

Cesare Pavese (1908–50)

Born on a farm in the Piedmont, the son of a judiciary official in Turin and a severely disciplinarian mother. Educated at the University of Turin where he studied English and American Literature and wrote a thesis on the poetry of Walt Whitman. Oppressed by thoughts of suicide as a student and unable to form stable and satisfying relationships with women, thereby establishing the pattern of his mature life. Awarded his doctorate in 1930, the year his mother died. Lived with his married sister in Turin thereafter. Began to write essays on and to translate American realist novelists, and made several vain attempts to gain a scholarship to Columbia University. Took up a part-time teaching post in Bra, where he met the woman he wished to marry, to whom he repeatedly proposed. Edited a literary review and worked briefly for the publishing house of Einaudi, later his primary source of income before his novels became known. Arrested for anti-Fascist activities in 1935 and imprisoned in Calabria for a year, where he wrote many of the poems of *Lavorare Stanca*, began the diary which was published after his death, and started to think in terms of the short stories and novels with which his name is now identified. Awarded the Strega Prize for the novel *Among Women Only*, and, two months later, partially prompted by the difficulties in his relationship with an American actress, took a fatal overdose of sleeping tablets in a Turin hotel room after a final telephone call to the woman he had wished to marry.

Cases of that 'bilingualism' which enables a writer to achieve excellence in both poetry and prose are sufficiently rare for readers to mistake them for something other than they are, and to stress one aspect of the accomplishment at the expense of the other. Pavese has been widely acclaimed as a major prose writer on the strength of such novels as *Among Women Only* and *The Moon And The Bonfires*, the mythological *Dialogues With Leucò* and the personal diary he kept between 1935 and his suicide in 1950. But Pavese's first impulses, and for that matter his last, were towards poetry; and it is his poetry which binds together what Pavese called 'the fundamental unity of what I have written or shall write'. It also provides access to that 'personal mythology (a feeble echo of some other one) which gives a value, an absolute value, to one's most remote world, endowing the slightest little element of the past with an ambiguous and seductive splendour in which, as in a symbol, the meaning of one's whole life seems to be summed up'. The words 'symbol' and 'personal mythology' are, however, being used here in a somewhat different sense from that in which a reader of modern poetry might be most likely to take them, for Pavese is anything but a recherché Symbolist exploring the arcana of his own idiosyncratic mythology. Nowhere does Pavese make this clearer than in the 1934 essay 'The Poet's Task' printed as an appendix to the revised and expanded edition of the only collection of poems he published during his lifetime – *Lavorare Stanca* (1936–1941). In this essay Pavese uncompromisingly states that 'every poetic impulse, however lofty, is an attempt to meet ethical demands'; it is the stance of a defiantly non-Symbolist poet. The 'essential expression of essential facts' required, in Pavese's view, not nuance but a clear, distinct and muscular language, the product of 'close, possessive and passionate adherence to the object' rather than attachment to the privacies of the perceiving subject. Pavese's diary is heavily introspective, indeed a classic document of modern introspection; but he was also, as the diary shows, a man possessed by a 'frenzy not to be myself'. It is no accident that he should have chosen the poetry of Walt Whitman to be the subject of his doctoral thesis. In an essay on

Whitman he applauds the poet's 'double vision through which, from the single object of the senses vividly absorbed and possessed, there radiates a kind of halo of unexpected spirituality', and in his own poetry he obviously enough aspired to precisely such a double vision. Attracted by the naturalistic tradition of American writing Pavese was intent on making naturalism serve as a medium for spiritual revelation, and thus by-passing the mystagogic elements in modern European poetry. The forthright foreword to his least naturalistic book, *Dialogues With Leucò*, is a reminder that even mythology has its origins in the mundane world:

I have nothing in common with experimentalists, adventurers, with those who travel in strange regions. The surest, and the quickest way for us to arouse the sense of wonder is to stare, unafraid, at a single object. Suddenly – miraculously – it will look like something we have never seen before.

This is more than just shrewd psychology; Pavese is confirming his preference for fact over fantasy and demonstrating that his early, and more naturalistic manner and his later, and more symbolic manner are essentially two sides of the same coin. The two editions of *Lavorare Stanca* effectively encapsulate Pavese's double vision: the first presents the poems in their chronological order, as if they were a poetic diary; the second thematizes them so that their symbolic and spiritual significance is foregrounded.

Pavese's poems are probably best read in the order in which they were composed, provided his stress on the 'spiritual meaning in every fact' is kept in mind. But both editions of *Lavorare Stanca* properly begin with the poem ('The South Seas') which he considered his first mature work in verse. The poem deals largely with childhood memories, and prefigures Pavese's later obsession with the question of what constitutes maturity. The memories are triggered by the few simple words uttered by the protagonist's elder cousin, who has returned to the land of his origins after travelling the world; the strategy is similar to that employed in Pavese's last and greatest novel, *The Moon And The Bonfires*. The two figures are strong and silent, like the landscape in which they walk and work; strength and silence are explicitly correlated, and are viewed as tokens of a weathered attitude to life, an adult wisdom of resignation as after the completion of a tiring task. The whole collection in fact explores the untranslatable ambiguities of the *Lavorare Stanca* title, which blends ideas of 'work is wearying', 'hard labour' (as in a prison sentence; Pavese was briefly imprisoned by Mussolini), and the rigours of the poetic 'task'. The much-travelled cousin walks the hills 'with the set expression I remember seeing as a child/in the faces of peasants who were tired'. But in the last lines of the poem this 'set expression' relaxes sufficiently for the decisive revelation, the spiritual message of the poem, to be made:

But when I say
how lucky he was, to have seen dawn
rising over the loveliest islands in the world,
he smiles at the memory and says that
at sunrise the day was already old for them.

Pavese's pervasive sense of time as a continuum is brilliantly embodied here by the subtle changes of tense found in all his poems; in novels like *The Moon And The Bonfires* the same effect is achieved by telling the story in a non-sequential way. In order to 'speak outside of time', as a late diary entry puts it, Pavese chose to speak from within its unstable rhythms, thereby acquiring what a poem of 1935 (appropriately entitled 'Myth') calls 'the dead smile of the man/ who understands'. This 'dead smile', as if in confirmation of its atemporal nature, points back to the smile of the cousin in 'The South Seas' and forward to the 'smile of the gods' developed in the *Dialogues With Leucò*.

'The South Seas' provided Pavese with a kind of matrix from which other poems might grow; the only significant element it lacks is the female figure who, both in his life and in his writing, provided Pavese with the possibility of relieving his solitude only to leave him with the realization that his solitude was unappeasable. Pavese's attitude to women has caused much controversy; it is not calculated to appeal to the diehard or narrow-minded feminist. But from the 'Fallen Women' poem of 1931 to the late novel *Among Women Only* Pavese is actually a very shrewd judge of feminine strengths and weaknesses; his image of women is far from being monovalent. Interestingly, in a letter addressed to a critic who had found some of the subject matter of *Lavorare Stanca* distasteful (primarily because it so often referred to prostitution), Pavese stressed that the poem 'Deola Thinking' was meant to be 'an act of kindness towards that unhappy woman'. 'Deola Thinking' is, indeed, a wonderfully compassionate poem; in a mode intermediate between internal monologue and third-person narrative Pavese conjures up the full reality of being Deola. She is just as much a worker as the men who till the Langhe hills of Pavese's boyhood, though as a despised creature in the city of Turin she experiences all the alienation of modern metropolitan life with none of the camaraderie which the farmhands enjoy. In another marvellous poem in the same mould, 'People Who Don't Understand', Gella is seen in transit between the country and the city, not properly appreciated in either, but credited with more understanding than the 'people' of the title, and wearing the smile which inseparably accompanies such an understanding in Pavese's 'personal mythology':

Gella's fed up of coming and going,
she smiles at the thought of coming into town
all dirty and dishevelled. As long as the hills and vines
are there and she can walk
through the streets, where the fields were, in the evening, laughing,
this will be what Gella wants, as she looks out from the train.

This blank and enigmatic 'look' which Pavese's figures direct at the world outside is at once a strength and a weakness; it is an index of their loneliness, and yet at the same time a sign of their disabused awareness of a harsh reality. The opening lines of 'Away From Home' are typical:

Too much sea. We've seen enough sea.
Late in the day, as the wide water stretches
into nothing, my friend stares at the sea,
I stare at him, and we do not speak.

As in 'The South Seas', however, this pervasive reticence is perpetually being broken in order that a disclosure may be made. An early example is 'Encounter', in which 'all at once there was a sound,/as if it came from the hills, a voice more pure/and more harsh, a voice from lost time'. In this case, as in many later ones (notably 'The Voice' of 1938), the voice belongs to a female created by, but not comprehended by, the poet, a figure generated, seemingly, out of the hills with which she is repeatedly equated. In this respect Pavese's poems present not so much 'figures in a landscape' as landscapes and figures which interpenetrate one another, as the eight 'Landscape' poems (written between 1933 and 1940) demonstrate with increasing finesse. 'Green Wood' and 'Afterwards' are particularly fine examples of the same technique, and 'Grappa In September' is perhaps the finest of all, with the morning atmosphere of Turin crystallizing as if in response to the poet's hunger for something he might relish. This magnificent poem is written in a kind of transfigured naturalism which wears its strangeness lightly, a seemingly effortless gloss on the 'yearning' more spectrally and more enigmatically treated in 'Sad Supper', where the scene is bathed in an ominous moonlight which points forward to *The Moon And The Bonfires*. In the first of the two appendices added to the second edition of *Lavorare Stanca* Pavese speaks in detail of the network of 'imaginative relationships' which provided him with a bridge between his early narrative mode and his more oblique later style, and there is arguably no better example than 'Grappa In September' of how compelling and subtle his construction of such a network could be.

At the proof stage of the first edition of *Lavorare Stanca* Pavese added eight poems 'written during the period of tranquillity I've recently enjoyed', as he wrote in a letter from his Calabrian prison; 'Grappa In September' was one of them. But when he returned to Turin after his imprisonment to find the woman he loved had married someone else, Pavese's always ephemeral tranquillity gave way to a mood of terrible desolation. In two great poems of October 1937

('Summer (1)' and 'Indifference') Pavese records his desperate hunger for a 'bitter ecstasy/that kills itself' to rekindle what has become only 'hard inhuman silence'. 'All life', he writes in 'Indifference' (confirming what the experience in 'Encounter' has prefigured), 'hangs on a voice.' This is consolidated in a chilling poem of 1938 ('The Voice'), where Pavese confronts, with something of the 'astonished calm' found in another poem of the same year ('Night'), the inescapable fact that the voice is 'remote/and does not ruffle the memory'. This uncanny tranquillity is developed to the point where it almost seems as if a disembodied voice from beyond the grave is addressing us, especially in three beautiful poems of 1940 dedicated to Fernanda Pivano, whom Pavese had long hoped to marry: 'Morning', 'Summer (2)' and 'Nocturne'. As in the early 'Encounter' poem, the female figure remains uncircumscribed by the poet's propostions about her, but by now the poet's own existence has shrunk to the point where he can no longer even use the first person pronoun with any confidence. In the 1945 sequence *Earth And Death* and the 1950 poems (published posthumously under the title *Death Will Come And Will Have Your Eyes*) Pavese is interested only in the 'you' figure, the 'other' whom he is trying to reach but who is by definition beyond him.

'You echo the ancient background/and make it purer' Pavese writes of Fernanda Pivano in 'Nocturne'; in the poetry written after *Lavorare Stanca* and in the *Dialogues With Leucò* Pavese attempted to emulate her achievement. In the *Dialogues* he certainly achieves this aim (he himself considered them his finest work), but the later poems become more and more terse, the images spiralling round and round one another, as if the poet were caught in a vortex. It is no surprise to learn that Pavese considered *Earth And Death* 'an explosion of creative energies which had been pent up for years'. Five years later, in the poems collected as *Death Will Come And Will Have Your Eyes*, a similar explosion evidently took place. It is virtually impossible in these later poems to distinguish between the female figure and the reality of which she is the instigator and guardian; in the 1950 poems, for example, the patter of rain (a motif originating in such earlier poems as 'Afterwards') and the sound of the woman's footsteps become inextricably linked. However the 'imaginative relationships' of the later *Lavorare Stanca* poems seem to have come dangerously close to having no basis in reality whatsoever. The external world has been reduced to a woman's smile, her closed lips and her silent eyes. The subtle oscillations between hope and despair which are such a marked feature of *Lavorare Stanca* yield here to a frenzy, a reflection of Pavese's ever-deepening conviction that the 'murmur in the blood' cannot be silenced, but that it is fatal to accede to it. The *Death Will Come* poems were actually inspired by Pavese's abortive relationship with an American actress; but to say so is to give them a biographical dimension which the poems themselves do not possess. Pavese's diary provides a useful corrective to the temptation to read them in terms of a particular event; five months before his suicide he wrote:

One does not kill oneself for love of *a* woman, but because love – any love – reveals us in our nakedness, our misery, our vulnerability, our nothingness.

In 1938 Pavese wrote to a friend: 'I live with the idea of suicide always in mind. That is far worse than having actually committed suicide, which, after all, is simply a sanitary operation.' Pavese carried out the operation in much the same way as the figure described in the 1940 poem 'Paradise On The Rooftops'. His diary for 1936 contains the entry: 'Who knows whether an optimistic suicide will come back to the earth again?' In 1940, after reading Freud, he wrote: 'The ego tends to revert towards calm, to be self-sufficient in its immobility and absence of desire.' Pavese's mythological studies consolidated his tendency to think of death as a sacrificial event offering the sufferer access to a world of perfect absolutes. Sceptical as he had always been about the relationship between the active and the contemplative life, he wrote the last entry in his diary: 'Not words. Action. I shall write no more.' Insofar as it is possible for us to think in such terms, it seems probable that Pavese saw it as the 'optimistic suicide' of which he had dreamed. By killing himself he partook definitively of the 'cure of silence' of which he had written in a letter to a friend four days before his death. And silence, as the first poem in *Lavorare Stanca* reminds us, was for Pavese an index of strength.

Yannis Ritsos (born 1909)

Born in Monembasia in Asia Minor, the son of a well-to-do landowner ruined on the defeat of the Greek forces by the Turks in 1924 and driven insane by the death of his wife and child from tuberculosis. Moved to Athens in 1925 where he did menial jobs and himself contracted tuberculosis, spending three years, there and in Crete, in sanatoria. Became a committed Marxist and spoke out openly against the Metaxas dictatorship, which prevented him from publishing freely for sixteen years. Fought for the radical cause in the First Civil War and was arrested by the authorities in 1948 during the Second Civil War. Spent four years in concentration camps. Returned to Athens in 1952; married in 1954. Wrote copiously until re-arrested in 1967 for his political beliefs; won the national poetry prize in 1956 and became internationally known, especially in Iron Curtain countries, though he has also won many prizes in Western Europe. Finally released from the detention camps of the Greece of the Colonels on grounds of ill-health and in response to an international public outcry, though kept under house arrest for long periods. Repeatedly nominated for the Nobel Prize, which he has never won.

Yannis Ritsos has been more widely translated than any other living Greek poet. There are no less than seven selections from his poetry, several of them very extensive, available in English and he has been similarly honoured in all the major, and most of the minor countries of Europe. In 1971, in one of the most prestigious French literary journals, the poet and novelist

Louis Aragon recommended Ritsos as 'the greatest living poet' to a public to whom he was little more than a name. In the past decade he has been repeatedly nominated for the Nobel Prize which he will now, after the adoption of his compatriot Odysseus Elytis in 1979, presumably never be awarded. He has won almost every other international literary prize of any significance. But he has never been avid of public recognition of this kind; his personal life has been one of almost unremitting hardship, fighting against illness and political harassment, and he would obviously sooner be read by the ordinary man in the street than acclaimed by the intelligentsia. Much of his poetry has been composed, as he puts it, 'under the nose of the sentry', though the restrictions under which he has been forced to operate seem to have galvanized him into writing almost continuously, in a manner that poets living under more liberal régimes and with unrestricted movement have found it impossible to match. His habit of dating his poems indicates that he frequently writes three or four a day; he has published more than fifty volumes of poetry, several volumes of translation (notably of Blok, Éluard, Mayakovsky and József) and also written studies of the poetry of Éluard and Mayakovsky. He is probably the most prolific of all modern poets of distinction, not excluding Neruda. And like Neruda he is a committed Communist and 'people's poet', though with a vein of folk poetry that marks him out from his Chilean predecessor, a vein that has made his work attractive to the composer Theodorakis, who has set several of his poems to music. The individual poem is inevitably almost buried by the sheer bulk of poems that surround it; a judicious pruning of his massive *oeuvre* is effectively forced upon anyone engaging with it. Yet the more one reads of Ritsos the deeper the impact; each separate volume presents at once different, yet kindred, configurations of image and situation in a manner that is unmistakably his own.

Ritsos published his first volume (*Tractor*, collecting poems from 1930 onwards) in 1934, and the first poem in the volume is an expression of the belief that has sustained him through all his subsequent crises: that poetry is a way of surviving. In this poem poetry is seen as a surrogate mother and in this respect poetry is the first of the multitude of females who, throughout his work, are fated to be the sufferers and survivors *par excellence*. In *Pyramids* (1935) there is a poem on the insanity of his sister, a subject to which he returned in the long poem *The Song of my Sister* (1937). But the most compelling female figure in early Ritsos is to be found in the poem *Epitaph* of 1936, where a mother laments the son she has lost in the police's brutal suppression of a worker's strike. This poem was publicly burned by the Metaxas régime and became the great rallying cry for those of a radical persuasion who wished to overthrow it. From the beginning Ritsos has been adamant that the private and the public utterance, the personal and the political gesture, cannot meaningfully be separated from one another, and that the poet, the representative figure of what he calls 'the final century before humanity', provides the ladder whereby humanity may ascend and resurrect itself. It is characteristic of him that, in a poem prompted by the Civil War which followed the German withdrawal at the end of the Second World War, he should have written a memorial to those who lost their lives which ends with an image of universal human brotherhood. The harsher his reality becomes, the more evidence he finds to suggest that such an ideal might be realized. Even when the only solidarity is that of the inmates of a concentration camp (as in the three-part *Chronicle of Exile*, 1948–1950), he thinks of the poet and the political detainees as more powerful than their oppressors. Like the domestic earthenware utensil celebrated in a long poem written at the same time (*The Blackened Clay Pot*) Ritsos and his fellow-sufferers are 'boiling and singing'. The great achievement of such poems is that, without in any way suggesting that poetry can be a substitute for the nourishing food of which the prisoners are deprived, poetry is shown to be the ideal medium to sustain morale when man persists in being a wolf to man.

In a period when few poets have departed from the gospel according to Poe, Ritsos has remained a practitioner of the long poem. Though he often gives way in long forms to the rhetoric from which he has elsewhere tried to school himself, *The Moonlight Sonata* (1956), *The Dead House* (1959), *The Window* (1960), *Beneath the Shadow of the Mountain* (1962) and the poems which retell classical legends catch the accents of a speaking voice in such a way as to make the rhetoric seem necessary. These are almost all dramatic monologues, and the speakers are characteristically women. The mood is sombre, and the sense of imprisonment is overwhelming. Ritsos's en-closed protagonists, framed still further by his 'stage direc-tions' at beginning and end, are the prey of unmistakable intimations of decay. Ritsos elaborates here, and objectifies, what in his more concentrated short poems may strike a reader as obscure or gnomic, sometimes too elusive to really benefit the mankind to which it is addressed. The long poems flesh out and make dramatic what the short poems render in a skeletal manner. They also enable him to speak of him-self without appearing to do so, in the full knowledge that 'what we hide is/what reveals us most'. And they provide the reader of the short poems with an invaluable compendium and key to Ritsos's favourite motifs: parts of the body (not-ably the hand, the finger and the foot), parts of the house (the corridor, the window, the stairs, the kitchen), seasons of the year (of which winter seems to be the most propitious for 'a return to the centre of our self') and the impersonal wit-nesses that embody his ideas on change and permanence: the moon, the mirror and the statue. *The Window* usefully pro-vides a gloss on the disjointed thumbnail descriptions which are the hallmark of the short poems: 'only dismemberment', Ritsos writes, 'can keep us intact'. The speaker in *Beneath the Shadow of the Mountain* also seems to be telling us something which will stand us in good stead on approaching the short poems when she remarks that silence is 'always more ex-pressive' than sound. Though most readers are naturally daunted by long poems, it would obviously be wrong to treat these elaborate structures as mere adjuncts to the more attrac-tive lyrics. They are dramatic expansions of the impulse that aligns Ritsos with his Greek forbears (Cavafy and Seferis), with other poets distressed by barbarism (Herbert and Brodsky), with all those 'quiet voices', in Brodsky's phrase, who write what Ritsos during the Metaxas régime understandably called *Notes in the Margin of Time*.

The brief, clipped utterances in Ritsos's vignettes are by no means marginal in their implications, however. 'Every word,' he writes in one of the most famous of them, 'is a doorway/to a meeting, one often cancelled/and that's when a word is true: when it insists on the meeting.' The success of his whole enterprise is dependent on instigating such a meeting; 'if you too don't see', as he puts it in 'Maybe, Someday', 'it will be as if I hadn't'. Despite developing privileged images in the manner of more private poets, Ritsos is not an introspective poet. The aptly-titled poem 'Understanding' demonstrates that 'to look outside yourself' is the indispensable prerequisite for 'Not [being]/"only you" but "you too"'. He adopts an idiosyncratic manner not to protect himself (though he could hardly be blamed for having done so, given the deprivations he has suffered), but rather to induce the reader to cooperate; in his own words, 'I hide behind simple things so you'll find me'. The simple things he records in his poems are there to activate engagement; they are what he calls 'a point of orientation'. A number of poems present a man sitting alone in the darkness of his room with only a cigarette for company; the cigarette is a point of light, an illumination which pierces the surrounding gloom. The figure is less solitary than he takes himself to be; his cigarette is as much of a consolation to him at this moment as the loaf of bread which offers more nourishing sustenance. Ritsos's points of orientation are generally familiar and humdrum things, the streetlights of a city, the knees of a silent woman in prayer, the noise of a train in the distance. His purpose is to organize a network of relationships around this given nucleus. In the poem 'Women', for example, from Ritsos's first collection of *Parentheses* (1946–7), the poet hears 'the train that's taking the soldiers to the front'. But his sensibilities have been quickened by the noise of a woman's footsteps and the clatter of her washing-up. 'Women are very distant' the poem begins; the soldiers going to the front are also very distant. Without suggesting that the distance between the woman and the man and between them and the soldiers can actually be collapsed, Ritsos shows that they are connected, however tenuously. He is not proposing anything so consolatory as the Symbolist doctrine of correspondences. The terse poem 'Miracle' (in the collection *Exercises*, written in the 1950s) is a warning against symbolic interpretations that depart too far from the facts of the case:

A man, before going to bed, put his watch under his pillow.
Then he went to sleep. Outside the wind was blowing. You who know
the miraculous continuity of little motions, understand.
A man, his watch, the wind. Nothing else.

It is continuity that matters to Ritsos, not correspondence; a timeless ecstasy would be foreign to a poet who, more than most, has had to survive the passing moment and hope for a better future. As he says in another of the *Exercises*, 'an endless exchange was shaping the significance of things'. Faced with a world in flux, the poet can only achieve a foothold by monitoring the exchanges that take place. The words he employs are only an approximation to the facts he records, some of which virtually defy description. But as he says in one poem: 'Poetry is in this "approximately". Can you see it?' It is not difficult to see it in a poem like 'Going Away' (in *Testimonies B*, 1966) where 'a big blood blotch' is all that is left of a person who has been arrested. Nor is it difficult to see the point of a poem like 'Exiled Twice' (from the same collection) where the poet's ability to see everything in terms of images understandably irritates a woman engaged in the tedious business of dusting. There are, however, times when the enigmatic smiles of Ritsos's personae remain almost impenetrable, as if the poet is loath to answer the question raised by one of the *Tanagra Women* poems of 1967: 'Face or Façade?'

The reader of Ritsos is often confronted by enigmas. In his second collection of *Parentheses* (1950–61), for example, there is the very brief 'Sound of Silence':

Night. No sound at all. Only the roaring of space and that
transparent undefined moon whose light remained still unformed
and hurt her.

Given Ritsos's conviction that words are only approximations
and that silence is an expressive medium in its own right –
a view shared by another very prolific poet, Joseph Brodsky
– it seems possible that this is a self-reflexive poem; the poet
is sympathizing with a moon whose anguish is expressed more
directly than any poet, even one who only stains the silence
with his own 'unformed' poem of three lines, could possibly
emulate. The sound/silence dichotomy is also present in a
compelling poem from *Testimonies A* (1963), 'Audible And
Inaudible':

An abrupt, unexpected movement; his hand
clutched the wound to stop the blood,
although we had not heard a shot
nor a bullet flying. After a while
he lowered his hand and smiled,
but again he moved his palm slowly
to the same spot; he took out his wallet,
he paid the waiter politely and went out.
Then the little coffee cup cracked.
This at least we heard clearly.

There are at least three 'points of orientation' in this poem:
the gesture of a man who mimes his own assassination, the
paying of the waiter and the fracture of porcelain. Which is
the most important? For the man the first, for the waiter the
second, for the audience the third? Possibly. But what the
poem unambiguously reminds us is that human life is as
fragile as porcelain under régimes which impose martial law
upon their citizens and that one does not have to strain to
see and hear this confirmed every day in the street. The in-
fluence of Surrealism on Ritsos is evident, but this poem is
much more openly socio-political than most Surrealist poems.
The punctilious language has nothing to do with the tur-
bulence of the unconscious mind; the impersonal tone is some-
what reminiscent of the parables of Kafka.

Ritsos has recently written more enigmatically than ever before; he seems to be intent on demonstrating that 'the word is signified by what it would conceal'. His increased sense of barriers to communication – exacerbated by his experiences in the Greece of the Colonels – is reflected in such collections as *Railings* (1969) and *Scripture of the Blind* (1972). 'The mask that protected your face,' he writes in a poem from the latter volume, 'has finally stuck to your skin.' This is true to a degree which might discourage a reader unfamiliar with what has gone before. But he has needed masks more than most poets in Western Europe; it is 'with such obscurities' that he 'seeks to escape the dark'. The stairs and corridors which were once images of escape from imprisonment are now full of people who, like the usher in 'Preparing The Ceremony' (in *The Distant*, 1975), are waiting to attack him. In *The Distant*, indeed, he is almost 'dumb, no gesture at all'. The vision has become bleaker, the possibility of human brotherhood more remote. A tragic sense of life seems to have supplanted the rhetoric of ideology; the 'people's poet' has withdrawn into a region where few will want, or be able, to follow him. There is a poem in *Scripture of the Blind* called 'Public Speech' which presents a figure who 'opened his mouth wide, but not a word came out'; but it is the poem's conclusion which is particularly memorable in the context of Ritsos's practice during the last ten years:

Who will grant pardon or punishment to the condemned? 'I', he shouted. 'I', he shouted again. 'What do you mean, you?' we asked him. Then with his scissors he cut off his left ear and stuffed it into his mouth.

Octavio Paz (born 1914)

Born in Mexico City and educated there. Began to publish poems in Mexican periodicals at the age of seventeen. Sided with the Republicans in the Spanish Civil War and visited Madrid, Valencia and Andalusia in 1937. Founded two literary journals on his return to Mexico, where he remained until 1943. Lived in the USA until 1945, studying and travelling on a Guggenheim fellowship. Visited Paris in 1945 and participated in Surrealist activities. Entered the Mexican diplomatic service and resident during the next twenty years in San Francisco, New York, Paris, Tokyo, Geneva and Delhi. First visited India and Japan in 1952 and deeply impressed by the native culture in each country. Mexican Ambassador to India from 1962 to 1968, during which time he studied Oriental art and philosophy. Married in 1964. Resigned as Ambassador in protest at the Mexican government's repressive measures against students before the 1968 Olympic Games. Professor of Latin American Studies at Cambridge University in 1970; returned to Mexico in 1971. Professor of Poetry at Harvard University 1971-2. Resigned from the editorial board of the literary review he had founded on returning to Mexico in protest at government intervention. Increasingly recognized in the last decade as one of the most significant poets and prose writers in Spanish America and a frequent recipient of literary and academic honours. Resident in Mexico City.

The international fame of the Mexican poet and essayist Octavio Paz has in recent years grown to the point where he threatens to dwarf all but Neruda of the Spanish American pantheon of poets. His prose writings alone place him in the front rank of discursive writers in Spanish in this century, alongside Ortega y Gasset and Unamuno. Like them, he is not so much a philosopher in the academic sense as a man of ideas committing himself passionately to the realities of the present, impatient of system and heedless of the contradictions generated by his prodigiously fertile intelligence. His analysis of Mexico and the Mexican temperament, *The Labyrinth Of Solitude* (1950; revised 1959) is the most widely admired of his books in prose. But the origins of his thinking are more clearly disclosed in *The Bow And The Lyre* (1956), *Quadrivium* (1965), *Alternating Current* (1967) and the book whose title provides us with the most concise summary of his position, *Conjunctions And Disjunctions* (1969). In all these cases the argument proceeds by daring but not always irresistible analogies and associations, with detail more important than structure, as is also true of his somewhat predictable lectures on modern poetry, *Children Of The Mire* (1974). The prose of Paz is an indispensable accompaniment to his poetry, which it is always impinging upon. But it can give the impression – which the poetry almost never does – that he possesses an opportunist's ability to assimilate each new intellectual vanguard as it appears. This is actually a reflection of his fascination with the idea at the heart of one of the major poems in the collection *Eastern Slope* (1969), that 'the present is perpetual'. This essentially Surrealist insight has recently been given a Structuralist colouring by Paz, but the manner in which he has conflated the two is his own, and in no sense doctrinaire. It may be that Paz will come to be thought of as the most accomplished and substantial poet to have emerged out of *la révolution surréaliste*, having kept his Surrealism open and flexible, and yet at the same time subjecting it to the modifications of a capacious intellect, much less capricious than it sometimes seems.

It is the later poetry of Paz which has brought him an international audience, and he himself has repudiated much of the poetry previous to his masterpiece, the long poem 'Sun

Stone' of 1957. His precocious first collection, *Rustic Moon* (1933), has not been reprinted, and only selections from the subsequent volumes (*Beneath Your Clear Shadow*, 1937; *Between The Stone And The Flower*, 1941; *On The Shore Of The World*, 1942), are included in the volume by which Paz himself wishes to represent his first twenty-five years of poetic activity. The title of this volume has untranslatable connotations of 'under oath' and 'under the breath' but unambiguously foregrounds the state Paz most prizes – liberty – and the medium – words – in which it may best be achieved: *Libertad bajo palabra*. And yet the Surrealist utopia in which love, poetry and freedom are indistinguishable seems utopian indeed in Paz's poetry of the 1930s and 1940s. In these poems the poet can only alleviate his loneliness with a frenzied eroticism and a vacillating faith in his violent words. 'I drown myself and do not touch myself', Paz writes in a poem of 1934 ('Mirror'). A decade later, under the 'transparent silence' of noon, the mood is calmer and the birdsong of the poet flies forth, but it is with death that the poem 'The Bird' ends. The agony and ecstasy of a condition with very marked similarities to those found in Symbolist, post-Symbolist and Surrealist poetry in France is organized in these poems around motifs which by their frequency indicate that they are peculiar to Paz, even when reminiscent of the French and Spanish poets he most admired. But the very fluidity with which the poet correlates his privileged images – of which the eye (as the source of all of them) is naturally the most dominant – suggests a freedom too indiscriminate to be ultimately liberating. There seems to be nothing which will establish dawn as more important than twilight, trees as more vital than stones, birds as more imitable than stars. Paz was evidently sufficiently contented with the position to compose a sonnet, or sequence of sonnets, with the same precision and bravura that distinguishes the Machado-like 'Loose Stones' at the other end of the scale. But there are signs, not confined to the poems of 1938–46 collected under the title *Condemned Door*, that this dispensation provided for as many calamities as miracles. The celebration of the Marquis de Sade in 'The Prisoner' (1948) is a critique of de Sade's inability to transcend himself, and clearly a reflection of (and a pointer beyond) Paz's own turbulent condition.

It is in the poetry written between 1948 and 1954, flanked on one side by his book on Mexico and on the other by his poem on the sun stone in Mexico City, that Paz decisively confronts and finds an exit from his labyrinth of solitude. The prose poems of *Eagle Or Sun?* (1949–50) describe a crisis and a crisis conquered, a season in hell which, like Rimbaud's, offers the possibility finally of possessing 'truth in one soul and one body'. These distressed and yet inspiring writings, which have been immensely influential on subsequent Spanish American literature, explore the implications of the last line of Paz's 'Hymn Among The Ruins' of Teotihuacan, where 'words which are flowers become fruits which are deeds'; they are devoted to 'removing the obstacles I placed between the light and myself in the first part of my life' ('The Poet's Labours', xiv). *Eagle or Sun?*, which begins under the sign of an 'implacable prohibition', ends with images of giving birth. This essentially entails a return – under the beneficent aegis of a fig-tree Paz remembers from his boyhood – to origins, the first fruits of which are the two great long poems of 1953 and 1955, 'The River' and 'The Broken Waterjar'. Neither of these poems is entirely free of the 'great helplessness' which surfaces half-way through the former; but the second rises at the end to one of Paz's most memorable affirmations. The correlations here seem less desperate, more inevitable, than in the pre-crisis poetry, and the cosmic implications are embodied in lines as long as those of Walt Whitman. The river is now flowing 'toward the living centre of origin, beyond the end and the beginning', and 'the day and night caress each other like a man and woman in love'. The title of the collection in which these poems first appeared, *The Violent Season* (1958), is taken from Apollinaire's poem 'The Pretty Red-Head', and both 'The River' and 'The Broken Waterjar' epitomize the 'ardent Reason' of which Apollinaire had spoken. Beside 'The Broken Waterjar', a much more affirmative hymn among the ruins than was possible in the poem of

1948, the *Seeds Towards A Hymn* (1954) seem like seeds indeed, still waiting for the liberation of the water which will enable them to grow.

In the long poem 'Sun Stone' (1957), Paz's supreme achievement and perhaps the outstanding long poem of the century, his concern for origins took on the mythic cast later deepened by his experiences as Mexico's ambassador to India. This circular poem, effectively a single utterance, is Paz's most inspired meditation on what Apollinaire called 'the long quarrel between tradition and invention', its length controlled by the number of days in the synodical period of the planet Venus, its immensely varied imagery (almost a compendium of Pazian motifs) radiating in all directions from its solar centre, the sexual act of origin. The massive pressure of a poem both formal and informal, closed and open, is towards a paradoxical 'enormous instant' where 'everything is transfigured and is sacred'. The figure who has fallen 'endlessly since my birth' is viewed as repeatedly approaching the 'door of being'. 'Sun Stone' synthesizes a wealth of correspondences which would have daunted even the most ardent Surrealist, and which were plainly beyond the capacity of the André Breton whom Paz is so often recommending for our admiration. The metapoetic features which might gladden the heart of a Structuralist, though much less marked than in the poetry of the following decade, are treated in 'Sun Stone' with an exemplary vibrancy, as if the love of language and the language of love were truly inseparable.

The poems of the collection *Salamander* (1962), written between 1958 and 1961, are equally concerned with the fundamentally mythic questions of death and rebirth and are orientated towards the life 'between two parentheses' of which the poem 'Certainty' speaks. Anguished by his 'Entry Into Matter' (the title of the first poem in the collection) the poet is heartened by the regenerative powers of the salamander of the title poem. But the controlled rhapsody of 'Sun Stone' is replaced in this collection by a much terser language; the landscapes (as in the powerful 'Ustica') are predominantly austere. The purgatorial mood is expressed most memorably in a poem on the winter solstice ('Solo For Two Voices') which acknowledges that 'Saying is a paring away', and dramatizes this insight in the stuttering wordplay with which it opens. A similar 'paring away' occurs at the end of the title poem, where the fire of words refines *salamandra* into *salamadre* and finally into *aguamadre*. For Paz the salamander is an erotic symbol, and the wordplay here eroticizes language in order to lay bare the salt water (*sala agua*) of our maternal origins.

All the poems in *Eastern Slope* were written in India, with the exception of the 'Fable Of Two Gardens' written on board the ship that was taking Paz and the wife he had married in the sub-continent to Paris. *Eastern Slope* is the volume which represents Paz at his most consistently invigorating and inviting, with a new expansiveness added to the fragmentary mode of *Salamander*, and a new eroticism which Paz derived from the creative-and-destructive Hindu goddess Kali. The extent of Paz's emergence from the labyrinth of solitude is made dramatically clear when we place the text 'Eralabán' from *Eagle Or Sun?* (describing a hypothetical and unsustainable magic land) beside a poem from *Eastern Slope* like 'Vrindaban' (the sacred site of one of Krishna's crucial battles with demons). 'Eralabán' ends with the protagonist devoured by cannibals; 'Vrindaban' is a poetic credo announcing (somewhat in the manner of Apollinaire's 'The Little Car', which it occasionally resembles) a new age:

I know what I know and I write it
The embodiment of time

It is precisely 'embodiment' which binds the collection together: in 'The Sacred Fig Tree' there is a 'thicket of hands' which 'reach for a body, not for earth'; in 'Wind From All Compass Points' the focus falls upon the bodies of lovers stretched out in the dawn. This is a poetry not so much of the present (though there are almost no past tenses) as of *presence*; the poet is crossing his 'fragile bridge of words' ('The Balcony') to a terrestrial paradise. The message is unambiguous, and fortified by poems addressed to the musicians and painters whom Paz considers have been engaged on a similar enterprise. The rhapsodic sexual intercourse of 'Maithuna' establishes unequivocally that the poet has accomplished Rimbaud's dream of possessing 'truth in one soul and one body'.

While still in India, Paz published his most obviously experimental poem, the apparently forbidding but in fact very crystalline *Blanco* (1966). This is a kind of homage to the Mallarmé of *A Dice Throw* (one of Paz's sacred texts), but also to the sexual rituals of Tantra, and to the 'intertextuality' of the Structuralists. Read in the context of *Eastern Slope* it actually presents few problems for the reader, though it will presumably never gain the wide audience it deserves. Together with *Eastern Slope* it is Paz at his most positive, though it has been followed (just as *Salamander* followed 'Sun Stone') by the less utopian poetry of Paz's return to Mexico. *Return* (1976) threatens to imprison Paz in the labyrinth of solitude from which he had seemingly decisively escaped, as the Babylonish dialect of 'The Petrifying Petrified' is not alone in indicating. The 'arrival' which seemed inevitable in 'The Balcony' has here receded to the point where Paz can categorically state (in 'At The Mid-Point Of This Phrase'): 'We never arrive'. By the end of this poem the poet has become a 'Tender of epitaphs', and the subsequent poetry never quite recaptures the affirmative power of Paz's experiences in India. In some of the recent uncollected poetry Paz actually becomes a *writer* of epitaphs in the manner of the Greek Anthology, though without abandoning his commitment to what Mircea Eliade has called 'the myth of the eternal return'. 'To die is to return,' Paz writes in 'Preparatory Exercise', and in the long autobiographical poem of 1975 (*A Draft Of Shadows*) he again returns to his childhood and to his favourite fig-tree. This is a renewed attempt to get beyond life and death into a third state, the 'empty plenitude' of 'being without being'. The attempt ends with Paz concluding: 'I am where I was'. But as the beautiful conclusion to 'Flame, Speech' indicates, in a kind of gloss on Heidegger's

notion that language is the house of being, Paz still retains
the power to transform elegy into praise:

The dead are mute
but they also say
what we are saying.
Language is the house
of all, hanging over
the edge of the abyss.
To talk is human.

Johannes Bobrowski
(1917–65)

Born in Tilsit, East Prussia, the son of a railway official.
Spent much of his boyhood in the village of his grandparents
on the Lithuanian border. Moved to Königsberg (modern
Kaliningrad) in 1928, where he learnt to play the organ and
clavichord and developed an interest in Baroque music.
Studied classical literature and later art history in Berlin.
Called up in 1939 and saw war service in Poland. A prisoner
of war in Russia until 1949. Later became a publisher's reader
in East Berlin, and wrote many of his poems whilst thus em-
ployed between 1952–63. Thereafter wrote two novels and
a considerable amount of short prose. Corresponded with
Paul Celan. Died suddenly of peritonitis in East Berlin.

The most impressive of the poets to have written in German
since the Second World War are Johannes Bobrowski and
Paul Celan, both of whom were brought up on the peri-
phery of German proper, and both of whom were conscious
that they were using a language that the rest of Europe had
little reason to feel affection for. In Bobrowski's case he had
begun (like Pasternak, whom he later translated) to express
himself in the wordless realms of music and painting, and
only as a prisoner of war in Russia did he see the possibilities
of forging a poetic language with its own peculiar painterly
and musical qualities. Bobrowski's place of origin, memor-
ably captured in his novel *Levin's Mill*, was in a region of
Poles with German names and Germans with Polish names,
which also offered him an intimate acquaintance with the
large number of Jews and gypsies who lived on the borders

of what used to be East Prussia and Lithuania. This clearly fostered in him an acute sense of continuities and discontinuities which was later to be reflected in his poetry, especially when, as an unwilling conscript to a cause in which he did not believe, he participated in the Nazi invasion of Russia, with its attendant suppression of precisely these beleagured minorities. Bobrowski's spiritual reaction to a period in which the political borders were constantly being rewritten was to reinvent a nomadic enclave under Roman jurisdiction for the four hundred years on either side of the birth of Christ, the Sarmatia which gives its name to his first book of poems, *Sarmation Time* (1961). He had, however, been far too moved by the contemporary reality to invoke Sarmatia in a politically reactionary spirit; indeed the distinguishing feature of Sarmatian time – most obviously reflected in the unstable tenses of the poems – is its effective timelessness, or more precisely its ability to suggest that each event, whether ancient or modern, subsists in a permanently contemporary continuum. Such an attitude enabled him to combine without undue difficulty a political commitment to Marxism and a religious commitment to Lutheran Christianity, and it ensured him an audience on both sides of the Iron Curtain, though inevitably without much agreement between them as to what his fundamental stance might be. Bobrowski was not, however, an ideological poet in any of the more usual senses of the phrase; his primary purpose was to express himself in a language which had been made to serve the interests of an ideology that had come uncomfortably close to destroying all culture whatsoever.

Although the title of Bobrowski's first volume indicates that time was one of his primary concerns, the proper name which it contains marks out no less precisely that space was of equal importance to him. The poems, both in this and in his two subsequent volumes, offer ample testimony – especially in something as fundamental as syntax and typography – of his deep need to investigate spatial relationships. Bobrowski's sense of space has led to him being labelled a 'nature poet', although he is only a 'nature poet' in the same way and to the same extent as Trakl may be said to be. And just as Trakl's 'evening land' is as much a state of mind as a reality, so the 'shadow land' of Bobrowski's second collection (published in 1962) – depicted with a Trakl-like concentration on a limited number of motifs – is at once conceptual and perceptual, a landscape of the mind even when the title of a particular poem acknowledges the stimulus of a specific geographical location. It does no disservice to poems that dramatize different aspects of a kindred reality to say that 'Lake Ilmen 1941', Kaunas 1941', 'Cloister Near Novgorod', 'North Russian Town', 'Vilna', 'The Volga Towns' and 'The Latvian Autumn' come to matter less to the reader of Bobrowski for their differences than for their similarities, and that they are easily related to poems that make no such precise reference to places on the map.

Bobrowski's ability to convince us of the reality of a particular motif and then to subject it to almost immediate metamorphosis makes any talk of constants seem a somehow improper response to his poetry. But certain features are so insistently foregrounded that they begin to seem inevitable concomitants of Bobrowski's vision: the river, the village, the road or track, the plains and the hills, the tree (especially the elder and the birch). His animals, whether human or otherwise (the distinction is often preserved only to reverse our expectations), reappear with the same regularity: the fish, the wolf, the hawk, the swallow, the fisherman, the hunter, the old who have remained behind, the young who (like the dead) have gone away. Bobrowski's *vie de province* is as sparse and rudimentary for his reader as for the people who inhabit it, and just as they must labour to derive sustenance from it, so must he. Bobrowski liked to stress, in a manner which makes him sound more Socialist Realist than he really is, that he was concerned to present 'a landscape in which men have worked, in which men live, in which men are active'. But the activity he is most concerned with is conjuring a language which will record and dynamically memorialize this landscape and these figures, a language with the same clear vital lineaments.

'Lake Ilmen 1941' presents a landscape fractured by the presence of the army which has invaded it, in which only the more heavily 'armoured flood' of the lake and the abiding presence of the wolf offer continuity in the aftermath of cataclysm. This wolf which 'listens for the bells of winter' and 'howls for the enormous/cloud of snow' initiates an imagery of sound and silence which runs throughout Bobrowski's work, more and more clearly identified as emblematic of the poet and the poetic act. In 'Kaunas 1941' the noise is associated with the Nazi murderers and the silence with the Jewish victims, and the poet's listening is rewarded only by a wood-pigeon reminding him of their fate. In 'The Road Of The Armies' memories of Napoleon's comparable failure to sub-jugate the Russians inspire in Bobrowski a realization that the earth ('the many-voiced Eurydice') will always prompt the poet, in his role as Orpheus, to lament. In 'The Memel', such a lament is juxtaposed with, and ultimately combined with, the 'image of silence' which the river embodies. Here, as elsewhere in Bobrowski (in 'By The River', 'The Jura' and 'Fishingport', for example), a poem of landscape is at the same time a poem of love, with a quite remarkable physical pressure propelling the language. The love is often familial – especially that of women for their sons and daughters – as in 'The Wives Of The Nehrung-Fishers' and in almost all the poems which take Jews for their subjects. For the Jews awaken in Bobrowski a respect for the wisdom which enables them to face, with a sad equanimity, the fact that 'Someone is always leaving'; 'the tree of [their] speech' remains standing. In Bobrowski's own case the Christian story – 'a story/which is as we are', tragic yet redemptive – offers similar sustenance, as 'The Animals At Christmas' demonstrates. The Ischtar of 'The Sarmatian Plain' and the strange gods of the 'Pruzzian Elegy' are even more ancient deities summoned up by this landscape, in which an almost pagan pantheism thrives. A comparable resurrection of the extinct language of the Pruz-zians (exterminated by the Teutonic Knights who created Prussia) occurs in this elegy, and surfaces again in the poem 'Dead Language'. We are reminded by Bobrowski, as often by Celan, that the Nazis did all they could to kill the German language as well as its people, notably by the brutally impersonal 'Report' on a girl who has managed to escape from the Warsaw ghetto.

In a sequence of poems concerned primarily with other poets – Villon, Else Lasker-Schüler, Gertrud Kolmar, Góngora, Dylan Thomas, Nelly Sachs and 'In Memory of B.L.' (Pasternak) – Bobrowski invokes dead spirits who nevertheless 'speak from the grave', sometimes in their own words, sometimes, as in the case of Mickiewicz (the great people's poet of Lithuanian Poland), as the 'I' of the poem. These, too, can be read as love poems, as 'Russian Songs' (where the 'Marina' is presumably Tsvetaeva) suggests. This is also true of the poems scattered throughout Bobrowski's three volumes which use composers (Bach and Mozart, for instance) and artists (Chagall, Jawlensky and Barlach) as their points of reference. But these also enable Bobrowski to express his feelings about the redemptive power of art. Of the poems addressed to dead poets, the 'Ode To Thomas Chatterton' and the poem 'To Klopstock' (the great practitioner of odes in German) are particularly fine, the latter a splendidly clear and affirmative *ars poetica*:

> I have
> gathered what I passed,
> the shadowed fable of guilt
> and atonement:
> just as the deeds
> I trust – you guided it – I trust
> the language of those who forget,
> deep into winters
> unwinged, I speak its word
> of reed.

Bobrowski's 'word of reed' is intended to perform the same function as the classical Orpheus's lute, as a poem in his third volume (*Weathersigns*, 1966) makes clear, a poem which bears a striking resemblance to the conclusion of Dylan Thomas's 'Over Sir John's Hill'. In 'Encounter' the poet-hunter who gives names to the natural world (uniting the roles of Orpheus and of Adam) finally becomes indistinguishable from that world until, with 'grass blade in mouth', he finds a way of expressing his shadow self's hopes of reintegration. Bobrowski's concern that he may be supplanting God by this naming activity is beautifully expressed in a poem from *Shadow Land* ('Always To Be Named'). But to name is essentially to praise, as 'The Call Of The Quail' makes plain. It is typical of Bobrowski that a poem called 'Lament' should end with a rainbow (the arc of the covenant between God and man) and a reminder that 'peace/is promised us'. Even when the weathersigns remain bleak, Bobrowski is always seeking some kind of reciprocation between self and world that will justify his calling. In 'Above The River' he calls upon the wind, emblematic of the wind of inspiration; in other poems, like 'Lament' and 'The Call Of The Quail', the natural world calls to him. The reciprocations are rare and temporary, and Bobrowski knows that a truly symbiotic relationship will have to wait until 'after the embrace' of death ('One Day'). This is why his tone sometimes sounds despairing, though never as anguished – even when 'I speak to you/ without a voice' ('Tale') – as that of his friend Paul Celan.

The poems of Bobrowski's third volume are predominantly autumnal in mood. The weathersigns seem to tell of approaching death, with the heavy footsteps of Saturn in 'Midnight Village' similar to those of the figure who, in 'Tolmingkemen Village', 'walks with white hair'. Images of a final sleep that will make the poet one with the dead he has so often conjured are made more poignant by the reminders of how sleepless our human lives must inevitably be, how separated we are:

you speak, alien voice,
I hear you with alien ear.

> ('Sanctuary')

Sometimes it seems, as in the earlier poem 'Log Cabin', that the house man has built will fall 'and the place thereof/shall know it no more'. But when the poet lodges in the calamus (or palm-tree), which provides this third volume with one of its most arresting images, a miracle like that experienced by St Veronica seems possible:

Inscribed
upon my palms
I find your face.

It is precisely when 'the rooms are deserted/in which answers are given' and when the poetry becomes a kind of bird's nest made of simple twigs that Bobrowski comes closest to achieving the kind of sanctuary he has hoped for. And although his voice diminishes almost to a whisper, or to the 'unspoken speech' of a shadowy Undine, he knows he is 'going to stay here/for a time' ('House'). Despite his early death, and the slight bulk of his work, this is exactly what Bobrowski has done.

The paradox of Bobrowski's achievement is that, like Celan, by using a

Language
worn out
by the weary mouth
on the endless road
to the neighbour's house

he can nevertheless reaffirm his faith in the great emotions which language can utter. This is particularly true of the poem written three months before his death, his last poem, aptly titled 'The Word Man':

Where there is no love,
do not speak the word.

The words 'man' and 'love' are here made indices of one another in a language that is teetering on the verge of silence despite its Biblical solidity and sublimity. The manner in which Bobrowski reaffirms old truths in a new way suggests he will increasingly come to be recognized outside Germany as one of its most important post-war voices; within the German-speaking world he was nothing less than one of the primary agents of cultural reconstruction.

Paul Celan (1920–70)

Born Paul Antschel in Czernowitz, Rumania, the only child of
German Jewish parents, and educated there. Spent a year
studying medicine in Tours in 1938. Studied Romance lan-
guages and literatures at Czernowitz University. In 1942 his
parents were deported to an extermination camp; he himself
was placed in a Rumanian labour camp. An editor and trans-
lator in Bucharest from 1945 to 1947, the year in which he
adopted his *nom de plume*. In Vienna in early 1948 and later
that year in Paris. Began the formal study of German litera-
ture in Paris in 1948; published and almost immediately
recalled his first collection of poems *The Sand From The Urns*
in that year. A friend of the multilingual Surrealist poet Yvan
Goll in 1949–50, but subsequently accused of plagiarism by
Goll's widow. A professor of German at the École Normale
Supérieure from 1950 onwards. Married the artist Gisèle Les-
trange; a son was later born to the couple. Awarded several
prestigious German literary prizes over the next fifteen years,
a period of marked mental instability and recurrent paranoia.
Made a trip to Israel in 1969, where he met a girl whom he
fell in love with. Drowned himself in the Seine for reasons that
have yet to be fully clarified. An accomplished translator of
Shakespeare, Rimbaud, Valéry, Blok, Mandelstam, Ungar-
etti, Jules Supervielle, Sergei Esenin and André du Bouchet.

It is generally agreed that the greatest of post-war German
poets is Paul Celan, although there has been no consensus as
to how his work may best be approached. The absence of a
consensus can be directly attributed to the fact that, in the

words of Michael Hamburger, 'the more we try to concentrate on [Celan's poetry] ... the more we are made aware that difficulty and paradox are of its essence'. In this respect, as in others, the case of Celan is similar to that of Mallarmé, or of Georg Trakl, or, of living poets, René Char, all of them poets who can seem forbidding to the common reader and who are often labelled 'cryptic', 'enigmatic' or simply 'obscure'. A representative instance of how even the uncommon reader may experience a problem of articulation when faced with Celan is a sensitive *TLS* review by George Steiner. After patiently characterizing the collections published in Celan's lifetime, Steiner was forced to admit that it was 'very difficult to say anything useful' about the posthumously published poems of Celan's last years. In a previous attempt to do so, in his study of 'Aspects of Language and Translation' *After Babel* (1973), Steiner quoted one of these late poems ('The Darkening Splinterecho' from *Snow-Share*, 1971) and commented:

The secrecy of the text stems from no esoteric knowledge, from no abstruseness of supporting philosophic argument. By themselves the words are nakedly simple. Yet they cannot be elucidated by public reference. Nor will the poem as a whole admit of a single paraphrase. It is not clear that Celan seeks 'to be understood', that our understanding has any bearing on the cause and necessity of the poem.

Steiner's primary concern at this point of *After Babel* is with translatability, Celan being called as a witness to prove that there is a distinctively modern 'revolt of literature against language'. But in the *TLS* he suggested that Celan may come to be 'more indispensable than Rilke', and it is difficult to see how this could ever be so if the question of whether Celan 'seeks "to be understood"' were doomed to remain as unclear as Steiner takes it to be.

Like most so-called 'difficult' poets, Celan was happy to avail himself of an opportunity to make his work more accessible to its potential audience. One such occasion offered itself in 1958, when Celan was awarded a literary prize by the city of Bremen and made a speech of acceptance. Celan began his address by reminding his audience that, both literally and figuratively, he had come from far away to be with them, from 'a region where people and books were alive ... a former province of the Hapsburg empire now buried in oblivion'. Celan's stance in the Bremen speech is that of a figure utterly disabused of the consolation that there exists a place of origin to which he might return, and conscious that circumstance has doomed him to be a wanderer upon the face of the earth. Out of this initial elegiac testament, however, there emerges an embattled faith which, without in any way making up for the loss of those near and dear to the poet (victims of the corporate madness of the German nation he is addressing), gives him grounds for a qualified hope and, as it were, ratifies his poetic enterprise:

> In the midst of the losses there was one thing that remained
> attainable, near and not lost: language.
>
> Yes, in spite of everything, language was preserved. But it had to
> cross its own answerlessness, its appalling silence, the thousand
> darknesses of deadly speech. It offered no words for what had
> occurred; but it crossed such things, and came into the light again,
> 'enriched' by them, During those years and the years that came
> after them I tried to write poems in this language: so as to speak,
> to orientate myself, to discover where I was and where I was going,
> to describe what was real to me.

Celan's deep need of therapy after trauma is evident; but he is also speaking in a spirit of general remedy, and obviously remembering Brecht's prediction, at the height of 'the dark times', that future ages would ask 'why were the poets silent?' Furthermore, he is attempting to present the very peculiarity of his language as a product of years of 'answerlessness' and 'deadly speech'. And over the whole address hangs the implication that no Jew, try as he may to relate to a Germany under reconstruction, can truly be said to have emerged from 'the dark times'. Celan's answer, as we might call it, his one compensation, was to believe that, in combating a vicious and degenerate rhetoric with a language purged and washed clean, his poetry might epitomize 'the one thing that remained attainable, near and not lost' and thus, in Milton's famous words, 'fit audience find, though few':

The poem is a message in a bottle, despatched in the – certainly not always hopeful – belief that sometime and somewhere it may know landfall, on heartland perhaps.

It is not only the poet who is travelling in search of an irretrievably lost point of origin and trying to content himself with a temporary dwelling-place; it is the poem also. And without being explicit about it, Celan is disassociating himself and his poetry from such predecessors as Gottfried Benn, self-confessedly a poet of 'monologue', whose partial rehabilitation in post-war Germany Celan naturally viewed with disquiet. Partially influenced by the Hasidic writings of Martin Buber (of whom he speaks warmly at the beginning of the Bremen speech), Celan saw himself as a poet of dialogue, an explorer and interpreter of the space in which a dialogue might take place. Typically, the 'message in a bottle' motif, for which Celan has subsequently become famous, is itself part of a dialogue which the poet saw himself conducting with Osip Mandelstam, whom Celan translated, whose later poems were all hostages to fortune, and who first used the phrase in an essay of 1913, 'On The Addressee'. Even in the genre of public address, Celan is in quest, obviously enough, of the appropriate addressee.

The Bremen speech suggests that Celan, like Mandelstam before him, believed in the capacity of 'the word' to find out its ideal auditor. But the tone of his remarks indicates that he lived in the tortured and distressful state of mind that Mandelstam's aesthetic of 'the word' was designed to combat. The mature Mandelstam evolved a system of belief in 'the word' which tempered the rigours he was doomed to suffer; Celan, on his own admission in a speech given in 1960, had 'a strong inclination towards silence'. Like the Mallarmé-inspired Mandelstam of a poem like 'Silentium' of 1910, Celan wished to 'discover/what has always been mute' and thus achieve fusion with 'the origins of life'. But he was equally a prey to the notion that what has always been mute must always remain so. Celan's origins in the Hasidic communities of Eastern Europe are sometimes cited as influential upon this 'strong inclination towards silence', and many commentators have compared it with Theodor Adorno's celebrated dictum that there could be 'no poetry after Auschwitz'. But Celan was sharply critical of poets who, by yielding to a comparable inclination, surrendered their claims to be considered witnesses in the fullest sense. He cannot have been unaware of the ironic potential inherent in one of Kafka's shrewdest parables:

Now the sirens have a still more fatal weapon than their song, namely their silence . . . It is conceivable that someone might possibly have escaped from their song; but from their silence certainly never.

It is not so much that Celan was, as Steiner would have him be, 'against language', rather that he was seeking to use language in a way that would enable him to traverse speechlessness and, as it were, come out on the other side of silence. Celan's dissociation of his own enterprise from that of Brecht is helpful here. Brecht's most famous lines occur in the poem of 1938 called 'To Those Born Afterwards':

What times are these, when
To speak of trees is almost a crime
Because it implies silence about so much injustice?

Celan answered Brecht's question with another question:

A leaf, treeless
for Bertolt Brecht:

What times are these
when to speak
is almost a crime
because it implies
so much made explicit?

To be explicit, as Brecht had been, was not Celan's way. He even came to regard his most anthologized poem (the early 'Death Fugue' from *Poppy And Memory*, 1952) as too explicit, though almost no two commentators have been able to agree on its meaning. As an enemy of the explicit, he left himself open to the suggestion that he sought obscurity for its own sake. But he was quick to retort that 'the concern of this language is ... precision'. And it is in fact precisely in his most stuttering and most autistic later poems that one can best appreciate the manic urgency with which he set about making an inherently imprecise medium of communication take on radically new forms of precision. Celan's method of constructing a space in which dialogue might take place was to subject a word or phrase to ruptures and fractures which rendered it incapable of communicating in the manner characteristic of most pre-Auschwitz poetry. In so doing he far surpassed even the most audacious experiments of Mallarmé, whose schemes he sought (as the 1960 speech 'The Meridian' indicates) to bring to fulfilment. By employing a language 'caught in its speech-seed' like that of the later Rilke (though shorn of Rilke's grandiloquence), Celan hoped to complete the task that had driven Mallarmé to despair: to make language speak. Like Mallarmé, though to an even greater degree, Celan subverted the traditionally stable spatial relationships created by a poem and existing between a poem and its reader. The morbidity of Celan's subject-matter (in which the tragic destiny of God's 'chosen' people and the image of those who perished in the death-camps are ever-present) is leavened by the dynamic manner in which it is presented. There is an aphorism of Karl Kraus's which proposes that 'the closer the look taken at a word, the greater the distance from which the word looks back' and, as the Bremen speech demonstrates, Celan was content that his audience should be aware of the distance between him and them provided they made every effort to collapse it by taking a closer look and engaging in dialogue.

Celan's first two collections – *Poppy And Memory*, 1952 (incorporating *The Sand From The Urns*, 1948, which he withdrew from circulation) and *From Threshold To Threshold*, 1955 – are his least characteristic; here the predisposing spirit is the essentially Surrealist doctrine of 'liberation of the image'.

Similarly Surrealist is the fascination with hallucinatory dream states, a subject on which Celan had spoken eloquently in his early prose piece 'Edgar Jené and the Dream of the Dream'. These early poems of Celan's are generally taken to be his least difficult, but except insofar as the language of dreams is available to the collective unconscious they seem to me to pose as many, if not more problems than the later poems. There is a diffuseness, a lack of control in these first two collections which threatens the integrity and coherence of the writing, memorable though individual images often are. Celan seems to recognize as much in the programmatic poems which conclude the second collection, where he resolves to 'keep yes and no unsplit' in a more rigorous manner in the future. Subsequently, far from liberating the image in the accredited Surrealist way, Celan subjected it to restrictions and constrictions that would have paralysed a Surrealist. Interesting in this regard is a curious prose piece called 'Conversation In The Mountains' (published in 1962), which amounts to something like a 'discourse on method':

Hardly has an image entered than it gets caught in the web, and already present is a thread which begins to spin, which spins itself around the image, a veil-thread; spins itself around the image and begets a child in conjunction with it, half-image, half-veil.

This has obvious affinities with Mallarmé's 'trembling of the veil' and, like Mallarmé's more or less discursive prose, Celan's may induce in a reader the same vertigo that it describes. But the image of begetting suggests that Mallarmé's notorious sterility has been transcended and, if a method is to be judged by the number of poems it generates, Celan's must obviously be regarded as a fruitful one. Whereas Mallarmé composed only some seventy poems, the complete corpus of Celan extends to over seven hundred.

The first collection in which Celan applied his new method was the 1961 volume *Speech-Grille*, a title with many meanings but all of them connected with the 'half-image, half-veil' notion. In *The No-One's-Rose* (1964) – arguably the most difficult collection for non-Jews to come to terms with – Celan explored the consequences of a return to religious orthodoxy. Thereafter he wrote in the ambivalent faith that there were 'still songs to be sung on the other side/of mankind'. These lines occur in a poem in *The No-One's-Rose* which provided Celan with the title for the last collection published in his lifetime: *Thread-Suns* (1968). As befits their content, they have an almost 'posthumous' tone. But the songs are still being sung *for* someone or *to* someone; even at his most terse Celan did not forget the claim made in the Bremen speech, that the poem was redeemed by its discovery of an addressee. Many of the later poems actually seek to create such a figure. Celan repeatedly speaks of a mysterious 'you' who seems to play a role similar to that of the unidentified 'you' so often encountered in the poems of Montale. In Celan's case this 'you' is a kind of composite figure: a lost mother, a lost beloved, a reader with whom the poet despairs of communicating, an 'other' with whom he might remain in dialogue. No one poem epitomizes all these aspects, though there is a poem in *Light-Compulsion* (1970; the title is effectively a gloss on the key utterance in the Bremen speech) which succinctly indicates how important the 'you' figure is:

I can still see you: an echo
to be grasped towards, on the ridge
of farewell, with antenna
words.

Your face shies softly
when there is suddenly
within me a lamplike
radiance, at the place
where, with the utmost pain, one says Never

Equally instructive is a three-line poem from *Thread-Suns*, which is obliquely prophetic of the mood in which he must have chosen to end his life:

You were my death:
you I could hold
while all else fell from me.

This brief and poignant utterance preserves the absolutely minimum requirements for a dialogue: an I and a you. Like Rilke's lovely 'Autumn' poem from *The Book of Images* it is concerned with salvation, with what will sustain one when all is failing or falling. And, as is characteristic of Celan, it situates salvation outside the confines of the solitary sensibility.

In the event, having paused to note in a poem posthumously collected in *Snow-Share* that 'they call life/our only refuge', Celan chose the ultimate 'other' of death for his refuge. The three-line poem in *Thread-Suns* suggests that, despite the Bremen speech, it was death which was the only thing 'near and not lost' for the traumatized Celan. Even his death, however, may be construed as a kind of dialogue: among the aphorisms of Novalis, whose writings Celan evidently knew intimately, is one which suggests that self-sacrifice is the only act which enables man to cast off his 'homesickness' and repossess his origins. It seems probable that Celan's death was not so much self-slaughter as self-transcendence, an analogue in the sphere of life for what he had preached and practised in the sphere of art.

Vasko Popa (born 1922)

Born in Grebenac, near Belgrade. Studied at the universities of Vienna, Bucharest and Belgrade, graduating in French and Yugoslav Literature in 1948 from the last-named. Awarded many Yugoslavian literary prizes and the Austrian Lenau prize in 1967. His poetry has been translated into all the major European languages.

It would be difficult to find a more dramatic illustration of the interest generated by the poetry of Eastern Europe than the publication in 1978 of the Yugoslav Vasko Popa's *Collected Poems*. There are, after all, many better-known English and American poets who have yet to gather their work together in this way, or be invited by their publishers to do so. But in the case of Popa perhaps only an extensive collection of his work could really be said to do justice to him, for he depends more than most poets on his audience being placed in full possession of the keys which might unlock a distinctly original but sometimes rebarbatively oblique vision of the world. Popa's practice of writing in cycles and of creating echoes within and between cycles by concentrating on a limited number of motifs gives his work a rigour and coherence that is rare in contemporary poetry, but it means that each individual poem can seem somehow impoverished when deprived of the poems designed to accompany and interact with it. It is as if Popa had been seeking to compensate for the potential shortcomings of a language shorn of almost all the rhetorical decorations present in most poetry (even in that which offers itself as 'minimalist') by subjecting his material to the kind of perspectival tests that attend the composition of an art object, such as a piece of sculpture, designed to be seen in more than one plane. This to some extent invalidates Ted Hughes's well-intentioned recommendation of Popa and his fellow Eastern Europeans as 'closer to the common reality, in which we have to live if we are to survive, than to those other realities in which we can holiday, or into which we decay when our bodily survival is comfortably taken care of, and which art, particularly contemporary art, is forever trying to impose on us as some sort of superior dimension'. Popa's poetry is so suspicious of rhetoric as to make any claim of this kind seem somewhat inflated. But it is in any case difficult to regard him as 'closer to the common reality' than, say, Brecht, and he frequently ventures into 'other realities' – admittedly at the furthest remove from the 'holiday' spirit of which Hughes speaks – in order to shed refracted light on this one. Furthermore, if he does not intend to 'impose' these realities on us as 'some sort of superior dimension', his very concentration on a world view that seems uniquely his own may make it seem like an imposition upon the reader approaching it from outside its peculiar frames of reference.

The strangeness of Popa's poetry has made comparisons with the Surrealists, by whom he was apparently influenced, inevitable. And yet the first poem of his first collection (*Bark*, 1953) stresses his resistance to Surrealist intoxications and concludes quite categorically: 'I'm not dreaming'. These nightmarish early poems, at once an objectification of and a stimulus for Popa's need to 'withdraw into my skin', were obviously conditioned by the macabre reality of 1943–5. Popa's 'withdrawal' is not escapist, however; it is part of a strategy of resistance. As the poem 'The Iron Apple' demonstrates, Popa is hungering for peace. And only if he can become 'the iron apple's/First rust and last autumn' (by actively fighting the Nazis) and (as in 'Echo') make his poetry 'a hundredfold/Echo of the howling' can he hope to find sustenance. To achieve these aims he must journey and traverse the peculiar topography of the 'Landscapes' that follow. The

'I' has disappeared from these 'Landscapes' and been re-placed by what have been aptly called 'objects in a void'. But by being placed in a void the objects seem to have recovered the mobility of human beings. This human dimension ex-plains why the mood remains sombre, though each of the 'Landscapes' ends with a mysterious intimation of tran-quillity or rebirth. In the 'List' of fifteen objects which com-prise the next sub-section of *Bark* these intimations are subjected to renewed evidence of anguish, as in 'Horse' for example:

In his lovely eyes
Sorrow has closed
Into a circle
For the road has no ending
And he must drag behind him
The whole world

However, the final poem of this sequence (a seminal influence upon the final subsection of Popa's second volume) concerns an object, a quartz pebble, that *is* a 'whole world', one that 'holds all/In its passionate/Internal embrace'. And it is with a similarly passionate 'internal embrace' that Popa brings his first volume to its conclusion, with a sequence of fifteen poems that return us to the human world of love and war. This sequence, called 'Far Within Us', begins in a mood of ten-tative optimism: 'From each pain/That we do not mention/A chestnut tree grows/And remains mysterious behind us// From each hope/That we cherish/A star arises/And moves unattainable before us'. And without ignoring grimmer truths ('We are two sheets of newspaper/Crudely pasted/ Over the evening's wound') the sequence ends affirmatively: 'We have lost each other/In the boundless forests/Of our meeting// . . . //We have found each other/On the golden plateau/Far within us'.

This 'golden plateau' is threatened by the 'unrest-field' which provides the title for Popa's second volume. The 'un-rest' begins as early as the epigraph, where the poet asks himself (in lines taken from 'Far Within Us') whether he will be able to 'set up a tent of my hands for you'. The 'you' of *Unrest-Field* (1956) seem unconcerned with a covenant such as the poet envisages. For the relationships between human beings in this collection (and especially in the subsection 'Games') are of a kind that can only find satisfaction in an endless round of torment and victimization. The poet stands at a distance from these games, a constant reminder that (as in the first poem of his first book) he is 'not playing'. Indeed he himself appears only in the last line of the melancholy epitaph for those who have gone from the game of life into the dance of death:

On one hand now the rain is falling
From the other grass is growing
What more should I say

That there is in fact much more to be said is clear from the 'conversation' sequence which follows ('One Bone To Another') and from the monologue which seeks to persuade and compel a 'monster' to 'Give Me Back My Rags'. 'One Bone To Another' is Popa's black humour at its blackest, as the bones at first congratulate themselves on escaping from the flesh and then find 'everything beginning again'. But there is no humour at all in 'Give Me Back My Rags', and the seven poems about 'The Quartz Pebble' end with a desolating confrontation between 'Two victims of a little joke/A bad joke without a joker'.

Popa's third collection, *Secondary Heaven* (1968), restores meaning to a world that has become 'a bad joke without a joker'. In each of the seven sections (each comprising seven poems) the world is haunted by the ghosts of things once meaningful that have become bad jokes. The traditional God, Light of Light, has become 'Yawn of Yawns', his acts the subject of 'Once upon a time' fairy-tales. In the vacuum created by his absence the poet is left with a world of signs to interpret, a world that he can only question without hope of an answer. The Godhead has been reduced to a cipher, as is clear from the sub-section 'Dissension'. But Popa is determined to demystify this cipher, or better still to have it condemn itself out of its own mouth. The structurally parallel sub-section 'Schism' continues this dialogue with the order of speakers reversed. Between these two sections Popa concentrates on the strategies that must follow from having 'gone down naked into ourselves'. The strategies themselves, however, cannot provide consolation: 'We wonder if these are really/Preparations for a welcome/Or only a farewell'.

The central poem of the sixth section explicitly acknowledges that 'It is dark now in our soul'. And only in the final section does Popa begin to find a 'you' he can take some comfort in, a constellation of animated symbols that he can address with tenderness. This enables the collection to end with a request quite different in character from that which makes 'Give Me Back My Rags' so turbulent:

Give me secret signs
I will give you a cherrywood staff

And one of my wrinkles as a path
And one of my lashes as a guide
To bring you home

It is Popa's homeland, and the history of his homeland, that forms the subject of his next collection, *Earth Erect* (1972). And although, as he announces at the beginning of it, he is 'still far from guessing their meaning', the 'secret signs' from the end of *Secondary Heaven* are soon full of the promise of ultimate salvation. To achieve it, the poet must become a pilgrim like Saint Sava before him. But his pilgrimage is through history and involves a confrontation with the disasters that have marked Serbia's relations with her oppressors. In surviving this pilgrimage, the poet can begin to carry out the task of providing sustenance for his people which he had hoped to fulfil in the poems of the war years:

I didn't know whether the white town [Belgrade]
Was coming down from the clouds into me
Or was growing from my womb into the sky

I came back from the journey
To share out the ripened stones from my bundle
Here on the city square

The fact that Popa is unable to distinguish between the inner
and outer worlds in this pivotal poem suggests that a kind
of primordial unity has been re-established, and that a new
covenant, a new faith, can be expressed. And without in any
way congratulating himself, Popa makes it clear that his
poetry's ability to make the 'secret signs' yield up their secrets
has been instrumental in bringing this about. For by placing
a limited number of sometimes arcane symbols in the crucible
of his imagination, Popa has created the 'incandescent kiss'
which (as a poem in *Secondary Heaven* suggests) will 'save our-
selves the cauldron's ears'.

This new faith takes on body in the new mythology of
Popa's collection *Wolf Salt*. The symbol of the wolf (which
the publishers of *Collected Poems* have sensibly placed on the
dustjacket) first occurs in the 'pilgrimage' poem that opens
Earth Erect, although the sevenfold structure of *Wolf Salt*
points back, beyond *Earth Erect*, to *Secondary Heaven*. The
backward glance that this entails is instructive. For whereas
the structure of *Secondary Heaven* places an 'Imitation of the
Sun' at its centre, *Wolf Salt* has a more substantial heart, the
'promised land'. This central poem has a prayer and a hymn
on either side of it and the whole collection seems to radiate
outwards in circles from it. Popa is at his most humble in
Wolf Salt, begging the lone wolf to

inspire me with fire from your jaws
That in your name I may sing
In our ancestral lime-tree tongue

Inscribe on our brow with your claw
The heavenly signs and runes
That I may grow to be the interpreter of your silence

If this makes for a radically hermetic poetry, it is at the same
time oddly accessible, more so perhaps than when Popa is
concerned with objects in a void. For the whole collection is

marked by a sense of plenitude, of brotherhood and of order. The 'howling/That comes from the heart of earth' is no less present than in the early poem 'Echo'. But the last poem of *Wolf Salt* demonstrates the poet's determination to persist in his quest, whoever or whatever tries to frighten him or advise him otherwise. There is no longer any question, as there once was, of whether he will be able 'to set up a tent of my hands for you'.

In a collection of quite unhermetic autobiographical poems published in the same year as *Wolf Salt* – *Raw Flesh* – Popa goes back to the world of his childhood (when he was nicknamed 'Wolf'). It is a pre-war world, destroyed for ever by the Second World War. Popa recovers it with warmth but without sentimentality. In the process he abandons the arcana he has previously depended on and begins to look more like the poet 'closer to the common reality' that Ted Hughes has spoken of. A particularly poignant example is the poem 'Poetry Lesson':

We're sitting on the white bench
Under the bust of Lenau

We're kissing
And just incidentally talking
About poetry . . .

The poet is looking out through us
Through the white bench
Through the gravel on the path

And is so splendidly silent
With his splendid bronze lips

In Vershats park
I'm slowly learning
What really matters in a poem

Many readers will find 'what really matters' to them in Popa in *Raw Flesh*, where he achieves something of the elemental simplicity of Lenau without Lenau's penchant for melancholy. There was poetic justice in Popa's being awarded the

1967 Lenau prize by the Austrian government. But the *Collected Poems* demonstrate that Popa has compressed a remarkable range into his ostensibly narrow cosmos, and may best be seen to matter when he is taken as a whole.

Yves Bonnefoy (born 1923)

Born in Tours, the son of a railway worker and educated there, specializing in mathematics and philosophy. Studied at Poitiers with a view to becoming a mathematician, but deflected from so doing by the poetic interests he developed on removing to Paris in 1943, stimulated primarily by the poetry of Paul Éluard and by the company of Surrealist painters whom he knew. Read very widely and was led to abandon pure Surrealism by reading Shestov's *Potestas Clavium*. Spent the years 1947–52 writing the poems for his first volume *Du Mouvement et de l'immobilité de Douve* (1953) which brought him immediate fame. Married his first wife in 1953 but later separated from her. Studied philosophy with Gaston Bachelard and wrote a dissertation on Baudelaire and Kierkegaard. Gradually allowed his interest in mathematics to decline. Visited Italy and was profoundly impressed by early Italian Renaissance art. Later studied French Gothic art and Italian Baroque art; began to translate Shakespeare into French. Has been a professor at the Universities of Geneva, Vincennes and Nice. Recently appointed Professor of Poetics at the Collège de France.

No French poet to have emerged since the end of the Second World War has made a greater impact than Yves Bonnefoy. On the publication in 1953 of his first volume of poems, Bonnefoy provoked a critical reaction in France comparable to that which had greeted Valéry's *La Jeune Parque* in 1917, and since then the many-sidedness of his activity has made analogies with Valéry, and beyond him Baudelaire, almost inevitable. Like his great predecessors Bonnefoy is almost as challenging in prose as in verse: his study of Rimbaud is perhaps the best single book on the subject, and his art criticism – of de Chirico, Miró, Piero della Francesca, Bernini and Poussin – is astonishingly wide-ranging. He is also an outstanding translator, notably of Shakespeare, and he has shown more interest in English literature than French poets usually do. This expertise has enabled him to develop very intelligent observations (in the 1965 essay 'French Poetry And The Principle Of Identity') on the advantages English has over French as a medium of expression. And it may help to explain why Bonnefoy has been more extensively translated into English than any other contemporary French poet. Only Bonnefoy's second collection of poetry, *Yesterday Reigning Desert* (1958) has yet to be made available in a bilingual edition, and most of the important poems from this volume were ably rendered in the selection made by the poet himself for the now sadly defunct 'Cape editions' of a decade ago.

Bonnefoy's discursive writings provide the best possible introduction to his poetry; he is in many ways his own best commentator, though he almost never talks directly about his own poems. The premise from which all his later conclusions derive is the first sentence of an essay of 1947 called 'Anti-Plato': 'It is really a question of *this* object.' This is an open riposte to the Greek philosopher who banished poets from his *Republic* and who separated the phenomenal world from the world of essences. But it is also an implicit critique of the Surrealists with whom Bonnefoy had briefly associated. For Bonnefoy's commitment to '*this* object' is effectively a commitment to the real rather than to the surreal. His complex feelings on the subject of Surrealism are made clearer in an essay of 1957 in which he stresses that he considers Surrealism 'the only genuine poetic movement this century has had', finally unsuccessful because of its excessive introversion, but admirable in the way it has attempted to 'reanimate in secular times . . . the feeling of transcendence'. In the decade between 'Anti-Plato' and this essay Bonnefoy had obviously concerned himself increasingly not only with the question of '*this* object' but also with its apparent opposite, the question of transcendence. Yet in the very act of dissociating himself from Plato Bonnefoy had begun a quest for a 'threshold' (as he would later call it) in which apparent opposites could be merged. In the essay in which he identifies what he takes to be the failure of the Surrealist ideal, Bonnefoy writes: 'In reading Kierkegaard, Shestov and Bataille, I grasped a better understanding of the powers and specificity of nothingness; but I also realized that it had to be conquered.' Of the authors referred to by Bonnefoy it seems probable that the one to provide him with his first weapon of conquest was the Russian theologian Shestov, for the idea which dominates Bonnefoy's essay 'The Tombs of Ravenna' (1953) – 'Nothing is less real than the concept' – is repeatedly expressed in Shestov's writings. But he must have arrived at this apparent irrationalism by way of more obviously rational thinkers; the epigraph to his first volume of poetry is taken from Hegel's *Phenomenology Of The Spirit* – 'the life of the spirit does not shrink from death ... [but] endures death and maintains itself alive within death'. It is, moreover, precisely this inescapable fact of death which, for Bonnefoy, makes nothing less real than the concept. Much more real for him, indeed the ultimate reality, is the inscription he found on a tomb in Ravenna: *hic est locus patria*, here is a place of origin. In the prevailing pessimism of post-war France, Bonnefoy was evidently seeking something upon which to rejoice, something positive which would nevertheless not falsify the fact that death was life's ultimate horizon. His reading of the so-called 'irrationalist' philosophers, together with his frequent trips to Italy, evidently led him to seek consolation in the transient fact of presence; his essays indicate that he was led to conceive of this consolation in heterodox theological terms. It is clear that his 'conversion' (as he has since called it) took place along the lines marked out by negative mysticism. But it was Earth and not Paradise that he was seeking to regain; hence his description of his enterprise as a 'theology of earth'. 'The true place,' he suggests in 'The Tombs Of Ravenna', 'is always a here'; the Latin inscription in Ravenna was obviously a potent reminder that 'here' is always, whatever else it may be, a place of death. The poet's task, under such conditions, becomes akin to that identified by Shestov in the final section of his book *Potestas Clavium*: his role is to provide a *memento mori*. Yet at the same time he also provides the 'words of communion' and consolation which will make the fact of death meaningful. 'I am concerned with transcendence,' Bonnefoy has written, 'but also with the place where it is rooted.'

The paradoxical nature of Bonnefoy's enterprise is advertised in the very title of his first collection of poems: *On The Motion And Immobility Of Douve*. Here, in accordance with Bonnefoy's anti-conceptual stance, Douve resists translation into other terms. Douve is at once a female figure, a landscape, an exemplification of Hegel's 'life of the spirit', a reminder that the poet is engaged in an act of naming, and ultimately poetry itself. Bonnefoy habitually quotes with approval Coleridge's description of a Beauty in which 'the many still seen as many becomes one,' and this is clearly true of Douve also. As in the Coleridge quotation, and as we might expect of a poet who has written such fine art criticism, Bonnefoy begins his book with what he has *seen*, and subtitles the first section of his five-act drama (no doubt prophetic of his later interest in Shakespeare) 'Theatre'. We are obviously intended to recall this section when we come to the fifth and final section, 'True Place'. For in 'Theatre' Bonnefoy is dramatizing the decomposition of his residual temptation to think conceptually. As poem XV of the sequence suggests, he is engaged in '[burning] to ashes/The old bestiary of the mind'. This is primarily in order to avoid making the same mistakes as, in Bonnefoy's opinion, Valéry had made with Monsieur Teste. But the decomposition is so brilliantly rendered that the poems come disconcertingly close to being incoherent. Each individual utterance is clear and forthright, but collectively they seem too dynamic to be really accessible. This is because, as poem IV admits, 'each instant I see you being born, Douve/Each instant dying.' Only in the more austere terrain of the second section ('Last Acts') does a certain coherence begin to emerge. Symptomatically perhaps, despite its title, 'Last Acts' is essentially concerned (as the 'Phoenix' poem suggests) with rebirth; Bonnefoy, like Hegel, has realized that 'You will have to go through death in order to live.' Encouraged by this, the poet begins to reconstruct what one poem calls a 'True Body' out of the ashes:

Douve, I speak in you; and clasp you
In the act of knowing and naming.

The last poem in this section is therefore rightly an *ars poetica*, preparing us for the central section to follow. It is in this third section ('Douve Speaks') that Bonnefoy dramatizes poetry's need to be 'propitious earth' and to 'take on meaning'. For this to occur, as one of the voices within Douve makes clear, the poet must extend Mallarmé's belief, as expressed in his celebrated riposte to Degas, that 'poetry is made of words'. 'To be words only,' Bonnefoy counters, 'is to die out soon.' In the fourth section, however, in constructing a place of origin comparable to that embodied in the inscription on the Ravenna tomb, Bonnefoy stresses that words remain important; he even uses the Latin inscription as a title for one of the poems in this section. The two-line poem which ends this fourth section, the pivotal poem of the collection as a whole, is itself little more than an inscription, and yet it summarizes the whole network of concerns that Bonnefoy has been developing up to this point:

You took up a lamp and now you open the door.
What use is a lamp, it is raining, the day breaks.

Only in the fifth section ('True Place') does Bonnefoy conceive of a place that can actually be lived in. And here, despite the singular form of the title, we once again encounter the 'many' of Bonnefoy's favourite quotation from Coleridge. *Douve* as a whole ends (as section four has prefigured) with intimations of daybreak. Yet its last words are a question, with Bonnefoy asking himself whether poetry will actually have the power to 'pierce the rampart of the dead'. This is the question which Bonnefoy's subsequent volumes will ultimately answer in the affirmative.

Douve is an extremely difficult book, much more complex in its infrastructure than I have space to suggest here. But the five years spent writing it had given Bonnefoy an immense authority over his material, so that even a bewildered reader could not fail to recognize it as a masterpiece. *Yesterday Reigning Desert* is in every sense slighter, and important primarily as a transitional stage which reaches fulfilment in *Words In Stone*. There are, however, some very beautiful poems in Bonnefoy's second volume, none more so than the one addressed 'To The Voice Of Kathleen Ferrier' in which Bonnefoy reminds himself that 'beyond any pure form' there is the 'only absolute [of] another song'. Here, as in *Douve*, voice becomes an agent of vision, and it is right that the turbulent questions which begin the collection should be finally quietened by the impersonal, but at the same time very emotional, voice with which it ends. The essay on the Ravenna tombs had described the 'true place' as 'always a here'. *Yesterday Reigning Desert* ends with Bonnefoy giving the notion one of his most riveting poetic utterances:

Here, in the bright place. It is no longer dawn,
It is already the day of speakable desires.

Between this marvellous conclusion to his second collection and *Words In Stone* (1965) Bonnefoy wrote his outstanding study of Rimbaud, which requires us from the start to 'listen to [Rimbaud's] voice', to assess his desires and finally to accept him – despite his abandonment of poetry – as 'the Phoenix of freedom, who comes to life in the ashes of hope'. It is very characteristic of Bonnefoy to end his study of Rimbaud on a hopeful note. In the 1958 essay 'The Act And Place Of Poetry' he had begun by saying that he would like to think of poetry and hope as 'almost identical'. By the end of *Words In Stone* this identity is established beyond all doubt. And it is symptomatic that the first poem in the book should climax with an augury of the terrestrial paradise which Bonnefoy has for so long been in search of. As in his other books, Bonnefoy is determined to confront, with whatever anguish of spirit it may entail, the stonier words that give the book its title. But this is in order that the inscriptional aspects of the title, dramatically embodied in the last poems in the volume, and ultimately affirmative, shall be seen to have been earned against all odds. Writing of a painting by Tintoretto (the *Crucifixion* in the Scuola di San Rocco in Venice), Bonnefoy once again emphasizes the word which was so prominent at the end of his second volume: 'Here/A great hope was the painter.' The next poem (the last but one in the collection) strikes the same note:

Yes, I can live here. The angel, who is the earth,
Enters each bush, to appear there and burn.

And the final poem places this benediction, as its title acknowledges, under the sign of 'The Art Of Poetry':

There was a bloody disconsolate voice in the mouth,
It was washed and called forth.

The triumph of Bonnefoy's book-length poem *In The Lure Of The Threshold*, which is certainly one of the great long poems of the century, is that it shows how this 'bloody disconsolate voice' is continually being called forth and superseded. In a manner which his essays suggest is incumbent upon French poetry if it is not to surrender to abstraction, Bonnefoy has reaffirmed that man's abiding need to undertake a return to origins is at once beyond the capacity of words to express and yet conditioned by the fact that it must be expressed.

Words in the sky
Today,
Something which gathers, disperses.

Words like the sky,
Infinite
And yet contained in this moment within the brief pool.

All Bonnefoy's writing, but especially the poems from *Words In Stone* onwards, confirms Sartre's punning intuition (in chapter four of *What Is Literature?*, 1947) that '[his] name seems predisposed to the utmost honesty'. He has never relapsed into *mauvaise foi*. Yet it is as much his energy as his honesty which makes him an impressive figure. Bonnefoy has stressed that it is the energy of English poetry that makes it attractive to him, which makes it particularly ironic that no living English poet has matched the range and quality of his own achievement. Only posterity can decide which of the French poets of the post-war period possess the classic status of their forbears. But it seems inconceivable that it will deny Bonnefoy's entitlement to such an eminence.

Yehuda Amichai (born 1924)

Born in Würzburg of German Jewish parents who emigrated to Jerusalem in 1936; educated at a Jewish school before emigration, though his first language was German. Fought in the British Army's Jewish Brigade during the Second World War, in the 1948 Israeli War of Independence, and again in the subsequent conflicts of 1956 and 1973. His first collection of poetry in Hebrew appeared in 1955, since when he has published many volumes of poetry, short stories, plays and one novel. Teaches in Jerusalem. Visiting poet at the University of California at Berkeley in the autumn of 1971. Now writes with equal facility in Hebrew and English.

Amichai is one of the three poets writing in modern Hebrew who have made a profound impression on those who cannot read a word of the language of Israel; the others are T. Carmi and Dan Pagis. Like Pagis, Amichai is of European origin and writes in a language different from that which he spoke as a child, indeed in a language which Michael Hamburger has aptly characterized as a 'historical anomaly'. He has recently, moreover, attempted self-translation into English with the help of Ted Hughes, a dramatic illustration of his claim to Antony Rudolf that 'English is a language I really like ... that speaks to me more than all other languages apart from Hebrew'. Yet somehow it does not seem wrong to think of Amichai as a European poet, even though he now seems intent on making a reputation for himself in his second non-native language. The spirit of his early work seems, in fact, to have as much in common with his German origins as with the Jewish culture he has steeped himself in. Though by no means so inaccessible a poet as Paul Celan, and actually becoming more and more accessible in his 'English' poems, Amichai's clipped and metaphorical utterance is not unlike Celan's, whose death in the Seine is commemorated in one of the finest of Amichai's *Songs Of Jerusalem And Myself*. Like Celan, though in a much less extreme manner, Amichai is sceptical of the stain on the silence which his words leave, which is no doubt why he has confined himself almost exclusively to the short lyric poem. Yet unlike Celan, indeed more like those German poets who have followed Brecht's example, Amichai has not allowed his scepticism to interfere with his clarity and his 'lowbrow' power to communicate. It is ultimately the declarative simplicity of Amichai which, beneath his very considerable verbal ingenuity, lives longest in the mind.

'Of all the things I do,' Amichai writes in an early poem ('In My Worst Dreams'), 'parting is the inevitable one.' Almost all his numerous love poems confirm that this is indeed the case, and the best of them, very much like 'In My Worst Dreams', treat the subject in the context of the inevitable parting of death. Amichai is a predominantly elegiac poet, convinced that 'Whatever was not of the body will leave no memory' ('Farewell You'). His sense of the shocks that flesh is heir to is so acute that he suspects

> even Newton discovered
> Whatever he discovered
> In the lull between
> One pain and another.

However it is also in such lulls that Amichai makes his own discoveries, not all of which are painful, as the poem which speaks of Newton demonstrates:

> in the nights it is written:
> Despair which despairs of us
> Became hope.
>> ('The Heart Is A Corrupt Director')

If Amichai cannot sustain this hope, as he clearly cannot, it is because what is written, as in Talmudic texts, is susceptible of such radically divergent interpretations that it becomes inherently ambivalent and unstable. Reality, as 'If With A Bitter Mouth' indicates, is unchanged by the constructions we are pleased to place upon it; to be human is to discover in 'the coming nights' that there are strangers as well as sweet words, and to be perpetually a prey to alteration:

And it is written in the book that we shall fear.
And it is also written, that we shall change,
Like words,
In future and in past,
Plural or alone.

An equally paradoxical sensitivity to changelessness and change is found in the very fine poem 'As For The World.' Here Amichai cannot but say ('like one of Socrates' disciples') 'Indeed your words are true' when faced with the indisputable evidences of the real world. But his true faith is in the even less consoling realm of learned ignorance, however much he may be aware, as the biblical allusion suggests, that this may lead to him being weighed in the balance and found wanting:

As for the writing on the wall,
I am always ignorant . . .
Knowing only the rustle and drift
Of the wind
When a fate passes through me
To some other place.

It is precisely this movement 'to some other place' which makes Amichai's love poems so poignant. In the poem 'In The Middle Of This Century,' for example, he strokes his loved one's hair 'in the opposite direction to your journey' in the full knowledge that this will not fend off the journey and the farewell. The very powerful 'Like Our Bodies' Imprint' is also informed by the certainty that:

Already a wind blows
Which will not rain on us both.

It is typical of Amichai that, in 'A Pity. We Were Such A Good Invention' – where the journey of marriage has come to a disastrous end and the 'aeroplane made from a man and wife' has crashed – he should bring the poem to its laconic and regretful end not with the memory of the tangled bodies in the wreckage but with the memory of the fact that at least a journey had been attempted: 'We even flew a little.' These poems are much more than mere exercises in nostalgia, for memories remain part of Amichai's 'now' even when, as in 'Farewell You', he realizes that it is 'No longer ours to say: Now, Now'. This is particularly clear in a poem ('My Mother Once Told Me') which describes his mother's solicitude for him when he was a child and confronts the fact that:

> persons I love are already pushing themselves
> Away from my life, like boats
> Away from the shore.

For although in the last stanza of this poem Amichai acknowledges that his childhood world is irretrievably lost, he remains – despite his maturity – clinging desperately to the 'persons I love,' in the same mood of helplessness and defiance which characterized his behaviour as a child.

'We always write about what we have lost,' Amichai told Antony Rudolf, and there are times when his 'tired man' pose and his Indian summer mood can seem somewhat reflex. But the range of his early poems is rather wider than it at first appears. 'It Was Summer, Or The End Of Summer,' for instance, is as much about 'the world' as about love, and the excellent 'Out Of Three Or Four In A Room' is clearly a public statement, contrasting the 'people who left whole' to go and fight and who are 'brought home in the evening, like small change' with the figure of the poet who, standing at the window, is engaged in a different kind of battle:

> Behind him, the words.
> And in front of him the words, wandering, without luggage.
> Hearts without provision, prophecies without water
> And big stones put there
> And staying, closed, like letters
> With no addresses; and no one to receive them.

Amichai is clearly conscious here, having fought in four wars, of the difference between art and action, and he is no more confident than Paul Celan that his words will actually reach his neighbour. But his images – which are almost always familiar, domestic and mundane – indicate a hope that there will be someone to receive them. Although he is more immediately attractive in his private poems, he can be very impressive (as 'My Parents' Migration' and 'National Thoughts' show) in the more public mode. These two poems are organized around his favourite habitual images, which accumulate meanings and become clearer when placed beside their counterparts in the more personal poems.

The best of the *Songs Of Jerusalem And Myself* (the second collection of Amichai to be translated into English) confirm the accuracy of the insight offered in the second of the 'Songs To Myself':

The world and I have eyes in common:
I look with them into it, it looks with them into me.

This is essentially written with what another poem calls 'all the severity of compassion.' A severe compassion is the hallmark of all Amichai's poetry. It is evident in love poems ('We Did It', 'During Our Love Houses Were Completed') in sequences that are at once public and private (the Buenos Aires and Achziv poems), and in poems which, like 'Jerusalem 1967', show Amichai addressing himself to the tragic dramas contingent upon the Jews being restored to the holy land of Israel. In the poem 'Darwin's Theory' (which postulates a quite different kind of survival from Darwin's natural selection), Amichai blends his two modes:

to remember my son and Jerusalem is . . .
The same pain. The same peace.

There is, however, more pain than peace in this collection, even when Amichai is exhorting either his child or his city to take refuge in sleep, and writing lullabies for them. There are wry poems which, like 'I've Been Invited To Life,' temporarily keep the pain at bay. And there is a great moment in 'My Father, My King' when the poet prays that

>   all things
> I do against my will
> [May] seem by my will. And my will
> like flowers.

But the love poems are without exception sad, the 'uselessness of returning' of which one poem speaks categorically confirmed by another which states finally: 'We did not return.' Life for Amichai remains an irreversible journey, 'a constant departure from houses'. Even the simple 'Poem On The Renovation Of My House' forces the poet to recognize that it is his biography, as well as his house, which has been altered. The images of communication which are so prevalent in these poems – there are repeated references to words, to what has been written, and frequent quotations in direct speech (a very marked feature of the 'English' collections) – are almost always accompanied by reminders that to create (whether in words or stones) is to be part of an inexorable process of decay and destruction. 'I gave you a watch instead of/A wedding ring' Amichai writes in 'Just As It Was'; it is the erosion of time that rivets his attention. His remarks on his loved one's gift to him are equally devastating, the image one of sudden earthquake rather than gradual erosion:

> You gave me a letter opener of silver:
> Letters like this aren't opened like that. They're
> torn open, torn open.

('Love Gifts')

Amichai is on record as saying that he considers English 'a much richer language' than the 'tired language/Torn from its sleep in the Bible' which he has until recently used as his primary medium of expression. Yet the fact that, in a recent interview, he aligns himself with Cavafy, Seferis and Montale would not encourage us to look for anything other than 'counter-eloquence' in the 'English' collections *Amen* and *Time*. Even so, both volumes actually seem more impoverished than those which preceded them, a little like Ingmar Bergman's periodic excursions into English. Love and war have remained Amichai's preferred zone of investigation, but neither is mapped with quite the precision or the ingenuity or the attention to formal properties that are manifest in the poems he had previously allowed others to translate. Isolated images, like the snake of 'Once A Great Love' and the leprosy of 'A Majestic Love Song' (both from *Amen*) retain the power to surprise and to focus the emotion. But Amichai is elsewhere, like other prolific poets, too garrulous and diffuse to rivet the reader's attention:

Sometimes I love water, sometimes stone.
These days I'm more in favour of stones.
But this might change.

('Patriotic Songs', xxxiii)

Amichai's hunger for life has increasingly tended to be confined to 'the generation machine ... still sweet/between my thighs' ('To Speak About Change Was To Speak About Love'). This has made 'the loneliness of the body' not only inevitable but predictable. Alongside this, the propositional strain:

To remember is a kind of hope.

The desert is a mirror for those looking at it.

seems to be surfacing more frequently, or to be less protected by ironies than in his previous writing. Perhaps he is tending to overcompensate for the unavoidably arid stretches in what he calls his 'dry weeping.' There is, symptomatically perhaps, a poem in Amichai's first translated collection which suggests that the 'intricate network' of imagery is something that he could do without; in *Amen* and *Time* the intricacy of his early image patterns has certainly been replaced by a more skeletal utterance in which it is the single item which is the vehicle of meaning – the house, the harbour, the beach, the loved one's face, the dream and, as so often, the written word. It would be premature to speak of a decline in the career of a poet whose best work will withstand comparison with much more famous names. But it may be that Amichai has yet to find the flexibility that other poets of self-imposed limitation have been forced to seek, that 'skill in the varying of the serenade' which, as Wallace Stevens knew, is the precondition for 'all manner of favours' to be extended to the poet.

Zbigniew Herbert (born 1924)

Born in Lvov; fought in the underground resistance against the Nazis during the Second World War, when he began to write poetry. Studied at the Academy of Fine Arts in Krakow from 1944 to 1945, and in 1947 received a Master's degree in economics from the Krakow Academy of Commerce. Studied Law at Torun university; awarded the degree of Master of Law in 1950. Studied philology at Torun. Lived briefly in Gdansk before moving to Warsaw, where he occupied a number of clerical posts. First visited Western Europe in the 1950s, spending time in France, England, Italy and Greece. Poet in Residence at the Free University in West Berlin from 1965 to 1969; taught at the City College of Los Angeles in 1970–71, after which he returned to Poland.

Much of the best poetry of the present century has originated in traumatic personal experience. But the poetry of modern Poland has inevitably stemmed from traumatic experience of a more collective kind. Poland, reunited in 1918 after over a hundred years of partition, survived only some twenty years before being invaded by the Nazis and, after sufferings second only to those of the Soviet Union during the Second World War, found its borders shifted several hundred miles westwards by a superior power at once its liberator and new oppressor. It is from this 'Poland' that three important poets have emerged and been accepted in the West as major voices: Czeslaw Milosz (an *émigré* since 1951, a distinguished prose writer, and the most recent recipient of the Nobel Prize), Tadeusz Rozewicz, and Zbigniew Herbert. Herbert, the most extensively translated and perhaps the finest of the three, was first published in Poland in the years of 'thaw' which followed the death of Stalin and has since come to be thought of in many quarters as the leading European poet of his generation. Since Polish is one of the 'minor' European languages, this is not a judgement that can be authoritatively tested out by many readers, who are obliged to take on trust the assurance that the structures and even the tone of his poetry will withstand translation. Yet Herbert makes so deep an impression that one is content to do so, even after pondering the implications of the 'awkward bumble bee' who figures in his poem 'On Translating Poetry'.

Herbert's voice, 'casual and whispering' as Milosz describes it, seems perfectly attuned to the fate of a country that has suffered tragic upheaval; it is too austere to be considered hopeful, too compassionate to be considered nihilistic. 'It is nihilism which menaces culture the most,' Herbert has written, deeply distressed by the apparent absence of values in the contemporary world. The Romantic or individualistic varieties of nihilism seem to him a particular menace: 'Beyond the poet's ego there extends a different, obscure but real world. One should not cease to believe that we can grasp this world in language and do justice to it.' Herbert is inevitably, therefore, 'classicist' in orientation, turning to history 'not for lessons in hope but to confront my experience with the experience of others'. In this way he hopes 'To win for myself ... a sense of responsibility for the state of the human conscience.' In accordance with this classicist stance he rejects a merely 'verbal art' and at times approaches the condition of anti-poetry as practised by Rozewicz. But it is precisely because he employs verbal art as a means of gaining access to the truth that he is never merely utilitarian. There is a prose poem of his the title of which – 'Ornamental Yet True' – seems to describe his *oeuvre* as a whole. It is the manner in which he makes ornament subservient to truth that marks Herbert out as a representative figure of a powerful strain in post-war European poetry.

Despite his suspicion of his own medium, and at the same

time because of it, Herbert frequently writes poems about poetry. But because his eye remains fixed on a reality outside the ego, he writes something quite unlike the 'meta-poetry' of some of his Western counterparts. In 'A Tale', for example, which is at once a critique and an affirmation of the necessity of art, Herbert concludes:

what would the world be
were it not filled with
the incessant bustling of the poet
among the birds and stones

And in a similarly bifocal poem, 'Why The Classics', he ends by disclosing the consequences of not addressing oneself to the world outside the self:

if art for its subject
will have a broken jar
a small broken soul
with a great self-pity

what will remain after us
will be like lovers' weeping
in a small dirty hotel
when wall-paper dawns

In the poem 'I Would Like To Describe' Herbert openly attacks the Romantic sundering of subject and object; his desire to 'give all metaphors/in return for one word/drawn out of my breast like a rib' seems here at once both partially fulfilled and partially unfulfillable. In the absence of such a word, as 'Voice' makes clear, the dumb world and the deaf poet can only:

go blindly on
towards new horizons
towards contracted throats
from which rises
an unintelligible gurgle

In 'Inner Voice' this 'unintelligible gurgle' is located within the poet's conscience and mocks his failure to engage with it. And something similar occurs in 'Revelation', where the contemplative poet is forced to turn from thoughts of essences by the postman ringing his doorbell; having banished the 'perfect peace' which the poet has been laboriously constructing, this occurrence forces him to fix his eyes upon the real 'heart of things'. The heart of things for Herbert is neither perfect nor peaceful; nor, therefore, as the poem 'Attempt At A Description' suggests, can the poem be:

only blood
busy with scansion of dark tautologies
binds together distant shores
with a thread of mutual agreement

This is why he views the senseless shedding of blood with utter horror, and why in 'Classic' he reminds his audience that the poet is not, however classical he may be, simply someone who reads inscriptions on stones:

the marble veins in the Baths of Diocletian are
the blood vessels of slaves which have burst in the quarries

Herbert confronts his own fondness for stones (as reflected in poems like 'Pebble' and 'White Stone') in 'Sense Of Identity', where he experiences 'a feeling of profound unity' with stone, but is careful to point out that 'it wasn't at all the idea of invariability' which made the stone attractive. His recurrent studies of objects in no way betoken a heart of stone. For although he knows that it is 'impossible to lay foundations for the psychology of a stone ball, of an iron bar, of a wooden cube', these objects are nevertheless continually telling him something about the psychology of humanity. Herbert may try to look at the world with the 'calm and clear eye' of one of his pebbles; but the world he has grown up in is neither calm nor clear. The poet therefore occupies, as the prose poem 'Violins' shows, an intermediate position between extremes of subjectivity and objectivity; his perspective is inevitably a humanizing one. Herbert's violins are not the instruments of the famous Romantic concertos; instead they bear all the hallmarks of an inhabitant of the ghetto and the concentration camp:

Violins are naked. They have thin arms. Clumsily they try to
protect themselves with them. They cry from shame and cold.
That's why. And not, as the music critics maintain, so it will be
more beautiful. This is not true.

It is Herbert's need to establish a perspective, bred of
conditions in which all perspective seems to have been lost,
that makes meaningful the act of producing an artistic object
like a poem. But the horizon, or vanishing-point, is always the
inescapable human fact of death. In 'Study Of The Object'
Herbert obeys all the prescriptions of the Cubist aesthetic (in-
cluding Apollinaire's ideas on order and adventure). But he
gives his object – a humble domestic chair – a human and
tragic dimension which is quite unique:

let it have the face of the last things

we ask reveal O chair
the depths of the inner eye
the iris of necessity
the pupil of death

This is an attitude clearly forced upon the poet by a world in
which human flesh has been used to make lampshades, as
the prose poem 'Armchair' obliquely suggests:

Who ever thought a warm neck would become an armrest,
or legs eager for flight and joy could stiffen into
four simple stilts? . . . The despair of armchairs is
revealed in their creaking.

This kind of perspective, which violates neither the reality
of the object nor the reality of the subject, is not some-
thing which Herbert prides himself on possessing. And his
attacks on those who lack it is always oblique. The chorus
who are watching 'The Sacrifice of Iphigenia' find the view
'superb, with the help of the proper perspective'; the gods
who have a new political policy to implement are concerned
only with whether Hermes's act of self-destruction is a good
or bad omen ('Attempt To Dissolve Mythology'). Herbert
uses classical and mythological figures to gain a purchase
upon the contemporary world, dissolving mythology by

rewriting it. This is what makes 'Apollo And Marsyas' such a compelling portrait of the choices available to the modern poet, and why the revised 'History Of The Minotaur' is as acute as any of the better-known parables of Kafka. Herbert's *personae* are always, like Cavafy's, recognizably human. In 'Hermes, Dog and Star', for example, the god Hermes, craving human companions, is taught a wisdom greater than his own by a dog and a star; but he ends up thinking that 'if he sets out to find friends another time he won't be so frank'. Similarly, in 'The Return Of The Proconsul', the speaker's hope that 'things will work out somehow' in the Rome of the Caesars is plainly an absurd one, given the political corruption and disguises which the rest of the poem describes. But the hope is not belittled; it remains real, however much Herbert may have given a 'nudge to the balance' (like the painters he speaks of in the third of his 'Three Studies On The Subject Of Realism'). The very fine 'Elegy Of Fortinbras' is perhaps the best index of Herbert's habitual position; here he takes on the personality of those who inhabit the mundane world, belittling ('The rest is not silence but belongs to me') and yet bereft ('what I shall leave will not be worth a tragedy'). 'Nothing is more ordinary than the dreams of Emperors,' Herbert writes sardonically in a prose poem. But elsewhere he shows that we all, himself included, habitually act as if it were otherwise:

When [the emperor] died, nobody dared to remove his portraits.
Take a look, perhaps still you have his mask at home.

Herbert writes out of an awareness that the barbarian is always a potential custodian of the citadel of the human heart, that he is always at the gates: his book of essays is significantly titled *The Barbarian In The Garden*. The barbarian is especially difficult to resist when, like the Stoic moralist and suicide Seneca of the poem 'Maturity', he poses as a man of culture. Culture remains an ideal, however, difficult as it may be to achieve:

Is it truly impossible to have at the same time
the source and the hill the idea and the leaf

and to pour multiplicity without devils' ovens
of dark alchemy of too clear an abstraction

The man of culture cannot expect love, for 'nobody loves moralists'. Yet he cannot really be a moralist, for 'slowly the water fills/the shapes of feet which have vanished' ('Episode'). This does not leave him without resources: he can proclaim a mystery (as in 'Rosy Ear') without being mysterious about it; he can even provide 'Practical Recommendations In The Event Of A Catastrophe' so absurdly pragmatic that they may prevent the need to implement them. The man of culture is often close to despair because 'That which struggles for light is mortally fragile' ('Dawn'); but he continues to struggle. Like his own Mr Cogito, one of the great personae of modern poetry (though by no means always to be trusted), Herbert 'accepts an inferior role' to that of the policy makers and is content not to 'inhabit history'.

And yet the poet inhabits history in a more fundamental way. Herbert seems to have realized at the age of ten (if we read the prose poem 'Conch' autobiographically) that 'even if we love someone very much, at times it happens that we forget about it'. He has tried ever since to remember. This is why his very early poem 'Two Drops' opposes 'the fragile power of love' to the cruelty of the bombs that threaten it. Without having written anything resembling what we ordinarily think of as a love poem, Herbert has written out of a love for people and objects. Brotherhood, especially the brotherhood which (as in 'Rain') survives death, is what moves him to utterance. This is why he is the most accomplished living writer in 'the language of history'. Yet only occasionally does Herbert speak with the public voice that speaks for all, as in the conclusion to 'Prologue':

The ditch where a muddy river flows
I call the Vistula. It is hard to confess:
they have sentenced us to such love
they have pierced us through with such a fatherland.

Elsewhere Herbert does indeed find it 'hard to confess', seeking instead the more limited company of those who will puzzle out his meaning and get beyond his irony. Insofar as this is a kind of 'inner emigration' (like that practised by some of his Western and Eastern counterparts), it is not always easy to do this. The last lines of 'Parable Of The Russian Emigrés', a relatively straightforward poem up to this point, suddenly take on all kinds of unexpected facets, not the least of which is that the speaker who is counselling him not to emigrate has the same name as the last of the Romanov Tsars:

This parable is told by Nicholas
who understands historical necessities
in order to terrify me i.e. to convince me.

Certainly it has seemed necessary to Herbert, despite six years abroad and frequent trips to the West, to remain in Poland, although his native city (because of what some would call 'historical necessities') is now part of the Soviet Union. Perhaps this is what has forced him to keep his voice 'casual and whispering'. Yet he has tried to demonstrate that, even if 'heaven is talking some foreign tongue' and the 'fragile human land' is continually threatened by 'terror' (as in 'To Marcus Aurelius'), there are still poets trying to understand the former and to stiffen our resistance to the latter.

Joseph Brodsky (born 1940)

Born in Leningrad of Russian Jewish parents. Left school at the age of fifteen; outraged by the Soviet brutalities in Hungary and Poland in 1956. Began to study Polish, in which he was fluent by 1958, the year in which he began to write poetry. Worked as a translator. A friend of Anna Akhmatova's from 1961 onwards. Arrested in December 1963 for 'social parasitism' and sentenced to five years exile. In a labour camp in the vicinity of Archangel for twenty-one months, during which time he taught himself English by reading the poetry of Eliot, Yeats, Auden, Dylan Thomas and Wallace Stevens. Became known in the West by virtue of the fact that he was a dissident writer who had been brought to trial. Returned to Leningrad in November 1965; continually harassed thereafter and prevented from accepting invitations to poetry readings abroad. Chose exile in June 1972. After brief stays in Vienna and London became Poet in Residence at the University of Michigan. Later taught at Columbia University and at New York University. Awarded the honorary degree of Doctor of Letters by Yale University in 1978; principal guest at the Cambridge Poetry Festival in 1979. Now writes with equal facility in Russian and English.

Although 'discovered' after Yevtushenko and Voznesensky had already made an impact in the West, Brodsky is the first post-war Russian poet to have successfully survived comparison with the exceptionally brilliant generation of poets born before the Revolution. Like them, he has proved unacceptable to a repressive régime; in 1964, after a show trial in which he was accused of being a 'parasite' and a 'cosmopolitan', he was sentenced to five years in a labour camp. Released after twenty months, Brodsky continued to be harassed until 1972, when he was 'invited' to leave the Soviet Union. After brief sojourns in Vienna and London, Brodsky took up a post as Poet-In-Residence at the University of Michigan, and has since occupied similar positions in other distinguished American colleges. Unlike those poets and writers who left Russia for Western Europe after the Revolution, Brodsky has found a fame and fortune commensurate with his abilities. But although the USA has proved a more secure second home than the Paris, Berlin and Prague of the first *émigré* generation, Brodsky's poems remain a testimonial to the anguish of permanent exile from one's native country and from those who speak one's native language. Although he has now reached a level of competence in English which enables him to translate himself without undue difficulty, Brodsky at present prefers to 'oversee' the efforts of others, and thus to maintain at least one link with his origins.

As a Jew born in the most European of Russian cities (Leningrad), Brodsky's sense of dislocation would have to have been extremely acute even without the experience of imprisonment and exile; but poetry has offered him an arena in which such dislocations may be overcome. Brodsky conceives of poetry as a heroic deed analogous to those performed in classical mythology by such figures as Hercules, in which the poem transcends the poet's personal grief and, by being raised to the 'metaphysical level', becomes 'a linguistic event'. Art for art's sake is therefore anathema to him; but art for politics' sake (represented for him by the poetry of Neruda and Mayakovsky) is no less unacceptable. Brodsky's preference is for writers who bring 'a new spiritual idea into the world': Dostoevsky and the Pasternak of the *Zhivago* poems; Kierkegaard, Pascal and Shestov, and a host of other 'quiet voices' (as he calls them) in world literature – Cavafy, Horace, the Polish poet Cyprian Norwid, and the English and American poets through whom (with the help of a dictionary) he taught himself English. Brodsky's acquaintance with

poetry written in English is more extensive than that of most
other European poets of comparable stature, and he has
written powerful elegies either in memory of beloved figures
(W. H. Auden and Robert Lowell), or in imitation of par-
ticular poems (Byron's 'Stanzas To Augusta', Wallace
Stevens's 'To An Old Philosopher In Rome'), or both –
notably the 'Verses On The Death Of T. S. Eliot' which bor-
row their form and structure from Auden's 'In Memory Of
W. B. Yeats'. Brodsky has also made brilliant translations of
Donne and the Metaphysical poets, concerned as he is (like
Eliot) with the dangers of a 'dissociation of sensibility'. But
an even more fundamental influence on him has been the
Bible, in particular the Old Testament writings which speak
of a covenant between God and man; quotations from the
Bible are very common in Brodsky's poems. The words of the
scriptures give an extra edge to his abiding sense of separa-
tion; 'separation,' he has said, 'is no longer a matter of human
choice; it is determined by history and geography'. Yet the
act of writing offers him at least the possibility of a covenant,
the chance that prayer will not remain unanswered for ever.
If all life is repetition (in the special sense given to the word
by Kierkegaard), an original covenant may be reconsti-
tuted, and order may triumph over disorder. Even if life is a
matter of permanent separation – of man from God and of
man from man (or, as frequently in Brodsky, woman) – the
apparently absurd act of writing betokens the persistence of
faith.

The best of Brodsky's early poems show him at the
beginning of a quest which is still in progress. 'Memories' –
he has remained very much a poet of memory and memorial-
ization – raises the question of whether the business of
'rhyming dactyls' can really be a source of spiritual sus-
tenance; 'The Jewish Cemetery Near Leningrad' stresses the
survival of idealism in an 'inescapably materialist world'; an
untitled poem of 1960 studies the distance between 'deeds of
domestic handicraft' (of which poetry is, for Brodsky, plainly
one) and the passage of the soul into eternal life. But none
of these short poems have the power of 'The Great Elegy For

John Donne', which deals with all these subjects at once. By the end of the elegy, when the whole material world has fallen asleep and only the poet's soul is left alive, Brodsky has achieved the 'metaphysical' level which he regards as crucial to a poem's success. Conscious of separation:

For though our life may be a thing to share,
who is there in this world to share our death?

he nevertheless finds something in which to believe:

Only the far sky,
in darkness, brings the healing needle home.

The falling snow joins body to soul and earth to heaven; in this respect it is a 'healing needle' of a kind. But, as if in confirmation of Brodsky's claim that 'the poem is an instrument of survival', it is clear that the act of writing a poem is also a kind of 'healing needle'.

Brodsky's experiences in the labour camp inevitably concentrated his attention on survival. But even under such conditions he did not give way to despair. His 'inner life' (as he calls it in 'Autumn In Norenskaya') attached itself to whatever crumbs of comfort it could find – the constellation of Pisces ('Sadly And Tenderly'), the flying cranes ('Spring Season Of Muddy Roads'), a hibernating moth ('Evening'). His sense of loss is visibly at its most exacerbated in the poems addressed to a beloved woman ('M.B.'), of which 'New Stanzas To Augusta' is one of the most impressive. With only the freedoms of the imagination left him, Brodsky in his poem 'A Prophecy' envisages a future domestic bliss which will acknowledge the harsh realities that he, and those like him, have had to confront:

And if
we make a child, we'll call the boy Andrei,
Anna the girl, so that our Russian speech,
imprinted on its wrinkled little face,
shall never be forgot. Our alphabet's
first sound is but the lengthening of a sigh
and thus may be affirmed for future time.

The Tolstoyan allusions here are much more than an aesthete's recourse to literature as an agent of continuity; the whole stance is an index of what Brodsky calls the *homo cultus*, whom he sees as the saviour of *homo sapiens*. In his 'Christmas Poem', Brodsky demonstrates this by linking the dying Prince Andrei of *War And Peace* to the birth of the Christ-child. Knowing it to be 'too late for miracles', he nevertheless raises his eyes heavenwards and celebrates the fact that he has been given the gift of life. The Eliot elegy, written whilst still under detention, makes it clear that even death cannot diminish such a gift, its mood reminiscent of the speaker in Eliot's 'Journey Of The Magi' (a favourite poem of Brodsky's) who says: 'I should be glad of another death'.

On returning to Leningrad, as 'A Halt In The Desert' demonstrates, Brodsky found the animals to be more aware of the possibility of a covenant than the human beings; 'it is difficult in Russia,' Brodsky has said, 'to know who is a human being.' Human beings remained his principal concern, however, and especially the woman or women he was in love with. As if continually aware of the fact that to cross the desert would involve going beyond the Russian frontier, Brodsky's mood became noticeably more elegiac, the poems a prolonged gesture of leavetaking, as 'Stanzas', 'Adieu, Mademoiselle Véronique' and 'On Washerwoman Bridge' are not alone in showing. But the title of one of them – 'Almost An Elegy' – is a reminder that these are really valedictions which, like Donne's famous poem, forbid mourning. Certainly they make lamentation seem a secondary matter to telling the truth. Refusing to dwell on his personal woes, Brodsky concerns himself with being faithful to details (like Pasternak before him) and hence impersonal (like Eliot before him):

It seems that what art strives for is to be
precise and not tell us lies, because
its fundamental law undoubtedly
asserts the independence of details.

('The Candlestick')

'Aeneas And Dido' is one of many poems of great precision which Brodsky wrote at this time, with the familiar story given much of the tragic finality of Virgil's famous account. But two other 'classical' poems – 'To Lycomedes On Scyros' and 'Odysseus To Telemachus' (both epistolary poems, like the later 'Letters To A Roman Friend' and 'Letters From The Ming Dynasty') – are even more powerful. Behind the Theseus and Ulysses *personae* in these poems we can see Brodsky squarely facing the fact that from now on he can only be a wanderer on the face of the earth, as solitary as his Biblical predecessor the Wandering Jew. 'To stretch the time/ of our connectedness' will be possible only if he can 'eclipse the world' ('Postscriptum'). Prior to his departure Brodsky endeavoured to do this through the medium of his imagination, especially that reason-ridden aspect of it which had attracted him to Donne; the fantastic realism of 'A Song To No Music' is the inevitable result of the competing strains in his sensibility. But it is his less elaborate poems on the realities of disconnectedness – 'A Second Christmas', 'On Love' and 'Six Years Later' – which show Brodsky at his most controlled and moving.

The poems which Brodsky has written since leaving Russia suggest that the idea of eclipsing the world has itself suffered eclipse. Some lines in the long 'Lullaby Of Cape Cod' are particularly desolate:

> Having sampled two
> oceans as well as continents, I feel that I know
> what the globe itself must feel: there's nowhere to go.

This insight, and the stark manner in which it is expressed, derive from a sharpened sense of loneliness; as Brodsky says elsewhere in the poem, 'Being itself the essence of all things, solitude teaches essentials'. Even here, however, Brodsky is wavering, like the Eliot of *Ash Wednesday*, between the profit and the loss:

> All that I could have lost has been totally
> lost. But also I've gained approximately

all those things I was in for.

('1972')

Despite there being 'nowhere to go', Brodsky has gone far afield. And he has tended to place himself, when he halts in the desert, in the vicinity of water: at Cape Cod, 'In The Lake District' of Michigan, by 'The Thames At Chelsea'. The most recent of his very fine Venice poems ('San Pietro') explains why:

Only water, and it alone,
everywhere and always stays true to itself.

In striving to emulate this fundamental element, Brodsky has created a new kind of utterance, at once as substantial and as ephemeral as water. The magnificent 'Butterfly' poem, which is addressed to precisely this paradox, contains a descriptive term for it: 'silent speech'. In Brodsky's silent speech the accents of the human voice remain as recognizable and distinct as in the 'quiet voices' that Brodsky admires so much, although they can be strangely muffled at times and are sometimes in danger of disappearing, like the object at the end of 'San Pietro':

A tin can launched skyward
by the tip of a shoe goes sailing
out of sight, and a minute later
there is still no sound of it falling on
wet sand. Or, for that matter, a splash.

Brodsky's voice is at its quietest in the autobiographical sequence which provides the title for his latest volume ('A Part Of Speech'); perhaps he is remembering Cyprian Norwid's claim that silence is as much a part of speech as any noun or verb. But in his own translation of this sequence Brodsky has chosen to emphasize the act of speech more strongly than in the Russian original:

What gets left of a man amounts
to a part. To a spoken part. To a part of speech.

No one who has heard Brodsky read his own poems can be

left in any doubt of his conviction that a residue of 'connected-ness' survives even the severest losses; 'to speak humanly', as Brodsky must have read in Wallace Stevens, 'that is acutest speech'.

Any judgement of Brodsky must perforce be an interim one, for he is still only forty years of age, and his poetry has been more praised than paraphrased. His genius has enabled him to write, with apparently equal facility, both very short and very long poems, and in all forms: sonnets, elegies, epistles, love poems, 'occasional' poems of travel, *divertisse-ments*. Like other poets who have pondered the problem of 'tradition and the individual talent' he can be rebarbatively difficult. But the 'wan flat voice' of his most recent poems has a purity that some of his earlier exercises in fantastic realism lacked. Even at his most garrulous, Brodsky seems to possess the elemental force of a poet like Donne, another master of the speaking voice. He has almost certainly written too much, and will want in time to prune his *oeuvre* of what is expend-able. But even what is expendable is a reminder of how important the fact and act of writing are to him. It is sympto-matic of Brodsky's ideas on the centrality of writing that he should consider Beckett's *Malone Dies* 'the greatest book ever written'; an absurd heroism is at the heart of his own en-deavours also. In a desolate recent poem ('Strophes') Brodsky ends with a 'nothing' reminiscent of Malone's final words. But it is inconceivable that this very prolific poet will not continue to act like the 'new Dante' at the end of a poem written before leaving Russia, who 'bends to the empty page and writes a word', trusting that – despite exile – a kind of covenant can be repeatedly confirmed.

Bibliographies

These bibliographies are restricted, except in a very few cases, to books published in England or America; I have supposed that those who wish to consult the poems as written in the original languages will do their own research. The word 'Collections' therefore designates not the individual volumes of the poet as originally published (except in a few self-evident cases which are usually bilingual editions), but rather *selections* made either by the editor or by the translator or, in some cases, by the poets themselves. The standard bibliographical practice of listing a poet's volumes in their order of appearance cannot therefore be applied in most cases, although I have tried to suggest an optimum order, as close as possible to the real order in which the poetry appeared, in which each poet's work might be approached. Secondary literature is listed in alphabetical order, except in the case of the first three sections where I have applied a chronological criterion.

GENERAL WORKS OF REFERENCE

Horatio Smith (ed.), *Dictionary of Modern European Literature*, Columbia UP, 1947.
Geoffrey Grigson (ed.), *Concise Encylopaedia of Modern World Literature*, Hutchinson, 1963.
Richard Ellmann and Charles Feidelson, Jr (eds.), *The Modern Tradition: backgrounds of modern literature*, Oxford UP, 1965.
Anthony Thorlby (ed.), *Companion to Literature, vol. 2: European*, Penguin, 1969.
Martin Seymour-Smith, *Guide to Modern World Literature*, Wolfe, 1973.
Alex Preminger (ed.), *Encyclopaedia of Poetry and Poetics*, Princeton UP, 1974.
Malcolm Bradbury and James McFarlane (eds.), *Modernism 1890–1930*, Penguin, 1976.

J.-A. Bede and William B. Edgerton (eds.), *Dictionary of Modern European Literature*, Second edition, Columbia UP, 1980.

GENERAL CRITICAL WORKS

J. M. Cohen, *Poetry of This Age 1908–58*, Arrow Books, 1959.
Michael Hamburger, *The Truth of Poetry: tensions in modern poetry from Baudelaire to the 1960s*, Penguin, 1972.
Hugo Friedrich, *The Structure of Modern Poetry: from the mid-nineteenth century to the mid-twentieth century*, Northwestern UP, 1974.
Octavio Paz, *Children of the Mire: modern poetry from Romanticism to the Avant-Garde*, Harvard UP, 1974.

ANTHOLOGIES

General:
Stanley Burnshaw (ed.), *The Poem Itself*, Penguin, 1964.
Willis Barnstone (ed.), *Modern European Poetry*, Bantam, 1966.
Michael Benedikt (ed.), *The Prose Poem*, Dell, 1976.
Robert Lowell, *Imitations*, Faber and Faber, 1962.
W. S. Merwin, *Selected Translations 1948–68*, Athenaeum, 1968.
Edwin Morgan, *Rites of Passage: selected translations*, Carcanet, 1976.

By country:
Anthony Hartley (ed.), *The Penguin Book of French Verse, vol. 3; the nineteenth century*, 1957; plain prose trs.
Anthony Hartley (ed.), *The Penguin Book of French Verse, vol. 4: the twentieth century*, 1959; plain prose trs.
Angel Flores (ed.), *An Anthology of French Poetry from Nerval to Valéry*, Anchor, 1958.
Leonard Forster (ed.), *The Penguin Book of German Verse*, 1957; plain prose trs.
Angel Flores (ed.), *An Anthology of German Poetry from Hölderlin to Rilke*, Anchor, 1960.
Patrick Bridgwater (ed.), *Twentieth Century German Verse*, Penguin, 1963; plain prose trs.
Babette Deutsch and Avrahm Yarmolinsky (eds.), *Contemporary German Poetry*, John Lane, 1923.
Michael Hamburger (ed.), *East German Poetry*, Carcanet, 1972. (bilingual).
Michael Hamburger (ed.), *German Poetry 1910–75*, Carcanet, 1975 (bilingual).

George Kay (ed.), *The Penguin Book of Italian Verse*, 1958; plain prose trs.

Vittoria Bradshaw (ed.), *From Pure Silence to Impure Dialogue: a survey of post-war Italian poetry*, Las Americas, 1971 (bilingual).

J. M. Cohen (ed.), *The Penguin Book of Spanish Verse*, 1956; plain prose trs.

Angel Flores (ed.), *An Anthology of Spanish Poetry from Garcilaso to García Lorca*, Anchor, 1961 (bilingual).

Dimitri Obolensky (ed.), *The Penguin Book of Russian Verse*, 1962; plain prose trs.

Jack Lindsay (ed.), *Russian Poetry 1917–55*, Bodley Head, 1956.

Vladimir Markov and Merrill Sparks (eds.), *Modern Russian Poetry*, MacGibbon and Kee, 1966 (bilingual).

Olga Carlisle (ed.), *Poets on Street Corners: portraits of fifteen Russian poets*, Random House, 1968 (bilingual).

George Reavey (ed.), *The New Russian Poets 1955–65*, Calder and Boyars, 1968 (bilingual).

Daniel Weissbort (ed.), *Post-War Russian Poetry*, Penguin, 1974.

Carl Proffer (ed.), *Modern Russian Poets on Poetry*, Ardis, 1976.

The Poets

Charles Baudelaire

Collections:

Poems, Penguin, 1961; plain prose trs. Francis Scarfe.

Flowers of Evil, New Directions, 1962; trs. Jackson and Marthiel Mathews (bilingual).

Selected Poems, Penguin, 1975; tr. Joanna Richardson (bilingual).

Paris Spleen, tr. Louise Varèse, New Directions, 1970.

Prose:

The Mirror of Art, Phaidon, 1955; tr. Jonathan Mayne.

The Painter of Modern Life and other essays, Phaidon, 1964; tr. Jonathan Mayne.

Art In Paris 1845–62, Phaidon, 1965; tr. Jonathan Mayne.

Selected Writings on Art and Artists, Penguin, 1972; tr. P. E. Charvet.

Intimate Journals, Panther 1969; tr. Christopher Isherwood.

Biography:

L. B. and F. E. Hyslop (eds.), *Baudelaire: a self-portrait* (selected letters with a commentary), Oxford UP, 1957.

Edwin Morgan, *Flower of Evil*, Sheed and Ward, 1944.
Enid Starkie, *Baudelaire*, Penguin, 1971.

Criticism:

Walter Benjamin, *Charles Baudelaire: a lyric poet in the era of high capitalism*, New Left Books, 1973; tr. Harry Zohn.
Michel Butor, *Histoire Extraordinaire*, Cape, 1969; tr. Richard Howard.
D. J. Mossop, *Baudelaire's Tragic Hero: a study of the architecture of Les Fleurs du Mal*, Oxford UP, 1961.

Stéphane Mallarmé

Collections:

Poems, Penguin, 1965; plain prose trs. Anthony Hartley.
Poems, Penguin, 1977; tr. Keith Bosley (bilingual).

Prose:

Selected Prose Poems, Essays and Letters, John Hopkins, 1956; tr. Bradford Cook.

Biography:

Austin Gill, *The Early Mallarmé*, Oxford UP, 1979.
Cecily Mackworth, 'The young Mallarmé', *English Interludes*, Routledge and Kegan Paul, 1974.

Criticism:

Malcolm Bowie, *Mallarmé and the Art of Being Difficult*, Cambridge UP, 1978.
Gerald L. Bruns, 'Mallarmé: the transcendence of language and the aesthetics of The Book', *Modern Poetry and the Idea of Language*, Yale UP, 1974.
Robert Greer Cohn, *Mallarmé's 'Un Coup de Dès': an exegesis*, Yale UP, 1949.
Robert Greer Cohn, *Toward the Poems of Mallarmé*, California UP, 1980.
Wallace Fowlie, *Mallarmé*, Chicago UP, 1953.
Judy Kravis, *The Prose of Mallarmé: the evolution of a literary language*, Cambridge UP, 1976.
Paul Valéry, 'On Mallarmé', *Selected Writings*, New Directions, 1950.

Paul Verlaine

Collections:
Selected Poems, Penguin, 1974; tr. Joanna Richardson (bilingual).
Women/Men, Anvil Press, 1979; tr. Alistair Elliot (bilingual).

Biography:
Joanna Richardson, *Paul Verlaine*, Weidenfeld and Nicolson, 1971.

Criticism:
C. D. Chadwick, *Verlaine*, Athlone Press, 1973.
C. D. Chadwick, 'Introduction', *Sagesse*, Athlone Press, 1973.
D. Hillery, 'Introduction', *Romances sans paroles*, Athlone Press, 1976.
Pierre Martino, *Verlaine*, Paris, 1951.
Arthur Symons, 'Paul Verlaine', *The Symbolist Movement in Literature*, Dutton, 1958.
Paul Valéry, 'Villon and Verlaine', *Variety: second series*, Harcourt, Brace, 1938; tr. W. A. Bradley.

Tristan Corbière

Collections:
Les Amours jaunes: a selection, California UP, 1954;
tr. C. F. MacIntyre (bilingual).
The Centenary Corbière: poems and prose, Carcanet, 1974;
tr. Val Warner (bilingual).

Criticism:
Randall Jarrell, 'Tristan Corbière', *Poetry and the Age*, Knopf, 1953.
R. L. Mitchell, *Tristan Corbière*, Twayne, 1980.
Edgell Rickword, 'Tristan Corbière', *Essays and Opinions 1921–31*, Carcanet, 1974.

Arthur Rimbaud

Collections:
Collected Poems, Penguin, 1962; plain prose trs. Oliver Bernard.
Complete Works, Harper and Row, 1976; tr. Paul Schmidt.
A Season In Hell; The Illuminations, Oxford UP, 1973;
tr. Enid Rhodes Peschel (bilingual).

Biography:
Edgell Rickword, *Rimbaud: the boy and the poet*, Heinemann, 1924.
Enid Starkie, *Arthur Rimbaud*, Faber and Faber, 1947.

Criticism:
Yves Bonnefoy, *Rimbaud*, Harper and Row, 1973; tr. Paul Schmidt.
Wallace Fowlie, *Rimbaud*, New Directions, 1946.
Henry Miller, *The Time of the Assassins: a study of Rimbaud*,
New Directions, 1946.

Constantine Cavafy

Collections:
Poems, Chatto and Windus, 1951; tr. John Mavrogordato.
Complete Poems, Harcourt, Brace, 1961; tr. Rae Dalven;
introd. W. H. Auden.
Collected Poems, Chatto and Windus, 1975; trs. Edmund Keeley and
Philip Sherrard (bilingual).

Biography:
Robert Liddell, *Cavafy: a critical biography*, Schocken, 1976.

Criticism:
C. M. Bowra, 'Constantine Cavafy and the Greek Past',
The Creative Experiment, Macmillan, 1949.
Joseph Brodsky, 'On Cavafy's Side', *New York Review of Books*,
February 1977.
Edmund Keeley, *Cavafy's Alexandria*, Harvard UP, 1976.
Patrick Leigh-Fermor, 'The Landmarks of Decline', *Times Literary
Supplement*, October 1977.
Philip Sherrard, 'Constantine Cavafy', *The Marble Threshing-Floor*,
Vallentine, Mitchell, 1956.

Stefan George

Collections:
Poems, Kegan Pual, 1944; trs. Ernst Morwitz and C. N. Valhope
(bilingual).
Works, North Carolina UP, 1949; trs. Ernst Morwitz and
Olga Marx.

Criticism:
Theodor Adorno, 'The George – Hofmannsthal Correspondence
1891–1906', *Prisms*, Neville Spearman, 1967.
E. K. Bennett, *Stefan George*, Bowes and Bowes, 1954.
C. M. Bowra, 'Stefan George', *The Heritage of Symbolism*,
Macmillan, 1943.

Ulrich K. Goldsmith, *Stefan George: a study of his early work*,
Colorado UP, 1959.
Georg Lukács, 'The New Solitude and its Poetry: Stefan George',
Soul and Form, MIT Press, 1974; tr. Anna Bostock.
M. and F. Metzger, *Stefan George*, Twayne, 1975.

Christian Morgenstern

Collections:
Gallows Songs, California UP, 1964; tr. Max Knight (bilingual).
Gallows Songs, Michigan UP, 1967; tr. W. D. Snodgrass and
Lore Segal.
The Daynight Lamp and other poems, Houghton Mifflin, 1973;
tr. Max Knight (bilingual).

Criticism:
Leonard Forster, *Poetry of Significant Nonsense*, Bowes and Bowes,
1962.
Erich P. Hofacker, *Christian Morgenstern*, Twayne, 1978.

Paul Valéry

Collections:
Collected Works, Routledge and Kegan Paul, 1961–75; fifteen
volumes; ed. Jackson Mathews; volume 1, *Poems* and volume 2,
Poems In The Rough (bilingual).
Selected Writings, New Directions, 1950; trs. various hands (bilingual).
Le Cimetière Marin, Edinburgh UP, 1971; tr. and ed. G. D. Martin
(bilingual).

Biography:
Cecily Mackworth, 'Aestheticism and imperialism: Paul Valéry in
London', *English Interludes*, Routledge and Kegan Paul, 1974.

Criticism:
C. M. Bowra, 'Paul Valéry', *The Heritage of Symbolism*, Macmillan,
1943.
W. N. Ince, *The Poetic Theory of Paul Valéry*, Leicester UP, 1961.
James Lawler, *Paul Valéry: the poet as analyst*, California UP, 1974.
Agnes Mackay, *The Universal Self: a study of Paul Valéry*, Routledge
and Kegan Paul, 1961.
Francis Scarfe, *The Art of Paul Valéry*, Heinemann, 1954.
Elizabeth Sewell, *Paul Valéry: the mind in the mirror*, Bowes and
Bowes, 1952.
Alastair W. Thomson, *Valéry*, Oliver and Boyd, 1965.

Hugo von Hofmannsthal

Collections:
Lyrical Poems, Humphrey Milford, 1918; tr. Charles Wharton Stork.
Poems and Verse Plays, Pantheon, 1961; ed. Michael Hamburger;
trs. various hands (bilingual).

Prose:
Selected Prose, Routledge and Kegan Paul, 1952; trs. Mary Hottinger,
James and Tania Stern; introd. Hermann Broch.
Plays and Libretti, Pantheon, 1963; ed. Michael Hamburger;
trs. various hands (bilingual).
'Poetry and Life' and 'Three Short Iniquirties', in *Symbolism: an
anthology*, ed. and tr. T. G. West, Eyre Methuen, 1980.
The Correspondence of Richard Strauss and Hugo von Hofmannsthal,
trs. Hanns Hammelmann and Ewald Osers, Collins, 1961.

Criticism:
Theodor Adorno, 'The George – Hofmannsthal Correspondence
1891–1906', *Prisms*, Neville Spearman, 1967.
Ronald Peacock, 'Hofmannsthal', *The Poet in the Theatre*, Hill and
Wang, 1964.
J. B. Bednall, 'From High Language to Dialect: a study in
Hofmannsthal's change of medium', *Hofmannsthal: studies in
commemoration*, ed. F. Norman, Institute of Germanic Studies,
London University, 1963.
Ernst Robert Curtius, 'To the Memory of Hofmannsthal', *Essays on
European Literature*, Princeton UP, 1973; tr. Michael Kowal.
Hanns Hammelmann, *Hofmannsthal*, Bowes and Bowes, 1965.
Alexander Stillmark, 'The poet and his public: Hofmannsthal's
"ideal auditor"', *London Germanic Studies*, 1, Institute of Germanic
Studies, 1980.

Rainer Maria Rilke

Collections:
Visions of Christ, Colorado UP, 1967; tr. A. Kramer; introd. by
S. Mandel (bilingual).
The Book of Hours, Hogarth Press, 1961; tr. A. L. Peck (bilingual).
Poems, Hogarth Press, 1934; tr. J. B. Leishman.
Requiem and other poems, Hogarth Press, 1949; tr. J. B. Leishman.
New Poems, Hogarth Press, 1979; tr. J. B. Leishman (bilingual).
Poems 1906–26, Hogarth Press, 1978; tr. J. B. Leishman.

The Life of the Virgin Mary, Vision Press, 1971; tr. Stephen Spender (bilingual).
Duino Elegies, Hogarth Press, 1968; trs. J. B. Leishman and Stephen Spender (bilingual).
Sonnets to Orpheus, Hogarth Press, 1936; tr. J. B. Leishman (bilingual).
From the Remains of Count C. W. and other poems, Hogarth Press, 1952; tr. J. B. Leishman (bilingual).

Prose:
Ewald Tragy, Vision Press, 1958; tr. Lola Gruenthal (bilingual).
Stories of God, Sidgwick and Jackson, 1932; tr. William Rose.
The Notebooks of Malte Laurids Brigge, Norton, 1949; tr. M. D. Herter Norton.
Selected Works, Hogarth Press, 1954; tr. G. Craig Houston.
Selected Letters 1902–26, Macmillan, 1946; tr. R. F. C. Hull.
Letters to a Young Poet, Sidgwick and Jackson, 1945; tr. Reginald Snell.
Letters 1892–1910 and 1910–26, Norton, 1972; two volumes; trs. J. B. Greene and M. D. Herter Norton.

Plays:
Nine Plays, Ungar, 1979; trs. Klaus Phillips and John Locke.

Biography:
Nora Wydenbruck, *Rilke: man and poet*, John Lehmann, 1949.

Criticism:
E. M. Butler, *Rilke*, Cambridge UP, 1941.
Timothy J. Case, *Rilke: a centenary essay*, Macmillan, 1976.
Hans Egon Holthusen, *Rilke*, Bowes and Bowes, 1952.
Eudo C. Mason, *Rilke*, Oliver and Boyd, 1963.
Eudo C. Mason, *Rilke, Europe and the English-Speaking World*, Cambridge UP, 1961.
John Sandford, *Landscape and Landscape Imagery in Rainer Maria Rilke*, Institute of Germanic Studies, University of London, 1981.
Frank Wood, *Rainer Maria Rilke: the ring of forms*, Octagon, 1972.

Antonio Machado

Collections:
Eighty Poems, Las Americas, 1959; tr. Willis Barnstone; introd. John Dos Passos; memoir by Juan Ramon Jiménez (bilingual).

Selected Poems, Penguin, 1974; trs. Charles Tomlinson and
Henry Gifford.
Selected Poems, Louisiana State UP, 1978; tr. Betty Jean Craige
(bilingual).

Prose:
*Juan de Mairena: epigrams, maxims, memoranda and memoirs of an
apocryphal professor*, California UP, 1963; ed. and tr. Ben Belitt.

Biography:
Alice Jane McVan, *Antonio Machado*, Hispanic Society of America,
1959; includes a selection of poems.

Criticism:
Carl W. Cobb, *Antonio Machado*, Twayne, 1971.
Norma Louise Hutman, *Machado: a dialogue with time*, New Mexico
UP, 1969.
Howard T. Young, 'Antonio Machado', *The Victorious Expression*,
Wisconsin UP, 1964.

Guillaume Apollinaire

Collections:
Selected Poems, Penguin, 1965; tr. Oliver Bernard.
Alcools, California UP, 1965; tr. Anne Hyde Greet (bilingual).
Calligrammes, California UP, 1980; tr. Anne Hyde Greet (bilingual).
Selected Writings, New Directions, 1971; tr. Roger Shattuck
(bilingual).
Julie or the Rose, Transgravity Press, 1978; trs. C. and G. Tysh
(bilingual).

Prose:
Apollinaire on Art: essays and reviews 1902–18, Thames and Hudson,
1972; ed. Leroy C. Breunig.
The Wandering Jew and other stories, Hart-Davis, 1967; tr. R. I. Hall.
The Poet Assassinated, Holt, Rinehart and Winston, 1968;
tr. Ron Padgett.

Criticism:
Scott Bates, *Guillaume Apollinaire*, Twayne, 1967.
C. M. Bowra, 'Order and Adventure in Guillaume Apollinaire',
The Creative Experiment, Macmillan, 1949.
Margaret Davies, *Apollinaire*, Oliver and Boyd, 1965.
Roger Shattuck, *The Banquet Years: the origins of the avant-garde in
France*, Cape, 1969.

Aleksandr Blok

Collections:
The Twelve and other poems, Eyre and Spottiswoode, 1970;
trs. Jon Stallworthy and Peter France.

Prose:
The Spirit of Music, Lindsay Drummond, 1948; tr. I. Freiman.

Biography:
Avril Pyman, *The Life of Aleksandr Blok*, Oxford UP, 1978, 1980;
two volumes.
Lucy E. Vogel, *Aleksandr Blok: the journey to Italy*, Cornell UP,
1973; includes trs. of the poems and prose sketches on Italy.

Criticism:
C. M. Bowra, 'Alexander Blok', *The Heritage of Symbolism*,
Macmillan, 1943.
Sergei Hackel, *The Poet and the Revolution: Blok's 'The Twelve'*,
Oxford UP, 1975.
Cecil Kisch, *Blok: prophet of revolution*, Weidenfeld and Nicolson,
1960.
F. D. Reeve, *Aleksandr Blok: Between image and idea*, Columbia UP,
1962.

Juan Ramón Jiménez

Collections:
Selected Writings, Farrar, Straus, Giroux, 1957; tr. H. R. Hays
(bilingual).
Three Hundred Poems 1903–53, Texas UP, 1962; tr. Eloise Roach.
Selected Poems, Penguin, 1974; tr. J. B. Trend.

Prose:
Platero and I: an Andalusian elegy, Signet, 1960; tr. William and
Mary Roberts.

Criticism:
Donald Fogelquist, *Juan Ramón Jiménez*, Twayne, 1979.
Paul Olson, *Circle of Paradox: time and essence in the poetry of
Juan Ramón Jiménez*, Johns Hopkins UP, 1967.

Umberto Saba

Collections:
Thirty-one poems, Carcanet, 1980; tr. Felix Stefanile.

Criticism:
Joseph Cary, 'Umberto Saba', *Three Modern Italian Poets: Saba, Ungaretti, Montale*, New York UP, 1969.

Dino Campana

Collections:
Orphic Songs, October House, 1968; tr. I. L. Salomon (bilingual).

Criticism:
Gino Gerola, *Dino Campana*, Florence, 1955.
Frederic J. Jones, 'Dino Campana: un orfico tra i vociani',
La poesia italiana contemporanea, Florence, 1975.
Eugenio Montale, 'Dino Campana', *Selected Essays*, Carcanet, 1978;
tr. G. Singh.

Gottfried Benn

Collections:
Primal Vision: selected writings, Bodley Head, 1961; ed. E. B. Ashton,
trs. various hands (bilingual).
Selected Poems, Oxford UP, 1970; ed. F. W. Wodtke; German text;
introd. and notes in English.

Criticism:
Michael Hamburger, 'Gottfried Benn', *Reason and Energy*,
Weidenfeld and Nicolson, 1970.
J. Ritchie, *Gottfried Benn: the unreconstructed Expressionist*, Wolff, 1972.

Georg Trakl

Collections:
Twenty Poems, Sixties Press, 1961; trs. James Wright and Robert Bly
(bilingual).
Selected Poems, Cape, 1968; ed. Christopher Middleton; trs. various
hands (bilingual).

Criticism:
Timothy J. Casey, *Manshape that shone: an interpretation of Trakl*,
Basil Blackwell, 1964.

Michael Hamburger, 'Georg Trakl', *Reason and Energy*,
Weidenfeld and Nicolson, 1970.
Martin Heidegger, 'Georg Trakl', *Merkur*, 1953.
Theo Hermans, 'Georg Trakl: existential conception and semantic
ambience', *The Structure of Modernist Poetry*, Croom Helm, 1981.

Fernando Pessoa

Collections:
Poems, Carcanet, 1971; four volumes; tr. Jonathan Griffin.
Selected Poems, Edinburgh UP, 1971; tr. Peter Rickard (bilingual).
Sixty Portuguese Poems, Wales UP, 1973; tr. F. E. G. Quintanµha
(bilingual).
Selected Poems, Penguin, 1974; tr. Jonathan Griffin.
There is as yet no selection of Pessoa's prose available in English but
the four volumes of prose published by Atica Editions of Lisbon
contain much material in Pessoa's awkward and sometimes
antiquated English.

Criticism:
Gabriel Josipovici, 'Fernando Pessoa', *The Lessons of Modernism*,
Macmillan, 1979.

Guiseppe Ungaretti

Collections:
Selected Poems, Penguin, 1971; tr. Patrick Creagh.
Selected Poems, Cornell UP, 1975; tr. Allen Mandelbaum (bilingual).

Criticism:
Frederic J. Jones, *Giuseppe Ungaretti: poet and critic*, Edinburgh UP,
1977.

Pierre Reverdy

Collections:
Poems, Unicorn Press, 1971; tr. Anne Hyde Greet (bilingual).
Selected Poems, Cape, 1973; tr. Kenneth Rexroth (bilingual).

Criticism:
Michael Bishop, 'Eyes and Seeing in the poetry of Pierre Reverdy',
Sensibility and Creation: Studies in twentieth-century French poetry,
ed. Roger Cardinal, Croom Helm, 1977.

Robert W. Greene, *The Poetic Theory of Pierre Reverdy*, California UP, 1967.

Robert W. Greene, 'Pierre Reverdy', *Six French Poets of our time*, Princeton UP, 1970.

Theo Hermans, 'Reverdy: the poem as object', *The Structure of Modernist Poetry*, Croom Helm, 1981.

Jean-Pierre Richard, 'Pierre Reverdy', *Onze études sur la poésie moderne*, Paris, 1964.

Antonio Rizzuto, *Style and Theme in Reverdy's 'Les Ardoises du Toit'*, Alabama UP, 1971.

Anna Akhmatova

Collections:
Forty-seven Love Poems, Cape, 1927; tr. Natalia Duddington.
White Flock, Oasis Books, 1978; tr. Geoffrey Thurley (bilingual).
Way of All the Earth, Secker and Warburg, 1979; tr. D. M. Thomas.
Selected Poems, Penguin, 1969; tr. Richard McKane.
Selected Poems, Collins-Harvill, 1974; trs. Stanley Kunitz and Max Hayward (bilingual).
Selected Poems, Ardis, 1976; ed. Walter Arndt.
Requiem and Poem without a Hero, Paul Elek, 1976; tr. D. M. Thomas.

Prose:
Selected Prose, Persea Books, 1977; tr. Daniel Weissbort.

Biography:
Amanda S. Haight, *Anna Akhmatova: a poetic pilgrimage*, Oxford UP, 1976.

Criticism:
Sam Driver, *Anna Akhmatova*, Twayne, 1972.

Boris Pasternak

Collections:
The Poetry of Boris Pasternak 1914–60, Putnam's, 1960; tr. George Reavey.
Sister, my Life: summer 1917, Washington Square Press, 1967; tr. Phillip C. Flayderman (bilingual).
Prose and Poems, Benn, 1959; ed. Stefan Schimanski.
Safe Conduct and other works, Paul Elek, 1959; ed. Alec Brown.
Poems, Michigan UP, 1959; tr. Eugene Kayden.

Fifty Poems, George Allen and Unwin, 1963; tr. Lydia Pasternak Slater.

In The Interlude: poems 1945–60, Oxford UP, 1962; tr. Henry Kamen.

Poems of Doctor Zhivago, Manchester UP, 1965; tr. Donald Davie (bilingual).

Prose:

Collected Prose, Praeger, 1977; ed. Christopher Barnes.

The Last Summer, Penguin, 1960; tr. George Reavey.

Letters to Georgian Friends, Penguin, 1971; tr. David Magarshack.

Doctor Zhivago, Fontana, 1961; trs. Max Hayward and Manya Harari.

An Essay in Autobiography, Collins-Harvill, 1959; tr. Manya Harari.

Play:

The Blind Beauty, Collins-Harvill, 1969; trs. Max Hayward and Manya Harari.

Biography:

Olga Ivinskaya, *A Captive of Time: my years with Pasternak*, Fontana, 1979.

Guy de Mallac, *Boris Pasternak: his life in art*, Oklahoma UP, 1982.

Gerd Ruge, *Pasternak: a pictorial biography*, Thames and Hudson, 1959.

Criticism:

C. M. Bowra 'Boris Pasternak 1917–23', *The Creative Experiment*, Macmillan, 1949.

Donald Davie and Angela Livingstone (eds.), *Pasternak: modern judgements*, Macmillan, 1969.

Victor Erlich (ed.), *Pasternak: twentieth-century views*, Prentice-Hall, 1979.

Lazar Fleishman, *Boris Pasternak in the 1920s*, Munich, 1981.

Henry Gifford, *Pasternak*, Cambridge UP, 1977.

Olga Hughes, *The Poetic World of Boris Pasternak*, Princeton UP, 1974.

Krystyna Pomorska, *Themes and Variations in Pasternak's Poetics*, The Hague, 1975.

Osip Mandelstam

Collections:

Stone, Princeton UP, 1981; tr. Robert Tracy (bilingual).

Selected Poems, Paul Elek, 1980; tr. James Greene.
Selected Poems, Oxford UP, 1972; trs. Clarence Brown and
W. S. Merwin.
Selected Poems, Persea Books, 1977; tr. Bernard Meares;
introd. Joseph Brodsky.
Selected Poems, Rivers Press, 1973; tr. David McDuff (bilingual).
Complete Poetry, SUNY, 1973; trs. Burton Raffel and Alla Burago.

Prose:
The Prose of Osip Mandelstam, Princeton UP, 1967;
tr. Clarence Brown.
Selected Essays, Texas UP, 1977; tr. Sidney Monas.
Complete Critical Prose and Letters, Ardis, 1979; trs. Jane Gary Harris
and Constance Link.

Biography:
Nadezhda Mandelstam, *Hope Against Hope*, Penguin, 1975;
tr. Max Hayward.
Nadezhda Mandelstam, *Hope Abandoned*, Penguin, 1976;
tr. Max Hayward.

Criticism:
Jennifer Baines, *Mandelstam: the later poetry*, Cambridge UP, 1976.
Clarence Brown, *Mandelstam*, Cambridge UP, 1973.
Stephen Broyde, *Mandelstam and his Age*, Harvard UP, 1976.
Kiril Taranovsky, *Essays on Mandelstam*, Harvard UP, 1976.

César Vallejo

Collections:
Selected Poems, Beacon Press, 1971; ed. Robert Bly (bilingual).
Selected Poems, Penguin, 1976; trs. Ed Dorn and Gordon Brotherston
(bilingual).
Trilce, Grossman/Mushinsha, 1973; tr. David Smith (bilingual).
Human Poems, Grove Press, 1968; tr. Clayton Eshleman (bilingual).
Complete Posthumous Poetry, California UP, 1979;
trs. Clayton Eshleman and José Rubia Barcia (bilingual).

Criticism:
Jean Franco, *César Vallejo: the dialectics of poetry and silence*,
Cambridge UP, 1976.
James Higgins, 'Introduction', *César Vallejo: an anthology*, Pergamon,
1970.

Marina Tsvetaeva

Collections:
Selected Poems, Oxford UP, 1981; tr. Elaine Feinstein.
The Demesne of the Swans, Ardis, 1980; tr. Robin Kemball
(bilingual).

Prose:
'Art in the Light of Conscience', *Modern Russian Poets on Poetry*,
Ardis, 1976; tr. Angela Livingstone.
A Captive Spirit: selected prose, Ardis, 1980; tr. J. Marin King.

Biography:
Ellendea Proffer (ed.), *Tsvetaeva: a pictorial biography*, Ardis, 1980.

Criticism:
Joseph Brodsky, 'A poet on prose: Marina Tsvetaeva', *Parnassus*,
Summer 1981.
Simon Karlinsky, *Marina Tsvetaeva: her life and art*, California UP,
1966.
D. S. Mirsky, 'Marina Tsvetaeva', *The Bitter Air of Exile: Russian
Writers in the West 1922–72*, California UP, 1977; Simon Karlinsky
and Alfred Appel, Jr (eds.).

Jorge Guillén

Collections:
Cántico: a selection, André Deutsch, 1965; ed. N. T. di Giovanni
(bilingual).
Affirmation: a bilingual anthology 1919–66, Oklahoma UP, 1968;
tr. Julian Palley (bilingual).
Guillén on Guillén: the poetry and the poet, Princeton UP, 1979;
trs. Reginald Gibbons and Anthony L. Geist (bilingual).

Prose:
Language and Poetry: some poets of Spain, Harvard UP, 1961.

Criticism:
Ernst Robert Curtius, 'Jorge Guillén', *Essays on European Literature*,
Princeton UP, 1973; tr. Michael Kowal.
Ivar Ivask and Juan Marichal (eds.), *Luminous Reality: the poetry of
Jorge Guillén*, Oklahoma UP, 1969.
F. A. Pleak, *The Poetry of Jorge Guillén*, Oxford UP, 1942.

Vladimir Mayakovsky

Collections:
The Bedbug and Selected Poetry, Weidenfeld and Nicolson, 1961;
trs. Max Hayward and George Reavey (bilingual).
Poems, Progress Publishers, Moscow, 1972; tr. Dorian Rottenberg
(bilingual).
Wi' the haill voice, Carcanet, 1972; tr. Edwin Morgan.
Mayakovsky and his poetry, Bombay, 1955; tr. Herbert Marshall.

Prose:
How are Verses made?, Cape, 1970; tr. G. M. Hyde.

Biography:
Ann and Samuel Charters, *I Love: the story of Vladimir
Mayakovsky and Lili Brik*, André Deutsch, 1979.
Viktor Shklovsky, *Mayakovsky and his Circle*, Pluto Press, 1972;
tr. Lily Feiler.

Criticism:
C. M. Bowra, 'The Futurism of Vladimir Mayakovsky',
The Creative Experiment, Macmillan, 1949.
Edward J. Brown, *Mayakovsky: a poet in the revolution*, Princeton UP,
1973.
Lawrence Stahlberger, *The Symbolic System of Mayakovsky*,
The Hague, 1965.

Paul Éluard

Collections:
Thorns of Thunder, Europa Press, 1936; tr. Samuel Beckett and
others (bilingual).
Uninterrupted Poetry: selected writings, New Directions, 1952;
tr. Lloyd Alexander; introd. Louis Aragon (bilingual).

Criticism:
Mary Ann Caws, 'Paul Éluard', *The Poetry of Dada and Surrealism*,
Princeton UP, 1970.
Robert Nugent, *Paul Éluard*, Twayne, 1974.

Eugenio Montale

Collections:
Selected Poems, New Directions, 1965; trs. various hands (bilingual).

Selected Poems, Penguin, 1969; tr. George Kay.
Provisional Conclusions, Regnery, 1970; tr. Edith Farnsworth.
New Poems, New Directions, 1976; tr. G. Singh (bilingual).
It Depends: a poet's notebook, New Directions, 1980; tr. G. Singh (bilingual).
Xenia/Motets, Agenda Editions, 1981; tr. Kate Hughes (bilingual).

Prose:
Selected Essays, Carcanet, 1978; tr. G. Singh.
The Butterfly of Dinard, Alan Ross, 1970; tr. G. Singh.
Poet In Our Time, Marion Boyars, 1976; tr. Alistair Hamilton.

Biography:
G. Nascimbeni, *Montale*, Milan, 1969.

Criticism:
Guido Almansi and Bruce Merry, *Eugenio Montale: the private language of poetry*, Edinbugh UP, 1977.
Joseph Brodsky, 'The Art of Montale', *New York Review of Books*, June 1977.
Glauco Cambon, 'Eugenio Montale's *Motets*: the occasions of epiphany', *PMLA*, 1967.
Arshi Pipa, *Montale and Dante*, Minnesota UP, 1968.
Arshi Pipa, 'Memory and Fidelity in Montale', *Italian Quarterly*, 1967.
G. Singh, *Eugenio Montale: a critical study of his poetry, prose and criticism*, Yale UP, 1973.
Sergio Solmi, 'The Poetry of Montale', *Quarterly Review of Literature*, 1962.
Rebecca J. West, *Eugenio Montale: poet on the edge*, Harvard UP, 1981.

Federico García Lorca

Collections:
Selected Poems, Penguin, 1960; plain prose trs. J. L. Gili.
Selected Poems, Grove Press, 1961; trs. various hands (bilingual).
Poet in New York, Grove Press, 1955; tr. Ben Belitt (bilingual).
The Cricket Sings, New Directions, 1980; tr. Will Kirkland (bilingual).

Prose:
Deep Song and other prose, Marion Boyars, 1980; tr. Christopher Maurer.

Plays:
Three Tragedies, New Directions, 1947; trs. James Graham-Lujan
and Richard L. O'Connell.
Five Plays: comedies and tragicomedies, New Directions, 1963;
trs. James Graham Lujan and Richard L. O'Connell.

Biography:
Ian Gibson, *The Death of Lorca*, Paladin, 1974.

Criticism:
Arturo Barea, *Lorca: the poet and his people*, Faber and Faber, 1944;
tr. Ilsa Barea.
Roy Campbell, *Lorca*, Bowes and Bowes, 1952.
Gwynne Edwards, *Lorca: the theatre beneath the sand*, Marion Boyars,
1980.
Edwin Honig, *García Lorca*, Cape, 1968.

Bertolt Brecht

Collections:
Manual of Piety, Grove Press, 1966; tr. Eric Bentley (bilingual).
Selected Poems, Grove Press, 1959; tr. H. R. Hays (bilingual).
Poems 1913–56, Eyre Methuen, 1976; eds. John Willett and
Ralph Manheim.

Prose:
Diary 1920–22, Eyre Methuen, 1979; ed. Hertha Ramthun;
tr. and with an introd. by John Willett.
The Threepenny Novel, Grove Press, 1956; tr. D. I. Vesey.
Tales from the Calendar, Methuen, 1961; trs. Yvonne Kapp and
Michael Hamburger.

Plays:
Collected Plays, Eyre Methuen, 1970–   ; trs. various hands (in
progress).

Biography:
Klaus Völker, *Brecht: a biography*, Marion Boyars, 1979;
tr. John Nowell.

Criticism:
Hannah Arendt, 'Bertolt Brecht', *Men in Dark Times*, Penguin,
1973.
Walter Benjamin, *Understanding Brecht*, New Left Books, 1977;
tr. Anna Bostock.
Martin Esslin, *Brecht: a choice of evils*, Eyre and Spottiswoods, 1959.

Jorge Luis Borges

Collections:
Selected Poems 1923–67, Allen Lane, 1973; ed. N. T. di Giovanni;
trs. various hands (bilingual).
Dreamtigers, Texas UP, 1964; trs. Mildred Boyer and Harold
Morland.
In Praise of Darkness, Dutton, 1964; tr. N. T. di Giovanni (bilingual).
The Book of Sand, Penguin, 1979; trs. N. T. di Giovanni and Alastair
Reid (bilingual).

Major prose:
Fictions, Grove Press, 1962; tr. Anthony Kerrigan.
Labyrinths, New Directions, 1962; tr. James E. Irby.
Other Inquisitions 1937–52, Texas UP, 1965; tr. James E. Irby.
A Personal Anthology, Grove Press, 1967; tr. Anthony Kerrigan.
The Aleph and other stories 1933–69, Dutton, 1970;
tr. N. T. di Giovanni.
Doctor Brodies's Report, Dutton, 1972; tr. N. T. di Giovanni.
A Universal History of Infamy, Dutton, 1972; tr. N. T. di Giovanni.

Biography:
Richard Burgin, *Conversations with Jorge Luis Borges*, Holt, Rinehart
and Winston, 1969.
Emir Rodriguez Monegal, *Jorge Luis Borges: a literary biography*,
Dutton, 1978.

Criticism:
Ronald Christ, *The Narrow Act: Borges's Art of Allusion*, New York
UP, 1969.
J. M. Cohen, *Jorge Luis Borges*, Oliver and Boyd, 1973.
John C. Murchison, 'The Greater Voice: on the poetry of
Jorge Luis Borges', in *Prose for Borges*, eds. Charles Newman and
Mary Kinzie, Northwestern UP, 1974.
Martin Stabb, *Jorge Luis Borges*, Twayne, 1970.
Guillermo Sucre, *Borges el Poeta*, Caracas, 1968.

George Seferis

Collections:
Poems, Atlantic, Brown, Little, 1960; tr. Rex Warner.
The King of Asine and other poems, John Lehmann, 1948; trs. various
hands.

Collected Poems 1924–55, Cape, 1969; trs. Edmund Keeley and
Philip Sherrard (bilingual).
Three Secret Poems, Harvard UP, 1969; tr. Walter Kaiser.

Prose:
A Poet's Journal: Days of 1945–51, Harvard UP, 1974;
tr. Athan Anagnostopoulos.
On the Greek Style: selected essays in poetry and Hellenism, Bodley Head,
1967; trs. Rex Warner and T. D. Frangopoulos.

Criticism:
Philip Sherrard, 'George Seferis', *The Marble Threshing-Floor*,
Vallentine, Mitchell, 1956

Salvatore Quasimodo

Collections:
Selected Writings, Farrar, Straus, Cudahy, 1960;
tr. Allen Mandelbaum.
Selected Poems, Penguin, 1965; tr. Jack Bevan.
Debit and Credit, Anvil Press, 1972; tr. Jack Bevan.

Criticism:
Frederic J. Jones, 'Salvatore Quasimodo e la dissoluzione dell'
ermetismo', *La poesia italiana contemporanea*, Florence, 1975.

Lucio Piccolo

Collections:
Collected Poems, Princeton UP, 1972; trs. Brian Swann and
Ruth Feldman (bilingual).

Criticism:
Leonardo Sciascia, *La corda pazza*, Turin, 1970.
Interview with Piccolo in *Books Abroad*, 1974.

Attila József

Collections:
Poems, Danubia Book Co., 1966; trs. various hands.
Selected Poems and Texts, Carcanet, 1973; tr. John Bátki.

Criticism:
István Mezáros, *Attila József e l'arte moderna*, Milan, 1964;
tr. from the Hungarian.

Pablo Neruda

Collections:

Twenty Love Poems and a Song of Despair, Cape, 1969;
tr. W. S. Merwin (bilingual).
Residence on Earth, Souvenir Press, 1976; tr. Donald D. Walsh
(bilingual).
The Captain's Verses, New Directions, 1972; tr. Donald D. Walsh
(bilingual).
Extravagaria, Cape, 1972; tr. Alastair Reid (bilingual).
A New Decade: poems 1958–67, Grove Press, 1969; trs. Ben Belitt and
Alastair Reid (bilingual).
Fully Empowered, Souvenir Press, 1976; tr. Alastair Reid (bilingual).
New Poems 1968–70, Grove Press, 1972; tr. Ben Belitt (bilingual).
Selected Poems, Beacon Press, 1971; ed. Robert Bly (bilingual).
Selected Poems, Penguin, 1975; ed. Nathaniel Tarn (bilingual).

Prose:

Memoirs, Souvenir Press, 1977; tr. Hardie St Martin.

Criticism:

Salvatore Bizzarro, *Pablo Neruda: all poets the poet*, Scarecrow Press,
1979.
René de Costa, *The Poetry of Pablo Neruda*, Harvard UP, 1979.
Manuel Duran and Margery Safir, *Earth Tones: the poetry of
Pablo Neruda*, Indiana UP, 1981.
Jorge Edwards, 'The Posthumous Fame of Pablo Neruda',
Times Literary Supplement, August 1976.
John Felstiner, *Translating Neruda: the way to Macchu Picchu*,
Stanford UP, 1980.

René Char

Collections:

Hypnos Waking, Random House, 1956; ed. Jackson Mathews
(bilingual).
Poems, Princeton UP, 1976; trs. Mary Ann Caws and
Jonathan Griffin (bilingual).

Prose:

Leaves of Hypnos, Grossman/Mushinsha, 1973; tr. Cid Corman
(bilingual).

Criticism:

Mary Ann Caws, *René Char*, Twayne, 1977.

Virginia A. La Charité, *The Poetics and the Poetry of René Char*,
North Carolina UP, 1968.
James R. Lawler, *René Char: the myth and the poem*, Princeton UP,
1978.
Special Char issue of *World Literature Today*, Summer 1976.

Cesare Pavese

Collections:
Selected Poems, Penguin, 1971; tr. Margaret Crosland.
Hard Labor, Grossman/Viking, 1976; tr. William Arrowsmith.

Prose:
Dialogues with Leucò, Peter Owen, 1965; trs. William Arrowsmith and
D. S. Carne-Ross.
American Literature, California UP, 1970; tr. Edwin Fussell.

Major novels:
The Devil in the Hills, Penguin, 1967; tr. D. D. Paige.
Among Women Only, New English Library, 1964; tr. D. D. Paige.
The Moon and the Bonfires, Penguin, 1963; tr. Louise Sinclair.

Biography:
Selected Letters 1924–50, Peter Owen, 1969; tr. A. E. Murch.
This Business of Living: a diary 1935–50, Peter Owen, 1961;
tr. A. E. Murch.

Criticism:
Gian-Carlo Biasin, *The Smile of the Gods: a thematic study of the works of
Cesare Pavese*, Cornell UP, 1968; tr. Yvonne Freccero.
Leslie Fiedler, 'Introducing Cesare Pavese', *Kenyon Review*, Autumn
1954.
Susan Sontag, 'The artist as exemplary sufferer',
Against Interpretation, Farrar, Straus, Giroux, 1966.

Yannis Ritsos

Collections:
Selected Poems, Penguin, 1974; tr. Nikos Stangos.
Corridors and Stairs, Goldsmith Press, Ireland, 1976;
tr. Nikos Germanacos (bilingual).
Chronicle of Exile, Wire Press, 1977; tr. Minas Savvas (bilingual).
The Fourth Dimension, Donker, 1977; tr. Rae Dalven.

456   Bibliographies

Ritsos in Parentheses, Princeton UP, 1979; tr. Edmund Keeley (bilingual).
Scripture of the Blind, Ohio State UP, 1979; tr. Kimon Friar (bilingual).
Subterranean Horses, Ohio State UP, 1980; tr. Minas Savvas (bilingual).

Octavio Paz

Collections:
Early Poems 1935–55, New Directions, 1973; trs. various hands (bilingual).
Eagle or Sun?, New Directions, 1976; tr. Eliot Weinberger (bilingual).
Configurations, New Directions, 1971; trs. various hands (bilingual).
A Draft of Shadows, New Directions, 1979; tr. Eliot Weinberger (bilingual).
Selected Poems, Penguin, 1979; ed. Charles Tomlinson (bilingual).
Renga, Penguin, 1979; ed. Charles Tomlinson.
Airborne, Anvil Press, 1981; in collaboration with Charles Tomlinson (bilingual).

Prose:
The Labyrinth of Solitude, Grove Press, 1961; tr. Lysander Kemp.
Alternating Current, Viking, 1973; tr. H. Lane.
Conjunctions and Disjunctions, Viking, 1973; tr. H. Lane.
The Bow and the Lyre, Texas UP, 1973; tr. R. Simms.
The Siren and the Seashell, Texas UP, 1976; trs. L. Kemp and M. S. Peden.
Marcel Duchamp or the Castle of Purity, Cape Goliard, 1971; tr. D. Gardner.
Claude Lévi-Strauss: an introduction, Cape, 1972; trs. J. S. and M. Bernstein.

Criticism:
Ivar Ivask (ed.), *The Perpetual Present: the poetry and prose of Octavio Paz*, Oklahoma UP, 1973.
Rachel Phillips, *The Poetic Modes of Octavio Paz*, Oxford UP. 1972.
Jason Wilson, *Octavio Paz: a study of his poetics*, Cambridge UP, 1979.

Johannes Bobrowski

Collections:
Shadow Land, Rapp and Carroll, 1966; trs. Ruth and
Matthew Mead.
From the Rivers, Anvil Press, 1975; trs. Ruth and Matthew Mead.

Prose:
Levin's Mill, Calder and Boyars, 1970; tr. Janet Cropper.

Criticism:
Brian Keith-Smith, *Johannes Bobrowski*, Wolff, 1970.

Paul Celan

Collections:
Poems, Carcanet, 1980; tr. Michael Hamburger (bilingual).
Speech-Grille and other poems, Dutton, 1971; tr. Joachim Neugroschel
(bilingual).
Breath Crystal, Rigmarole, Melbourne, 1975; tr. Walter Billeter.

Prose:
Prose Writings and Selected Poems, Paper Castle, Carlton, Victoria,
1977; trs. Walter Billeter and Jerry Glenn.

Criticism:
Jerry Glenn, *Paul Celan*, Twayne, 1973.
James K. Lyon, 'The Poetry of Paul Celan: an approach',
Germanic Review, January 1964.

Vasko Popa

Collections:
Collected Poems 1943–76, Carcanet, 1978; tr. Anne Pennington;
introd. Ted Hughes.
The Little Box, Charioteer Press, Washington, 1978;
tr. Charles Simic.
The Golden Apple, Anvil Press, 1980; tr. Anne Pennington and
Andrew Harvey.

Yves Bonnefoy

Collections:
On the Motion and Immobility of Douve, Ohio State UP, 1965;

tr. Galway Kinnell (bilingual).
Selected Poems, Cape, 1968; tr. Antony Rudolf (bilingual).
Words in Stone, Massachusetts UP, 1976; tr. Susanna Lang (bilingual).
In The Lure of the Threshold, Massachusetts UP, 1981; tr. Susanna Lang (bilingual).
The Origin of Language and other poems, George Nama, New York, 1980; tr. Susanna Lang (bilingual).

Prose:
Miró, Faber and Faber, 1967; tr. Judith Landry.
Rimbaud, Harper and Row, 1973; tr. Paul Schmidt.

Criticism:
Mary Ann Caws, 'Yves Bonnefoy', *The Inner Theatre of Recent French Poetry*, Princeton UP, 1972.
John E. Jackson, *Yves Bonnefoy*, Paris, 1976.
Richard Vernier, 'Yves Bonnefoy and the Conscience of Poetry', *Sub-Stance*, nos. 23–4, 1979.
Special Bonnefoy issue of *World Literature Today*, Summer 1978.

Yehuda Amichai

Collections:
Selected Poems, Cape Goliard, 1968; tr. Assia Guttman.
Songs of Jerusalem and Myself, Harper and Row, 1971; tr. Harold Schimmel.
Selected Poems, Penguin, 1971; compiled from the above two volumes.
Travels of a latter-day Benjamin of Tudela, Menard Press, 1978, Cauldron Books, 1977; tr. Ruth Nevo.
Amen, Oxford UP, 1978; tr. by the author and Ted Hughes.
Time, Oxford UP, 1979; tr. by the author and Ted Hughes.

Prose:
Not of this time, not of this place, Harper and Row, 1968; tr. Shlomo Katz.

Criticism:
Interview with Anthony Rudolf, *London Magazine*, January 1980.

Zbigniew Herbert

Collections:
Selected Poems, Penguin, 1968; trs. Czeslaw Milosz and Peter Dale Scott.
Selected Poems, Oxford UP, 1977; trs. John and Bogdana Carpenter.

Prose:
The Barbarian in the Garden, Carcanet, 1982.

Joseph Brodsky

Collections:
Selected Poems, Penguin, 1973; tr. George Kline.
A Part of Speech, Oxford UP, 1980; trs. various hands.

Criticism:
Henry Gifford, 'The Language of Loneliness',
Times Literary Supplement, August 1978.
Rosette Lamont, 'A Poet's Schoolroom', *Massachusetts Review*,
Autumn 1974.
Czeslaw Milosz, 'A Struggle against Suffocation', *New York Review of Books*, August 1980.
R. D. Sylvester, 'The Poet as Scapegoat: Joseph Brodsky's *Halt in the Desert*', *Texas Studies in Literature and Language*, 1975.

Index